A publication of the Seventy-fifth Anniversary Year
of THE UNIVERSITY OF CHICAGO

The
Limits
of
Symbolism

Studies of Five Modern French Poets

By

Bernard Weinberg

The University of Chicago Press
Chicago and London

Library of Congress Catalog Card Number: 66–23703

THE UNIVERSITY OF CHICAGO PRESS, CHICAGO & LONDON

The University of Toronto Press, Toronto 5, Canada

Printed in the United States of America

To My Father

Four of the essays included here were published previously, the first as many as twenty years ago. I am grateful to the *Romanic Review* for permission to republish the study on *Le Cimetière marin;* to the *Publications of the Modern Language Association* for *Le Bateau ivre;* to the *Chicago Review* for *Anabase;* and to *L'Esprit Créateur* for *Le Tombeau d'Edgar Poe.* All four have been modified slightly. The Appendix, "The Limits of Hermeticism, or Hermeticism and Intelligibility," translates and expands upon a paper originally printed in the *Cahiers* of the Association Internationale des Etudes Françaises. *Le Cimetière marin* and *Les Grenades* were first printed in Valéry's collection, *Charmes,* in 1922, © Editions Gallimard. Saint-John Perse graciously authorized me to quote freely from *Anabase.*

B.W.

Contents

Introduction / 1

1. A Statement of Method: Baudelaire's *Le Cygne* / 8

2. Baudelaire, *Spleen* ("Quand le ciel bas et lourd") / 37

3. Baudelaire, *Recueillement* / 51

4. Baudelaire, *Un Voyage à Cythère* / 64

5. Rimbaud, *Le Bateau ivre* / 89

6. Mallarmé, *L'Après-midi d'un faune* / 127

7. Mallarmé, *Le vierge, le vivace et le bel aujourd'hui* / 170

8. Mallarmé, *Toast funèbre* / 187

9. Mallarmé, *Le Tombeau d'Edgar Poe* / 225

10. Mallarmé, *Un Coup de dés jamais n'abolira le hasard* / 236

11. Valéry, *Le Cimetière marin* / 322

12. Valéry, *Les Grenades* / 353

13. Saint-John Perse, *Anabase* / 365

Appendix: The Limits of Hermeticism, or Hermeticism and Intelligibility / 420

Introduction

Several basic assumptions underlie the analyses that make up the present volume of essays on modern French poems. They are general assumptions about the art of poetry in terms of which the method employed in the individual analyses is justified. I think it useful to state them here briefly.

My first assumption is that an art of poetry does exist. I am not sure whether, for the individual poet who uses it, it is a set of principles, or a collection of habits, or a complex of feelings about the "rightness" or the "wrongness" of elements that might go into the making of the poem. But we know that as the poet composes, he constantly makes choices: where to begin his poem, how to continue it, where to end it; the object or the word or the figure to be introduced at each point; the sounds and the rhythms to be developed; the emotions to be aroused and directed. These choices result from his art. They are not accidents, they do not just happen. In each case, the choice depends upon a conception or an instinct relative to the form that the whole poem will ultimately take, and the "art" consists in determining, at every point, which of the alternative solutions is to be adopted. The poem that results is thus a product of the poet's art, and as such it is ultimately a product of the whole art of poetry. For the "art" belongs to the art and not to the artist; that is, the making of the individual poem is related to the making of all poems as the particular is related to the general. The poet makes each poem in a separate and special way; but he also makes it in terms of the general conditions of the art of poetry and of the general ways in which poems of any kind may be organized. In this sense he uses an "art" of poetry.

I do not mean to imply by this that the individual poem is not unique; for it is. Its uniqueness consists in the presence and ordering of elements that are present in that order in no other poem. Yet in so far as it is a poem it is composed of elements like those in other poems, organized in a way resembling that used in other poems; hence it belongs to the art. Nor do I wish to suggest how, by what psychological processes or what personal habits, the individual poet has made the individual poem. This we cannot know; or in any case, it is not the subject of my present inquiry. We may assume that each poet works in a special way for each poem, and that no generalization is possible. Some write quickly on the basis of a feeling or instinct about the poem; others more slowly and on intellectual grounds. Some use their art deliberately and self-consciously; in others the art must be present only as impulse and suggestion. But this we need not attempt to discover. We have the poem before us; it is our only sure document; and it is the only document which need concern us.

Second, I assume that, as a product of the art, any poem is the possible objective of an analysis that will discover, not by what creative process it was made, but what it is and in what particular form it exists. The assumption here is that it should be possible to describe that final form which, as the ultimate goal of the poet, determined his individual choices. This means that the relationship of any element to the whole poem should be discernible, the reason for its presence and its place. The problem in the analysis is not to recreate or reproduce the operation by which the poem was made, but rather to see the existing whole as a whole and the relationships of all the parts to one another and to the whole. It is a problem of "inspection" in the light of a large number of questions whose purpose is to help the "inspector" see with sharpness and definition every aspect of the work. If the creative process was directed toward the making of the poem, the analytical process is directed toward the understanding of the poem.

Understanding is of various kinds. It is intellectual in so far as it attempts to adduce reasons for what it discovers, to state in language as much of one's apprehension of the poem as is reducible to discourse, to explain the particular in terms of general considerations. It is sensitive in so far as it depends upon feelings and insights, upon the initial instinctive reactions that lead one into the poem and that are constantly renewed as one's readings of the poem are multiplied.

It is evaluative each time that one decides (or feels) that a given detail—discovered by analysis or apprehension—is good or bad for the poem as a whole, or that the poem as a whole is better or less good as a result of one's most recent discovery about it; and these evaluations may depend upon intellectually formulated criteria or upon the educated insights that come from long experience as a reader. I assume generally, though, that in the total analytical process the intellectual phases will dominate; that they are the ones that can most readily be refined and developed in the critic; and that they in turn may contribute to an education of sensitivity itself.

Third, I assume that the art of poetry, like any body of habits or processes or operations, is subject through the years to change, to increase and expansion, to renewal and refinement. No art ever stands completely still. It changes within the career of each artist as each new work raises new problems that require different solutions; it changes within an artistic tradition as each artist adds, to what he has learned from his predecessors in the tradition, his own private way of conceiving the art and of making works. Through all this the art itself retains its identity, since it uses the same general means to represent the same general objects in works that are essentially similar; but no work of the art is ever identical with another. The literary critic may therefore take into account a historical dimension if he so wishes. He may ask about a group of poems, by one or several poets, what changes in the art are perceptible as one passes from earlier poems to later poems. If he cares to call upon historical hindsight, he may seek in earlier poems the techniques and devices that are fully developed in later ones. This historical process, however, should not be accompanied by any sense of predictability, by any notion that because certain things are happening in a given poet, other things must necessarily happen in the next poet. The expectations of "natural" evolution do not apply in the arts, where every work is particular, discrete, and "artificial."

Finally, we must assume that the effect produced by the poem in a reader is a result of what it is, as a particular thing, rather than of what he is, as a particular person. Granted that each reader brings to the poem his own sensitivity and his own experience, that every reading will be slightly different from every other, nevertheless there is a central, essential reading of the poem that is basically the same for all readers who read it well. (The purpose of any analysis of a poem is to help the reader to a better reading.) If this is so, it is because the poem exists and persists as an object, as a work of art presenting a unique combination of elements in a unique form. The totality of the form produces a total effect, each part contributes a part of the total effect. It is thus possible to speak of the whole and of its parts as potentials for certain effects in the reader—thinking always of the reader as possessed of general rather than of particular capacities for experiencing those effects—and to speak of the "effects" themselves as resident in the poem rather than in the individual reader. I assume that, by so doing, one may avoid what is idiosyncratic in the response of any single reader and distinguish instead what might be expected to be the response of all good readers.

Every analysis of a poem is a hypothesis. It does not claim to give the last word or ultimate truth with respect to the interpretation of the poem. It does not pretend to be permanent and unchanging—or unchangeable. At best, an analysis represents one reader's best reading of a poem at a given moment in his career of studying that particular poem and in his career of studying poetry in general. At such a moment, the reader brings to bear upon the interpretation of the individual work all that he has learned about the interpretation of works—all his habits of analysis and synthesis, all the techniques and devices that he has developed for penetrating into the work, all the questions he has learned to ask about poetic structures, all the force of his educated sensitivity. One supposes that as he goes on reading this work and other works, the reader's habits and methods will improve, that they in turn will contribute to the further refinement of his sensitivity. The next reading of the poem should be a better one than the last.

It is as hypotheses that the readings of the eleven poems in this volume are presented. They are what I make of the poems after many years of study and after innumerable examinations. I hope that they profit from my experience with other kinds of poetry, narrative and dramatic as well as lyric, and with poetry in literatures other than the French and from times other than the modern. It seems to me that the whole of one's literary life is called upon each time that one reads and interprets a given work. Each one of the analyses gives witness to my way of understanding the poem at the time the analysis was written—and the writing covers a period of almost twenty years. I do not guarantee that if I were to do over, today, one of the earlier ones, it would not be quite different from the reading as originally published; nor that if I were to do them all over some years hence, they would not all show important variations from their present form. I think that essentially the analyses would be the same, since I believe that they represent the essential structures of the poems as I understand structure and poetry. But there would, I hope, be new discoveries about details and particulars, perhaps even new insights and new emphases.

The individual analyses of poems are not isolated. There is a kind of historical line that connects them. If the arrangement is chronological, it is only as far as authors are concerned, and very rough at that. The real order is determined by my wish to follow, through a small number of selected poems, the emergence of those techniques and those poetic devices that we now commonly associate with "modern" poetry. Beginning with Baudelaire, French poets add to the traditional methods of the art of poetry certain new ways of building the poem and of finding or making the language used to represent its substantive elements. They do not do this in any calculating fashion, with any coordinated effort to advance French poetry into modern times. Rather, each one, as he experiments with fresh solutions to the problem of his art, seeks and finds the ways of writing that seem to him to improve upon the ways of his predecessors. At times these new ways are merely subtle variations of older habits and methods; at other times, however, they constitute such radical departures from the usual solutions as to mark major advances in the potentialities of the art.

The "emergence" of which I speak is thus not a regular or orderly process; it is not susceptible of arrangement in any historical order nor of explanation through any historical causes. But it forms a part of the history of the art. The poets whose poems I here analyze developed their art as they practiced it—in one way in one poem, in another way in another poem. They set themselves, for each poem, a fresh and challenging artistic problem; and to the extent to which they found satisfactory answers, they augmented the powers of the poetic art. As we read their poems, we may ask not only what each one is and how it is put together, but also what signs it contains of the appearance of the new poetry.

Several years ago, in July of 1962 to be precise, I made a first attempt to suggest some of the lines of development or emergence of the new art. That was in a paper given in Paris at the Fourteenth Congress of the Association Internationale des Etudes Françaises; it was entitled "Les Limites de l'hermétisme, ou Hermétisme et intelligibilité." The paper is translated as an appendix to the present volume, since I think that it may assist the reader in seeing more clearly the nature of those lines. Still earlier, in March of 1957, I had published the essay on *Le Bateau ivre,* also included here, with the subtitle, "The limits of symbolism." It is from that subtitle that I borrow the title for this volume. If I have found the notion of "limits" useful to me, it is not because I think or wish that limits should be imposed upon a poet either by persons or by traditions outside himself. Rather, it is apparent that the poet, working with his art, finds that there are natural limits to the degree to which he can extend a given device or a given kind of structure. Beyond those limits, the nature of the device changes or the poem fails of producing the effect for which it is intended. Through intellectual or through instinctive processes, the poet discovers what those limits are and builds his poem accordingly.

However, the choice of the title, *The Limits of Symbolism,* is not meant to indicate that all or most of the poems studied here are symbolist poems; most of them are not. Yet because of a loose way of talking in our time, the terms "symbol," "symbolism," and "symbolist" have been indiscriminately applied to all these poems and all these poets, and to countless others. We have come to equate "symbolist" with "modern" and to see the symbol as the sole instrument of the modern poet. I have therefore been insistent upon the desirability of defining the symbol carefully and of describing fully how it is used when it serves as the basis for a symbolist poem. I have wished—and this is one of the "lines of development"—to distinguish as technical terms and as technical devices the simple comparison or simile from the metaphor, the metaphor from the "occa-sional" symbol, the occasional symbol from the "structuring" sym-bol. The last is the only kind that makes for the true symbolist poem. In other essays, I have wished to show that such poems as *L'Après-midi d'un faune* and *Anabase* are not symbolist poems at all, that we need to discern other devices as organizing them, call these devices by other names—if names are inevitable. If I myself have any intention to "limit," it is only to limit the unthinking and almost mechanical use of a technical term for works to which it is not really appropriate.

Poetry itself has no limits; the art is always powerful to find new directions and new techniques. It is new in every poem that it produces. But the criticism that deals with it is limited by the very nature of the poems that it studies and analyzes. A criticism that would be valid must read those poems singly and separately, in terms of what they are as individual and independent works of art.

I

A Statement of Method

Baudelaire's *Le Cygne*

Formal analysis of poetic works has as its purpose to discover, in each poem, its total form, in order to make possible (1) an understanding of the principle of organization that underlies the structure of the work, (2) a full and proper response to the emotional or intellectual potential of the work, and (3) evaluative statements about the quality of the poem. Total form is taken to be the composite of all the elements of which the poem is made (down to the last significant word, when that is possible) in the order in which they are arranged. The analysis may be applied to poems of any kind, narrative or dramatic or lyric, but the structural bases that it discovers are apt to be more different from kind to kind than they are among works within the same kind. Any description of the structure of a poem should seek that sort of unique appropriateness to the poem which corresponds to the uniqueness of the poem itself. The purpose is not to place the work in a class or to find bases of comparison with other works, but rather to separate and distinguish it from others through concentration on its special essence.

For many works, especially those that are fairly remote in time, the process of formal analysis needs to be preceded by a process of historical and philological recovery. Before we can begin to talk about the form of any poem of the Middle Ages or the Renaissance, for example, we must make a considerable linguistic effort in order to be sure that we are understanding each word or construction as it should be understood. Before we can assign a proper meaning to

8

names and allusions in a more recent poem, we must pursue various lines of historical investigation in order to fill in or to clarify the references. For more recent poems still, those in which an allusive technique is employed, we cannot hope to penetrate into the meaning or the form of the poem until we have not only run down the allusions, but also reread the texts to which allusion is made—sometimes in their totality; for this reason, T. S. Eliot provides a certain number of notes (although not all that are needed) to *The Waste Land*. In all cases, our problem is to use those kinds of philological or historical disciplines which will clarify for us the superficial, grammatical, external meaning of the text; we must understand the text as words and as things signified by words before passing on to questions of structure.

Historical recovery of this kind is usually more necessary the farther back we go in time—with the exception of some very modern poems. Yet even poems of the past century may require a modest historical effort as a preparation for analysis. Baudelaire's *Le Cygne* is one of these. It was published first in *La Causerie* on Jan. 22, 1860, then in the second edition of *Les Fleurs du mal,* 1861.

Le Cygne

À Victor Hugo

I

Andromaque, je pense à vous! Ce petit fleuve,
Pauvre et triste miroir où jadis resplendit
L'immense majesté de vos douleurs de veuve,
Ce Simoïs menteur qui par vos pleurs grandit,   4

A fécondé soudain ma mémoire fertile,
Comme je traversais le nouveau Carrousel.
Le vieux Paris n'est plus (la forme d'une ville
Change plus vite, hélas! que le cœur d'un mortel);   8

Je ne vois qu'en esprit tout ce camp de baraques,
Ces tas de chapiteaux ébauchés et de fûts,
Les herbes, les gros blocs verdis par l'eau des flaques,
Et, brillant aux carreaux, le bric-à-brac confus.   12

Là s'étalait jadis une ménagerie;
Là je vis, un matin, à l'heure où sous les cieux
Froids et clairs le Travail s'éveille, où la voirie
Pousse un sombre ouragan dans l'air silencieux,　　　　16

Un cygne qui s'était évadé de sa cage,
Et, de ses pieds palmés frottant le pavé sec,
Sur le sol raboteux traînait son grand plumage.
Près d'un ruisseau sans eau la bête ouvrant le bec　　　20

Baignait nerveusement ses ailes dans la poudre,
Et disait, le cœur plein de son beau lac natal:
"Eau, quand donc pleuvras-tu? quand tonneras-tu, foudre?"
Je vois ce malheureux, mythe étrange et fatal,　　　　24

Vers le ciel quelquefois, comme l'homme d'Ovide,
Vers le ciel ironique et cruellement bleu,
Sur son cou convulsif tendant sa tête avide,
Comme s'il adressait des reproches à Dieu!　　　　28

II

Paris change! mais rien dans ma mélancolie
N'a bougé! palais neufs, échafaudages, blocs,
Vieux faubourgs, tout pour moi devient allégorie,
Et mes chers souvenirs sont plus lourds que des rocs.　　　32

Aussi devant ce Louvre une image m'opprime:
Je pense à mon grand cygne, avec ses gestes fous,
Comme les exilés, ridicule et sublime,
Et rongé d'un désir sans trêve! et puis à vous,　　　36

Andromaque, des bras d'un grand époux tombée,
Vil bétail, sous la main du superbe Pyrrhus,
Auprès d'un tombeau vide en extase courbée;
Veuve d'Hector, hélas! et femme d'Hélénus!　　　40

Je pense à la négresse, amaigrie et phthisique,
Piétinant dans la boue, et cherchant, l'œil hagard,
Les cocotiers absents de la superbe Afrique
Derrière la muraille immense du brouillard;　　　44

A quiconque a perdu ce qui ne se retrouve
Jamais, jamais! à ceux qui s'abreuvent de pleurs
Et tettent la Douleur comme une bonne louve!
Aux maigres orphelins séchant comme des fleurs!　　　48

Ainsi dans la forêt où mon esprit s'exile
Un vieux Souvenir sonne à plein souffle du cor!
Je pense aux matelots oubliés dans une île,
Aux captifs, aux vaincus! . . . à bien d'autres encor!   52

Many of the allusions that require clarification for us were perfectly clear to the reader of Baudelaire's time; but even for that
reader, some needed to be explained or commented. In 1860 the
dedication of a poem "À Victor Hugo" carried with it an awareness
of the fact that Hugo at that time was in exile; he had left Paris for
Brussels in 1851, moved to Jersey in 1852, and taken up residence in
Guernsey in 1855. It might thus provide a first indication of the
subject of the poem about to be read. On the other hand, the
epigraph accompanying the poem in its first form, "Falsi Simoentis
ad undam" (quoted from Book III, line 302 of the *Aeneid*), might
require a return to one's Virgil if one were to discover that this, too,
alluded to a person in exile. Almost any reader, save those who had
their Virgil at their fingertips, would have to reread the whole of the
passage in Book III if he were to get the full emotional impact of
lines 1–4 and 36–40 in *Le Cygne*. All would have to make the
connection with that version of the Andromache story (rather than
Racine's or anybody else's) in order to feel the right emotion relevant to Andromache and her situation. The presence of the epigraph
in the earliest text made the connection immediately; its absence
from later texts puts an additional burden on the reader.

The text to which Baudelaire refers describes a meeting between
Aeneas and Andromache at the time when she was in exile; she had
built a false tomb for Hector beside an artificial river, and there wept
her dead husband:

> sollemnis cum forte dapes et tristia dona   [301]
> ante urbem in luco falsi Simoentis ad undam
> libabat cineri Andromache, Manisque vocabat
> Hectoreum ad tumulum, viridi quem caespite inanem
> et geminas, causam lacrimis, sacraverat aras.
>
> . . . .
> 'Hector ubi est?' dixit lacrimasque effudit et omnem
> implevit clamore locum. vix pauca furenti

subicio et raris turbatus vocibus hisco:

. . . .

'heu! quis te casus deiectam coniuge tanto
excipit? aut quae digna satis fortuna revisit,
Hectoris Andromache? Pyrrhin conubia servas?'

. . . .

'me famulo famulamque Heleno transmisit habendam.'

A reference to the full text not only completes the allusion and supplies all the necessary details, it also enriches the reader's emotion and hence fulfills the purpose of the allusion: to transfer to this poem a state of feeling associated with a personage and a situation in another poem. The figure of Andromache in exile, at both points in Baudelaire's text, carries with it a complex visual image and a highly developed emotional context.

There are two, perhaps three other literary allusions in *Le Cygne* whose clarification will add dimensions of understanding and feeling to the poem. At line 25, "l'homme d'Ovide" is a reference to the *Metamorphoses,* Book I, lines 84–86:

pronaque cum spectent animalia cetera terram,
os homini sublime dedit caelumque videre
iussit et erectos ad sidera tollere vultus.

Here consultation of the original text will serve to emphasize the bitter irony of Baudelaire's verse; for while in Ovid man is distinguished from other creatures and ennobled by his capacity to look heavenward, the swan raises his head toward the sky in a ridiculous gesture and in order to reproach God. In lines 46–47, the allusion may be rather mythological than literary: "ceux qui s'abreuvent de pleurs / Et tettent la Douleur comme une bonne louve!" We are supposed to be reminded, I think, of the Roman wolf who suckled Romulus and Remus—orphans, we should remember, deprived of their proper mother, hence in that special state of exile that forms the subject of the poem. Lines 49–50, "Ainsi dans la forêt où mon esprit s'exile / Un vieux Souvenir sonne à plein souffle du cor!" may contain an allusion to Vigny's poem on Roland at Roncevaux, especially to the well-known verse,

Dieu! que le son du cor est triste au fond des bois!

If they did, overtones of the sadness and nostalgia contained in that poem would be transferred to this one.

Besides the literary references in *Le Cygne* we find a group of what we might call local and contemporary references; these pertain primarily to the area of the Carrousel and the Louvre, site of the speaker's present recollection of past events and especially of his vision of the swan. The poem distinguishes three separate moments in the history of this area: the present, time of the "nouveau Carrousel" and of "ce Louvre"; a recent past when the new Carrousel was being constructed, time of "ce camp de baraques" and of the "échafaudages"; and a more remote past, before the area had been cleared for reconstruction, time of the "ménagerie." In a way the poem recreates these all for us and we do not need to call upon history. Still, a simple consultation of works treating the successive stages in the development of the area (even so casual a one as the Marquis de Rochegude's *Guide du Vieux Paris*) might assist us in correcting our image of the area, might permit us to see it roughly as Baudelaire saw it rather than as we see it now. It is important that our visual image should be brought into some kind of correspondence with the realities of the time, since visual images are a strong factor in the creation of emotional effects.

There might well be other passages in *Le Cygne* for which historical or philological explanation would be necessary. That would depend, in each individual case, on the knowledge and the experience of the reader; and he would have to decide. The object of the reader should at all times be to make himself as nearly as is possible a contemporary reader of the poem—contemporary readers are always the best ones—by augmenting his store of relevant information. His purpose should not be merely to find sources and analogues or to collect miscellaneous facts, but rather to refresh his memory and to learn those things which, because they are directly pertinent to the reading of the text, will enable him to understand it more completely and to feel its emotions more adequately.

The formal analysis of a poem does not itself depend upon the findings of the pre-critical investigation; it considers them as preliminary but of a different order than its own methods of approach. It concerns itself directly and exclusively with the text, making outside reference—and that remotely and almost instinctively—only to the principles of the art and to certain criteria that derive from those principles. A large number of questions, always generally the same but each time asked in a different way, lead the critic into the text; they all are parts of the single, central question: How is this poem organized and ordered? The order of the asking of the questions is unimportant, as long as all are ultimately asked. Similarly, the way in which the answers are presented is secondary to the completeness of the final presentation. One may begin with a summary statement of one's conclusion about the form and proceed from it to a study of the substantiating details; or one may start from the *mot-à-mot* and lead into the general formulation. Two items of caution: it should not be thought that the critic's exposition of his case in any way follows the progress of his own discovery of the poem; and what he has to say about the poem should not be interpreted as an account of the creative act by which the poem was made. That is, the analytical process is to be kept distinct from the artistic process on the one hand and from the expository process on the other.

In my discussion of *Le Cygne,* I am going to follow the poem through from beginning to end, departing from a strict chronological order only when reference back and forth seems to serve some useful purpose.

The poem begins with the words "Andromaque, je pense à vous!" Two persons are presented here, primarily the speaker in the poem ("je"), then the person whom he addresses in an apostrophe, Andromaque ("vous"); the act that links them is an act of thought ("je pense") or of reminiscence—the latter suggested by the fact that somebody in the present is "thinking" of a mythological Greek princess. We should take care to note the nature of this act; for throughout the poem, what will be important will be the thoughts and feelings of the speaker about the things that he relates or describes—not the things themselves. The poet properly lays this as one of the bases of development of the poem. The rest of the first stanza specifies the "thought":

> . . . Ce petit fleuve,
> Pauvre et triste miroir où jadis resplendit
> L'immense majesté de vos douleurs de veuve,
> Ce Simoïs menteur qui par vos pleurs grandit . . .   [4]

The thought about Andromaque involves a number of elements that will recur in other contexts throughout the poem: (1) the throwing back of the whole event into distant past time through the use of "jadis"; (2) the situation of the personage; (3) her passions or feelings in that situation. Andromaque's basic situation is that of the "veuve" deprived of her husband; but it is also that of a person in exile from her proper place of existence. Her essential passion is that of sorrow. All three of these elements are assigned to the initial object in the poem not because they belonged to Andromaque in the legend, but because they introduce probabilities that will be useful throughout the rest of the poem. Indeed, it may be that the "example" or "case" of Andromaque was chosen for presentation at this point precisely because these probabilities were built into it.

One may properly ask (at this point or at some other) why the poem should begin with Andromaque rather than with the swan, who gives it its title. The answer, I think, is multiple. First, if the poem is to create and sustain a given state of feeling or passion, this is more immediately and more directly accomplished through association of that feeling with a human being rather than with a dumb creature. (In fact, all thoughts and passions assigned to non-human beings or objects are necessarily human ones that have been transferred to these beings or objects by an analogical or metaphorical operation. Human thoughts and passions are the only ones that the poet can know and that the reader can recognize.) When, later, the swan is introduced, the feelings already existent will easily be adapted to him. Second, a mythological personage provides the occasion for a kind of emotional shorthand: a few suggestions, a name, the brief sketching of a situation, summon up a whole complex of memories and of passions associated with them. This was the way in which the Renaissance poets, at their best, made use of mythology, and this is what Baudelaire does in *Le Cygne*. Third, the choice of a person out of the distant past makes it possible for the poet to establish, right off, one of the bases of the organization of his poem: an opposition of past time to present time, of a special kind, with the accompanying passion.

In the first appearance of Andromaque in the poem, lines 1–4, only one time is explicitly indicated, the time of her exile and sorrow; but the other time, that of her happiness as Hector's wife in their own country, is everywhere implicit. It is implicit both in the way the present locale is described and in the way the emotion is stated. Every device is used to disparage the place of exile: the repetition of the demonstrative in "Ce petit fleuve, Ce Simoïs menteur"; the use of "menteur" to distinguish the artificial rivulet (made by Andromaque) from the real and famous river alongside of which Hector had been buried; the epithets "Pauvre et triste miroir." Each time, one is to think of the distant reality as contrasted to the present reality—of a happy past opposed to a sorrowful present. These details in themselves serve, by opposition, to magnify Andromaque's sorrow. Against the "Pauvre et triste miroir," "L'immense majesté de vos douleurs de veuve"; against the "petit fleuve," the double meaning (material and moral) of "qui par vos pleurs grandit." When one realizes that sorrow and tears are for a dead husband, one senses a time of joy (in another land) when the husband was still alive.

The first stanza, therefore, introduces two sets of relationship, one between Andromaque in exile and Andromaque before the exile, the other between Andromaque and the present thoughts of the speaker. The latter is the one continued in the next two lines,

> A fécondé soudain ma mémoire fertile,
> Comme je traversais le nouveau Carrousel. [6]

The poem thus returns to its starting point, to the thoughts of the speaker, and indicates at what recent point in time, and in what place, the recollection of Andromaque had come to him. The time was "Comme je traversais," the place "le nouveau Carrousel." We should note that it is "le nouveau Carrousel"; for here again is a probability of the recall of an "old" or former Carrousel. The motion backward to time past is by now built into the poem. The speaker indicates the precise nature of his thought when he refers to "ma mémoire," and he prepares for the multiplication of memories later in the poem through "fécondé" and "fertile." The numerous repetitions of "je pense" are in this way announced, a constant device of the poem is introduced: again and again, a present object will bring the remembrance of a past time and a past event, with the emotion proper to them. That emotion is as yet unspecified.

Our expectations with respect to an "old" Carrousel are fulfilled in the seven lines that follow; but before we come specifically to the Carrousel, we shall have the first of a series of generalizations in the poem—generalizations which translate the successive metaphors into a literal meaning for the speaker.

> Le vieux Paris n'est plus (la forme d'une ville
> Change plus vite, hélas! que le cœur d'un mortel).   [8]

The first hemistich of line 7 states, with respect to "le vieux Paris," a sentiment of regret arising from the comparison of the new with the old, and from the passing of the old. It expands the reference by opposing "le vieux Paris" to "le nouveau Carrousel." These two places become another figuration of the difference between past time and present time. Then the generalization: in it, the speaker expresses the reason for his sorrow; objects and situations may change, but the human heart either does not change or changes less rapidly. It remains attached to the former state, resents the present. "La forme d'une ville" encompasses both "Carrousel" and "Paris," with "forme" designating the element that changes. Contrariwise, "le cœur d'un mortel" includes the speaker primarily, Andromaque next, and all those persons who will follow in the poem, with "cœur" designating the element that does not change. Hence the basic opposition:

> forme : ville | cœur : mortel.

This opposition will be pursued throughout the poem, where changes in circumstances or situations will be set against the unchanging human heart. The resultant emotion of sorrow, first contained in Andromaque's "douleur," now simply reiterated in "hélas!" will likewise be variously formulated.

I should emphasize the fact that with this generalization, the emotional potential of the poem increases sharply. The passion that accompanies the speaker's thought about Andromaque and his thought about Paris becomes one with Andromaque's own passion. This is as it should be if, before the swan is introduced, our feelings toward it are to be surely and properly directed.

In the next stanza, one of the past forms of the Carrousel is described; it no longer exists except as a memory—"je ne vois qu'en esprit"—and it may thus serve as a basis for comparing present with past. We shall see, however, that the "form" and the time that concern the speaker are not the ones described in this stanza; these are merely the means for moving one step back into time on the way to a more remote period.

> Je ne vois qu'en esprit tout ce camp de baraques,
> Ces tas de chapiteaux ébauchés et de fûts,
> Les herbes, les gros blocs verdis par l'eau des flaques,
> Et, brillant aux carreaux, le bric-à-brac confus.   [12]

The time is that of the construction of the "nouveau Carrousel," of "ce Louvre" (line 33); a fairly recent past. This is clear from a number of details: the "camp de baraques," the "chapiteaux ébauchés" and the "fûts," the "gros blocs verdis," the "bric-à-brac confus." There are also indications of disorder and neglect: the "herbes," the water of the "flaques," the green moss on the building stones. Such a detail as the last indicates the passage of a period of time. The whole of the description may be useful, in fact, to put the episode of the swan farther back into time, more distant from the present, as well as to prepare for the swan an "artificial" milieu as different from his "beau lac natal" as could be imagined. In this transitional passage, representing a time of transition, we have above all a set of "thoughts" or impressions on the part of the speaker, signifying a reaction to the human activities producing change—all of them far from being admirable or pleasant.

Then comes the episode of the swan, the most completely developed of the examples or parallels that the speaker will use:

> Là s'étalait jadis une ménagerie.   [13]

While "Là" refers back to the "camp de baraques," immediate predecessor to the "nouveau Carrousel," the "jadis" (repeating the "jadis resplendit" of line 2) moves into a more remote period; the operation upon the essential element of time continues. What was to be found on the site of the Carrousel before the construction is simply indicated by "une ménagerie"; but its size is shown through the verb "s'étalait." No further description; yet the impressions associated with the time of construction are vaguely transferred to the notion of "ménagerie," and they will be corroborated by later details. Then the ever-present speaker puts into the menagerie the event that interests him most:

> Là je vis un matin . . .   [14]

The repetition of the "Là" (in the insistent initial position) solidifies the allusion, "je vis" is opposed to the present tenses of "je pense" and "je vois," and "un matin" (for all its indefiniteness) puts the episode in a definite time.

> . . . à l'heure où sous les cieux
> Froids et clairs le Travail s'éveille, où la voirie
> Pousse un sombre ouragan dans l'air silencieux . . .   [16]

We may wonder why, before the direct object of "je vis" is presented, we should have this long description of the early morning hour when the swan was seen. I think that there are several reasons.

On the whole, the speaker wishes to generalize about the milieu and the climate in which the swan will be presented; he also wishes, specifically, to show the extent to which that milieu, produced by man, is inimical to the swan. The important thing will be the state of mind of the reader (reflecting that of the speaker) at the moment when the swan enters. "Sous les cieux froids et clairs" may apply generally to any early-morning hour; for the swan, it denotes the absence of certain elements which might make its existence possible and happy. With "le Travail s'éveille" (and the capital "T" gives a general and almost symbolic meaning to the word) we have the first of two human references that will characterize the morning hour— and make it a very early hour. "Le Travail" of course means "les travailleurs," and a notion of the hard work to come attaches to "s'éveille." That same hard work, in one manifestation, is described in the rest of the stanza. I have held various hypotheses about the meaning of these lines. I now think that the simplest is the best: these are the workmen who, at dawn, sweep the streets, raising a "sombre ouragan" of dust before them. The earliness of the hour is emphasized in "l'air silencieux." With respect to the swan, whom we are to see first in this cold light of dawn, the "sombre ouragan" and the "air silencieux" predispose us to an impression of the milieu in which he now finds himself.

The next stanza, at last, introduces the swan (object of "je vis") and begins to describe his situation and his feelings:

> Un cygne qui s'était évadé de sa cage . . .   [17]

There is a dramatic quality about the introduction, after the long delay, at the beginning of a line and the beginning of a stanza. The action described—"s'était évadé de sa cage"—is also dramatic and calculated to win our sympathy at once. For the "cage," sign of the swan's captivity, is antipathetic to us, and we applaud the swan's escape from it. It is also the captivity and the "cage" that links the swan with Andromaque. We are now able to reconstruct the temporal sequence in the speaker's "thoughts": the traversing of the new Carrousel, followed by the memory of the time of construction, followed by the recollection of the menagerie and the swan in captivity, followed by the thought of Andromaque in captivity—almost the reverse of the order of presentation of these events in the poem. The cage, sign of captivity, is also a place of exile, as is the menagerie (Carrousel) into which the swan has escaped. We should note that we as readers are called upon to establish the correct associations between Andromaque and the swan without direct statements by the poet (through the speaker); those statements will come only later, in Part II.

There follow now several stanzas, completing the first Part, that have as their aim to stress the intolerability of the swan's circumstances and the nature of his (like-human) feelings in these circumstances. One by one, actions and thoughts are depicted:

> Et de ses pieds palmés frottant le pavé sec,
> Sur le sol raboteux traînait son grand plumage.   [19]

Both details contrast a natural part of the swan's being with an unnatural use to which it must now be put. The "pieds palmés," made for smooth paddling through water, are now "frottant le pavé sec"; the "grand plumage," made for flight in the air, now must be dragged on the "sol raboteux" (both "pavé sec" and "sol raboteux" are such in order to contrast as violently as possible with the swan's native habitat). With both activities we associate a sense of the ridiculous, of the awkward, of the ungraceful, merely because the activities are so improper to the agent; and they are so because the agent has been violently removed to an alien milieu. The same is true for the next activity:

> Près d'un ruisseau sans eau la bête ouvrant le bec
>
> Baignait nerveusement ses ailes dans la poudre . . .   [21]

With "ruisseau sans eau" and "la poudre" the difference between the present, unnatural setting and some past, natural setting continues to be emphasized; but the past is merely implied. Then two more actions: "ouvrant le bec" and "baignait nerveusement ses ailes." These begin to assign a moral attitude, a state of feeling to the "beast" (now so designated); they are as ridiculous and erroneous as the others, with in addition a sense of frustration and despair accompanying them. The vision both of the beast and of its surroundings is completed before the speech of protest is quoted.

It is in the quotation of that speech that we have the sure sign that human passions and thoughts are being assigned to a non-human creature, and for purposes of making his case as illustrative as is Andromaque's of the human situation central to the poem.

> Et disait, le cœur plein de son beau lac natal:
> "Eau, quand donc pleuvras-tu? quand tonneras-tu foudre?" [23]

"Disait" is of course analogical, turning the supposed feelings and thoughts of the swan into words that a man might utter. In "le cœur" there is a reference back to "le cœur d'un mortel" (line 8), stressing once more the analogical character of the swan, and in "son beau lac natal" we find a quintessence of all that the swan now lacks: the "lac," diametrically opposed to his present surroundings, "beau" as different from the multiple ugliness around him, "natal" containing the essence of his situation of exile. It is the last word, especially, that points forward to other examples later in the poem. In what he says, the swan expresses a yearning for return to a place of water, unlike the "pavé sec," the "sol raboteux," the "poudre"; rain and thunder would merely presage the coming of this water—replacing the "cieux froids et clairs." The "donc" emphasizes the length of the time of waiting already elapsed, and the repetition of "quand" may serve the same function.

To this point, the swan and his situation and his feelings have been presented without commentary; our own thoughts and feelings about him have been directed only by the ways in which we have been led to associate him with Andromaque and with the speaker. In the five lines that terminate the first Part the speaker comments, specifies, and interprets:

> Je vois ce malheureux, mythe étrange et fatal . . .   [24]

Returning to the present tense of his original formula, "je pense," the speaker in "je vois" (now replacing "je vis") shows that he is now again in the time of meditation; what he sees is in the mind's eye, "en esprit." He calls the swan "ce malheureux," thus creating a category for all those who figure in the poem, including himself; misfortune consists in being removed in time and place from a situation where happiness was possible. Because he represents others who are "malheureux" in the same way, the swan is a "mythe"; also, because he is a dumb creature who represents the sufferings (and the speech) of a man. The quality of "étrange" perhaps relates to these ways of representation, whereas "fatal" adds some suggestive or prophetic virtue, as if the case of the swan might be taken as generally predictive:

> Vers le ciel quelquefois, comme l'homme d'Ovide,
> Vers le ciel ironique et cruellement bleu,
> Sur son cou convulsif tendant sa tête avide . . .   [27]

The speaker now describes the swan's gesture as he remembers or imagines it—before interpreting it. Again, the insistence of repetition, "Vers le ciel quelquefois, Vers le ciel," involving the sky which now stands for the radically changed milieu; it is described as "ironique" because, through the absence of rain and thunder, it mocks at the swan's prayer; and as "cruellement bleu" because of its indifference (through the absence) to that same prayer. "Cruellement bleu" adds another needed quality to the "froids et clairs" of line 15. Both of these epithets add an affective quality that had not previously appeared, needed because of the coming interpretation of the "myth." They also help to augment the reader's feeling of sympathy with the plight of the swan. The next line (27) associates the same kind of moral attitude with one of the swan's gestures: "avide" gives to him the eagerness of hope, just as "son cou convulsif" describes the only way in which he is able to express that eagerness (we should not miss the ridiculous image of that gesture).

Those human references implicit throughout the description of the swan are made explicit in two formulas, and first of all in "comme l'homme d'Ovide" of line 25. The poet makes a simple simile; but for the reader who remembers Ovid's man it has an ironic twist, the nature of the gesture for man and swan being so completely different and the two moral attitudes being so irreconcilable. Ovid's man raises his head nobly toward the heavens to thank the gods for having granted him that special privilege; the swan stretches his head heavenward with a convulsive motion in order to reproach God. That, at least, is the interpretation which the speaker puts upon his gesture:

> Comme s'il adressait des reproches à Dieu! [28]

The simile, again introduced by "comme," is needed in order to liken the swan further to a man, to find an explanation for his misfortune, and to propose a possible meaning for the "fatal" of line 24. If God was responsible for the swan's exile and unhappiness—or if the speaker sees the matter in that light—then there is a kind of fatal necessity connected with it which makes his prayer and his gesture more futile than ever.

Part I of *Le Cygne* comes to an end with this stanza. In it, three things have been accomplished. First, the recollection of Andromaque has provided the first example of a person suffering in exile (although the state of exile must still be inferred) and a feeling of pity for such a state has been initiated. Second, in a fuller and more complete way, the parallel case of the swan has been developed, expanding the feeling of pity as it expands both the circumstances and the passions involved. Third, the thoughts of the speaker have been introduced, repeated, diversified; but, as it were, in passing and without insistence. They appear most specifically in the generalized reference to "le cœur d'un mortel" with the accompanying "hélas!"; they appear also in the interpretation that the speaker gives to the swan's adventure. But the fact that everything in the poem refers, ultimately and intimately, to the passions of the speaker, is not yet clearly stated. That statement will be the function of Part II.

The first words of Part II accomplish the clear reference:

> Paris change! mais rien dans ma mélancolie
> N'a bougé! . . .   [30]

With the words "Paris change!" the speaker collapses into a briefer formula all the elements of lines 7–8: "Le vieux Paris n'est plus (la forme d'une ville / Change plus vite . . .)." The device serves economically to transfer the emotion from those lines to the new section, and in a concentrated way. Besides, what had been parenthetical before becomes now the main line of exposition: it is the change in his own situation that primarily interests the speaker. Time has passed and external things have changed, but in his heart "rien . . . n'a bougé." We are thus returned to the old opposition:

> forme : ville | cœur : mortel.

Now, however, it is the speaker's own passion that is involved, and this is specified as "ma mélancolie"; melancholy is the form that his suffering takes as he compares present with past. It is significant that the poet here names unequivocally the passion attributed to his speaker. Baudelaire constantly does so, as a means to directing the feelings of his reader; his successors in the nineteenth century will seek rather to avoid such clear identification, for the purpose of achieving new effects.

In the rest of the stanza the speaker develops the ideas simply stated in the first words:

> . . . palais neufs, échafaudages, blocs,
> Vieux faubourgs, tout pour moi devient allégorie,
> Et mes chers souvenirs sont plus lourds que des rocs.   [32]

Each of the four items in the enumeration is a reprise of something alluded to earlier in the descriptions; "palais neufs" pluralizes the "nouveau Carrousel" (soon to reappear as "ce Louvre"), "échafaudages" recalls the period of construction and the "camp de baraques," the "blocs" are the "gros blocs verdis," and the "vieux faubourgs" are probably at once "le vieux Paris" and "une ménagerie."

The enumeration again provides a summary statement—only to be finally collapsed into the "tout" of "tout pour moi devient allégorie." With "pour moi" (as in *"ma* mélancolie") the speaker clearly displays his intention throughout the poem: to relate everything to himself. "Devient" shows a return to the present time of meditation (cf. "je pense, je vois"). But what about "allégorie"? The meaning is close to if not identical with that of "mythe" at an earlier point; all the other things contemplated by the speaker have meanings beyond themselves, and these are specifically meanings for the thoughts and feelings of the speaker—"pour moi." These constitute their "allégorie." We are thus now authorized to construct a proportional metaphor:

$$\frac{\text{exil d'Andromaque : sa douleur}}{\text{cage du cygne : son malheur}} :: \frac{\text{changement dans}}{\text{ma situation}} : \text{ma mélancolie}$$

The metaphor is related to our earlier opposition, since in each case the passion—persistent in the heart—results from a change in circumstances, from good to bad, through time. The last line of the stanza reflects such a change; in "mes chers souvenirs" the speaker shows the persistence of a past (cf. "ma mémoire," line 5) that was "dear" to him, but in a form at present barely tolerable ("plus lourds que des rocs"). This is the form of his melancholy.

Interpretation and "allegorical" meaning are extended in the next two stanzas, first to the swan, then to Andromaque. Line 33 leads to a restoration of the correct order of associations and memories:

> Aussi devant ce Louvre une image m'opprime . . .   [33]

The sight of "ce Louvre," "le nouveau Carrousel," recalls the "image" of the swan, which in turn brings the memory of Andromaque ("je pense à vous"); that is the order now followed in these two stanzas. "Aussi" at the beginning has a resumptive or conclusive function, making the transition from the generalization in the preceding stanza to the two repeated examples now to come. They come, however, with the emotional accompaniments that were not possible during the first presentation. Then, the speaker's own situation and feeling had not been clarified; at this point, they have been. They are recapitulated in "m'opprime"; for the vision of the swan is one of his memories that are "plus lourds que des rocs," and it arouses the unhappy emotion in him. The restatement of the first example will have the needed emotional overtones:

> Je pense à mon grand cygne, avec ses gestes fous,
> Comme les exilés, ridicule et sublime,
> Et rongé d'un désir sans trêve! . . .
>
> [36]

Repeating "je pense" of the first line of the poem, the speaker connects the swan definitely with Andromaque; we now appreciate the emotional content of his "thought." When he says "mon grand cygne," the "mon" functions like a special kind of ethical dative: the swan is "his" because of the "allegorical" significance of its situation and feelings for him. The swan is "grand" rather morally than physically, through the magnitude of his misfortune—we are to think back to the "majesté" of Andromaque's sorrows and to the false Simoïs which "grandit" through her tears—"grand" especially through his mythical or allegorical virtue. The phrase "avec ses gestes fous" brings to the summation of those gestures—"frottant le pavé sec," "traînait son grand plumage," "ouvrant le bec," "baignait nerveusement ses ailes," "sur son cou convulsif tendant sa tête avide" —a judgment: the gestures are "fous" because they are at once inappropriate and futile.

The swan's allegorical value (in the particular sense adopted here) is specified in the next line: he is like all those who are in exile. The central term, "exilés," has now been used. We know that, since it includes Andromaque and the speaker as well as the swan, it must be used in an extraordinary and private way; and we shall discover, as we go on in the poem, that that is true and that the meaning is even more special than we had thought. Each of the "exilés" will be (like the swan) "ridicule" and "sublime"; "ridicule" is again a generalization of all that had been said about the swan's gestures, but as an abstraction it may apply to others and other acts; and "sublime" contains everything noble both in the swan and in Andromaque, again as an abstraction. Similarly, the passion ascribed to the swan, "rongé d'un désir sans trêve," will be applicable to all the other exiles; the desire is for a return to the place or a recovery of the time of happiness, and besides being unremitting, "sans trêve," it is basically hopeless and impossible. The use of the verb "rongé" shows to what an extent the whole being is possessed by this passion, made to suffer by it.

Andromaque in exile is again evoked in the following stanza, and with the same devices as had been used for the swan:

> . . . et puis à vous,
> Andromaque, des bras d'un grand époux tombée,
> Vil bétail, sous la main du superbe Pyrrhus . . .   [38]

"Puis" reestablishes the correct order of the associations and "à vous" is to be linked with "je pense," just as it had been in the first line of the poem. The initial formula, "Andromaque, je pense à vous," is merely dismembered and inverted. There had been, previously, no statement about Andromaque's happy state, preceding her "exile"; now both are described in the formula, "des bras d'un grand époux [i.e. Hector] tombée." The "grand" is sufficient to characterize her husband and her former state, "époux" completes the "veuve" of line 3, and "tombée" epitomizes the passage to the state of misfortune. This same state is further described in the following line, where "Vil bétail" denotes the passage to the condition of property or slave and "sous la main" indicates her servitude. Pyrrhus is "superbe" through his haughty attitude towards her. The whole of the description is overlaid with affective elements, expressing the speaker's feelings towards Andromaque. Those feelings find their final and most telling expression in the line that concludes the stanza:

> Veuve d'Hector, hélas! et femme d'Hélénus!   [40]

"Veuve" is repeated from line 3 and, for the first time, the husband's name is given; it had been saved for this point in order to make a dramatic opposition to the inconsequential Hélénus, thereby stressing the extent of Andromaque's "fall." All elements in the line are carefully balanced for the sake of this effect: "veuve" against "femme," "Hector" against "Hélénus," with the "hélas!" in the middle (echoing the "hélas!" of line 8 in an identical position) again giving the measure of the speaker's sympathy.

After the resumption of his two major examples, the speaker passes on to an enumeration that will conclude the poem. It points, in more or less detail, to other persons or groups of persons whose fate has been the same, with the purpose of generalizing the situation and the attendant emotion. By now the central passion is fully specified and implanted; each further generalization will augment it. All the new examples will be parallel to the old. The first is that of the negress exiled from her native Africa, presumably in Paris:

> Je pense à la négresse, amaigrie et phthisique,
> Piétinant dans la boue, et cherchant, l'œil hagard,
> Les cocotiers absents de la superbe Afrique
> Derrière la muraille immense du brouillard . . .   [44]

The procedure used for the negress will be the same as that used for the swan. She is described in a condition diminished and deteriorated from that original and proper to her: "amaigrie" (note the progressive force of the epithet) and "phthisique." In an unsympathetic milieu ("la boue," "la muraille immense du brouillard") contrasting with that of her native land ("Les cocotiers absents de la superbe Afrique"), she acts in ways that are exactly parallel to those of the swan. "Piétinant dans la boue" recalls his awkward gestures, "cherchant, l'œil hagard," his avid straining of his head toward heaven. Since it is introduced by "Je pense," which is by now an organizing formula, the example is charged with the speaker's emotion and his own experience. Hence the "absents" can evoke the whole of a lost past, the "superbe" (here meaning splendid and wonderful), the whole of a distant place of happiness.

There follows now one of several generalizations which will play a double role, that of extending the sense of "exile" and that of specifying the category of unfortunates into which the speaker himself must fit. The construction still depends upon "Je pense":

> A quiconque a perdu ce qui ne se retrouve
> Jamais, jamais! . . .   [46]

"Quiconque" extends the group of persons envisaged far beyond those already presented, just as "a perdu" makes way for many other kinds of loss besides those of husband, of country, of past time. The generality of the loss is indicated by "ce qui ne se retrouve / Jamais, jamais!" with the insistent repetition of the last word showing the degree of hopelessness and of despair. Still continuing from "je pense," the speaker summons up another large group:

> . . . à ceux qui s'abreuvent de pleurs
> Et tettent la Douleur comme une bonne louve!   [47]

Here there are (in addition to the possible mythological reference that I have already suggested) two quotations from the first stanza. Andromaque's "douleurs de veuve" are changed into "la Douleur" —the capital letter makes the general abstraction—and her "pleurs" become the "pleurs" of all those who weep, "ceux qui." "S'abreuvent," "tettent," and "une bonne louve" metaphorize their sorrow, relate it to the myth of Romulus and Remus, and, combining as they do that myth with Andromaque's story, add an extremely pathetic note to the enumeration. The same note is present in the next line:

> Aux maigres orphelins séchant comme des fleurs!   [48]

I see in "orphelins" a possible association with the myth just alluded to, in "maigres" a variant on the "amaigrie" of line 41, and in "séchant comme des fleurs!" a radical diminution from an original state. These are not "exiles," but they have lost the possibility of health and happiness in the loss of the suckling mother (perhaps a recall of the "tettent" of the preceding line); now they, too, feed and wither on sorrow. Such a line as this might, by itself, seem to be sentimental; but it does not create that impression because the whole context of the poem is condensed into it, with its notions of the "grandeur" and the sublimity of those who suffer.

Having specified and generalized the emotion at one and the same time—specified with respect to its quality, generalized with respect to its application—the speaker may now conclude. He does so by completing the application, first to himself, then to the widest possible category of sufferers. The "Ainsi" introducing the last stanza is the sign of the coming conclusion:

> Ainsi dans la forêt où mon esprit s'exile
> Un vieux Souvenir sonne à plein souffle du cor!   [50]

Having already stated, in line 32, that his memories were the source of sorrow, making present as it were a state of past happiness, he now connects his own memories with the exile of others, bringing the emotions together. He uses several devices to do so. "Les exilés" (line 35) is turned into the verb "s'exile," to which he gives the restricted meaning of a change in time; but in order to retain something of the conventional meaning, he makes the metaphor "dans la forêt." His mind ("mon esprit"), moving into the past, is like an exile moving into a forest. What it finds there is not "mes souvenirs," but "Un vieux Souvenir"; again the abstraction (with its capital letter) for the whole process of remembrance, and the "vieux" (remember "le vieux Paris") to signify not only the return to the past but also the length of time covered in that return. The memory is a vigorous and dominating one which, like the exile "rongé d'un désir sans trêve," fills his whole being: "sonne à plein souffle du cor." The metaphor of the forest is further exploited, perhaps (as I have suggested) through an allusion to Vigny's poem. It has the virtue of all metaphorical expression, that of augmenting the emotional potential through imagery and association. The speaker has now fully identified with himself all those of whom he had previously spoken, he has made their passion his, he has transferred to himself all the feeling that the reader had been induced to associate with them.

After the contraction to himself, the expansion to all other sufferers in the closing lines of the poem:

> Je pense aux matelots oubliés dans une île,
> Aux captifs, aux vaincus! . . . à bien d'autres encor!

This time "Je pense" (the refrain that introduces his remembrance of all the exiles and like-exiles in the poem) evokes three categories of men, the "matelots" (exiles when they are "oubliés dans une île"), the "captifs," the "vaincus." The captives and the conquered have forever lost something: their freedom or the chance of victory; they are in the broader class to which the notion of exile has been extended. Finally, the all-inclusive formula, "à bien d'autres encor!" sufficiently vague to admit unlimited groups of those who sorrow through loss, through exile, through the unhappy memory of past happiness. As it closes, the poem opens up, to the imagination of the reader, unlimited possibilities of associating the emotion with other individuals and groups.

Such generalization has been the main function of Part II. Beginning with the three singular examples that had occupied Part I—the speaker, Andromaque, the swan—it has added group after group of persons whose situation is identical with or similar to that of the three. At the same time it has moved away from a kind of technical meaning of "exile" towards a related or metaphorical one; "exiles" are all those who, in the present, suffer from the loss of something out of the past. To achieve this extension, it has developed further the idea (present from the outset) that present time may be made equivalent to present place, past time to distant places. Concurrently the emotions of sorrow in Andromaque, of longing in the swan, of painful nostalgia in the speaker, have been blended into a single emotion, general enough to accommodate all the related emotions of the people introduced. This last step was necessary so that the situations and the feelings of a variety of persons might be made comparable to the speaker's—the really important ones.

I should point out that (as is generally the case in poetry) the reader's emotion by no means coincides with that of the people in the poem. In *Le Cygne,* we should really distinguish three separate emotions: that of the persons whom the speaker contemplates (and this one Baudelaire names clearly for us), that of the speaker as he meditates upon them (and this is also fairly clearly defined), and that of the reader. But while the first and the second gradually come together into one, as the speaker identifies his plight with that of his examples, the third remains essentially distinct. The reader understands the emotions of the people in the poem—of Andromaque, the swan, the negress, the speaker—and he is sympathetic to their plight; but he neither is himself in that same plight, nor does he suffer the same passions. There is a proper metaphorical relationship between the emotion of the speaker and that of his examples; there is no such relationship between these persons and the reader. What the reader feels, instead, is a product or an offshoot of situation and emotion in the poem—in a way perpendicular to them; it is aroused, directed, conditioned by them; but it is not one with them. That is to say, it is an aesthetic emotion rather than a real one. The distinction is important for our understanding of poetic form. For were this not so, it might be thought that in poetry the reader's emotions are manipulated directly as they are in rhetoric. Instead, they are manipulated indirectly, through the intermediary of the poetic form.

How, in the case of *Le Cygne,* is the poetic form achieved as a means to the achievement of the aesthetic effect? We may suppose that the central emotion to be aroused within the poem is one of sorrow, and that we as readers will feel, with respect to all those who suffer that sorrow in the poem, something akin to pity. The sorrow within the poem is a result, in each case, of a change in circumstances from fortunate to unfortunate, involving a change in time from the past to the present and in place from a "native" to an "alien" country. The totality of the change is thought of, in metaphorical terms, as an "exile." This way of conceiving the central situation and its resultant emotion gives rise to a basic metaphor:

> past time :
> past place : present time : : past happiness : present sorrow
> past situation :

Once we conceive of this as the metaphor about which the poem is organized, we may see each of its examples as a variant upon the metaphor. The most complete ones are those of Andromaque and of the swan. Andromaque's situation has changed from that of Hector's wife to that of Pyrrhus' wife, then Helenus'; from noble station to slavery; in place, from Troy to the "false Simois"; in time. The swan's change has essentially been one of place, from the "beau lac natal" to the cage and the dry and dusty menagerie; but there is enough of a human awareness of time in him to permit the comparison of his two states and the resultant painful nostalgia. In a way, the speaker is a counterpart to the swan. His situation represents primarily a change in time from a happy past to an unhappy present, and the change in place (from "le *vieux* Paris" to "le *nouveau* Carrousel") consists merely in the operation of time upon a single place.

The virtue of a metaphorical structure resides precisely in the possibility it affords of transferring the whole or any part of an image or an emotion from one of the elements in the metaphor to the other. Thus Andromaque or the swan (or any of the others later mentioned) may be "myths" or "allegories" to the speaker's suffering; time may be substituted for place, place for time, one form of "exile" for another. So long as the fundamental set of relationships is retained, the correct emotion will be present in the poem (and the derivative emotion in the reader). Moreover, a kind of compression or condensation becomes increasingly feasible: at the end of his poem, Baudelaire may write simply "Aux captifs, aux vaincus," and all of the passions accompanying exile (as it has been developed in *Le Cygne*) will be felt. He could not have done so at the beginning, when the bases of the metaphor remained to be established. Once they have been set down, all statements about separate cases or examples tend to become equivalent statements—equivalent in their emotional context and in their emotional potential.

In terms of the operation of this metaphorical structure, the order of the poem may be plainly perceived. It begins with its two most fully developed examples, since through these it introduces the whole range of conditions that determine situation and emotion. And of these two, it presents Andromaque first, rather than the swan, because of her more ready human accessibility and because of the mythological echoes that accompany her. At the same time, it states not only the interest of the speaker in these examples, but more importantly his identification (to a point) with them. Afterwards, it may exploit separately the constituent elements of time, place, situation, emotion, either through further examples or in general statements. Concurrently, the speaker's own state is regularly brought into comparison with that of his examples, so that it may grow and be enriched through each of them. When all the useful and appropriate elements of his emotional state have been presented, and when the related examples have been multiplied to the fullest, the poem may end; for both the internal emotion and the potential for an emotional effect upon the reader will have reached their full realization.

From the point of view of the development of the techniques of French poetry, this poem may be regarded as essentially traditional. Metaphorical structures of the kind had been used by many poets before Baudelaire, and frequently by himself, although perhaps not so subtly nor with the same richness of exploitation. There is one respect, however, in which what Baudelaire does in *Le Cygne* may be related to one of the main lines of innovation in modern French poetry. Let us look at the following passage, ripped out of context and isolated:

Un cygne . . . s'était évadé de sa cage,
Et, de ses pieds palmés frottant le pavé sec,
Sur le sol raboteux traînait son grand plumage.
Près d'un ruisseau sans eau la bête ouvrant le bec

Baignait nerveusement ses ailes dans la poudre,
Et disait, le cœur plein de son beau lac natal:
"Eau, quand donc pleuvras-tu? quand tonneras-tu, foudre?"
. . . .

Vers le ciel quelquefois . . .
Vers le ciel ironique et cruellement bleu,
Sur son cou convulsif tendant sa tête avide,
Comme s'il adressait des reproches à Dieu!

I have done two things to this passage. Besides separating it from the rest of the poem, I have removed from it all traces of the speaker and his commentary (as in line 24) and the overt comparison of the swan to a man. I have made of it something that might (with a few syntactical alterations) stand by itself as a separate poem. Now since all direct allusion to the speaker or to man in general has been cut away, one half of the metaphor has disappeared. The swan, who was "like" the speaker (and others) in his situation and his emotion, is now no longer in that relationship. He stands by himself and for himself. Yet, if we were to reread closely this new "poem," we would see that there are enough segments of the original metaphor remaining in it to permit us to see the swan as somehow representing a man, both in his plight and in his feelings.

In a word, we have here all the features of a modern symbolist poem. As practiced by the French poets of the late nineteenth century, the symbolist poem was one in which a half-metaphor served as the basis of the structure; that is, the object or the person represented throughout the poem was one which, in a metaphorical structure, would have been analogical to another object or person (as the swan, in *Le Cygne,* is to the speaker). Only, that other object or person was nowhere explicitly identified. Instead, the analogies were implicit and they had to be inferred from the half of the metaphor presented; inference was made possible by various signs or pointers that the poet built into his poem. That is to say that if the symbol is a kind of truncated metaphor (but one which persists throughout the poem as the basis of its structure), then symbolist structure is in a way implicit in metaphorical structure. All the symbolist poet needed to do was to handle metaphorical structure in a particular way to arrive at his innovation. Baudelaire, in *Le Cygne,* does not by any means go that far; his swan is only one of several "persons" analogized to the speaker, and he appears only occasionally in the poem. Yet in the way in which Baudelaire handles this particular passage he shows a mastery of a technique which, with slight modifications, will be that of the symbolist poets. He himself uses that technique, fully realized, in certain others of his poems.

Since I have called this chapter "A Statement of Method," and since I have wished not only to present an analysis of Baudelaire's *Le Cygne* but also to use that analysis as an exemplification of a method, I think it not inappropriate now to state explicitly what I have been trying to do.

1. I have attempted to fill in as much of the literary and historical background of the poem as might be useful for its understanding. This is not properly part of an analytical method; but it is antecedent and propaedeutic to the application of analysis to certain poems. I shall probably have occasion to engage in this kind of study only rarely in the succeeding chapters.

2. In the analysis proper, I have tried first to find the meaning, for the whole, of each separate word or formula; and this meaning has been sought always from the context of the total poem. This is the first point at which a rigid discipline is necessary in order to avoid the temptation of "reading into" the poem meanings which are not there.

3. Once the meaning of the smallest parts was made clear, I have looked for all the appropriate relationships among those parts. The word "appropriate" indicates again the need for great care; for it is easy to find chance connections that are not meaningful for the poem.

4. In turn, once the relationships among the parts were made clear, I have asked to what central whole these parts belonged—assuming that they were parts of something. In a work of the poetic art, which moves through time, the central or organizing structure will be a temporal one; hence my question about the whole sought

an answer that would include a dynamic element, a line of development and change, a movement from the beginning through the middle to the end.

5. Only when that central organizing principle had been discovered was it possible to discuss the nature of the basic structure. In that discussion, I have tried to do two things: to describe or characterize the structure of *Le Cygne* as a particular and unique thing; and to relate that structure to a class of structures, thereby describing it generally and making possible comparison with other structures.

6. Throughout the discussion of the parts and the whole, I have thought of them in terms of the emotion that they were meant to evoke—an emotion resulting from situations, images, passions assigned to the persons. This is the "internal" emotion present as a result of the moral conditions of the poem.

7. But I have hoped, at the same time, not to neglect giving some attention to the "external" emotion, derived from the other and felt by the reader as the effect produced by the work of art.

8. Since the work of poetry moves through time, I have looked for the chronological development, within the poem, of both these emotional lines, especially the first.

9. With respect to each of the separate devices used by the poet, I have raised questions about its usefulness specifically for the arousing of the internal emotion and for the achievement of the external emotional effect.

10. This means, in the last analysis, that I have everywhere tried to establish the relationship between structure and effect, to think of each in terms of the other, to predict effect from structure and to judge structure in terms of effect.

A final word of caution: What I have not wanted to do was to make any guesses about the creative act, or rediscover the processes by which the poet made the poem, or reconstruct the poet's psychology. I insist upon considering the creative process and the analytical process as separate and distinct—and upon devoting myself exclusively to the analytical.

2

Baudelaire

Spleen ("Quand le ciel bas et lourd . . .")

Spleen

Quand le ciel bas et lourd pèse comme un couvercle
Sur l'esprit gémissant en proie aux longs ennuis,
Et que de l'horizon embrassant tout le cercle
Il nous verse un jour noir plus triste que les nuits;   4

Quand la terre est changée en un cachot humide,
Où l'Espérance, comme une chauve-souris,
S'en va battant les murs de son aile timide
Et se cognant la tête à des plafonds pourris;   8

Quand la pluie étalant ses immenses traînées
D'une vaste prison imite les barreaux,
Et qu'un peuple muet d'infâmes araignées
Vient tendre ses filets au fond de nos cerveaux,   12

Des cloches tout à coup sautent avec furie
Et lancent vers le ciel un affreux hurlement,
Ainsi que des esprits errants et sans patrie
Qui se mettent à geindre opiniâtrément.   16

—Et de longs corbillards, sans tambours ni musique,
Défilent lentement dans mon âme; l'Espoir,
Vaincu, pleure, et l'Angoisse atroce, despotique,
Sur mon crâne incliné plante son drapeau noir.   20

The title *Spleen* indicates the state of feeling that will be attributed to the speaker in the poem that follows. It is, of course, an ambiguous indication: several other poems in the group bear the same title, yet the feeling in each is particular and distinct from the others. Only the whole of the poem itself will delimit and refine upon the feeling, providing the particular connotations that will distinguish this *Spleen* from the others.

We noted, in *Le Cygne,* the fact that Baudelaire had clearly named such emotions as "Douleur" as one of his devices for assuring comprehension and for directing the passions. In *Spleen,* he extends the same practice, not only by multiplying the specific identifications, but also by providing occasional opposites. Thus if we run through the poem, we find on the one hand such affective terms as "l'esprit gémissant," "longs ennuis," "triste," "infâmes," "affreux," "geindre," culminating in the formula at the end (line 19), "l'Angoisse atroce, despotique." On the other hand, "l'Espérance" at the beginning (line 6) and "l'Espoir" at the end (line 18) are represented as timid, futile, vanquished. The intentions are clear: "spleen" is characterized positively and as it were circumscribed by a number of related feelings, negatively by its opposition to anything that might be thought of as hope. We might call it, using the terms of the poem, something like "an anguish of hopelessness."

But so to call it would not be, in any sense, to reproduce the effect and the effectiveness of the poem. A poem is not a collection of terms naming the passions; it cannot and does not achieve its ends merely by listing the emotions sought. When such listing occurs, it is ordinarily for purposes of clarification or for reinforcement of more properly poetic means. In the case of *Spleen,* the poetic means chosen by the poet is a composite visual image all of whose component images are similarly related to a central conception and are at the same time appropriate to the central emotion. This means, really, that the visual image is selected or invented because of its usefulness in expressing that emotion.

The first form of the image is found in the first stanza:

> Quand le ciel bas et lourd pèse comme un couvercle
>
> . . . .
>
> Et que de l'horizon embrassant tout le cercle . . .   [3]

We are to see two things here, first and foremost an image of a completely enclosed space ("couvercle," "tout le cercle"), then a heavy (and presumably dark) object effecting the enclosure. In the second stanza, another such image of rigidly enclosed space appears in the form of the "cachot humide" with its "murs" and its "plafonds pourris." This dungeon becomes, in the third stanza, the "prison" simulated by the falling rain:

> Quand la pluie étalant ses immenses traînées
> D'une vaste prison imite les barreaux . . .   [10]

Whether it be small or vast, formed by the sky or the horizon or the rain, circular or square, the kind of space that one sees is closed, contained, restricted on all sides. Indeed, the impression is cumulative as one passes from image to image, and the variations are less important than the basic similarity.

Likewise, the series of details associated with the enclosed space is cumulative; there are no repetitions, but the details are complementary and constitute a filling out of the central image. We have already seen, in connection with the initial statement, not only the adjectives "bas et lourd" but also a kind of consequence of their idea in the verb "pèse." More details come in line 4, concluding the first image:

> Il nous verse un jour noir plus triste que les nuits.

"Noir" and "nuits" complete an impression that we formed at the beginning, although without specific direction. The "humide" applied to the dungeon and the "pourris" describing the ceilings add a new notion, having moral as well as physical overtones, and this is confirmed in the "traînées de pluie" of line 9. One descriptive element is particularly worthy of remark, and that is the "muet" applied to the mass of spiders: it emphasizes the fact that throughout the preceding description all has been silent except for such dull sounds as one might associate with "verse," "battant les murs," "se cognant la tête." In so far as motion has been suggested, it has been vertical and downward motion, such as the "pèse" and the "verse" for the sky, the "traînées" and the "barreaux" for the rain. Both of these, the silence and the descending motion, are needed preparations for a later "event" in the poem.

The covered vessel, the dungeon, the prison; darkness, humidity, oppressiveness and silence; obviously, these are meant for one who is a prisoner and oppressed. In fact, such a one is present from the outset. He is "l'esprit gémissant en proie aux longs ennuis" (line 2) upon whom the lid weighs; he belongs to the "nous" (line 4) who must also include the speaker, although no firm identification is made as yet. In the second stanza, it is he in whom hope struggles:

> Où l'Espérance, comme une chauve-souris,
> S'en va battant les murs de son aile timide
> Et se cognant la tête à des plafonds pourris . . .   [8]

Through the personification of Hope, made into the imprisoned bat, a passion of some person is expressed and clarified; the person must be the "esprit gémissant," one of "nous." Similarly, the same general person is alluded to in the last two lines of the third stanza:

> Et qu'un peuple muet d'infâmes araignées
> Vient tendre ses filets au fond de nos cerveaux . . .   [12]

Here we have the first indication that "nos cerveaux" may likewise be considered as dark enclosed spaces, in the depths of which spiders spin their webs. The thought is again expressed through the occasional metaphor.

Whoever this person may be—"l'esprit gémissant," "nous," "nos cerveaux"—it is he who feels or suffers the dominant passion of "spleen" toward which everything, from the outset of the poem, has been pointing. By the time we reach the end of the third stanza, the visual imagery, the names or abstractions for the feelings, such occasional metaphors as those of the bat and the spiders, the suggestion of complete silence, all have contributed to the generation and the growth of a strong central impression, equivalent to what the person in the poem must be feeling. I have discussed so far only these first three stanzas, for one thing because they have as their function to create the impression of which I have been speaking, for another because—introduced as each of them is by "quand"—they specify a single point in time anterior to the first "event" of the poem. This convergence in time of the various objects and feelings described is another device for making the objects themselves converge into one object, the feelings into one feeling.

The "event" is the tolling of the bells:

> Des cloches tout à coup sautent avec furie
> Et lancent vers le ciel un affreux hurlement . . .   [14]

Two things distinguish the event from the circumstances that had
prepared it: the loud noises replacing the silence ("sautent avec
furie," "affreux hurlement") and the upward motion replacing the
downward ("sautent," "lancent vers le ciel"). It is apparent now
that both features had been made one way at the beginning so that
their opposites might lend a dramatic quality to the event; the
sounds are the louder for the silence that had preceded them, the
upward movement is more violent because of the slow downward
movement to which it is contrasted. In its turn, this "event" is
followed by another to which it was really merely an accompaniment. The bells that toll are funeral bells, and the funeral is the
metaphor for the death, within the speaker, of struggling Hope,
vanquished by "l'Angoisse atroce, despotique." We are now authorized in saying "within the speaker," for he identifies himself at two
points: "dans mon âme" (line 18) and "Sur mon crâne incliné"
(line 20). In the funeral, the silence, the blackness, and the downward motion of the early parts of the poem return; and both the
"âme" and the "crâne" of the speaker become the human counterparts of the enclosed spaces that had previously been described.

Through these various devices—the creation and exploitation of a
central visual (and auditory) image, the naming of the related
passions, the use of occasional metaphors, and the final allegorical
episode—the meaning and the effect of "spleen" are built and fully
realized in the course of the poem. The passion of "spleen" is the
object represented in the poem; but it is represented first as belonging to a definite person, the speaker, at a given time, and second as
analyzed into its constituent thoughts and sensations. In itself,
"spleen" is one and indivisible; as such, it can neither be adequately
expressed by the speaker nor felt by the reader. For purposes of
expression and effect, it must be taken apart, spread out, looked at in
various ways, compared to various things that will make it comprehensible. All this must take place through time—analysis is always a
spreading out in space or in time, and poetry is a temporal art—and

42

hence one of the poet's problems is the discovery of the most useful
order for the chronological disposition of the parts. What Baudelaire
did for the solution of that problem may be seen by a running
analysis of the poem that he produced.

The first stanza is the first of three, as I have pointed out, to begin
with a temporal indication, "Quand," of such nature as to require a
kind of temporal resolution; when such-and-such is true, then such-
and-such happens. It also presents the first of the exemplary images:

> Quand le ciel bas et lourd pèse comme un couvercle
> Sur l'esprit gémissant en proie aux longs ennuis,
> Et que de l'horizon embrassant tout le cercle
> Il nous verse un jour noir plus triste que les nuits . . .   [4]

The initial statement of the visual image, in lines 1 and 2, contains
all the elements (lowness, heaviness, enclosure) that will recur in
the later treatments; hence it may begin to suggest the pertinent
emotion. It does so immediately in connection with a person suffering the emotion; and two conditions are specified. For one, the
person so suffering (and his mind is already "gémissant" at this
point) is a victim, a prey. For the other, his present state results from
a long history ("aux longs ennuis"), and the time indicated by the
"quand" may thus be a time of crisis or culmination. We should note
that neither here nor later does the speaker give any suggestion as to
the causes of the feeling or the precise form that it takes; our
attention will thus be throughout on the passion itself, not on persons or circumstances or events that might have brought it on. This
is one way of abstracting the passion, a lyrical way rather than a
narrative or dramatic way since it has no direct reference to situation, character, or action. The "triste" of line 4, assigning an attribute to the daylight, really represents an attribute of the emotion,
while "jour noir" and "nuits" complete the visual image; at the same
time, they introduce elements that will be useful in the final stanza.

A similar plan determines the content of the second stanza: the
visual image of an enclosed space imprisoning the speaker. But only
one part of the speaker, the emotion of hope that will be vanquished
at the end, is here present:

Quand la terre est changée en un cachot humide,
Où l'Espérance, comme une chauve-souris,
S'en va battant les murs de son aile timide
Et se cognant la tête à des plafonds pourris . . .   [8]

In the second image, the extent of the pressing inward of all limits of the enclosed space is emphasized by the reduction of "la terre" to a "cachot humide." Added to the impressions already aroused in Stanza I, the image we see is darker, tighter, more oppressive. All these aspects are enhanced by the introduction into the space of a flying creature who represents Hope. Much is achieved, for the growing emotional effect, through the personification of Hope. The comparison to a bat, with its sinister connotations, reduces Hope to a weak, fluttering creature, and these characteristics are repeated in the "aile timide" and the "se cognant la tête." The space becomes progressively smaller as the bat's flight is limited by "les murs" and the "plafonds pourris," and the last detail in particular stresses the hopelessness of Hope's struggle; a reason is provided for the state of the "esprit gémissant." In a sense, the effect achieved by introducing a rapidly moving object into the motionless space is similar to the one that will be obtained, later, by introducing violent sound into the silent space. The moral plight of the speaker is made accessible to the senses; but we should note that the identity of the sufferer is still no more definite than it was in the first stanza. This generality of the reference (added to the non-circumstantial character of the emotion) permits us to enter more readily into the state of feeling than if that state were highly specific.

There is no further specification of the reference in the third stanza, where a new form of the central image is developed; the "nos" still gathers in the reader with the unidentified speaker and others.

Quand la pluie étalant ses immenses traînées
D'une vaste prison imite les barreaux,
Et qu'un peuple muet d'infâmes araignées
Vient tendre ses filets au fond de nos cerveaux . . .   [12]

Once more the repetition of the "Quand" shows that the point of time is still the same as it was at the beginning—that the three images are simultaneous and superimposed rather than successive—while the punctuation itself (in the full text, semicolons follow the first two stanzas and a comma the third) indicates that the mind is to be held in suspense while it awaits the solution, just as the voice (in the reading) is to repeat the intonational pattern that precedes the climax. As far as the image is concerned, whereas the first form was an expanded form, embracing the whole horizon, and the second form a contracted one, reducing the whole earth to a dungeon, this third form is again "vaste." Space is limited by the "immenses traînées" of the rain which, because of their verticality, are likened to prison bars; the "cachot" is now the "prison." All the feelings attached to the first two images are poured into the third, and that precisely because certain elements have persisted or been repeated. The device is an eminently poetic one, but one which can be used only in the "middle" of a poem (or at the "end") after the conditions have been initially established in the "beginning."

With the metaphor in lines 11 and 12, a number of earlier poetic probabilities are realized. First of these is the reduction of space (again) to that of "nos cerveaux"; this is the very basis of the metaphor. Second is the presentation (again) of living creatures within that space, the "araignées" succeeding the bat. Third, the spinning of the spiders' webs exploits the image of linear movement; because of what we have seen before, we will see it as largely vertical. The metaphor works roughly in this way: the silent working of the passions in the depths of our minds or souls is like the silent spinning of webs in the far reaches of a prison. Certain aspects of those passions have already been named in "ennuis," "triste," "pourris"; the "infâmes" used as an epithet for the spiders is now added to the characterization. Other details are suggested in the multiplicity of "un peuple muet" and in the progressive sense of "vient tendre"; each attaches to the passion an impression of slow and secret movings within the dark and unbearable space. In this way, new emotional overtones are made to fill out the passion just as new images completed the central visual impression. When we arrive at the end of the third stanza—of that "conditional" temporal development introduced by the series of "quand"—the complex passion and the complex vision that represents it have both been pushed to a degree of completeness that almost demands a new turn if additional effects are to be achieved.

Temporal resolution and rhythmical climax, in the fourth stanza, are the outward marks of this new turn, which consists in reversing some of the previous impressions; but the reversal merely has as its purpose to intensify:

> Des cloches tout à coup sautent avec furie
> Et lancent vers le ciel un affreux hurlement,
> Ainsi que des esprits errants et sans patrie
> Qui se mettent à geindre opiniâtrément.   [16]

"Tout à coup" answers the expectations of the three "quand." It signalizes the event that occurs against the background that has been described; both background and event will be "moral." I have already pointed out how both sound and motion here are contrasted with their predecessors, and the dramatic effect that results. But the epithet used for the sound of the bells, "affreux," and even the noun "hurlement" itself—so contrary to one's associations with the sound of bells—are meant to coincide with the rest of the feeling previously created. Indeed, the phrase summarizes the whole of the emotional "tone" that rings within the speaker's mind. And it is apparently designed to be metaphorical in that very way.

The bat, the spiders had moved silently within the prison spaces that contained them. Now, within the totality of the enclosed space that represents the speaker's mind ("nos cerveaux"), and where the bells toll, other creatures move to and fro. They are not, however, living creatures (another opposition), but rather "esprits errants," set in motion or awakened by the tolling bells. The extent of their desolation is stressed by "sans patrie"; since they, too, represent the speaker's passion of "spleen," the notion of the homeless dead brings a new dimension to that passion. Besides, rather than keeping the silence of bat and spiders, they begin (and this is the spiritual event that accompanies the sensible one) to "geindre opiniâtrément." There is in "geindre," which must be taken as concomitant with the "hurlement," another representation of the despair that is one of the components of "spleen," and its adverb "opiniâtrément," occupying the entire hemistich, repeats what "longs ennuis" had earlier said about the interminable nature of the passion. It does so with increased insistence, seems to constitute a climax to the whole statement that has preceded.

What had seemed to be climax and conclusion (the fourth stanza completes the long sentence and ends with a period) could not, however, properly be so. For the poem still lacked both an identification of the speaker and the application of the passion to him. The abstract "esprit gémissant," the general and impersonal "nous" and "nos," needed to be specified and personalized. Besides, all the suggestions of decay and death, bringing about the suggestion of the funeral knell, demanded clearer statement and fuller realization. All these probabilities for further development of the poem are satisfied in the final stanza:

> —Et de longs corbillards, sans tambours ni musique,
> Défilent lentement dans mon âme; l'Espoir,
> Vaincu, pleure, et l'Angoisse atroce, despotique,
> Sur mon crâne incliné plante son drapeau noir.   [20]

Each element, here, does constitute a realization of something introduced earlier in the poem, does conclude. "Mon âme" and "mon crâne" not only reduce the plural "nous" to the singular speaker, they also represent the last of the enclosed spaces—and the ones to which all the others stood in an analogical relationship. All the spaces were, in a word, metaphors for the speaker's soul. Within that prison space, there are again beings in motion. They are in the first place the unnamed beings who walk in the funeral processions; the "longs corbillards" parallel in space the movement of the "longs ennuis" in time, while "défilent lentement" carries echoes of the "filets" (line 12) and the slow motion intimated in the earlier stanzas. In the second place, the personified passion of Espérance, which in the second stanza had been represented as struggling, is now represented, under the form of "l'Espoir," as vanquished; it again inhabits the space of the soul. I have wondered why "Espérance" should be changed to "Espoir"; perhaps it is because there is in the former a sense of dynamism and activity that is lacking from the latter. Another being appears in the scene, although outside the enclosed space of "mon crâne." This is the conquering "Angoisse" who now becomes a personification of all the feelings associated with "spleen." Through these beings and activities, the whole body of feeling comes to be intimately connected with the speaker.

Moreover, the tonality of the passion is preserved through other references to antecedent parts of the poem. With "sans tambours ni musique" we return to the silence of the beginning, now enhanced by the intervening furious pealing of bells. Hope, characterized as vanquished, now weeps with a sound that must recall the "geindre" of line 16. Two epithets, "atroce, despotique," applied to "l'Angoisse," make of him at once the jailer of the "cachot" and the "prison" and the cause, in the speaker, of the death of anything that might oppose "spleen." At the same time, they describe the hold that "spleen" has upon the speaker. The last line of the poem, describing the action of "l'Angoisse," is composed of elements derived from earlier stanzas. I see two vertical, downward movements that fit into the established pattern, the "inclining" of the speaker's head under the weight of all the things (spiritual things) that bear down upon him, and the "planting" of the flag by Anguish. Verticality is stressed both in the action itself and in the position of the flag standard that results from it. The flag is black not only because it is a symbol of death but because it summarizes all the visual impressions that have preceded and all the emotional tonality of "spleen."

By this time, the emotional tonality to be associated with "spleen" has been completed and accomplished. The visual impressions of darkness, humidity, downward weighing, oppressiveness and restriction, the impression of silence (interrupted briefly by the tolling of the bells), have been synthesized into the final death scene. They have been translated back into the emotions that they stood for from the beginning, and these too have been synthesized into the central passion of Anguish. As for the function of Hope, it has been throughout to stand as an opponent to "spleen," as something that prevents its complete domination; when hope is defeated, "spleen" may take over the speaker's soul. The very nature of "spleen" becomes clearer as we see it, "atroce, despotique," juxtaposed to the timid, fluttering, vanquished and weeping Hope. One of the devices for directing the emotion is thus a negative and contrasting one; our sense of what "spleen" must be is enhanced by our knowledge of what it is not. The direct and the indirect statements of the central emotion—direct through the abstractions and the personifications, indirect through the multiple imagery—have run parallel through the poem; at the end, they coincide. The feeling is thereby augmented and intensified.

In its structure, *Spleen* thus exemplifies a general poetic principle of organization. Its beginning consists in initial statements of probability—a purely poetic probability that resides in incomplete or unrealized potentials—and the rest in realizations of that probability. The probability is complex and varied, affecting the person who speaks throughout the poem, the central passion that he feels and expresses, the images and the metaphors that he uses to express it, the syntactical and prosodic structure through which the expression is made. Whichever one of these lines we may choose to trace in the poem, we shall find a similar pattern of initial presentation, leading to expansion and development, culminating in a final climactic form. The derivative emotion of the reader follows a similar evolution. But *Spleen* also has its own particular principle of organization. It develops an overall, inclusive image made up of secondary or contributory images; these serve as background for an event, itself presented through an image; and both background and event represent a passion that turns out to be the speaker's. The passion is called "spleen" and all the sensory images are chosen for their usefulness in suggesting that passion or in eliciting it. The passion thus comes to be known to us through two processes, through the metaphors involved in the various images and through a kind of allegorizing connected with certain abstractions that belong to the passion.

Both metaphors and allegorizing are occasional. I mean by this that there is no single metaphor about which the whole of the form is constructed, just as there is no allegorical basis for the entire poem. Such metaphors as that of the bat or that of the spiders appear at a given point in the poem, make their contribution, and then disappear. If they were "structural" rather than "occasional" metaphors, they would persist from beginning to end and the whole of the structure would depend upon the working out of the metaphor. When "Espoir" and "Angoisse" are capitalized, personified, and made to act, this happens only for a moment; there is no attempt to create a total allegory which, throughout, would supply the basis for the organization of the poem. *Spleen* is thus built upon a principle of translating the central passion into a series of related images, meta-phors, allegorizations, even direct namings of elements of the pas-sion, every one of which is appropriate to that passion but none of which reduces all the others to a subsidiary status.

During the analysis of *Spleen,* as in the summarizing remarks just concluded, I have been applying two criteria which should be gener-ally useful in the study of lyric poetry. Asking, with respect to each detail, to what extent it contributed to the developing central image, I have in each case referred to a criterion of "belongingness," or "usefulness," or appropriateness. The underlying assumption was that any detail of the poem must be studied and judged in terms of its relationship to the whole. If we ask whether the comparison "comme un couvercle" is a good one, and if we answer that it is because it introduces, at the very beginning, two visual qualities that will be exploited throughout the development of the image—the closing in of a space and the downward-weighing motion—then we have applied a criterion of usefulness and found an affirmative answer. We have also derived that affirmative answer from a total reading of the poem which discovered for us the nature of the central image. That is, the application of this criterion to any detail demands a prior conception of the whole, found through many readings that related part to whole and whole to part in a series of constantly shifting hypotheses. Moreover, if we raise the identical question with respect to each and every detail, we can reach some conclusions about the total unity of the poem. For if our answer is always affirmative, if every element seems justifiable through its usefulness for the whole, then we have a convincing witness to the total unity of the poem. If, on the contrary, we find no such possibil-ity of justifying every part in terms of the whole, then our judgment must be that the unity of the poem is only imperfectly achieved.

The second criterion was one of order. For example, I pointed to the progression, within the poem, from "l'esprit gémissant," to "nous," to the abstract "l'Espérance," to "nos cerveaux," before the arrival at "mon âme" and "mon crâne." If I introduced this consid-eration at all, it was because of a conviction that (in any poem) some principle of order must be discoverable, some basis for the succession of the various elements. Apparently, in this *Spleen,* the reason for the order here discovered is the wish to present the central passion in an abstract and general way before limiting it to the single speaker, and that as a device for involving the reader immediately in the passion. A related order would seem to be present in the passage from descriptive background to event (clearly signified by the triple use of "quand" followed by "tout à coup") and in the gradual accumulation of the feelings that constitute the full emotion of "spleen." This criterion is applicable in the same way as the first one: we try first to distinguish a total movement within the poem (and "first" should probably be "last," since this is something we arrive at rather than starting with it), then we seek to find the relationship of partial progressions to that total progression, finally we make judgments. The total movement must itself be judged in terms of its adequacy for effecting in "time" that whole complex of poetic relationships that proper unity effects in "space." Unity and order are really two ways of looking at the same object, the one from the point of view of the interrelationships among the elements, the other from the point of view of their sequence or succession.

In a sense, there is no need to make a special, summary statement about the extent to which Baudelaire's *Spleen* satisfies these two criteria, just as there is no need to apply the criteria in any separate way. The criteria are present implicitly throughout the reading, they direct the kinds of questions that one asks at every point, they lead to many of the discoveries that one makes about the structure of the poem. If those discoveries reveal a high degree of integration of all the parts and an order that develops the emotion from its initiation to its fulfilment, then the criteria have been satisfied. The judgment is made *pari passu* with the discoveries of the reading, and the growing sense of the structural qualities of the poem is equivalent to a growing judgment as to its excellence.

3

Baudelaire

Recueillement

In the discussion of *Le Cygne,* I suggested that one section of the text, separated from the rest, might almost be considered as a symbolist poem. It could be made, with certain changes and distortions, to satisfy the fundamental conditions of the poetry practiced by the full-blown Symbolists: a structure based on the full statement, through the course of the poem, of one half of a metaphorical relationship (this statement would constitute the "symbol"); the almost total suppression of the other half of the metaphor (that is, of the object "symbolized"); and the provision, at useful points, of a sufficient number of signs or pointers to permit the inference of the suppressed half and hence the identification and the interpretation of the symbol. I also stated that Baudelaire, in other poems, did practise an integral symbolism. His *Recueillement* is such a poem.

Recueillement

Sois sage, ô ma Douleur, et tiens-toi plus tranquille.
Tu réclamais le Soir; il descend; le voici;
Une atmosphère obscure enveloppe la ville,
Aux uns portant la paix, aux autres le souci.   4

Pendant que des mortels la multitude vile,
Sous le fouet du Plaisir, ce bourreau sans merci,
Va cueillir des remords dans la fête servile,
Ma Douleur, donne-moi la main; viens par ici   8

Loin d'eux. Vois se pencher les défuntes Années,
Sur les balcons du ciel, en robes surannées;
Surgir du fond des eaux le Regret souriant;   11

Le Soleil moribond s'endormir sous une arche,
Et, comme un long linceul traînant à l'Orient,
Entends, ma chère, entends la douce Nuit qui marche.   14

Many of the analytical procedures used in the study of a non-symbolist poem are of course immediately transferable to a symbolist poem; the art is essentially the same, and so must be the criticism. Yet symbolist poetry presents certain special problems to the critic, and he must think about special techniques for their solution. I think of the component parts of an analysis applied to a symbolist poem as the following:

1. The study of the "symbol" itself, with the goal of determining its structure. This study is exactly like that of any kind of poem.

2. The search for the "signs" or "indicators" or "pointers" that permit the identification of the object "symbolized." This is a special function in the analysis of symbolist poetry.

3. The identification and description of the object "symbolized"— of that second, unexpressed half of the metaphor.

4. The interpretation of the "symbol" in terms of what it is meant to represent; that is, the translation of the "symbol" into the object "symbolized." This amounts, really, to a complete statement of all elements entering into the metaphorical relationship.

5. The determination of what special effects result from the use of a symbolist structure.

The order of these procedures is by no means a fixed or necessary order; they may be pursued simultaneously or in any sequence that best corresponds to the character of the poem itself and to the needs of the analyst.

In *Recueillement,* one of the first indications of the existence of a non-literal meaning comes in the first line, with the capitalized and personified "Douleur." We meet, immediately, two persons, a speaker who identifies himself in "ma Douleur," and a person to whom he speaks. The latter is addressed as a child—not only through the *tutoiement,* but also through such phrases as "Sois sage" and "tiens-toi plus tranquille"—but it is not a child: it is a passion that belongs to the speaker as a child might belong to him. We know something else about this "child"; it has been unruly, needs to be chided and called to obedience. The emotion contained in the "ô" of "ô ma Douleur" is not yet specified; from what follows we shall learn that it mingles exhortation with tenderness. The opening line of the poem thus establishes these probabilities: for a continued apostrophe to a personified passion; for the father-child relationship, particularly the request for compliance with a mild command; for revelations about the nature and the causes of the child's restiveness —hence of the speaker's "Douleur." In connection with this last, we can expect the appearance of images or of circumstances that will represent the "Douleur" and that will arouse reactions appropriate to it.

Several of these expectations begin to be fulfilled in the next line:

> Tu réclamais le Soir; il descend; le voici. [2]

As he continues to address the child, the speaker indicates the nature of her "untranquillity": she had been asking for the coming of evening; and the speaker can now appease her by announcing its arrival. But "le Soir" is more than evening itself, both because of its capital letter and because it is such an evening as "la Douleur" might demand. Questions are raised and left unanswered—just as they have been before and as they should be in the opening lines of a poem. The speaker also announces the time of day, the falling of evening—"il descend; le voici"; and he does so not because of the picturesque possibilities it entails, but because this moment of the day will come to have its special meaning in the poem. The remaining lines of the quatrain both describe this falling of evening and suggest its consequences for two categories of men:

> Une atmosphère obscure enveloppe la ville,
> Aux uns portant la paix, aux autres le souci. [4]

Line 3 specifies the setting, "la ville," which will be expanded upon later, and its particular aspect as evening falls: "Une atmosphère obscure enveloppe . . ." This, too, introduces probabilities for a future picturesque development, perhaps even some consequences

for the symbolic meaning. As evening comes, it brings to the inhab-
itants of the city two differing moral states, to some "la paix," to
others "le souci"; that is, some men will find a cessation of their
suffering, others merely an increase. As we look back in the first
stanza, we see that the speaker (one of the men in the city) might
fall into either category; but, since his "Douleur" has impatiently
awaited the evening, it is more probable that she (or he) hopes to
find "la paix." As we look forward to the rest, we shall see that what
evening brings to any man will depend upon his own particular
choice of activity.

Stanza I thus presents a very complex poetic situation. A speaker is
introduced, his passion named. His passion has hoped for some kind
of solution with the coming of evening, and evening falls. The two
alternative solutions are proposed. Besides, the first visual image to
be associated with evening has been suggested. In the apostrophe by
the speaker to his passion and in the relationship established between
them, in vague intimations about a derived sense to be given to
"Soir," and in the generalization of the last line, we have indications
both that the situation will be applicable to others besides the
speaker and that there will be derived or secondary meanings in the
poem.

Both categories of men, those who will now find peace and those
who will find unhappiness, are more fully described in the second
quatrain; but by no means to the same extent. Essentially, the
quatrain is devoted to the latter group. With its first word, "Pendant . . . ," line 5 sets up an opposition between the two groups
which, significantly, is an opposition in time:

> Pendant que des mortels la multitude vile . . .   [5]

We can expect, soon, to have the contemporaneous but alternative
situation. "Mortels" restates either "Aux uns" or "aux autres"; this
remains to be seen. In any case, the word itself denotes not only
living beings but also those who are subject to death. It comprises the
whole of humanity; yet in this verse a restriction immediately follows: "la multitude vile [des mortels]." Just as the "Pendant que"
had indicated a kind of exclusion or separation, so the "vile" (with
its tone of contempt and condemnation) shows that the speaker

removes himself from the group that he is about to characterize. The many and the vile: we expect him to be the one and the better-than-vile. What separates him from the many is stated in the next two lines:

> Sous le fouet du Plaisir, ce bourreau sans merci,
> Va cueillir des remords dans la fête servile . . .   [7]

The many are those who seek only pleasure; but every phrase used to characterize their pleasure is a condemnation comparable to that contained in "vile." Pleasure itself is personified (hence the "P") as a "bourreau sans merci"; he is an executioner who spares none, who kills all. He also wields the whip that holds the multitude in slavery ("la fête servile"). The life they lead is called by the bitter name of "la fête servile," and it brings them (before their ultimate execution) only remorse. In "cueillir des remords" the speaker expresses his contempt for those who deliberately go about creating their own unhappiness.

So much for the others; we shall hear no more about them. It was necessary, however, to describe the large mass of men from whom the speaker distinguishes himself, merely so that the nature of the withdrawal or separation might be perfectly clear. If "les autres" are the living who seek pleasure and find only remorse, then he (as one of "les uns" who find peace) will have to choose other ways and goals. The initial grouping into two categories is still present, although only partially and implicitly for the first group. Everything becomes explicit in the next line, which runs on into the first tercet:

> Ma Douleur, donne-moi la main; viens par ici
>
> Loin d'eux. . . .   [9]

Repeating his apostrophe to "Ma Douleur" (hence addressing again his own passion), the speaker uses formulas similar to those with which he had originally spoken to the child. "Donne-moi la main" urges the close association with him that will accompany the separation from all others contained in "viens par ici." When the invitation is completed by "Loin d'eux," we see the pair (father and child, speaker and passion) moving away from the "fête servile." This is their rejection of the whole way of life of the "multitude vile." For the completely simple ideas, completely simple language is used; we may compare "Tu réclamais le Soir; il descend; le voici," with "donne-moi la main; viens par ici / Loin d'eux."

"Loin d'eux" is very properly placed at the beginning of the first tercet. For if the quatrains, and especially the second one, had had as their function to characterize the city and the way of the "others," which the speaker wishes to leave, the tercets will conclude the sonnet with a description of that other city and way to which the speaker intends to move. The words just spoken to the child-passion are an invitation to accompany him there, and he will now proceed to depict that city in terms exactly opposed to those used for the other:

> . . . Vois se pencher les défuntes Années,
> Sur les balcons du ciel, en robes surannées . . . [10]

Two additional commands—they are really admiring recommendations—will be addressed to the child during this part of the poem; the first is the "Vois," which introduces a number of things to be seen, the other is the "Entends, . . . entends" of the last line, introducing something to be heard. All the things to be seen combine to form a single vision, one which extends and completes that originally presented in "Une atmosphère obscure enveloppe la ville." The time is still the coming of evening, and this explains the visual image of lines 9–10. We are to see the clouds that hang over the city ("Sur les balcons du ciel"), clouds of faded and darkened colors ("en robes surannées"). But we are also to "see," with the mind's eye, something else in these clouds: the past and dead years ("les défuntes Années") which hang over the city. An element of time is added to the vision, just as it was in "le Soir"; and the capital letters of both terms point to non-literal meanings. In this light, "robes surannées" also takes on an expanded context of reference. All these details and suggestions make of the present moment a culmination of a lengthy past.

To the dark air and the evening clouds are now added waters that flow through the city, presumably a river:

> Surgir du fond des eaux le Regret souriant . . . [11]

The waters, however, are only lightly traced in; what is striking is the vision of an allegorical figure that rises from the river. It is "le

Regret souriant," clearly a reference to the "remords" of line 7, but now smiling and benign rather than brutal; it rises like a nymph from deep within the waters. Again, the imagination of the speaker transforms a part of his emotion into an allegorical being who contrasts sharply, in this vision, with its real counterpart in the city of the "others." Another feature of the spiritual landscape appears in the first line of the second tercet:

> Le Soleil moribond s'endormir sous une arche . . .   [12]

It is, of course, the setting sun; but it is not merely the setting sun. For it is "moribond" and goes to sleep—both concepts are proper to a personified Sun. As a picturesque detail, the arch under which the sun sets—and it must therefore be on the west side of the city—now comes to join the river as an identifying landmark.

After what is seen in the West, what is heard in the East:

> Et, comme un long linceul traînant à l'Orient,
> Entends, ma chère, entends la douce Nuit qui marche.

The sonnet concludes with this auditory "image," not without its visual accompaniments, of the approach of night. At the beginning of the poem, the desired evening had arrived; it is now followed by the night coming in from the east. Or, I should say, the Night coming in from the East; better still, from the Orient. Both words are capitalized and the Night rises from the point where the now-falling Sun had risen. The speaker tenderly invites his child ("ma chère") to listen to the sound of the soft Night as she approaches, a sound of walking that is likened to the sound of a trailing shroud. But the invitation passes from tender to joyous: the first "Entends" is soft and appealing, the second "entends" is accompanied by a note of wonderment and delight—and must so be when the line is read aloud. In "long linceul traînant à l'Orient" there is again, I think, a visual image of clouds trailing off to the East (where they would by now be dark), just as we are meant to see a vague face and figure incorporating "la douce Nuit qui marche."

In its apparent and superficial form, then, the sonnet presents a speech addressed by a speaker to a child who represents his emotion. He calls her to calm and peace from her earlier restiveness, telling her that the evening which she had awaited is now falling. This evening, he tells her, will bring only unhappiness to those mortal men who take it as the occasion for their pursuit of pleasure. But to her and to himself, since they will withdraw themselves from the rest (hence the "recueillement"), it will bring a surcease of sorrow. The two alternatives are stated, not as abstract ideas, but as two contrasting pictures: on the one hand, the cruel and bustling image of the pleasure-seeking multitude, on the other hand, the quiet and tender image of sunset and evening followed by the approaching night. The speaker's choice is obviously the correct one, and the child should not hesitate to accept his invitation.

This the apparent and superficial content. It is evident from the outset, though, that beneath this surface there are other meanings to be discovered. Baudelaire uses several devices to suggest their existence to the reader. Most obvious of these is the use of capital letters to set off certain nouns. The series of these is long, considering the brevity of the poem: Douleur (twice), Soir, Plaisir, Années, Regret, Soleil, Orient, Nuit. These are in the first place passions or emotions (Douleur, Plaisir, Regret), in the second place references to the time of day (Soir, Nuit, perhaps the related Soleil and Orient), finally a more general term for the passage of time (Années). The purpose of the capitalization seems to be to personify, or to make an abstraction, or simply to emphasize relationships and oppositions. For it is clear that the words so capitalized not only fall into related groups, but that they stand in clear relationships to one another. Among the emotions, Plaisir is definitely opposed to Douleur; and, because it is both "smiling" and associated with the peaceful vision of evening, Regret is probably also so opposed. For the times of day, there seems to be a movement from the east (Orient) where the Sun rose to the west where he now sets, accompanied by a westward movement first of the Soir, then of the Nuit. If one takes this as a movement in time and then generalizes it, one passes from the total repeated course of a day to the repeated course of a year, and this gives the maximum generalization of time (in this poem) found in "les défuntes Années."

Another device for the suggestion of internal meanings is what we might call the grouping or concentration of objects, and therefore of the terms that represent them, around a single central concept. It becomes perfectly evident, for example, that after we have had "mortels" (line 5) followed by "bourreau" (line 6), we should be particularly watchful for things and words that belong to death— violent or otherwise. These begin to multiply immediately: in line 9, "les défuntes Années"; in line 10, "en robes surannées"; in line 12, both "moribond" and "s'endormir"; in line 13, "comme un long linceul." We may even be inclined, looking backward, to associate "Une atmosphère obscure" (line 3) with the same group. Such a piling up of objects, epithets, and actions cannot be fortuitous; nor can be the fact that they are associated with both visual images, with the city of the "others" and the city of the speaker. We are obliged to connect the idea of death with the whole of the poem, but especially with its dominant part, the depiction of the city of the speaker.

The consequence with respect to these two observations is that we give to the capitalized nouns, in all categories, meanings related to the concept of death. If the term is an abstraction or a personification, we will choose, from among many possible meanings, those suggested by the concentration of images and concepts. Thus both "Soir" and "Nuit" will be seen as signifying (in addition to their parts of day) aspects of death; and if there is a chronological separation between them, then "Nuit" will be death itself and "Soir" a time when death approaches. Similarly, if the "Soleil" now dying in the west, as Night is heard following upon Evening, stands for a progression through space as well as through the time that ends with death, then both the starting point and the beginning in time will be represented by "Orient"; "Orient" will be rising and origin and birth. One must be extremely scrupulous about adding such interpretations to the explicit terms of the text, one must do so only when the poet, through the devices he chooses, issues a forthright invitation to do so. Above all, it is important to avoid trying to find such "hidden meanings" in every word of the poem; for to attempt that is to risk turning the poem into an elaborate allegory or a puzzle or a "devinette."

For *Recueillement,* the many straightforward indications that we have, through the devices employed, justify a reading of the poem as a poem about death. If "Soir" is the approach of death and "Nuit" its arrival, the whole speech of the speaker to his "Douleur" may express his attitude toward his oncoming death, his preference for it. Read in that way, the object "symbolized" by the speech might be the following: The speaker addresses his sorrow, saying that it has called for the coming of death, and that the approach of death is now apparent. For most men, who wish only a continuation of their pleasure-seeking lives, only further servitude in this life which he calls "la fête servile," that approach means only further suffering. But for him, since he separates himself from the multitude, it is welcome as bringing the termination of sorrow and the peace that he has hoped for. He thus accepts it with a kind of quiet joy, which gives the general tone to his meditation. The whole of the metaphor is therefore present in the poem, the "symbol" as directly expressed and as providing the basis for the explicit structure, the object "symbolized" as only implicitly present but indicated and identified by a number of structural devices.

Perhaps the nature of this proportional metaphor may be more succinctly seen if we state it as a metaphorical relationship among a number of objects actually expressed in the sonnet. Such a statement does not yet take into account the overall analogy of the "symbol" to the "object symbolized"; but it may serve as a step on the way to the discovery of the analogy. There are difficulties attached to the making of such a statement, merely because of the way in which proportional metaphors work; since there comes to be, as the metaphor develops, a transferability of all elements from one "side" of the metaphor to the other, one may hesitate as to the proper place for any particular element.

coming of death :	*man's life* : :	*coming of evening* :	*day's course*
plus tranquille :	douleur	Soir :	Orient
par ici :	la ville	atmosphère obscure	
la paix :	le souci	Soleil moribond	
loin d'eux	: mortels	balcons du ciel	
	: multitude	robes surannées	
Regret souriant :	Plaisir	long linceul	
	: fête servile	douce Nuit	
	: bourreau		
	: remords		
défuntes Années :			

Two things are significant about such a statement, imperfect as it may be. On the one hand, we note that whereas the pairs of objects (and hence terms) are fairly completely worked out on the moral and human side—man's life and the speaker's death—there are by no means such exact correspondences on the physical side—the progress of a day from morning to evening. This is because the human side is the important one: the speaker's "moral" situation, the state of his soul, is such that he can see with equanimity the coming of death, even derive from it a sense of superiority to other men. It is this situation that is at the basis of the emotion in the poem and of the reader's response to that emotion. The physical side, all the imagery of sunset and evening, is merely meant to be suggestive and expressive of that same emotion, and its development can be secondary and auxiliary. On the other hand, while much attention is paid to the terminal point of the progress in space and to the terminal moment of the progress in time, to the West and to Evening or Night, little is said either about the point and time of beginning (except for the "Orient") or about the intervals between beginning and end. Again, the reason is that the important moment, for the emotion of the speaker, is the moment of approaching death; all of his concern is with it and he will think of the immediate and the remote past only as they enter into the preparation of the present.

If I have thought it useful, as I have done, to "analyze out" the component elements of the metaphor upon which the symbolic structure is based, it is because of my conviction that some such inferential process is necessary if the reader is to understand fully and to feel deeply such a symbolist poem as *Recueillement*. The process need not always be as deliberate and as intellectual a one as I have made it out to be; the reader may get the "feel" of the structural complexities and interrelationships without reducing them to precise statements or to tabular form. But make the inference he must, in one way or another, if he is to understand the symbol and interpret it correctly. Generally, the symbolist poet (like his colleagues in other recent poetic modes) makes a far greater demand upon his reader than had the more conventional poet. And that demand is essentially an intellectual demand. We can read such poems as *Le Cygne* and *Spleen* without much puzzling about meanings, relying upon our intuitive responses to provide us with the proper effect. In those poems, everything is explicit; and while there are subtleties and structural niceties, we can depend upon an educated sensitivity to make these apparent to us. But in a poem like *Recueillement* (and the problem will become more acute as we move on into later periods), much is implicit, much is left unsaid. Especially, the whole nature of the symbolic relationship needs to be the object of an inference. The symbolist method depends upon the suppression of part of the metaphor that would normally be clearly stated, and we must recover that part by means of the "signs" and "pointers" of which I have spoken. The process of recovery is an intellectual process.

The importance of making the inference and interpreting the symbol may be seen if we compare the emotional effect of *Recueillement* read literally with its effect when we read it as a symbolist poem. Even the surface meaning is, by itself, highly effective. As the speaker addresses his passion, as he throws into sharp contrast his vigorous condemnation of the involvement of others with his own retirement and meditation, he expresses a kind of noble and dignified sorrow that elicits the sympathy and to a degree the pity of the reader. The contrasting visual (and auditory) images are of special usefulness here: the speaker's sorrow attains a kind of tangible quality as the image of evening and approaching night is developed, with all of its suggestions of darkness and quiet and with its moral overtones. If one were to follow through the sonnet, word by word, the development of the central passion, one would discover the same careful, progressive, and efficacious treatment that we observed in the case of *Spleen*.

When, however, we add to the literal reading our interpretation of the symbol, the poem's effectiveness is considerably augmented. This is because of what we might call an increase in the moral dimension. It is one thing to express a quiet sorrow that leads one to withdraw from the violent activity of other men in order to contemplate the peaceful arrival of evening. It is another thing to express a sorrow so profound that it leads one to wish for death and to hail the coming of death with a satisfaction bordering on joy. We respond much more profoundly to the latter expression, merely because we recognize in the poem the representation of an object which is in itself of greater moral and emotional significance. The visual images remain the same, the devices for representing the passion remain the same; but all are now invested with a new meaningfulness and a multiplied potential for an effect upon our emotions.

4

Baudelaire

Un Voyage à Cythère

The ways of organizing a lyric poem are not infinite, but they are many. Each individual lyric, of course, has its own private structure, and since lyrics may be infinitely multiplied, in that sense there would be no end to the number of structures that might exist. As we continue to read more and more poems, however, we discover that their structures tend to fall into groups, or classes, or patterns of organization. Sometimes a lyric is a fairly simple exploitation of one of these formal possibilities, sometimes it develops more richly the same form. But there are many lyrics that achieve their distinction and to a degree their excellence through the combination of several structural modes. The result is an increased complexity of means and devices, leading to a deepening and an enrichment of the emotional effect. As the "art" gains in subtlety, the poem comes to have a kind of augmented internal magnitude, and this in turn produces a greater potential for variety and subtlety of effect.

Baudelaire's *Un Voyage à Cythère* is one of these, and in the discussion that follows I wish to point out how at least three distinct structural modes are brought together in order to give to the poem an extraordinary degree of complexity and of effectiveness.

Un Voyage à Cythère

Mon cœur, comme un oiseau, voltigeait tout joyeux
Et planait librement à l'entour des cordages;

Le navire roulait sous un ciel sans nuages,
Comme un ange enivré d'un soleil radieux.   4

Quelle est cette île triste et noire? —C'est Cythère,
Nous dit-on, un pays fameux dans les chansons,
Eldorado banal de tous les vieux garçons.
Regardez, après tout, c'est une pauvre terre.   8

—Ile des doux secrets et des fêtes du cœur!
De l'antique Vénus le superbe fantôme
Au-dessus de tes mers plane comme un arome,
Et charge les esprits d'amour et de langueur.   12

Belle île aux myrtes verts, pleine de fleurs écloses,
Vénérée à jamais par toute nation,
Où les soupirs des cœurs en adoration
Roulent comme l'encens sur un jardin de roses   16

Ou le roucoulement éternel d'un ramier!
—Cythère n'était plus qu'un terrain des plus maigres,
Un désert rocailleux troublé par des cris aigres.
J'entrevoyais pourtant un objet singulier!   20

Ce n'était pas un temple aux ombres bocagères,
Où la jeune prêtresse, amoureuse des fleurs,
Allait, le corps brûlé de secrètes chaleurs,
Entre-bâillant sa robe aux brises passagères;   24

Mais voilà qu'en rasant la côte d'assez près
Pour troubler les oiseaux avec nos voiles blanches,
Nous vîmes que c'était un gibet à trois branches,
Du ciel se détachant en noir, comme un cyprès.   28

De féroces oiseaux perchés sur leur pâture
Détruisaient avec rage un pendu déjà mûr,
Chacun plantant, comme un outil, son bec impur
Dans tous les coins saignants de cette pourriture;   32

Les yeux étaient deux trous, et du ventre effondré
Les intestins pesants lui coulaient sur les cuisses,
Et ses bourreaux, gorgés de hideuses délices,
L'avaient à coups de bec absolument châtré.   36

Sous les pieds, un troupeau de jaloux quadrupèdes,
Le museau relevé, tournoyait et rôdait;
Une plus grande bête au milieu s'agitait
Comme un exécuteur entouré de ses aides.   40

Habitant de Cythère, enfant d'un ciel si beau,
Silencieusement tu souffrais ces insultes
En expiation de tes infâmes cultes
Et des péchés qui t'ont interdit le tombeau.   44

Ridicule pendu, tes douleurs sont les miennes!
Je sentis, à l'aspect de tes membres flottants,
Comme un vomissement, remonter vers mes dents
Le long fleuve de fiel des douleurs anciennes;   48

Devant toi, pauvre diable au souvenir si cher,
J'ai senti tous les becs et toutes les mâchoires
Des corbeaux lancinants et des panthères noires
Qui jadis, aimaient tant à triturer ma chair.   52

—Le ciel était charmant, la mer était unie;
Pour moi tout était noir et sanglant désormais,
Hélas! et j'avais, comme en un suaire épais,
Le cœur enseveli dans cette allégorie.   56

Dans ton île, ô Vénus! je n'ai trouvé debout
Qu'un gibet symbolique où pendait mon image...
—Ah! Seigneur! donnez-moi la force et le courage
De contempler mon cœur et mon corps sans dégoût!   60

Most apparent among the structural bases in this poem is the narrative line. Superficially at least, *Un Voyage à Cythère* recounts a number of successive moments or episodes in a voyage, and it is this story that provides the chronological continuity. We learn at first of the situation preceding the first event: "Mon cœur . . . voltigeait . . . Et planait . . ."; "Le navire roulait . . ." Then the event: an island is sighted, a question is asked about its identity, an answer is given: "Quelle est cette île . . . ?"; "C'est Cythère, Nous dit-on . . ." As the voyagers approach, they describe the island as it appears to them, "Cythère n'était plus que . . . ," and the speaker begins to perceive something on the island: "J'entrevoyais . . . un objet . . ." They come closer, and he then sees it clearly: "voilà qu'en rasant la côte . . . , Nous vîmes que c'était un gibet . . ." He next describes what was going on on the island: "[Des] . . . oiseaux . . . Détruisaient . . . un pendu . . ."; "Les yeux étaient . . . , Les intestins . . . coulaient . . . ," "ses bourreaux . . . L'avaient . . . châtré

. . .' ; "un troupeau . . . tournoyait et rôdait . . . ," "Une plus grande bête . . . s'agitait . . ." The speaker addresses the hanged man, "Habitant de Cythère . . . ," and describes his own reaction to what he has seen: "Je sentis . . . , J'ai senti . . ." In a summary statement at the end, he compares the episode with his feelings about it: "Le ciel était . . . , la mer était . . . , Pour moi tout était . . . et j'avais . . . Le cœur"; "je n'ai trouvé debout Qu'un gibet . . ."

This is not to say that *Un Voyage à Cythère* is a narrative poem. If it were, the story itself would provide the central structure: initial statements about situation and character would prepare the way for the beginning of an action, and in that action one episode would lead to another as a result of the realization of the same probabilities. Here, there may be a story, but there is no action, if by action we mean a sequence of causally related events resulting from elements in character and circumstance. The story furnishes essentially a chronology, is in a sense predetermined and pre-existent, may be regarded not as an end in itself but as the occasion for something else. What the narrator says about the events of his narration is what really counts, and we may go so far as to say that the story is invented, or contrived, or organized to make it possible for him to say those things. The poem is thus truly lyric since it proceeds through the direct expression and evocation of the emotion.

The second structural basis, closely related to the progress of the narrative, is the extended opposition between the two islands of Cythère, the Cythère of mythology and legend opposed to the Cythère of the voyager's reality. These alternate through a large part of the poem; but the function of the opposition will perhaps be clearer if we collect the details belonging to each so as to see the totality of the impression intended for each. The legendary Cythère is "un pays fameux dans les chansons" (line 6), and the mere speaking of its name evokes in the narrator an image of a world fully given over to love: "Ile des doux secrets et des fêtes du cœur!" (line 9). The spirit of Venus hovers over the island, filling it with love and voluptuousness (lines 10–12). He may see it as a landscape, but he thinks of it above all as the eternal residence of love (lines 13–17); in this sense he imagines it as it might have been in antiquity, as a temple where the rites of love were celebrated (lines 21–24). It was, after all,

Venus' island: "Dans ton île, ô Vénus!" The total evocation is thus rather sentimental than picturesque, moral rather than physical, since the speaker wishes to attach to the island—as it had previously existed in the imaginations of men and in his own thought—the central idea of the delights of love.

But even before the first of these details is given, the speaker begins the characterization of the real island as he saw it during the voyage. Its essential features are part of the original question, "Quelle est cette île triste et noire?," and part of the answer, "c'est une pauvre terre." Later he calls it "un terrain des plus maigres" (line 18) and "Un désert rocailleux" (line 19). Above all, the island is the site of the gibbet and its hanged man, and soon the speaker's attention passes from the island itself to this "objet singulier." The whole tone and impression of the real Cythère comes to be epitomized by the "pendu," described so fully and so vigorously. He is, in a sense, the opposite of the "jeune prêtresse" earlier imagined by the narrator and, just as she had served to express the essence of the legendary island, he represents the spirit of the real island. In this way, the meager details about the physical appearance of Cythère are supplemented by the multiple impressions associated with its "pendu" and the two islands are equally well depicted in the poem.

If the narrative line served to provide a basic chronological organization to the poem, the contrast of the two Cythères adds two visual and moral landscapes that begin to justify the presence of the story. That is, the story may be said to exist as a framework for the description of the island that the voyager actually saw and for the evocation of the island that he imagined. To these a third device is added: the equivalence between the "pendu" seen by the voyager and the voyager himself. With the addition of the third device, we discover that the real purpose of the contrast was to throw into high relief the nature of the visible island and of its "objet singulier" so that, in turn, the equivalence might be established. That equivalence is not directly expressed until fairly late in the poem, in line 45: "Ridicule pendu, tes douleurs sont les miennes!" After that point, it becomes the central subject of the remaining verses, the speaker moving back and forth between the hanged man and himself: "Je sentis, à l'aspect de tes membres . . ." (line 46); "Devant toi, . . .

J'ai senti" (lines 49–50); "un gibet . . . où pendait mon image"
(line 58). In the last stanzas, indeed, the contrast and the equivalence come together; such lines as "Dans ton île, ô Vénus! je n'ai
trouvé debout / Qu'un gibet . . . où pendait mon image . . ."
(lines 57–58) collapse into a single expression all three structural
bases, in a way perfectly proper to the conclusion of a lyric.

I think that we may distinguish a fourth structural basis which,
unlike the other three, is not materially separable from them but
which, at certain points in the poem, is concomitant with them. This
is the ironic intention, which causes us to give to certain phrases or
lines a meaning other than the one overtly expressed, and in a sense
contradictory to it. The matter of irony is a difficult and subtle one
and its presence should never lightly be claimed for any poem. In
part, the difficulty arises from the fact that irony is never discernible
in an isolated part of the work; we attach it to any part only after we
have determined its relationships with other parts and with the
whole and have realized, in the light of those relationships, that a
literal reading is not compatible with our total understanding of the
work. To this degree it is "structural." Perhaps the parallel situation
of "dramatic irony" may help clarify what I am saying. Dramatic
irony is present when a reader or spectator, because of what he
knows about the total situation, sees in actions or words meanings
and consequences that are not apparent to the actor himself—merely
because the actor does not have that knowledge of the total situation.
In the kind of "lyric irony" that we find in *Un Voyage à Cythère,*
the speaker himself has the advance knowledge of all that he is
going to say; but the reader does not, and hence he can appreciate
fully what is said now only after he has read all that is to be said
later. The irony is anticipatory, and is appreciated in retrospect.

We may take as an example, in *Un Voyage à Cythère,* the very
first line:

> Mon cœur, comme un oiseau, voltigeait tout joyeux . . .

On first reading, and at face value, the line may be taken as expressing a joyous state of soul; it sets the tone for the gay description that
follows. But as we read forward into the poem, we become increasingly aware of the fact that we should not have interpreted the line

in that way. Since it begins a narrative of events already terminated, and since at the time the speaker makes this statement he has already gone through the whole range of his moral discovery, his "heart" cannot have been "joyous" as he spoke. Even if he had tried to reconstruct an original optimistic state, something of the later bitterness would have insinuated itself into his statement. That this is the case is evident from two elements in the line (and in the following description); the kind of exaggerated or extreme statement that we have in the comparison, "comme un oiseau," and in *tout* joyeux," and the anticipatory use of two terms that will undergo a radical evolution through the course of the poem, "cœur" and "oiseau." Each time we encounter them, we remember back to their use in the first line, and an additional ingredient of grimness is added to their meaning there. When we reread the line, each successive reading will carry with it more of the later associations, and the total ironic impression will result.

The interweaving of these various "structuring" devices, and the growth of the effect resulting from them, will be apparent if we follow the poem through from beginning to end. They are, indeed, separate only analytically, and in the poem represent parallel or simultaneous means of arriving at a total effect. The opening stanza presents at once the circumstances preceding the narrative event and the atmosphere surrounding the legendary island, both of them seen through the eyes of the speaker as he was before his moral discovery.

> Mon cœur, comme un oiseau, voltigeait tout joyeux
> Et planait librement à l'entour des cordages . . .   [2]

Introducing himself as main personage of the narrative ("Mon cœur"), the speaker emphasizes two qualities of his spiritual state at its beginning, joy ("tout joyeux") and freedom ("librement"). These are dramatized both by the comparison to the bird and by the choice of the two verbs, "voltigeait" and "planait"; the two movements are different, but they combine to create an impression of grace and absolute lack of constraint. With the formula "à l'entour des cordages," the speaker places himself on the ship in which the voyage is being made. I think that there is already, in the ultra-rosy details of the description and in the lilt of the rhythm that accompanies them, a suggestion that they are not to be taken too literally; and of course in the light of the rest of the poem we know that we are to be prepared, from the start, for the coming of their exact opposites. The second half of the stanza tells about the ship:

> Le navire roulait sous un ciel sans nuages,
> Comme un ange enivré d'un soleil radieux.   [4]

Again, the all-too-perfect conditions surrounding the ship, like those pertinent to the speaker's heart, are a source of suspicion. The "rou-lait" describing its motion is similar to the "planait" applied to the bird, and we are to see the flight of the "ange enivré" as like that indicated in "voltigeait." The sky is absolutely cloudless, the sun bright. We should note the parallelism of the two comparisons, "comme un oiseau" and "comme un ange," and interpret it again (I believe) as a sign of exaggeration or *charge*.

Our suspicions are confirmed at the beginning of the next stanza, when we discover that everything that had gone before was set up to contrast with line 5:

> Quelle est cette île triste et noire? . . .

We are to assume that the speaker asks the question; an island is sighted, he asks its name. Only two epithets are needed to characterize the island, "triste et noire," for each of them appears against the background of the preceding stanza. We see in "triste" the opposite of the whole context of "joyeux" and "enivré," in "noire" the opposite of "un ciel sans nuages" and "un soleil radieux." The black is immediately blacker because of the prevailing whiteness. It is significant that this contrast should be established so early in the poem; for not only does it prepare for the device of opposition-equivalence on the moral scale, but it also leads to the development of two distinct and opposed visual worlds in the poem, with their accompanying emotions. Now, a reply to the question is given by some unnamed person ("dit-on"):

> —C'est Cythère,
> Nous dit-on, un pays fameux dans les chansons,
> Eldorado banal de tous les vieux garçons.   [7]

Initially, the reply is simple enough, "C'est Cythère," since it merely confirms our knowledge, from the title, of the island's identity. But what is startling is that Cythère should turn out to be an "île triste et noire." Moreover, the person who replies to the assembled inquirers ("Nous dit-on") continues with mocking remarks about it. To say "un pays fameux dans les chansons" is to minimize a great legend in scornful terms, to reduce mythology to the level of the music-hall. The next line is even more disparaging; Cythère (and the love that it here represents) is not the dream of young lovers, but of "tous les vieux garçons," the disappointed men who have not found love. It is the unattainable Eldorado of their dreams, "banal" not only because all think about it but because they conceive of a commonplace and mediocre love as associated with it. Again, the myth has been diminished in the extreme, and the informant may therefore conclude:

> Regardez, après tout, c'est une pauvre terre. [8]

The summary states the judgment and the conclusion of the informant; it also denies, for the reader, any conflicting opinions that he may have held about the island. But it does not yet, as we shall soon see, invalidate any of the speaker's own illusions about Cythère.

Those illusions are described at length in the next nine lines, in a way to represent not only the speaker's feelings about it (and they are not the same as his informant's) but as well the standard features of the legend that we are all assumed to share. However, in the very exaggeration of its terms, the whole description carries with it that note of irony that was perceived in the first stanza. The dash at the beginning of line 9 returns us to the speaker:

> —Ile des doux secrets et des fêtes du cœur!

In a way, this constitutes an alternative and contradictory reply: "Quelle est cette île . . . ?" "Ile des doux secrets . . ." The island's "doux secrets" will be revealed later; when they are, all the bitter irony of this formula will become apparent to us. At the moment, the line introduces a depiction of this island of love that corresponds to the speaker's conception of it—from a distance and before he has come to know it. It is still the site of the "fêtes du cœur"; and the heart is still the one that had been "tout joyeux" at the beginning. It is not the heart that will come increasingly into prominence as the poem develops. Nor does the "feast" have any relationship to the one that will later be described, except by the kind of ironic indirection that is already expanding as a device.

> De l'antique Vénus le superbe fantôme
> Au-dessus de tes mers plane comme un arome,
> Et charge les esprits d'amour et de langueur.   [12]

With these words the speaker begins the evocation of the Cythère of ancient legend. We should note, though, that it is not a visual evocation, but rather one that seeks to form a sensuous impression of love, desire, and voluptuousness. Hence we do not see "l'antique Vénus" (goddess of the island) in any corporeal form, however beautiful; we see instead—or rather we sense—her "superbe fantôme," for it is the passion that she inspires and fosters that counts. A "superbe fantôme" because of her irresistible power. In line 11, one of the images of the first stanza returns, as "plane" repeats "planait"; the same motion is ascribed to the phantom of love as to the speaker's heart, establishing thereby a connection between the two. The sensuous quality of the evocation is emphasized in "comme un arome," which also becomes useful for "charging" men's hearts with love and languor. We might note that "les esprits" here have nothing to do with the "vieux garçons" of line 7; rather, they are in the true lovers among whom the speaker still classes himself.

The evocation becomes somewhat more physical and visual in the next line, but the passion still predominates:

> Belle île aux myrtes verts, pleine de fleurs écloses . . .   [13]

Again, the elements are meant to contrast with the informant's description. The "île triste et noire" of the questioner becomes the "Belle île" of the speaker; the "pauvre terre" is now covered with green myrtles, full of flowers. For the opposition of the two islands is being developed step by step. Thus the "pays fameux dans les chansons" and the "Eldorado banal" give way to the island that is

> Vénérée à jamais par toute nation . . .   [14]

This is another denial of the attitude of the "vieux garçons," hence an affirmation of the speaker's present opinion. Yet it contains, in the extreme form of its expression—"à jamais," "par toute nation"—the seeds of disbelief, and the same may be true of the use of "Vénérée" for the island of love. Throughout the passage, we realize that we are both being subjected to an excessively admiring description and being prepared for an event that will belie it. That becomes abundantly clear in the last three lines of the passage:

> Où les soupirs des cœurs en adoration
> Roulent comme l'encens sur un jardin de roses
>
> Ou le roucoulement éternel d'un ramier! [17]

At face value, the lines might be taken as merely expressing the extent to which love dominates the island. Once more, however, the expression is overdone, and when we find an accumulation of phrases such as "les soupirs des cœurs en adoration," "l'encens sur un jardin de roses," "le roucoulement éternel d'un ramier!" we see a highly sentimentalized picture of love such as one might encounter in a keepsake. It is almost as banal a vision as that of the "vieux garçons," but in a different way. We should note that "cœur" here appears for the third time, now with the ironic epithet, that "roulent" takes up the "roulait" of line 3 (just as "plane" had repeated "planait"), and that another bird, the "ramier," is added to the one to which the speaker had compared his heart.

These echoes, in the passage just considered, of elements in the first stanza, accomplish several things. They place the speaker's conception of Cythère firmly in the time of pre-knowledge, before he had actually seen the island at close range. In so doing, they make of the description a mere echoing of traditional ideas. Besides, as they unite the two passages in tone, they augment our feeling that even at this time the speaker, through the ways he chooses for expressing himself, is manifesting a mocking attitude towards the traditional island—an attitude that can only reflect the knowledge that in reality he already has of the island, but that the reader will not acquire until later. Indeed, the very next lines begin the revelation to the reader of what the speaker already knows. The dash now represents not a change of speaker but a change from the one speaker's imaginary vision of the island to his real vision of it:

—Cythère n'était plus qu'un terrain des plus maigres,
Un désert rocailleux troublé par des cris aigres.   [19]

An event has occurred. After the first sighting and the identification of the island (and the interpolated reverie-apostrophe of the speaker), the voyagers come close enough to see it clearly; the speaker tells what he has seen. As he does so, he repeats a pattern that is by now constant in the poem and that is essential to its emotional effect. The gay and free movement of the first stanza had been followed by the reference to the "île triste et noire," the description of the informant by "c'est une pauvre terre"; now the speaker's elegiac vision is replaced by the sight of "un terrain des plus maigres"—a formula very close to the preceding one. The really important phrase in line 18, though, is "n'était plus"; for it establishes the break in time, on the one hand between that of "l'antique Vénus" and the present, on the other between the time of ignorant imagination and that of the known reality. "Maigres" is meant to contrast with the visual details in lines 13 and 16, and the elements of the following line are equally produced by opposition. "Un désert rocailleux" is opposed to the whole impression of sensuous richness, "troublé" to the notions of peace and of graceful movement, the "cris aigres" specifically to the "roucoulement éternel d'un ramier"; we realize this later when they turn out to be the cries of birds of prey.

These descriptive elements are presented as the prelude and background for the discovery of a specific object by the approaching voyager:

J'entrevoyais pourtant un objet singulier!   [20]

The object is not yet clearly seen—that will constitute the next "event"—yet the "pourtant" indicates that it can be distinguished sufficiently to be recognized as "singulier." It is an "object" with no further specification, "singulier" without indication as to how or why. An air of mystery and suspense results (and this is a narrative device) and before the mystery is solved we will have another long interpolation that returns to the other "side" of the opposition. In this way the suspense is augmented and the emotional impact of the final identification is assured. Before that we learn, in the sixth stanza, what the object is not:

> Ce n'était pas un temple aux ombres bocagères,
> Où la jeune prêtresse, amoureuse des fleurs,
> Allait, le corps brûlé de secrètes chaleurs,
> Entre-bâillant sa robe aux brises passagères.   [24]

As we return to the evocation of the legendary and imaginary Cythère, we find that some of its features are the same as before, but that one important addition has been made: a person, a living human being, has been put into the landscape. A temple to Venus has been placed there and a priestess has been provided to celebrate her rites. Such details as the "ombres bocagères" (related to the "myrtes verts" of line 13), the "fleurs" (see the same line), and the "brises passagères" (vaguely recalling the "fantôme" and the "encens"), are repetitions. They establish the needed continuity. What is new about the priestess is that she introduces the body and the flesh into this mythological setting. Before, there had been the spirit and the goddess of love, now there is a woman who loves ("amoureuse des fleurs"). Only the heart had previously been mentioned—"fêtes du cœur," "cœurs en adoration"—whereas here it is the body, "le corps brûlé," that is involved in love and that presents itself to love, "Entre-bâillant sa robe." The vague sensuousness and voluptuousness of the earlier description lose their abstract quality and are concretized in a living being. The extent of this change is epitomized by the passage from the "doux secrets . . . du cœur" of line 9 to the "corps brûlé de secrètes chaleurs" of line 23.

Temple and priestess are not what the speaker now sees; they are another imaginary vision that he draws out of the legendary Cythère. But it was necessary to introduce them at this point, before introducing the "objet singulier," in order to prepare for the identification of that object. Hence the essential factors of the vision are anticipatory: the living woman, inhabitant of Cythère, leads to the dead man, inhabitant of Cythère, her body and its love to his body and its love, her rites to his rites. Besides, when the ultimate association between the dead man and the speaker is made, it will rest upon similarities both of heart and of body. Structurally, it was useful to complete the relationship heart : body in connection with the legendary island before transferring it to the real island and finally to the speaker; the poetic probabilities thus become fully established.

There will be several phases in the identification of the "objet singulier," and we shall learn first that it is a gibbet, then that it is a gibbet holding a hanged man; the man of course is the important object. Once more, the narrative line will be pursued:

> Mais voilà qu'en rasant la côte d'assez près
> Pour troubler les oiseaux avec nos voiles blanches,
> Nous vîmes que c'était un gibet à trois branches,
> Du ciel se détachant en noir, comme un cyprès.   [28]

Once more, also, many of the details in the narrative are derived from earlier parts of the poem. The stanza is related to the preceding one through the sequence "Ce n'était pas . . . ," "Mais . . . Nous vîmes que c'était . . . ," and the fact that this is the next event in a story is indicated by the "voilà que . . ." The ship, recognized first through its "cordages," is now characterized by "nos voiles blanches" and its progress across the sea brings it very close to the island; close enough, indeed, "Pour troubler les oiseaux . . ." "Troubler" takes up the "troublé par des cris aigres" of line 19 and the birds here mentioned are the same as the ones whose cries had broken the calm of the island. In the partial identification of the object, "un gibet à trois branches," there is already a suggestion of the tree to which it will be compared in the next line. That comparison is rich in references; "Du ciel" goes back to the "ciel sans nuages" (line 3), "en noir" directly to the "île triste et noire," by contrast to all of the original insistence on whiteness and light (cf. "nos voiles blanches"), and "comme un cyprès" is opposed to the "myrtes verts" of line 13. The last opposition is significant; for while the myrtle belonged on Cythère as part of the cult of Venus, the "cypress" seen there could be related only to death. The total effect of the stanza is to assign to the "object" traits that bring it into strong juxtaposition to all the images previously associated with the island of ancient legend.

The eighth stanza is the first of three that will be devoted to the description of the man hanged on the gibbet. In the development of the poem, we have thus completed the opposition of the two Cythères and are at the point where the "inhabitant" of the real Cythère will be presented, prior to the establishment of a moral equivalence between him and the speaker. The figure of the hanged man is in a sense transitional, since his physical features (and they are the ones that will be emphasized exclusively in the three stanzas) are related to the traits of the real island (hence opposed to those of the legendary island), while his moral person will contain the elements of the speaker's own history. The emotional effect of the description here presented gains much of its vigor from the fact that the visual image is violent, horrible, disgusting, in place of the sentimentally sweet image attached to the legendary island and the priestess. The devices of opposition here attain their maximum effectiveness:

> De féroces oiseaux perchés sur leur pâture
> Détruisaient avec rage un pendu déjà mûr,
> Chacun plantant, comme un outil, son bec impur
> Dans tous les coins saignants de cette pourriture.　　　[33]

As the narrative continues ("Détruisaient"), the divergence of direction—and at the same time the continuity—is indicated in the presence of the "féroces oiseaux," replacing the free birds of the voyage and the "ramier" of Venus' island; they are the birds disturbed by the approaching ship. What they are disturbed from is their feast upon the hanged man. The act of feasting occupies a part of the passage, "perchés" describing their position, "Détruisaient avec rage" the violence of their activity, and the whole of line 31, "Chacun plantant, comme un outil, son bec impur," its specific nature. The hanged man occupies the rest of the passage, appearing first as "leur pâture," then as "un pendu déjà mûr," finally in the summarizing formula, "cette pourriture"; activity and object are related in the phrase, "Dans tous les coins saignants." The whole picture is horrifying, both in its insistence on the state of decomposition of the hanged man and in its indignation at the voracity of the birds, expressed especially in "son bec impur."

But the picture will become more revolting still in the next stanza, where we discover the condition to which the birds of prey have already reduced their victim:

> Les yeux étaient deux trous, et du ventre effondré
> Les intestins pesants lui coulaient sur les cuisses,

Et ses bourreaux, gorgés de hideuses délices,
L'avaient à coups de bec absolument châtré.   [36]

The purpose for continuing the description in this way would seem
to be dual, first to raise the disgust to a point where the "Comme un
vomissement" of line 47 will be justified, second to attach the punishment specifically to the organs through which the hanged man
had sinned. Our reaction is thus one of physical revulsion, which
grows as we pass from the initial details—"Les yeux étaient deux
trous," "ventre effondré," "intestins pesants . . . coulaient"—to the
final fact of the destruction of his genitals. For obvious reasons, this
last is given special attention. Cythère is love's island, and the instruments of love must be responsible for the hanged man's fate. That it
is a punishment is shown by the use of "ses bourreaux" for the birds;
their ravenous activity, "gorgés," "à coup de bec," is made to apply to
his genitals (the speaker reveals his own horror when he calls them
"de hideuses délices") and the extent of their success is revealed in
the "absolument châtré." There is now neither irony nor a subtle
balancing of opposites, but rather a completely direct and forthright
depiction. We learn only the fact of the hanged man's punishment;
the reasons and the commentary will be provided later. Indeed, it is
in the light of this depiction that we read the irony into the description of the legendary Cythère; the recollection of the "hideuses
délices" and the "absolument châtré" gives a strange tone to "Entre-
bâillant sa robe aux brises passagères."

A further punishment awaits the hanged man, however, and it
will come when his rotted body falls from the gibbet:

Sous les pieds, un troupeau de jaloux quadrupèdes,
Le museau relevé, tournoyait et rôdait;
Une plus grande bête au milieu s'agitait
Comme un exécuteur entouré de ses aides.   [40]

The stanza is in some respects parallel to the preceding one. Like the
birds, the beasts of prey are called the hanged man's executioners:
"un exécuteur entouré de ses aides"; the notion of punishment is
reinforced. Their avidity is expressed in "jaloux" and in "Le museau
relevé." But their feast still lies in the future, and they now wait for
it; hence the "tournoyait, rôdait, s'agitait." It will be their job to

finish—"absolument"—the destruction of the man's body, begun by the natural processes of decomposition and continued by the birds. There is so far no specification of the beasts; we know only that they are beasts of prey, and that is all we need to know. The freedom given to our imagination is perhaps more effective than the names would be, since their activity and their intention are more important than any visual image. As for the effect, the stanza tends to project into the future the horror of the present scene—to add another "event" to the narrative—through its intimation of an even more cruel destruction. Our sympathy for the hanged man reaches a climax along with our sense of horror and distaste.

With the "objet singulier" not only identified but completely described, the speaker may now proceed to his interpretation of its meaning for himself; the rest of the poem contains the interpretation. In the three stanzas that now follow, the speaker addresses the hanged man (just as he had previously addressed the imaginary island) in order to do three things: to explain the victim's punishment, to declare the similarity of their lots, and to reveal his own suffering. Stanza XI begins the apostrophe with a kind of commentary on the hanged man's punishment:

> Habitant de Cythère, enfant d'un ciel si beau,
> Silencieusement tu souffrais ces insultes
> En expiation de tes infâmes cultes
> Et des péchés qui t'ont interdit le tombeau.   [44]

The speaker will use three forms of address for the hanged man; the first one identifies him as an "Habitant de Cythère" in order to associate him clearly with both the legendary and the real island— both of them still the island of love. This is apparent in the description, "enfant d'un ciel si beau," which refers to the "ciel sans nuages" of the speaker's voyage as well as to the imaginary vision; something of the ironic note returns as we join this image to that of the corpse. The same is true of "Silencieusement" in the next line, which has two references, one to the necessary silence of the dead man, the other (looking forward) to the final outcry of the living speaker in the last lines of the poem. Already, the dead and the living are beginning to be compared. With "tu souffrais," the speaker applies to the hanged man a verb which may be taken literally only for himself—only the living can suffer—and which must be taken figuratively for the hanged man—the dead can "suffer" only in the sense of undergoing. With "ces insultes," the punishment inflicted by the birds of prey takes on a spiritual meaning.

The interpretation of lines 43 and 44 raises some difficulties, probably because of our wish to inquire into the precise nature of the sins for which the dead man now atones. They are referred to only as "tes infâmes cultes" and "des péchés." I think that we do not need to know more than we are told: that is, that these are sins against love ("tes . . . cultes" is the counterpart of the rites celebrated by the young priestess, the hanged man is an "habitant de Cythère") and that in some way—in kind or in degree—they are violations of what was expected of the lover. Hence the "infâmes" and the formula "qui t'ont interdit le tombeau." What is important is the fact that the hanging itself and the leaving of the corpse to be destroyed by birds and beasts are a punishment, the suffering of the hanged man an atonement, an "expiation," for sins against love. And the reason why we need to know this is built into the structure of the poem: the hanged man exists in the poem in order to provide a comparison to and a clarification of the plight of the speaker. He will say so explicitly later. At this point he needs only to assert the relationship between sins of love and the horrible accompaniment that punishes them, the suffering that follows upon them. That is the function of Stanza XI, which prepares the reader for the inference that he will later have to make.

In the next stanza, the speaker proceeds to what has been, all along, the purpose of his narrative and his commentary: the discovery in the hanged man of a situation comparable to his own. Because of the general structural basis, the identification is linked to another step in the narrative:

> Ridicule pendu, tes douleurs sont les miennes!
> Je sentis, à l'aspect de tes membres flottants,
> Comme un vomissement, remonter vers mes dents
> Le long fleuve de fiel des douleurs anciennes. [48]

As the speaker addresses the dead man for a second time, he takes up the "pendu" of line 30; but he adds to it the epithet "ridicule," which in this context takes on a very special meaning. The hanged man is not "ridicule" in any funny way, but rather because he contrasts absurdly with his surroundings and with one's expectations for a man, a lover, and a native of Cythère; he is "ridicule" for an "Habitant de Cythère, enfant d'un ciel si beau." (We recall a similar usage in line 35 of *Le Cygne,* "Comme les exilés, ridicule et sublime." I shall have something to say shortly about the recurrence of this and other concepts in the two poems.) When he says, "tes douleurs sont les miennes!" the speaker suddenly effects the identification between the hanged man and himself. Suddenly, but not unexpectedly; for there had been certain indications along the way of the involvement of the speaker in the fate of the dead man. Yet there is a dramatic quality about the explicit revelation that produces a vigorous reaction in the reader, especially with his inference that the physical tortures of the hanged man are represented in the speaker by moral tortures of equal violence. The building of the emotional effect reaches a kind of climax with this first outcry of the speaker.

He then specifies by continuing his narrative: "Je sentis . . . remonter . . . Le long fleuve . . ." Physical sufferings, "l'aspect de tes membres flottants," are paralleled by moral sufferings, the "fiel des douleurs anciennes." But their response in the speaker is a physical one, "remonter vers mes dents / Le long fleuve de fiel," so strong that he can make the comparison, "Comme un vomissement." That is, the sense of disgust and revulsion created in the reader (and in the speaker) by the spectacle of the hanged man on the gibbet are now made a part of the speaker's spiritual state—the basic state underlying all that he says in the poem. The passage from physical to moral had previously been effected in the phrase, "tu souffrais ces insultes"; it is now reinforced by "[le] fiel des douleurs anciennes," where the metaphorical use of "fiel" helps make the transition. The speaker, however, is disgusted with himself (for reasons yet to be discovered), and it is in this sense that the emotion of the speaker and the emotion of the reader remain distinct. He reacts with bitterness to his "douleurs anciennes," whereas the reader reacts to them with sympathy and compassion.

In his third apostrophe to the hanged man, the speaker fills in the details of the torture common to himself and the hanged man, thereby completing the metaphor:

Devant toi, pauvre diable au souvenir si cher,
J'ai senti tous les becs et toutes les mâchoires
Des corbeaux lancinants et des panthères noires
Qui jadis aimaient tant à triturer ma chair.   [52]

In "Devant toi," he establishes the agency of his vision in recalling
his own sufferings; so that when he goes on to say, "pauvre diable au
souvenir si cher," the expression evinces not only sympathy for the
other man but a certain degree of self-commiseration; and the "souvenir si cher" is also his own. It is truly no more specific than had
been the "douleurs anciennes"—or, for that matter, the hanged
man's sins. The advantage of imprecision is the same in all cases; it
allows for concentration on the passion itself, on the suffering, rather
than on accidental causes. The remaining three lines of the stanza
depend entirely on the re-use of elements from the vision of the
hanged man. The birds of prey are now epitomized by the "corbeaux lancinants," the beasts of prey by the "panthères noires" (who
probably pluralize the "plus grande bête" of line 39). "Tous les becs"
not only refers to the "bec impur" of line 31 and the "coups de bec"
of line 36, but it also (through its superlative) marks the extent of
the speaker's suffering, as does "toutes les mâchoires" for the beasts.
The avidity of birds and beasts is translated by "aimaient tant" and
the effectiveness of their activity both by "lancinants" and by "triturer." Since all these terms have described a physical activity, the
speaker must say "triturer ma chair"; but the equivalence of heart
and flesh have long since been built into the poem, and we know
that this is a moral suffering represented by a material destruction.
The complex relationships in the poem are now clear: for the
speaker, the physical suffering of the "habitant de Cythère" is an
atonement for sins against love just as his own moral suffering is an
atonement for his own sins. Thus:

> *"habitant de Cythère"*   *speaker*
> physical suffering : sins : : moral suffering : sins

One of the particular features of the structure of *Un Voyage à
Cythère* is that the parts of the metaphor are successively presented
by means of the narrative, rather than being simultaneously present
throughout the poem.

In a poem like Ronsard's "Quand vous serez bien vieille," there is a constant metaphorical relationship between the life of a woman and the existence of a rose; but the second part of the relationship, concerning the rose, is expressed only at the very end. The reader makes all the necessary inferences from the statement in the last line, and applies them retrospectively to the antecedent parts of the poem. This is different from the case in "Mignonne, allons voir si la rose," where the total ratio *rose* : *woman* is implicit throughout and explicitly indicated at many points, almost from the beginning. In both cases, the metaphor is extremely simple. That of *Un Voyage à Cythère* is considerably more complex, and because of this complexity it presented a greater range of possibilities for presentation. The one chosen by the poet was that of the narrative, permitting a piecemeal introduction of the various constituents. One of the consequences of this choice is the subtlety of emotional effect as the successive elements are revealed—and the ironic overtones that result from the revelation.

Stanza XIV gives, in a way, the most overt statement of the irony that comes from the oppositions. Its first line is a reprise of the initial stanza of the poem:

> —Le ciel était charmant, la mer était unie. [53]

But the dash that precedes it signifies the passage to a conclusion in which beginning and end will be brought together and the oppositions clearly stated. The "ciel charmant" and the "mer unie" are physical details repeated from Stanza I; yet we no longer take them at face value. We know that they are now contemplated in terms of the speaker's later discoveries:

> Pour moi tout était noir et sanglant désormais,
> Hélas! et j'avais, comme en un suaire épais,
> Le cœur enseveli dans cette allégorie. [56]

It is the "Pour moi" that clarifies all the relationships: the speaker has become, from his original status as a member of a group of voyagers, a person of distinct moral quality and suffering, in every way parallel to the quality and the suffering of the "habitant de Cythère." And he has come to know of this identity. Hence the "désormais;" hence the impossibility, also, of interpreting line 53 literally. "Tout était noir et sanglant" expands the blackness of the island and the gibbet (lines 5 and 28) and the bloodiness of the spectacle (lines 29 ff.) to include all aspects of the speaker's moral existence.

Beginning with "Hélas!" a concise expression of the speaker's present emotional state, lines 55 and 56 achieve a total characterization of that state (resulting, as we have seen, from the discoveries concomitant with the "voyage"). The essential comparison is to death: his heart ("Mon cœur . . . voltigeait . . . et planait") is now buried "comme en un suaire épais"; what had been (apparent) freedom of motion and gayety has been changed into the immobility and the sorrow of death. The shroud is made "épais" to indicate the degree of the envelopment, hence the extent of his sense of moral death. "Dans cette allégorie": the meaning is clear, but it is particular to this passage. "Allégorie" is not to be taken in any technical literary sense, nor even in the broader construction of a way of representing abstractions by living persons. On the contrary, we are to understand by "allégorie" the general correspondence between what has gone on in the island of Cythère—the sins and punishment of the lover—and what is now going on in the heart of the speaker— his sins and moral suffering. It thus means something like "represent-ative value," "capacity to evoke similarities," just as it did in line 31 of *Le Cygne*. Both poems take external beings or objects and develop through them a discovery of the speaker's moral state; they are "allegorical" only in this way—and "allegorical" means "metaphori-cal." If here the speaker has his heart "buried" in the allegory, it is because his discoveries in *Un Voyage à Cythère* have brought him to a full awareness of his degree of moral despair.

Something of the same representative intent is contained in the concluding stanza of the poem. Just as, in *Le Cygne,* "mythe" had gone along with "allégorie" as an alternative term, so here the "gibet symbolique" is synonymous with the "allégorie." Once again, the speaker uses an apostrophe, this time to address Venus.

> Dans ton île, ô Vénus! je n'ai trouvé debout
> Qu'un gibet symbolique où pendait mon image... [58]

Cythère has not previously been called, specifically, Venus' island, although all that has been *said* about it identified it as the island of love. The effect of the appellation here ("ton île, ô Vénus") is to throw into sharp relief the rest of the sentence: the island has come to mean, for the speaker, everything but love. The "ne . . . que" of the construction takes care of the contrast. The gibbet is "symbolique" since the man hanged upon it "represents," "stands for" the speaker himself. The physical sufferings of the "habitant" (in death) are a concretization of the speaker's moral sufferings (in life). He sees the one, he feels the other. The "habitant" is his "image"—his myth, his "allégorie," his symbol in the particular sense in which these terms are used both here and in *Le Cygne*.

Another apostrophe concludes the poem. Addressed not to the Goddess of Love but to God, it appeals to God for assistance in this state of moral despair:

> —Ah! Seigneur! donnez-moi la force et le courage
> De contempler mon cœur et mon corps sans dégoût!   [60]

However, what we have here is not really a prayer to God for help; there is nothing earlier in the poem to make us think that it might be, no religious bent on the part of the speaker, no relationship between him and God. He uses this apostrophe just as he had used the other. He had spoken to Venus in order to reveal something about himself that he had discovered through the vision of "her" island; he speaks to God in order to express the full scope of the moral despair that he has there discovered in himself. The lines are summary in every respect; they conclude. If we think back to the long developments treating separately the hearts and the bodies of those who inhabit Cythère and then bringing them together, we see the justification for the final concise formula: "mon cœur et mon corps." If we remember the speaker's physical revulsion as he views the hanged man and then the "vomissement" that he senses within himself, we see that "sans dégoût" contains the whole of the wish for escape from his present moral state. The "contempler" of the last line is a transmutation, to the internal moral plane, of the material contemplation that had constituted much of the voyage. Finally, the wish for "force" and "courage"—a wish possible only for a living man—at once displays his realization of his present moral condition and his dissatisfaction with it.

If the last stanza epitomizes in this way the totality of the moral discovery, it also brings to full actualization the various lines of poetic development that I have been suggesting. The narrative strain is concluded with the sentence, "je n'ai trouvé debout / Qu'un gibet . . . où pendait . . ."; this tells the whole story briefly. The opposition between the two islands is also made concisely: on the one hand, "ton île, ô Vénus"; on the other (with the "ne . . . que") "un gibet." As for the identification between the hanged man and the speaker, it is collapsed into the two formulas, "un gibet symbolique" and "mon image." Such a procedure on the part of the poet shows to what a degree the various devices selected for the making of his poem really constitute a single device, a single structural concept that is realized through them.

As a consequence of this division of the central structural line, a number of special effects can be obtained in the creation and the development of the essential emotion. The gradual revelation of the speaker's own state of feeling—he passes from impersonal viewing to the sympathy of an outsider for another's suffering to a deep personal involvement—carries along with it a slow evolution of the reader's emotion. Especially if we take into account the ironic concomitant, which enhances the reader's emotion, we see the whole process as one of extending the affective distance between the reader and the speaker at the beginning, in order progressively to decrease that distance as the poem goes along. Perhaps I should say that we are set off on a false route by the excessively rosy description at the beginning, evoking an emotion directly opposite to the final one. But this only at first reading. We know, later, that we must begin at the beginning to perceive the speaker's despair and to sympathize with it. We know, too, that as soon as we come upon the "île triste et noire," we have had a first glimpse of the true state of affairs in the speaker's soul, and our sympathy for him is solidified. I suppose that basically what we feel for him is a kind of pity (perhaps the reason for the secrecy about his sins is to prevent the arousal of any sense of condemnation), and that pity is increased if we come to it through an apparent attitude of congratulation. Similarly, the arousal of physical revulsion, in us as in the speaker, renders more telling the pity we feel for a moral state that has all the features of the revolting physical object.

The intention to arouse and conduct a complex emotion like the one in *Un Voyage à Cythère* accounts for the length, the "magnitude" of the poem. The metaphorical parallels that I have cited from Ronsard, for example, were derived from sonnets or poems that were short and simple because the emotion sought was simple and clear. One of the discoveries of nineteenth-century French poetry, and especially of Baudelaire, was that the emotion expressed and aroused in a poem might be much more complicated, subtle, varied, refined. But in order to make such a poem, the conception of poetic structure needed also to be refined. This was not basically a question of length; the eighteenth and the early nineteenth centuries had produced many long lyrics that were as simple-minded as they were "simple-souled." It was rather a question of multiplication and integration of the useful poetic devices. None of the devices used by Baudelaire in *Un Voyage à Cythère* was new; all were traditional. His synthesis of these devices was new, however, in the sense that he wove together three or four poetic means for the creation of a very particular emotional effect. If not new, at least unique. For every poem, in whatever genre, is a private and independent structure of objects, chosen and organized for the achievement of a specific emotional effect.

5

Rimbaud

Le Bateau ivre

In Baudelaire's *Le Cygne,* where the structure is essentially meta-phorical, there are nevertheless the beginnings of a symbolist tech-nique in poetry—this in the sense that, were one to alter slightly the description of the swan by removing all overt reference to the man to whom he is compared, one would have a fairly complete and independent development of one-half of a metaphor in a way that would make a kind of elementary "symbolist" sense. So to alter the poem is of course to violate it; and if I suggested the possibility of so doing, it was merely in order to indicate how easy is the transition from a metaphorical to a symbolist structure. In such a poem as *Recueillement,* symbolist structure is full blown. The half of the metaphor relating to the coming of evening and night, to the "re-cueillement" itself, is stated completely, and a sufficient number of "indicators" is provided so that the reader may infer the other half, the approach and arrival of death. The typical symbolist situation is present, in a clear and simple form.

At an opposite end of the symbolist scale stands Rimbaud's *Le Bateau ivre.* For if the symbolism of *Recueillement* is clear and simple, that of *Le Bateau ivre* is unclear and highly complex. It is unclear not because we have doubts about the fact that the boat is a symbol for something else, but because that something else is not

This essay is a slightly modified version of an article entitled *"Le Bateau ivre,* or the limits of symbolism," *Publications of the Modern Language Association of America,* LXXII (March, 1957), 165–93.

readily identifiable. The thing symbolized, the "other half" of the metaphor, is vague and dubious, partly because there seem to be various conflicting suggestions within the poem, partly because certain partial and occasional indicators have led to a traditional reading that is not corroborated by the rest of the poem. *Le Bateau ivre* is complex through its length and the number of narrative episodes involved; through the many aspects of the symbol presented for consideration; through the multitude of descriptive details; and—resulting from all these—through the variety of emotions that succeed one another both in what the boat says about itself and in what the reader is made to feel with respect to the boat.

Complexity of this kind carries with it a great danger for the interpretation of the poem: the danger of an allegorical reading, the danger of seeing the poem as a vast enigma each part of which must be "solved" in terms of a central meaning. That danger raises a theoretical question with respect to the analysis of symbolist poetry in general: How much of a symbolist poem is actually involved in the central symbol about which the poem is built, and what purpose is served by such parts of the poem as are not involved in that symbol? Unless the poem is an allegory or an enigma, there will be parts of it that are not immediately translatable into terms of the central symbol and the thing symbolized. The artistic reasons for the presence of those parts, either in terms of internal structure or of external effect, need to be sought and discovered. Once found, they may be related both to the symbol and to the thing symbolized, to the literal meaning and the symbolic meaning, and the poem as a whole may be more fully understood.

Le Bateau ivre

Comme je descendais des Fleuves impassibles,
Je ne me sentis plus guidé par les haleurs:
Des Peaux-Rouges criards les avaient pris pour cibles
Les ayant cloués nus aux poteaux de couleurs.　　　4

J'étais insoucieux de tous les équipages,
Porteur de blés flamands ou de cotons anglais.

Quand avec mes haleurs ont fini ces tapages,
Les Fleuves m'ont laissé descendre où je voulais.   8

Dans les clapotements furieux des marées,
Moi, l'autre hiver, plus sourd que les cerveaux d'enfants,
Je courus! et les Péninsules démarrées
N'ont pas subi tohu-bohus plus triomphants.   12

La tempête a béni mes éveils maritimes.
Plus léger qu'un bouchon j'ai dansé sur les flots
Qu'on appelle rouleurs éternels de victimes,
Dix nuits, sans regretter l'œil niais des falots!   16

Plus douce qu'aux enfants la chair des pommes sures,
L'eau verte pénétra ma coque de sapin
Et des taches de vins bleus et des vomissures
Me lava, dispersant gouvernail et grappin.   20

Et dès lors, je me suis baigné dans le Poëme
De la Mer, infusé d'astres, et lactescent,
Dévorant les azurs verts où, flottaison blême
Et ravie, un noyé pensif parfois descend;   24

Où, teignant tout à coup les bleuités, délires
Et rhythmes lents sous les rutilements du jour,
Plus fortes que l'alcool, plus vastes que vos lyres,
Fermentent les rousseurs amères de l'amour!   28

Je sais les cieux crevant en éclairs, et les trombes
Et les ressacs et les courants: je sais le soir,
L'Aube exaltée ainsi qu'un peuple de colombes,
Et j'ai vu quelquefois ce que l'homme a cru voir.   32

J'ai vu le soleil bas taché d'horreurs mystiques,
Illuminant de longs figements violets,
Pareils à des acteurs de drames très antiques,
Les flots roulant au loin leurs frissons de volets!   36

J'ai rêvé la nuit verte aux neiges éblouies,
Baisers montant aux yeux des mers avec lenteurs,
La circulation des sèves inouïes
Et l'éveil jaune et bleu des phosphores chanteurs!   40

J'ai suivi, des mois pleins, pareille aux vacheries
Hystériques, la houle à l'assaut des récifs,
Sans songer que les pieds lumineux des Maries
Pussent forcer le mufle aux Océans poussifs!   44

J'ai heurté, savez-vous? d'incroyables Florides
Mêlant aux fleurs des yeux de panthères à peaux
D'hommes, des arcs-en-ciel tendus comme des brides,
Sous l'horizon des mers, à de glauques troupeaux. 48

J'ai vu fermenter les marais énormes, nasses
Où pourrit dans les joncs tout un Léviathan!
Des écroulements d'eaux au milieu des bonaces,
Et les lointains vers les gouffres cataractant! 52

Glaciers, soleils d'argent, flots nacreux, cieux de braises,
Echouages hideux au fond des golfes bruns
Où les serpents géants dévorés des punaises
Choient, des arbres tordus, avec de noirs parfums! 56

J'aurais voulu montrer aux enfants ces dorades
Du flot bleu, ces poissons d'or, ces poissons chantants.
—Des écumes de fleurs ont béni mes dérades,
Et d'ineffables vents m'ont ailé par instants. 60

Parfois, martyr lassé des pôles et des zones,
La mer dont le sanglot faisait mon roulis doux
Montait vers moi ses fleurs d'ombre aux ventouses jaunes,
Et je restais ainsi qu'une femme à genoux... 64

Presque île ballotant sur mes bords les querelles
Et les fientes d'oiseaux clabaudeurs aux yeux blonds.
Et je voguais, lorsqu'à travers mes liens frêles
Des noyés descendaient dormir à reculons!... 68

Or, moi, bateau perdu sous les cheveux des anses,
Jeté par l'ouragan dans l'éther sans oiseau,
Moi dont les Monitors et les voiliers des Hanses
N'auraient pas repêché la carcasse ivre d'eau; 72

Libre, fumant, monté de brumes violettes,
Moi qui trouais le ciel rougeoyant comme un mur
Qui porte, confiture exquise aux bons poëtes,
Des lichens de soleil et des morves d'azur; 76

Qui courais, taché de lunules électriques,
Planche folle, escorté des hippocampes noirs,
Quands les juillets faisaient crouler à coups de triques
Les cieux ultramarins aux ardents entonnoirs; 80

Moi qui tremblais, sentant geindre à cinquante lieues
Le rut des Béhémots et les Maelstroms épais,

Fileur éternel des immobilités bleues,
Je regrette l'Europe aux anciens parapets!   84

J'ai vu des archipels sidéraux! et des îles
Dont les cieux délirants sont ouverts au vogueur:
—Est-ce en ces nuits sans fond que tu dors et t'éxiles,
Million d'oiseaux d'or, ô future Vigueur?—   88

Mais, vrai, j'ai trop pleuré! Les Aubes sont navrantes.
Toute lune est atroce et tout soleil amer:
L'âcre amour m'a gonflé de torpeurs enivrantes.
O que ma quille éclate! O que j'aille à la mer!   92

Si je désire une eau d'Europe, c'est la flache
Noire et froide où vers le crépuscule embaumé
Un enfant accroupi, plein de tristesses, lâche
Un bateau frêle comme un papillon de mai.   96

Je ne puis plus, baigné de vos langueurs, ô lames,
Enlever leur sillage aux porteurs de cotons,
Ni traverser l'orgueil des drapeaux et des flammes,
Ni nager sous les yeux horribles des pontons.   100

On the literal level, *Le Bateau ivre* is a narrative which recounts in relatively short space the adventures of a boat and the emotions accompanying those adventures. The boat passes, at the beginning, from a state of servitude to one of liberty, and the joy of liberation is indicated. Next come the multiple voyages and adventures as the boat drifts or is blown over the surface of all the world's oceans, adventures accompanied by great exultation in the sense of boundless freedom, but also by a premonition of lassitude and regret. Finally, it is these latter emotions which dominate as the boat, its drunken career having ended in debilitation, disintegration, and a tragic sense of impotence, yearns to end its voyagings in a final sinking to the bottom of the sea—or else to return to its original state of servitude. The progression of the narrative is thus from liberation, to unrestrained adventure, to a disillusionment with adventure; the progression of the emotions is from joy, to exultation mixed with regret, to despair and a wish for an end of suffering.

On the symbolic level (and I suggest here a hypothetical interpretation which I hope to substantiate in the course of the following analysis), *Le Bateau ivre* is a narrative which recounts in relatively short space the passage of a man through several stages of his development, and the emotions accompanying that passage. The man passes, at the beginning, from the restrictions and servitude of childhood to a state of adult manhood, and the joy of liberation is indicated. Next come the multiple adventures as the man, free of all restraint, participates fully in all the activities of a certain kind of adult life, adventures accompanied by great exultation in the sense of boundless freedom, but also by a premonition of lassitude and regret. Finally, it is these latter emotions which dominate as the man, his adult life having brought a sense of discouragement, impotence, and corruption, yearns to end his life in final death—or, as an alternative, to return to the peace and the orderly security of his childhood years. The progression of the narrative is thus from a state of childhood, with all its restrictions, to a state of manhood involving disappearance of these restrictions and complete liberty of action, to a disillusionment with this liberty; the progression of the emotions is from joy, to exultation mixed with regret, to despair and a wish for an end of suffering.

I have purposely insisted upon these two aspects of the poem, the parallelism of the literal and the symbolic action, the identity of the emotion, because this is the poetic device by which the ultimate effect of the poem is achieved. The emotions attributed to the boat are from the outset those which belong not to a boat—which as an inanimate object would have none—but to a man in like circumstances and progressing through a similar series of episodes. The boat speaks throughout, saying what a boat might say about the actual adventures which it relates, but expressing an emotional accompaniment proper only to a man. The identity of the emotions is the basis of the symbolical relationship. The problem of the poet is so to express the literal action that the symbolic action becomes apparent through it, thereby rendering the expression of the emotions more vigorous and more poignant to the reader. The problem of the reader is to discover the symbolic meaning through the literal one; as he does so, he understands more clearly, the emotions become more intelligible and more personally alive for him, and his pleasure in the reading is enhanced.

In the analysis which follows, I shall attempt to show in considerable detail how Rimbaud handles the relationship between the literal and the symbolic meaning. I need hardly insist that any reading such as the one I propose is a hypothesis rather than a demonstration. One does not "prove" that one is "right"; one attempts rather to discover that reading which will most completely and most appropriately explain the whole of the text and all of its parts. The only proof is in reference to the text itself.

> Comme je descendais des Fleuves impassibles . . .   [1]

In the first line, Rimbaud gives three initial indications of high importance to the structure of the poem. First, in "Comme je descendais," the boat describes its state or condition in the past before the events of the poem actually begin. The "Fleuves" (capitalized because of their symbolic meaning [1]) designate a body of water of fixed boundaries and direction, determining the "descent" of the boat; symbolically, they represent those restrictions within which the man moves before his liberation. In "impassibles" we have again an ambivalent term, since the waters are as indifferent to the course of the boat as the forces controlling the man are to his wishes and feelings.

> Je ne me sentis plus guidé par les haleurs.   [2]

Again, we have three indications: in "Je ne me sentis plus," the moment of liberation, signified not only by the past absolute tense of the verb but also by the negation, "ne . . . plus"; in "guidé," a kind of summary of the action of the impassive Rivers, in both their literal and symbolic meaning; in "par les haleurs," a first identification of the human forces which restrict and control movement, the haulers for the boat, unidentified people for the man. It will be noted that the past, preceding the liberation, is only briefly touched upon here; additional statements will be made about it later.

> Des Peaux-Rouges criards les avaient pris pour cibles,
> Les ayant cloués nus aux poteaux de couleurs.   [4]

---

[1] I can only suppose that some of the capital letters represent the author's intentions, rather than merely the current editorial tradition. From the present state of editions of this text, one cannot be sure. So for the punctuation and other related matters.

The last two lines of the first strophe have a curious function in the poem. They denote, for the ship, the nature of the forces which had brought about the liberation. For the man, the "Peaux-Rouges" will again be the forces of freedom, but they are not further identified— and will not ever be in the course of the poem. One notes immediately, in comparison with the sketchy indications preceding, the extension and complication of the image here. The reason is that Rimbaud wishes to insist upon the visual quality, and at the same time on the unreal and intensely imaginative quality of the image. For this is a child's image, the kind of comparison that the boat would be making if it were (or had been until recently) a child, filled with visions of a story-book character. We have here then, in a very imprecise and indirect way, a first hint of the proportion *boat : child* which will be corroborated by later suggestions. One of the functions of these lines is thus to make the initial comparison. Emotionally, the image signifies the violence both of action and of feeling.

> J'étais insoucieux de tous les équipages,
> Porteur de blés flamands ou de cotons anglais. [6]

These two lines develop rapidly the elements earlier introduced. With "J'étais insoucieux" the boat returns to a description of the preceding condition, avowing an indifference and an impassivity toward its masters equivalent to that of the "Fleuves" for it; so for the child, living within himself. Those masters are identified, for the boat, as the "équipages"—plural and somehow anonymous; for the man, they are merely the persons who control and direct, without further identification. As for line 6, it has many references: in "porteur," to the useful functions of the boat while in servitude, a usefulness lost—and regretted—by the time the phrase "porteurs de cotons" is repeated in line 98; in "blés" and "cotons," a further specification of this usefulness, in the importance of the products themselves for man; in "flamands" and "anglais," an indication of the civilized and European nature of the masters, as against the barbarous and exotic savages who bring an end to servitude.

> Quand avec mes haleurs ont fini ces tapages,
> Les Fleuves m'ont laissé descendre où je voulais. [8]

The second strophe concludes with two lines which return, in point of time, to the event of liberation described in line 2. The "Quand" indicates such a return, as does the repetition of "mes haleurs." In "ont fini ces tapages," we have a formula which at once summarizes the cessation of activity of the "haleurs" and the "équipages" and indicates the attitude of the childish mind towards this activity, "tapage" being a child's word (or a parent's word) for any kind of undesirable action. The last line continues the repetitions from the preceding strophe with "Les Fleuves"; but from then on it operates rather by contrast, with "m'ont laissé descendre" indicating the same direction of motion as in the "descendais" of line 1 but declaring now that the action depends upon the volition of the boat ("où je voulais") rather than upon others as in the earlier "guidé." The passage from dependency to manifestation of volition is the first step, for both boat and child, in the process of spiritual liberation.

The first two strophes have, then, as their function to state the initial condition of servitude with its accompanying sentiments, to indicate the moment of release from such servitude, and to prefigure (if briefly) the passions attendant upon that release. All the statements are valid both for the boat and for the child, and some of them already suggest the nature of the proportion *boat : child*.

> Dans les clapotements furieux des marées . . .   [9]

The first line of the third strophe introduces a procedure which will become standard throughout the rest of the poem. This is the providing of descriptive detail concerning the sea, detail which has little if any symbolic value but which, because of its affective value, contributes to the total emotional impression of a given part of the poem. So, here, the "clapotements furieux" of the tides has emotional significance in its contrast with the "impassibles" of line 1—as an intimation of the joy, the liberty, the madness of the boat itself— and it also supplies directly the first visual and auditory images of the sea.

> Moi, l'autre hiver . . .   [10]

After juxtaposition of the boat to the sea, with the emphatic "moi" opposed to the preceding line, occurs the first indication of time with "l'autre hiver." It will be noted that these time indications, throughout the poem, are wilfully vague; their purpose is to suggest the passage of long periods of time without establishing anything resembling a strict chronology. In this way, "l'autre hiver" suggests that the event of liberation is already in a distant past, and warrants the change of feeling experienced since that event.

> . . . plus sourd que les cerveaux d'enfants,
> Je courus! . . . [11]

In the first overt comparison which it uses, the boat compares itself to a child, and its indifference and heedlessness (cf. the "insoucieux" of line 5) to the way in which a child succeeds in maintaining a voluntary deafness to the orders and entreaties of his elders. Here, it is to be assumed, the boat is excluding whatever final admonitions the forces of civilization may have to offer it, and at the same time is indifferent to the warnings contained in the "clapotements furieux." The "Je courus" must be combined with the earlier "Dans" (l. 9), for the event (not the activity) is being indicated; this is the moment of liberation and of entrance into the sea. "Courus" stands in sharp opposition to "me sentis . . . guidé" and demonstrates the act of volition characterized in "où je voulais."

> . . . Et les Péninsules démarrées
> N'ont pas subi tohu-bohus plus triomphants. [12]

First we have the event, then the emotion accompanying it—contained in the single word "triomphants." The event of liberation, of separation, is expressed in a kind of secondary symbol, the "Péninsules démarrées," where the peninsulas detached from their continents are not limited geographical entities but are the vast continents themselves which, in a primitive conception of the making of the Earth, broke apart and drifted through the oceans. The "tohu-bohus" (note the Biblical origins and meaning of the word) of severance is likened to the "clapotements furieux": both accompany movements of violently separated objects through the sea. It should perhaps be pointed out, however, that in "subi" there is an admission of passivity—of loss of control and of vigor—which will ultimately describe the state of the boat itself.

> La tempête a béni mes éveils maritimes. [13]

State of the sea ("La tempête"; cf. "les clapotements furieux") accompanying the event ("mes éveils maritimes") and, accompanying both, the augury of good fortune and happiness contained in "a béni." For the child, this is the original benediction given by life to those who enter it as adult novices.

> Plus léger qu'un bouchon j'ai dansé sur les flots . . . [14]

In this line (conveying so well by its rhythm the action which it describes), the boat expresses its feelings of joy, of lightness, of freedom, which characterize its first independent movements over the waters. The visual image comprises the notion of the smallness of the object as it compares itself with the "marées" and the "flots"; so for the young adult entering the vast adventure of manhood.

> Qu'on appelle rouleurs éternels de victimes . . . [15]

Joy and confidence lead boat and man to discredit the stories told about those who, having ventured on the sea or on life, have become victims rather than conquerors. But is the discrediting ("qu'on appelle") wise? Or should one admit the probability that the boat itself, and the man whom it symbolizes, may ultimately fall into the category of victims? In any case, the poetic probability is here established that such a fate might possibly overtake the adventurer of this poem. "Rouleurs" indicates the active potential of the greater force, the sea or life, and "éternels" its inevitable and final victory (if one credit the stories told about it).

> Dix nuits, sans regretter l'œil niais des falots! [16]

This second indication of time falls within the first and points only to the earliest period of the liberation. Then follows reaffirmation of the boat's joy in its independence ("sans regretter"). The "œil niais des falots," again, is an equivalent of the "équipages," of those forces which direct, control, and guide—and "niais" gives the point of view towards such guidance of the freed boat or man, thus reinforcing "sans regretter" and strengthening the sentiment of line 5.

> Plus douce qu'aux enfants la chair des pommes sures . . . [17]

In a second comparison which recalls by its very form the first (l.10), the boat again clarifies its feelings by reference to a childhood experience. The essential opposition is *douce : sures,* in which what would be sour to the adult is sweet to the child; so the still childish mind takes pleasure in a similar experience—

L'eau verte pénétra ma coque de sapin . . .   [18]

Several details are to be noted here. The water is "verte" not only because it is sea water, but because the analogy to the "chair des pommes sures" is still being developed. In "pénétra" (as in "subi") there is another intimation of what will be—if it is not already—the essentially passive nature of the boat's role. In "ma coque de sapin" we are given a material detail exclusively appropriate to the boat, which will always speak in such terms; moreover, there is perhaps in the specific terms used a suggestion of the fragility of the structure ("coque") and of the inferior quality of the materials used ("sapin"). The total effect of the line is to give the first intimations of that state of "drunkenness" which will characterize the rest of the boat's career. Perhaps, indirectly, it also gives some hint of the weaknesses of character which cause the man to choose this particular form of adult life and which lead ultimately to failure.

Et des taches de vins bleus et des vomissures
Me lava . . .   [20]

The first physical effect of the boat's adventure is the removal of all traces of the "équipages"—"taches de vins," "vomissures"—by the purifying action of the water. From the point of view of the man, all corrupting traces of his elders and superiors are thus removed as the adventure progresses. "Taches" is itself an affective word, serving object and symbol and adding a note of disparagement to the feeling attendant upon both.

. . . dispersant gouvernail et grappin.   [20]

The second material effect is the removal of the last instruments by which men might retain or steer the boat. Progressively, the boat well be freed of men and machines, "équipages," "falots," and so forth, which might retain it, just as all the forces tending to dominate the man are excluded. But we remark, even this early, that each one of these removals represents for the boat a loss and a diminution.

The function of the third, fourth, and fifth stanzas is thus to complete the account of the event of liberation, for boat and child, and to describe the first effects of that event. These are physical and material effects, but they are suffused with emotional overtones coincident with the sense of liberation and of joy. These stanzas also establish probabilities for the turn which the emotions will later take. The function of Stanzas 6–17 (ll. 21–68), on the other hand, is to recount in detail the adventures themselves. This section will be less exclusively symbolic than the preceding one, and it is here especially that we shall have to raise the question of the "limits of symbolism" and of the functions of those words which do not seem to contribute directly to the development of the symbolic meaning.

> Et dès lors, je me suis baigné dans le Poème
> De la Mer, infusé d'astres, et lactescent . . .   [22]

With a time indication that points forward to future events, the boat enters upon a description of those events. In "je me suis baigné," it insists at once upon the voluntary nature of its action and upon the completeness of its identification with the sea. Similarly, "le Poème de la Mer" has two intentions: it makes explicit, in a sense, the symbolic equivalence between the sea and life, and it has the form of a cry of exultation completely adequate to the boat's emotions. The words "infusé d'astres, et lactescent" present a special problem of interpretation. For I see no possibility of "translating" the two concepts into specific terms relevant to the man or to his adventure. Rather, the function of the words seems to be to lend concreteness and completeness to the image of the sea which is gradually being developed, and by so doing to enhance the emotional effectiveness of the passage. Here there is wilful confusion between sea and sky, giving an impression of limitless vastness and suggesting (through the objects and the colors assembled in the description) a kind of superior beauty whose total effect is pleasant. There may also be, in this confusion, a reflection of the "ivresse" already suggested.

> Dévorant les azurs verts . . .   [23]

With the verb, the boat once again indicates the eagerness and the joy of the adventure; the complement adds further to the description of the sea.

> . . . où, flottaison blême
> Et ravie, un noyé pensif parfois descend.   [24]

Shortly after its expression of doubt about the existence of victims of the sea, the boat admits that these do exist. The "noyé pensif" is one of these, and the fact that he is a "flottaison blême et ravie" shows his completely passive status. Two things need to be insisted upon: First, the presence of these occasional ("parfois") victims makes it more poetically probable that the boat may someday be of their number, especially since the word "descend" links the victim to the "descendais" and "descendre" already used for the boat. Second, this probability is reinforced by the terms here employed for the victim; for, like him, the boat is already a "flottaison" (cf. "subi," "pénétra") and is in a sense "ravi" (that is, carried away); only the qualification "blême" differentiates them—plus the fact that the boat is not yet a "noyé pensif." To "pensif," I believe, may be assigned not only the description of the intent and fixed stare of drowned men, but also the meaning of one who has learned, through experience, lessons which the boat has not yet learned. In terms of the man, these lines express a realization of the fact that the joys of adult manhood may not be completely unmitigated and that it may end in disaster.

The effect of the next passage,

> Où, teignant tout à coup les bleuités, délires
> Et rhythmes lents sous les rutilements du jour,   [26]

is not "pleasant" as was the description in the preceding stanza, although it is related to line 23 as "bleuités" is related to "azurs." For in between the two has come the image of the victims of the sea, and the passage itself is an introduction to another undesirable concept, the "rousseurs amères de l'amour." "Teignant tout à coup" thus suggests sudden and undesirable interruptions of the beautiful scene just painted; while "délires et rhythmes lents," as it opposes two different kinds of motion, shows a conflict between them; and the kind of light described in "les rutilements du jour" is hard and blinding. It should be noted, moreover, that "teignant" is directly related to "rousseurs" and to the cognate image of "fermentent," and that both "délires" and "rhythmes lents" are meant to characterize "l'amour" as well as to describe movements of the sea. The total effect of these lines is thus to add to the symbolical and the literal meaning a note of disturbance and even of unhappiness, consonant with the introduction of the general idea of corruption, of victims, and of failure.

> Plus fortes que l'alcool, plus vastes que vos [2] lyres,
> Fermentent les rousseurs amères de l'amour!   [28]

As a further overt identification of the symbol—these are the signs by which the symbolical meaning becomes apparent—the boat is made to compare its adventures to those of a man. Three forms of joyful adult activity are mentioned, "l'alcool," and "lyres" symbolizing not only poetry but all kinds of creative activity, and "amour." But whereas the epithets for the first two, "fortes" and "vastes" (transferred from the "rousseurs" to "alcool" and "lyres") are laudatory and joyful, that of the third, "amères," is of an opposite character. It is, moreover, stronger and vaster than the others, suggesting again the probability of passage, for boat and man, from joy to sorrow. The words "fermentent" and "rousseurs" are especially important; they are, apart from "flottaison blême," the first signs of a kind of decay and corruption which, as the adventure continues, will become an increasing part of it. It should be noted that in "vos" the boat indicates that it is not only comparing its experiences to those of a man, but that it is recounting them to men. Besides, the particular kinds of adult activities here mentioned (the "alcools" are related to the "bateau *ivre*") constitute a restriction and a choice of adult activity, and these factors may account for the ultimate failure of the adventure.

> Je sais les cieux crevant en éclairs, et les trombes
> Et les ressacs et les courants; je sais le soir,
> L'Aube exaltée ainsi qu'un peuple de colombes . . .   [31]

[2] Most modern texts read "nos"; so does the MS. in the hand of Verlaine (cf. *Le Manuscrit autographe*, II [Nov.–Dec. 1927], 76). But the MS. is in general careless and unreliable. Even if it were completely trustworthy I should be inclined to prefer the reading "vos" of the earlier editions, merely on the basis of internal evidence. Rimbaud is extremely careful to make the boat speak always in terms uniquely appropriate to a boat; since boats do not have lyres, it would be improper for the boat to say "nos lyres," whereas "vos lyres" addressed to the men to whom the boat is speaking is entirely acceptable.

There follows now a long enumeration of the component parts of the adventure, introduced by "je" or "j'ai" and expressed in parallel constructions. The first are discoveries leading to knowledge—"je sais, je sais." Discovery of evening and of dawn is not merely an apprehension of natural phenomena; "l'Aube" especially seems to symbolize the beginnings of all things with its epithet "exaltée"—at least, the beginning of each glorious day of the adventure. Both dawn and evening will appear later with opposite emotional connotations (cf. ll. 89–90); but at this point, close to the beginning of the adventure, the dominant feelings are still of joy, of power, of freedom. Hence these lines will present images characterizing the sea and the sky in terms appropriate to such feelings. The skies will be "crevant en éclairs"—adding a note of wildness and violence—and the sea will contain such phenomena as "trombes, ressacs, courants," all containing the idea of motion. The fact that all these phenomena depend upon the introductory "Je sais" makes of them a part of the boat's intimate experience and, inversely, their own character imparts an emotional tonality to that experience. In line 31, the essential reaction of joy is contained in the word "exaltée": it is the boat which feels "exalted" at the vision of the dawn. But the rest of the line indicates that "exaltée" needs to be taken, at the same time, in a second sense (almost an etymological sense) of "raised on high"; this is the rising of the dawn. But why "ainsi qu'un peuple de colombes"? I believe that the image is meant to impart a feeling composed of these elements: (1) a sense of the silvery color associated with both dawn and doves; (2) the upward motion; (3) the suggestion of a numberless multitude of objects forming this upward motion; (4) the joy in liberty of motion and freedom of flight. Thus the image is at once visual and affective, and through both of these aspects it contributes to the creation of the effect desired at this particular point in the poem.

> Et j'ai vu quelquefois ce que l'homme a cru voir!   [32]

From knowledge, the enumeration passes to vision. Here, the boat sees in himself a superiority to mankind ("ce que l'homme *a cru* voir"), which means that the man engaged in the adventure considers that he is better than other men and has achieved superior knowledge; but only "quelquefois"—somehow parallel to the "parfois" of the sea's victims.

> J'ai vu le soleil bas, taché d'horreurs mystiques,
> Illuminant de longs figements violets,
> Pareils à des acteurs de drames très antiques
> Les flots roulant au loin leurs frissons de volets!   [36]

If in the preceding stanza the boat was made to feel the glories of the dawn, in this stanza it experiences rather the horrors of oncoming night. The experience is not only completed, but it is also oriented in the direction of the ultimate intellectual and emotional conclusions. At this particular point, the feeling of horror will be aroused by suggestions of: (1) mystery, (2) colors associated with sunset and night, (3) remote times, and (4) vaguely unpleasant sounds. The suggestion of mystery is found in such phrases as "le soleil *bas*," "taché d'horreurs *mystiques*," "de longs *figements*" (where the metaphor for clouds is sufficiently remote to suggest uncertainty of form and consistency), "au *loin*," and "leurs frissons de volets" (here again the image is vague and mixed). The suggestion of night is of course found in the entire passage, but it is especially prominent in such phrases as "le soleil bas," "*Illuminant* de longs figements *violets*," and the overtones of the last line. The suggestion of remote times is contained above all in line 35, "Pareils à des acteurs de drames très antiques," but is reinforced by "longs," "au loin." Lines 35 and 36 need explanation. I believe that the central intention is to suggest for the waves both their motion ("roulant" and the suggestion of parallel moving lines found both in "frissons" and in "volets") and their sound (contained especially in "frissons"). But why "Pareils à des acteurs de drames très antiques"? Here again, the intention may be double: first, to evoke the sound of voices coming from a distance (and possibly through hollow-sounding amplifiers) like the sound of the distant waves; second, to sketch a visual seascape of the distant sea ("J'ai vu"), perhaps as an audience in a Greek theater might see it and might hence consider it as one of the actors. (We should remember that such theaters sometimes faced the sea and that the sea was visible in the distance at all times.) The suggestions of sound have already been indicated; I might point out that if "frisson" is one of these, it carries with it the implications of "shudder" as well as of "quiver." The total effect of the stanza is to add to the feeling of grandeur and violence one of vague uneasiness and foreboding.

> J'ai rêvé la nuit verte aux neiges éblouies,
> Baiser montant aux yeux des mers avec lenteurs,
> La circulation des sèves inouïes,
> Et l'éveil jaune et bleu des phosphores chanteurs!   [40]

The next stanza contributes further to these same effects. After knowledge and vision, dreams. "La nuit" is added to the series "soir, Aube," just as it will be included with them in the later passage already cited (ll. 89–90; cf. also l. 87). All these forms of activity constituting the adventure are of course literally possible only for the man in the ratio *boat* : *man,* and are only metaphorically possible for the boat. The "dream" is of the sea at night rather than at sunset, and elements of motion and of color are predominant, although there are still some references to mystery. The total effect will thus be one of wonder and of contained delight, not one of horror. I take it that "la nuit verte" is meant to refer to the color of the sea at night, and that the "neiges éblouies" are whitecaps and other kinds of foam appearing on the surface of the water. This would make the following line, "Baiser montant aux yeux des mers avec lenteurs," indicate both the internal movement of the water which produces such foam and the bursting forth of the foam itself; but the image is curious, since the sea is at once the seer and the seen, the kisser and the kissed. Such words as "éblouies" (the eyes of the seer would be so dazzled), "baiser," and "lenteurs" contain the essential effects of wonder and delight. In the next line, "La circulation des sèves inouïes," the boat once more returns to a description of the sea's motion. There is still something mysterious about this motion ("inouïes") and something of the "lenteurs" of line 38 carries over to it. The final line of the stanza combines, once more, motion ("l'éveil," comparable to "montant aux yeux") and the visual effect of motion ("jaune et bleu des phosphores"), with the kind of feeling involved being suggested in "chanteurs."

> J'ai suivi, des mois pleins, pareille aux vacheries
> Hystériques, la houle à l'assaut des récifs . . .   [42]

After contemplation, the first of several forms of action is shown ("j'ai suivi"), with another indication of the period of time through which the action takes place. To an image of motion is added an indication of the accompanying sound—motion in "la houle à l'assaut des récifs," sound in the simile. For I presume that "pareille aux vacheries / Hystériques" is meant to suggest above all the kind of noise which would be made by the raving of cattle gone mad. The basis for the comparison is probably the noise of water and wind on the reefs; multiplied and raised to a pitch of frenzy, this sound might resemble that of a "vacherie hystérique." But it should be noted that the additional intention to suggest a kind of madness and a kind of bestial stupidity is also present in the simile, and gives an additional overtone to the effect produced.

> Sans songer que les pieds lumineux des Maries
> Pussent forcer le mufle aux Océans poussifs!   [44]

In these lines, the boat points to an activity excluded from its adventures, and that activity is prayer. For if one finds the ocean recalcitrant and untractable, one may succeed in calming it by praying for the intercession of those Marys whose special domain it is to watch over boats and sailors and see them safely home. The "Océans," now a violent and inimical counterpart of the "Poème de la Mer," are compared to wild horses, both in the term "poussif" and in "forcer le mufle," and the "pieds lumineux" of the Saints give the impression of lighted statues in seaside shrines. The boat's failure to consider the possibility of prayer is consonant with its rejection of all restraining, controlling, or directing influences in life.

> J'ai heurté, savez-vous? d'incroyables Florides
> Mêlant aux fleurs des yeux de panthères à peaux
> D'hommes!   [47]

Another form of action is denoted, more violent than the preceding; and another form of direct address to the men to whom the boat is speaking. Among the descriptions of the sea which constitute the burden of this section, we now have a description of the land masses encountered. "Florides" is used in the original sense of a flowered land or island; but with suggestions of wildness, uncivilized nature, strangeness ("incroyables"); these latter to emphasize the vastness of the adventure, its contrast with the earlier civilized pursuits of the boat, and its mystery. "Mêlant aux fleurs" repeats the idea of "Florides." The phrase "des yeux de panthères à peaux / D'hommes!" belongs to both boat and man. But it has a special meaning for each; for the boat, a visual observation—men with panther's eyes; for the man, a moral overtone allowing one to judge of the actions of other men with respect to him. The latter forms a part of the discovery and education which will lead the man from joy to its opposite. Here again, in the mixture of flowers and men, there may be some reference to the kind of drunken confusion which had earlier mixed sea and sky.

> . . . Des arcs-en-ciel tendus comme des brides
> Sous l'horizon des mers, à de glauques troupeaux.   [48]

A visual image is drawn this time, with a simile which attaches to it once more the notions of vastness and of mystery. Perhaps there is, in the "glauques troupeaux," a recollection of the earlier image in lines 41–42; but the effect is entirely different, with the emphasis being now placed upon the color of the sea and its movement. The mysterious overtones come from the color itself, from the mention of the horizon, and from the idea that the rainbow is bound to something indeterminate beneath the horizon.

> J'ai vu fermenter les marais énormes, nasses
> Où pourrit dans les joncs tout un Léviathan!   [50]

Among "things seen," the catalogue of which is now resumed, the boat here lists another example of decay and corruption. The word "fermenter" is used again (cf. l. 28), now applied to a part of the sea itself, and the newest victim discovered is not a man—whose plight would be less close to the sympathies of the boat—but the great sea monster who somehow represents all the power and the mystery of the sea itself, or even a monstrous ship. For the man who is symbolized by the boat, the leviathan must of necessity have social and political overtones, and the rotting of "tout un Léviathan" presents an image of whole civilizations in decomposition. Both the still waters of the "marais" and the traplike effect of the "nasses" and the "joncs" are meant to stand in sharp contrast to the complete liberty

of the open sea—and, indirectly, to the "où je voulais" earlier boasted
by the boat (l. 8).

> Des écroulements d'eaux au milieu des bonaces,
> Et les lointains vers les gouffres cataractant! [52]

In the light of the two preceding lines, these two take on an ominous
significance. The sea (for the boat) and life (for the man) are not
always benevolent and beneficent, but they present instead certain
violent aspects ("écroulements," "cataractant") which may account
ultimately for the death of victims and the rotting of leviathans.
Such passages as "au milieu des bonaces" are meant to emphasize, in
their context, the multiplicity and variety of the adventure, the sharp
contrast between kinds of weather and spectacle encountered, and
the strong variations in the feelings experienced by the boat.

> Glaciers, soleils d'argent, flots nacreux, cieux de braises . . . [53]

Again in this line the intention is to generalize, to ascribe to the
sea and the sky a variety of aspects and of accompanying moods. But
this is done, in the present case, by an alternation of "sea elements"
and "sky elements," and by a concentration upon certain central
effects. There is something in common, that is, to the three notions
of "glaciers," of "soleils *d'argent*," of "flots *nacreux*," if only in the
suggestion of white and cold and a kind of shininess. At the same
time, the "soleils" and the "cieux de braises" suggest radiance of a
sort. The total effect is one of distance, reflecting surfaces, faint
outlines, with (in the final "braises") a sharply contrasting redness
which adds the note of mystery and conflict. The line, after all,
introduces a stanza in which the predominant idea is that of corruption and decay, and it must prepare the emotions for what follows in
the stanza.

> Échouages hideux au fond des golfes bruns
> Où les serpents géants dévorés des punaises
> Choient, des arbres tordus, avec de noirs parfums! [56]

Among the "things seen" (the stanza continues the construction
of the preceding one) are—aside from the natural phenomena in
line 53—new examples of corruption and decay. It may be presumed
that the "échouages hideux" are sunken and stranded vessels, even

closer to the feelings of the boat than had been the leviathan, and that for the man they suggest also the notion of disaster and failure. All the images, visual and olfactory, accumulated in these lines add to the feeling of disgust, of horror, of dismay which boat and man experience when they find others like themselves who have undergone a tragic fate—which might later be their own.

> J'aurais voulu montrer aux enfants ces dorades
> Du flot bleu, ces poissons d'or, ces poissons chantants.   [58]

For the third time childish images and childish associations are recalled by the mind recently removed from childhood; as in the other instances, it is a pleasant and nostalgic picture. Here, as in the comparisons "plus sourd que les cerveaux d'enfants" and "Plus douce qu'aux enfants la chair des pommes sures," when the boat who is also a man wishes to make a direct and telling reference, it derives its materials from childhood memories. It is important in the structure of the poem that this should be done consistently and strikingly, since the last and most striking image of all (ll. 93–96) will belong to this same series and conclude it. In all cases, the recollection is a tender one and regret is mingled with the other emotions. Here, in contrast with the violent and catastrophic events just presented, the image is a happy and delicate one, and this impression is enhanced by such prosodic elements as the rhythmic pattern of line 58 and the harmonic juxtaposition of "d'or" and "dorades." For the boat is still at a point in its narration where the acceptable and joyful elements of its adventure ("Du flot bleu") outweigh and overbalance the others. But the others will of necessity, in the development of the poem, achieve the dominant position.

> —Des écumes de fleurs ont bercé mes dérades
> Et d'ineffables vents m'ont ailé par instants.   [60]

The impression of pleasure and delight continues in these lines, with a kind of quiet joy expressed in the phrases "des écumes de fleurs," "ont bercé," "d'ineffables vents." The continuation of the adventurous movement is indicated by "mes dérades" and "m'ont ailé." But there are restrictions; both "bercé" and "m'ont ailé" indicate, once more, passivity rather than active will on the part of the boat, and the inclusion of the phrase "par instants" shows the occasional and momentary nature of these pleasures.

> Parfois, martyr lassé des pôles et des zones . . .   [61]

Intermittently ("Parfois"), movement and pleasure cease. The endless wanderings ("des pôles et des zones") produce only weariness ("lassé"), and for the first time the boat recognizes its own status as a victim in the word "martyr"; so, presumably, does the man. It is important that the recognition should come toward the end of the present section; the events comprising the adventure cannot produce their ultimate emotional state until the adventure itself is concluded. One should oppose, here, the feeling of "martyr" to that of "où je voulais" (l. 8) and that of "lassé" to that of "triomphants" (l. 12).

> La mer dont le sanglot faisait mon roulis doux . . .   [62]

The activity of the sea and the passivity of the boat are here again stated ("faisait"), but the motion is at this point a pleasurable one ("doux") as in lines 57–60. Should one see, in the "sanglot de la mer," a possible suggestion that the sea—or life—itself experiences feelings of lassitude and sorrow parallel to those of the boat or man?

> Montait vers moi ses fleurs d'ombre aux ventouses jaunes
> Et je restais, ainsi qu'une femme à genoux . . .   [64]

In the first of these lines, the boat is really using an inverted figure; for the fact is not that the sea is lifting up its flowers to the boat, but that the boat, dipping farther into the waters, comes closer to the flowers. This interpretation is confirmed by the following line, where the boat first comes to rest ("Et je restais"), then dips down into the sea, assuming an almost vertical position. I take this to be the meaning of "ainsi qu'une femme à genoux." But there is also contained in the latter an attitude of prayer, and for the man at least this represents a reversal of his attitude as compared with lines 43–44, just as "restais" is a reversal of the violent motion described in such words as "Je courus!" (l. 11). In a stanza in which the dominant note will be one of intimacy, calm, and arrested motion, the image chosen for affective purposes, "fleurs d'ombre aux ventouses jaunes," will be of a different kind from those used earlier. The suggestions will be of color, a dark yellow resulting from "ombre" and "jaunes," and of form, circular and cuplike. One sees the flowers suspended in the water, moved and darkened by it; and from this vision comes a feeling peculiarly appropriate to this stanza. As the end of this section approaches, the opposites of the terms used at the beginning of the poem come into increasing prominence.

> Presque île, ballottant sur mes bords les querelles
> Et les fientes d'oiseaux clabaudeurs aux yeux blonds.   [66]

If one recall, now, the triumphant "Péninsules démarrées" of line 11, the modest "Presque île" which opens this stanza, with its notion of smallness and immobility, presents another of these oppositions. So does the rest of the passage quoted here. For if one of the first effects of the sea adventure was to wash away the stains left by man ("Et des taches de vins bleus et des vomissures / Me lava," ll. 19–20), in the end the sea element deposits its own discord and corruption on the boat ("les querelles / Et les fientes d'oiseaux clabaudeurs"). These the boat carries with it for the remainder of its journey ("ballottant sur mes bords"). The detail of the "yeux blonds" merely provides (since they are extraordinary, repellent, and a little eerie) a sense of distaste for an item included in the adventure. Symbolically, we may state that the man, coming into adult life cleansed and purified of all traces of his former masters, eventually is befouled by life itself, by the quarrels of other men and the corruption they produce. So the corruption and decay seen and discovered in the course of the journey finally come to affect the adventurer himself.

> Et je voguais, lorsqu'à travers mes liens frêles
> Des noyés descendaient dormir, à reculons!   [68]

The adventurer himself is subject to corruption and begins to fall apart ("mes liens frêles") as a result of his aimless wanderings ("je voguais"). And again we see, for the third time, the victims, the dead men produced by the sea ("Des noyés") and the failures produced by life, described again with the same verb ("descendaient"), but with the additional notice that this is the end of the journey ("dormir"). Death will thus naturally propose itself, later, as one of the solutions available to boat and man in their final emotional dilemma. It is, indeed, already a closely personal matter in the formula *"à travers mes* liens frêles." Finally, "à reculons" presents the exact antithesis to the vigorous forward movement which had at first characterized the adventure.

Stanzas 6–17, constituting the long central section of the poem, thus accomplish a complicated set of aims, both narratively and emotionally. Narratively, they enumerate the multitude of things seen, discovered, and experienced by the boat and by the man whom it symbolizes. As before and as throughout, the events are specific, material, visually identifiable for the boat. But when translated into terms of the man, they become very generalized forms of experience, identifiable at best as moral states and describable only in terms of their emotional tonality, which is the same as that felt by the boat. These events involve, for both, endless wandering, visions of all kinds of natural phenomena, acquisition of many forms of knowledge, discovery of decay and corruption and death as well as of beauties and of objects of admiration. They also involve, progressively, the personal experience of decay and corruption, with the passage from an active to a passive role in the adventure. For the man, this means discovery of facts about other men, about society, and about himself, which leave him with a certainty of his own degeneration and a premonition of his own ultimate death. Emotionally, these events are accompanied by an initial joy, followed by an admixture of wonder and horror, followed in turn by the beginnings of despair.

But the development of the feeling of despair is reserved for the following section, consisting of Stanzas 18–23 (ll. 69–92). In these stanzas the adventure continues, but seen now in retrospect rather than in the present of participation, and from the point of view of the defeated victim rather than of the hopeful novice.

> Or moi, bateau perdu sous les cheveux des anses,
> Jeté par l'ouragan dans l'éther sans oiseau . . .   [70]

The initial word of the new section, "Or," is adversative rather than transitional. Opening a period which ends only with line 84, "Je regrette l'Europe aux anciens parapets," it signifies that, in spite of all else that might be said of a positive nature, the events which are about to be summarized again had an essentially negative result.

The emphatic "moi" has the effect of returning the emphasis from the adventures to the feelings of the boat themselves. Then comes the significant formula "bateau perdu," indicating finally that the boat accepts its status as a victim, along with the others encountered; that its wanderings have been without direction and goal; and that its present "position" is unknown. The image "sous les cheveux des anses" gets its forcefulness from the recollection of an earlier line, "nasses / Où pourrit dans les joncs tout un Léviathan!" For the "cheveux" come to constitute a trap or net in which the boat is caught. Moreover, the use of "anses" with all its restrictive connotations, rather than some vaster body of water, provides an emotional contrast to the sense of liberty earlier experienced and in a way prepares for the "flache" of line 93. The state of passivity and helplessness is confessed in "Jeté par l'ouragan," and a kind of isolation and abandon in "dans l'éther sans oiseau." These are the final physical circumstances which will bring on the final emotional state.

> Moi dont les Monitors et les voiliers des Hanses
> N'auraient pas repêché la carcasse ivre d'eau.   [72]

A part of this emotional state is a sense of uselessness, springing from a recognition of physical decay. The "carcasse ivre d'eau"— note the difference of feeling between this and the earlier "L'eau verte pénétra ma coque de sapin" (l. 18)—is held together, now, only by its "liens frêles" (l. 67) and is of no further use to man or to society, which would not even attempt to retrieve it ("repêché") from the sea. Man and society are here represented by vessels which have clear and recognized utility, warships such as the Monitors, merchant vessels such as the "voiliers des Hanses." It will be remembered that the boat itself was once in this category—"Porteur de blés flamands ou de cotons anglais"—and that among its feelings must be included regret and disappointment at the loss of this usefulness and at the realization of the failure of its present adventure. The idea will reach its final development in the last stanza of the poem.

> Libre, fumant, monté de brumes violettes,
> Moi qui trouais le ciel rougeoyant comme un mur . . .   [74]

From this point until the end of the period (l. 84), the boat will be speaking of the past—of what used to be—from the perspective of the present; the emotions will be mingled, the present feelings of despair and discouragement alternating with the exultation of a former time. That exultation is epitomized in "Libre, fumant," where the first word is a key word for the earlier material situation and the second a kind of glorification of the attendant passion. In "Moi qui trouais le ciel" there is the additional implication of a personal importance, of self-assertion of an object which stands against the whole expanse of the sky. But this condition no longer exists; the verb is in the past. The "longs figements violets" of line 34 and the "cieux de braises" of line 53 are here brought together in an image whose main effects are of color. Since the boat is here speaking of its moments of triumph, the color will be violent and deep, unlike some of the indications for other moments of the adventure. "Monté de brumes" defines the preceding "fumant" and creates a totality of image appropriate to the totality of feeling.

> Qui porte, confiture exquise aux bons poètes,
> Des lichens de soleil et des morves d'azur.   [76]

The metaphor here presented has a usefulness for the development of the symbol, and this consists precisely in the suggestion of another kind of utility for the boat. For even if all else had been lost, for a time at least the boat existed as a beautiful object, such as a good poet might love and describe, with those standard clichés of the poets, bright sun and blue sky, for its components. However, in the case of the boat these components exist in a form specifically proper to the boat and attached to it, the "lichens" and the "morves." In this sense the totality of the simile, "comme un mur qui porte," exists as a present generalization.

> Qui courais, taché de lunules électriques,
> Planche folle, escorté des hippocampes noirs,
> Quand les juillets faisaient crouler à coups de triques
> Les cieux ultramarins aux ardents entonnoirs.   [80]

Except for "Qui courais" (with its idea of violent and free movement) and "Planche folle" (expressing the drunken joy accompanying that movement), these lines add little to the symbolic meaning. There is perhaps in "Planche" a suggestion of the further reduction of the great boat to a rudimentary structure. But occurring in a section in which the boat wishes to describe the violence and the glory of its complete freedom, the stanza assembles a group of seemingly disparate objects and images, each of which makes a peculiar contribution to the total impression. From the phrase "taché de lunules électriques" comes a dual effect, a visual image in which certain shapes and luminosities are contained and an indirect and very tenuous suggestion of the night sky. "Escorté des hippocampes noirs" again makes two suggestions: first, that the presence of an "escort" in a way implies the glory and the greatness of the boat; second, that since the escort is made up of "hippocampes" (with their mythological overtones), it lends a supernatural air to the whole procession. The next two lines, taken as forming a single image, produce a singularly vigorous effect in which heat, violence, and sharply contrasting color are the predominant elements. Impressions of heat come from the personified "juillets," from the "ardents entonnoirs," perhaps even from the rich color "ultramarins"; of violence, from "faisaient crouler" and "à coups de triques"; of color, from the combination of "juillets," "ultramarins," and "ardents." Against this background, the "planche folle" becomes an extraordinary, almost supernatural object participating in a stupendous adventure. Something of the character of the adventure rubs off on the adventurer itself, and an emotional state is created, which will stand in sharp opposition to the "Moi qui tremblais" beginning the following stanza.

> Moi qui tremblais, sentant geindre à cinquante lieues
> Le rut des Béhémots et les Maelstroms épais . . .   [82]

Repeating the "Moi" of line 67, the boat recalls another aspect of its adventure—this time a less joyous one—in the fear which grew out of a realization of its own smallness and weakness as compared with the gigantic and mythological vastness of the sea—and of life—itself, suggested by the references to the "Béhémots" and the "Maelstroms." Moreover, the vastness is creative and productive ("sentant geindre . . . le rut"), whereas the activity of the boat has no such consequences.

> Fileur éternel des immobilités bleues . . .   [83]

The penultimate line of the period prepares for the last line by way of sharp contrast. To unlimited space is added unlimited time ("éternel") and the feeling that there is no possible end or limit to the adventure as now pursued ("immobilités bleues"). The last notion is further enhanced by use of the word "fileur."

> Je regrette l'Europe aux anciens parapets.   [84]

Each word, in the final verse of the period, is intended to strike a sharp opposition to what has preceded. "Je regrette"—the final emotional conclusion to the whole adventure—stands alone against all the preceding words of joy and exultation. "L'Europe" is meant to stand, contrary to the wildness and the barbarity of lands and seas encountered in the adventure, for all that is civilized and reduced to the domination of men. And "aux anciens parapets" adds to the idea of civilization the idea of restriction and circumscription both in time and in space. Europe is an island, enclosed within space and time, and the man symbolized by the boat now wishes for a return to that island. I say "return" because in "Porteur de blés flamands ou de cotons anglais" the original European associations of the boat had been indicated. In a final figure, lines 93–96, time and space will be even more restricted.

The next two stanzas complete the section, and in a sense they generalize all that has preceded in it. They give, alternately, an epitome of the adventure itself and a quintessence of the intellectual and emotional conclusions.

> J'ai vu des archipels sidéraux! et des îles
> Dont les cieux délirants sont ouverts au vogueur.   [86]

This is the epitome of the adventure, stated in the broadest and the most "expansive" terms, in the sense that vastness and limitless space are suggested. The boat begins with the formula "J'ai vu," recalling its use in lines 32, 33, 49 (recalling also the related and variant formulas), and indicating thus the wish to generalize. Both words in "archipels sidéraux" have the "expansive" meaning already suggested, the first denoting as it does innumerable islands stretching across vast bodies of water, the second indicating that stars and skies are involved, not islands and water, and that hence the image is even more unrestricted. In what follows, the image is in a way reversed, since islands themselves are referred to and the skies are theirs. The last words of line 86, "sont ouverts au vogueur," again emphasize the intention, with "ouverts" insisting upon the limitlessness of the adventure and "vogueur" becoming a kind of generic term for the boat itself.

> —Est-ce en ces nuits sans fond que tu dors et t'exiles,
> Million d'oiseaux d'or, ô future Vigueur?—   [88]

In these lines, the boat reveals what it has sought and failed to find— "Vigueur." We are to take this, I believe, as meaning a complete realization of one's potentialities in action and achievement; and it strikes us immediately that each of the boat's losses and diminutions through its career, each of its invasions by decay and corruption, has constituted a loss of this "vigor," a step away from such realization. Structurally, then, the word illuminates a whole series of earlier sections in the poem and stands as a kind of contrast to the notion of "victims" so prominent throughout. The epithet "future" (added to the "ô" and the apostrophic form) shows the extent of failure and the abandonment of an original hope. Failure is emphasized further in "tu dors et t'exiles," with both verbs pointing out the inaccessibility of such vigor to the boat during all its wanderings. Finally, "en ces nuits sans fond" does two things: it removes the locale of some future adventure from that of the past adventure, displacing it from earth to the skies, showing thereby the hopelessness of success on earth; and it establishes a parallelism between the infinite space involved in the heavenly adventure and the limitless expanses of the waters already visited. But why the metaphor "Million d'oiseaux d'or"? We may conjecture that the notion of "oiseaux" is meant to suggest beings capable of penetrating into the "endless night" of the heavens; that the epithet "d'or" not only supplies a contrast of light to darkness but also suggests a kind of victory of the former over the latter; and that the "million" (somehow parallel to "un peuple de colombes" in l. 31) indicates the transcendence, through the multitude both of beings and of actions, of the victory achieved, of the vigor obtained.

Mais, vrai, j'ai trop pleuré! . . .   [89]

The final stanza of the section will have as its function to state, in a concentrated form, the degree of discouragement and disappointment at which the boat has arrived, the emotional upshot of the whole adventure, and the first of two possible solutions: death. The phrase "j'ai trop pleuré" comes as a surprise, since no weeping has been previously indicated; but if one looks back one finds that all the earlier manifestations of regret and frustration might have been accompanied by weeping and may be epitomized by the term. The "trop" shows the extent of the suffering, and the need for a cessation.

. . . Les Aubes sont navrantes.
Toute lune est atroce et tout soleil amer.   [90]

In these lines the boat takes three elements of the adventure, which had earlier been sources of joy and exultation, and states that they are now sources of despair and weeping. (1) "Les Aubes": Compare in line 31 "L'Aube *exaltée*" with the description of "navrantes" now used. (2) "Toute lune": Compare (although the comparison is not as precise here) in line 30 "je sais le soir" and in line 37 "j'ai rêvé la nuit," in each case accompanied by expressions of pleasure, with "atroce" here used. (3) "Soleil": Compare, in addition to all the indirect allusions to sunlight, in line 53 the "soleils d'argent" with the "amer" now employed. The three epithets, "navrantes . . . a-troce . . . amer," provide a summary of the present feeling towards the whole adventure, and they stand in direct contrast to the feelings previously experienced.

L'âcre amour m'a gonflé de torpeurs enivrantes.   [91]

All three epithets and their antecedent emotions are combined in the phrase "l'âcre amour," where "âcre" characterizes the present bitterness and "amour" the past elation. In "m'a gonflé" we have a kind of reprise of line 18, "L'eau verte pénétra ma coque de sapin," except that now both cause and effect are moral rather than physical, and that the emotion is opposite. The last words of the line, "torpeurs enivrantes," again reverse the earlier situation; "enivrantes" carries into the present the former general state of the "bateau ivre," but it is now a drunkenness of sorrow and of lethargy ("torpeurs") rather than of joy and of activity. The boat has gone full circle in its adventure, and the man whom it symbolizes has completed the voyage through all human joys to the ultimate disillusionment.

> O que ma quille éclate! O que j'aille à la mer!   [92]

To the dilemma in which the boat finds itself—its inability longer to endure the pain which has taken the place of joy—one of the solutions is death. The wish for death is expressed in this line, in terms appropriate not only to the boat but also to its present condition. Only the "quille" is now left to the boat, which has lost anything else giving it character and individuality; should this sink down into the sea, all suffering would be brought to an end.

The remaining two stanzas of the poem serve two functions: to state the alternative for solution and to indicate, once again and finally, why solution is necessary. These things they do in the order stated, curiously enough, so that the very last stanza is a summation of the emotions now present in the boat and man; but these emotions are themselves more poignant and telling because they are experienced in juxtaposition to another set of emotions involved in the second solution. The poem will thus end with a heightened expression of the total and final effect which it is seeking.

> Si je désire une eau d'Europe, c'est la flache
> Noire et froide où vers le crépuscule embaumé
> Un enfant accroupi, plein de tristesses, lâche
> Un bateau frêle comme un papillon de mai.   [96]

Each one of the elements in this penultimate stanza is intimately related, by way of opposition, to the materials which have preceded it in the poem. The second solution, here presented, is for the boat to return to its original state of confinement and servitude—which would be accompanied by many desirable things now lost and regretted. The wish is expressed in the phrase "Si je désire une eau d'Europe," where "une eau d'Europe" recalls "l'Europe" of line 84 as well as the original associations of the boat. This European water, so far unspecified, soon becomes "la flache"; against all the limitless expanses of "Océans, mer, marées," with their possibility of endless adventure, the boat sets the smallest imaginable body of water which could sustain a boat, the tiny, circumscribed pool. And against the brilliant colors, the sunlight, and the great variety of conditions experienced during the adventure stand the descriptive details of line 94, "Noire et froide" and "vers le crépuscule embaumé." It will be noted that the suggestions here increase the effect of smallness, of intimacy, and of pleasurableness. The "Noire et froide" is already a premonition of the sadness of the child, and the "embaumé" of his essential happiness. As for "Un enfant accroupi," this is the last of the images of childhood and justifies—as it explains—all the others. If the boat wishes now to be a child's boat, it is because the man who was only recently a child now wishes to return to the conditions of his childhood. Just as he had throughout compared his impressions with those of a child, so now he compares his whole adult life with childhood—and is driven to prefer and to accept the latter. "Plein de tristesses" describes the basic mood of the child; but it does so (perhaps because of the plural) in a way which makes that mood desirable rather than painful. The whole attitude of the child is one of smallness, immobility (cf. the "accroupi" and the kind of motion involved in the later "lâche"), and concentration upon himself. With "lâche un bateau" the boat provides, with striking conciseness, a contrast to his own voluntary and violent entrance into a career of adventure. And to his own strength and vigor, present at first but now lost, he opposes the weakness and fragility contained in the final phrase of the stanza, "frêle comme un papillon de mai." The simile serves not only to emphasize this fragility but also to add to the whole of the preceding description a note of softness and intimacy.

> Je ne puis plus, baigné de vos langueurs, ô lames . . . [97]

The final stanza is devoted to a statement of the cause for the boat's present emotional dilemma, his impotence and discouragement which are the only results of his adventure. That impotence is contained in the first words, "Je ne puis plus," upon which depend all the forms of impotence which follow in the stanza. The rest of line 97 again summarizes the adventure, with an intimation still of the joys associated with it. Throughout the poem, indeed, both elements of joy and of sadness are present; but the balance changes as one passes from the beginning to the end. So here, at the very end, "baigné de vos langueurs, ô lames" contains (through the words themselves and through the remarkable harmonic effects) a reminiscence of the earlier sense of exultation.

Enlever leur sillage aux porteurs de cotons . . .   [98]

The first form of present impotence is the boat's incapacity to compete with the merchant vessels among which it originally belonged; "porteurs de cotons" makes the identification through the partial repetition of line 6, "Porteur de blés flamands ou de cotons anglais." The loss of its crew, of all signs of human control, of the devices for steering and guiding it, has rendered the boat incapable of a utility which it once had, expressed in the "enlever leur sillage." For the man, this is tantamount to an admission of diminution of his powers, of loss of his vigor, of a sense of uselessness.

Ni traverser l'orgueil des drapeaux et des flammes . . .   [99]

The second form of impotence is the boat's incapacity to vie with the naval vessels, the warships, earlier mentioned in the "Monitors" of line 71 (just as the merchant vessels had been mentioned in the "voiliers des Hanses" of the same line). "Traverser" again carries with it the notion of equality of effectiveness, "orgueil" that of a quality once present in the boat but now lost, while "des drapeaux et des flammes" is a kind of glorification of power and pageantry which the boat no longer possesses.

Ni nager sous les yeux horribles des pontons.   [100]

The final form of impotence is the boat's incapacity to stand the gaze (which we must regard as reproachful and accusing) of prison ships (the eyes would be the portholes, through which peer imprisoned men). The implications here are multiple. For prison ships represent authority, law and order; the boat has defied or ignored these, and a sense of guilt results. Prison ships also represent the subjection of human beings to cruel and enforced bondage (in this way they merit the characterization "horribles"); the boat has proclaimed the glories of liberty and freewill, and failure has ensued. Hence it feels the deep frustration of its adventure, along with a sense of sympathy, and even of community of revolt and failure, with those men who constitute the human freight of the "pontons." Whereas in the distant past, before the adventure, it might have sailed ("nager") unashamed before the prison ships, it is now no longer capable of so doing. For the man symbolized, the implications are clear: his soul has been reduced from an original state of pride and independence and confidence to a final state of abjection, uselessness, and frustration.

I do not think that I need to insist further on the symbolical relationship between boat and man and on the successive stages of development through which the symbol moves, each accompanied by a meaning for the man symbolized and by an emotional effect proper both to boat and to man, but especially to man. In so far as emotions are involved for the boat, they are those of a man in like circumstances, and they are recognized by a reader who identifies them as such and who feels them as a man having similar capacities for feeling. But several problems of interpretation of the symbol still remain. One may ask whether the "man" represented is all mankind or a particular man, whether the "adventure" symbolizes the passage of everyman from childhood to adult life or the passage of one particular man from childhood to a particular kind of adult life. The text, I believe, corroborates the latter hypothesis. For rather than attempting to generalize, it speaks constantly of a specifically "drunken" boat in a peculiarly "drunken" adventure: of complete liberation from restraint and restriction, of wild passage through every variety of episode and circumstance, of passivity, of confusion and disorder. In this way it perhaps answers another question, that relative to the causes of the boat's and the man's failure. The causes lie in part in the choice of this life rather than another, in part in the character which led the man to make this choice rather than another. I do not mean that there is any moral lesson present or implied; merely that action in the poem comes from a particular choice and that this choice springs from character. The indications of character are however of the most summary, and are for the most part derived by working backwards from action.

As for the problem of the nonsymbolic elements of the poem, the solution should now appear fairly simple. I have from the start insisted that the poem, both on the literal and on the symbolic level, possessed an essentially narrative form. The emphasis, however, is not on the series of events which constitute the narrative, but rather on the series of emotions which accompany those events (hence its essential lyricism). The structure is one which effects the passage from an initial emotional state to a final emotional state. The function of the symbolic elements is to state the events and the essential emotions which they produce. The function of the nonsymbolic elements—those which seem not to lend themselves to direct identification with any specific aspects of the thing symbolized—is to contribute to the nature and the intensity of the emotions aroused. This they do by rendering action and circumstance more concrete, more sensible, by surrounding them with affective accompaniments. In a sense, they prolong and complete the symbol.

One must therefore apply to them a canon of appropriateness which involves not only the poem as a whole as point of reference, but the particular place in the order of the poem at which the passage appears. This is abundantly clear in such a poem as *Le Bateau ivre,* where the emotional effects change so subtly and so clearly as one passes from one part of the poem to another. Any judgment of the usefulness or the "goodness" of any such nonsymbolic passages must thus depend (as must, indeed, any judgment of a detail) upon a prior analysis of the total structure of the poem. Since in *Le Bateau ivre* the total emotional range is considerable, the variety of effect possible in the individual images will be commensurately large. This does not mean that "all" emotions are treated or suggested either in the poem or in the individual passages; for the boat and the man (and the contemplator) move in the essentially restricted area between "joy" and "despair." As a matter of fact, the unity of the poem and of its effect is a function of the fact that the adventure and its accompanying emotions (either on the literal or on the symbolic level) are restricted to and productive of a single emotion contained in the passage from one state of feeling to another. It is indeed very difficult to describe or define the exact accretion to emotion made by an individual passage or image; for the language of the passions is extremely inexact and imperfect, and this inexactness and imperfection must reflect itself in the language of criticism. The best that one can do is to "classify" the particular effect of a passage under the general effects of the poem, then to indicate what nuances are produced by it, how they are produced, and what they contribute to the formation and the development of the general effect.

Perhaps this last statement may be used as a basis for asking a final question about these nonsymbolic passages. Suppose that they had not been included in the poem; what then would be lacking from it? Clearly, the whole of the central structure, both literal and symbolic, would still be present. Moreover certain passages, especially at the beginning and at the end of the poem, would be unchanged. But from the two long central sections of the poem something would indeed be lacking. The statements of the boat would be skeletal. They would say what was essential, but would not add to it those "supplementary" or "auxiliary" elements which either provide the shades of feeling desired or reinforce the statement of the central emotions. The poem might produce the same overall effect; but it would do so less fully, less richly, less successfully. The function of these "additional" passages would seem to be to provide the nuance and the shading, the color and the differentiation; and in this sense they are not additional at all, since the poem produces not its general effect but its specific effect, and this specific effect results from the combination of all its particular elements.

To suggest that the nonsymbolic elements of the poem are "additional" or "excessive" would be to posit a lack of unity which, in the case of *Le Bateau ivre,* is corroborated neither by sensitivity nor by analysis. Rather, one feels and one discovers that both symbolic and nonsymbolic elements are integral to the creation of the total resultant effect. Perhaps we might say that the broad general character of the emotions is determined by the development which the symbol undergoes, both in its literal and in its symbolic phases, and that the other "unilateral" components add to these general emotions nuance and color and specification. I do not wish to intimate that, from a theoretical standpoint, the symbol itself can do no more than establish the general emotion; although since it depends upon likeness or comparison it might tend to establish such likeness on the basis of common characteristics which cannot become too specific. I merely wish to say that in the present poem the two types of development work in the kind of relationship indicated. Again from the theoretical standpoint, one might presumably say that the totally symbolic poem would be extremely difficult if not impossible of achievement; but the poet who achieved it would display the folly of any such generalization. In this particular poem, the poet has preferred not to do so. He has effected, instead, a combination of symbolic and nonsymbolic elements, in a proportion and in a relationship demanded by the peculiar conditions of his poem. The limits which he placed upon his symbolism were such as to assure on the one hand the intelligibility and the emotional accessibility of his poem, on the other hand the maximum creation of the desired poetic effect.

6

Mallarmé

L'Après-midi d'un faune

To the problem of poetic organization, of the achievement of special and original poetic effects, Mallarmé constantly sought and found new solutions. He sometimes (as we shall see later) used the symbolism of Rimbaud, pushing it farther in the direction of obscurity and hermeticism; but the basic technique remained of necessity the same. In *L'Après-midi d'un faune* he worked with other means; it is not a symbolist poem (although others have sought to interpret it as such), simply because it fails to satisfy any of the conditions of symbolism as I have been describing them here. Besides, our analysis will demonstrate, I hope, that there is an entirely different and independent basis of organization.

As we go into the reading of the *Après-midi,* we should bear in mind certain aspects of its history and of its superficial form. It was first written as a dramatic eclogue, with indications of setting and action and with several interlocutors. Some of the original features disappeared through the successive reworkings of the poem; but we still have a dramatic monologue in which the faun speaks throughout, and the earlier versions may help us to interpret passages which are less clear in their final form. In the definitive version, Mallarmé clearly wrote to be read rather than heard; hence he could rely upon typographical devices that would have been useless in a recited text. Capital letters for a few words and above all the division of the monologue into sections printed in Roman characters and others printed in italic characters, make it possible for him to emphasize certain words and to distinguish two basic parts of his text. (We might note here that this is a kind of experiment in typography which will lead, ultimately, to the full-scale exploitation that we shall find in *Un Coup de dés . . .*)

L'Après-midi d'un faune

Églogue

Le Faune

Ces nymphes, je les veux perpétuer.
                    Si clair,
Leur incarnat léger, qu'il voltige dans l'air
Assoupi de sommeils touffus.

                  Aimai-je un rêve?
Mon doute, amas de nuit ancienne, s'achève   4
En maint rameau subtil, qui, demeuré les vrais
Bois mêmes, prouve, hélas! que bien seul je m'offrais
Pour triomphe la faute idéale de roses.
Réfléchissons...

            ou si les femmes dont tu gloses   8
Figurent un souhait de tes sens fabuleux!
Faune, l'illusion s'échappe des yeux bleus
Et froids, comme une source en pleurs, de la plus chaste:
Mais, l'autre tout soupirs, dis-tu qu'elle contraste   12
Comme brise du jour chaude dans ta toison?
Que non! par l'immobile et lasse pâmoison
Suffoquant de chaleurs le matin frais s'il lutte,
Ne murmure point d'eau que ne verse ma flûte   16
Au bosquet arrosé d'accords; et le seul vent
Hors des deux tuyaux prompt à s'exhaler avant
Qu'il disperse le son dans une pluie aride,
C'est, à l'horizon pas remué d'une ride,   20
Le visible et serein souffle artificiel
De l'inspiration, qui regagne le ciel.

O bords siciliens d'un calme marécage
Qu'à l'envi de soleils ma vanité saccage,   24
Tacite sous les fleurs d'étincelles, CONTEZ
Que je coupais ici les creux roseaux domptés

Par le talent; quand, sur l'or glauque de lointaines
Verdures dédiant leur vigne à des fontaines,   28
Ondoie une blancheur animale au repos:
Et qu'au prélude lent où naissent les pipeaux
Ce vol de cygnes, non! de naïades se sauve
Ou plonge...

           Inerte, tout brûle dans l'heure fauve   32
Sans marquer par quel art ensemble détala
Trop d'hymen souhaité de qui cherche le *la*:
Alors m'éveillerai-je à la ferveur première,
Droit et seul, sous un flot antique de lumière,   36
Lys! et l'un de vous tous pour l'ingénuité.

Autre que ce doux rien par leur lèvre ébruité,
Le baiser, qui tout bas des perfides assure,
Mon sein, vierge de preuve, atteste une morsure   40
Mystérieuse, due à quelque auguste dent;
Mais, bast! arcane tel élut pour confident
Le jonc vaste et jumeau dont sous l'azur on joue:
Qui, détournant à soi le trouble de la joue,   44
Rêve, dans un solo long, que nous amusions
La beauté d'alentour par des confusions
Fausses entre elle-même et notre chant crédule;
Et de faire aussi haut que l'amour se module   48
Évanouir du songe ordinaire de dos
Ou de flanc pur suivis avec mes regards clos,
Une sonore, vaine et monotone ligne.

Tâche donc, instrument des fuites, ô maligne   52
Syrinx, de refleurir aux lacs où tu m'attends!
Moi, de ma rumeur fier, je vais parler longtemps
Des déesses; et par d'idolâtres peintures,
A leur ombre enlever encore des ceintures: 56
Ainsi, quand des raisins j'ai sucé la clarté,
Pour bannir un regret par ma feinte écarté,
Rieur, j'élève au ciel d'été la grappe vide
Et, soufflant dans ses peaux lumineuses, avide   60
D'ivresse, jusqu'au soir je regarde au travers.

O nymphes, regonflons des SOUVENIRS divers.
Mon œil, trouant les joncs, dardait chaque encolure
Immortelle, qui noie en l'onde sa brûlure   64
Avec un cri de rage au ciel de la forêt;
Et le splendide bain de cheveux disparaît

Dans les clartés et les frissons, ô pierreries!
J'accours; quand, à mes pieds, s'entrejoignent (meurtries   68
De la langueur goûtée à ce mal d'être deux)
Des dormeuses parmi leurs seuls bras hasardeux;
Je les ravis, sans les désenlacer, et vole
A ce massif, haï par l'ombrage frivole,   72
De roses tarissant tout parfum au soleil,
Où notre ébat au jour consumé soit pareil.
Je t'adore, courroux des vierges, ô délice
Farouche du sacré fardeau nu qui se glisse   76
Pour fuir ma lèvre en feu buvant, comme un éclair
Tressaille! la frayeur secrète de la chair:
Des pieds de l'inhumaine au cœur de la timide
Que délaisse à la fois une innocence, humide   80
De larmes folles ou de moins tristes vapeurs.
Mon crime, c'est d'avoir, gai de vaincre ces peurs
Traîtresses, divisé la touffe échevelée
De baisers que les dieux gardaient si bien mêlée: 84
Car, à peine j'allais cacher un rire ardent
Sous les replis heureux d'une seule (gardant
Par un doigt simple, afin que sa candeur de plume
Se teignît à l'émoi de sa sœur qui s'allume,   88
La petite, naïve et ne rougissant pas:)
Que de mes bras, défaits par de vagues trépas,
Cette proie, à jamais ingrate se délivre
Sans pitié du sanglot dont j'étais encore ivre.   92

Tant pis! vers le bonheur d'autres m'entraîneront
Par leur tresse nouée aux cornes de mon front:
Tu sais, ma passion, que, pourpre et déjà mûre,
Chaque grenade éclate et d'abeilles murmure;   96
Et notre sang, épris de qui le va saisir,
Coule pour tout l'essaim éternel du désir.
A l'heure où ce bois d'or et de cendres se teinte
Une fête s'exalte en la feuillée éteinte: 100
Etna! c'est parmi toi visité de Vénus
Sur ta lave posant ses talons ingénus,
Quand tonne un somme triste ou s'épuise la flamme.
Je tiens la reine!

          O sûr châtiment…

                    Non, mais l'âme   104
De paroles vacante et ce corps alourdi
Tard succombent au fier silence de midi:

Sans plus il faut dormir en l'oubli du blasphème,
Sur le sable altéré gisant et comme j'aime   108
Ouvrir ma bouche à l'astre efficace des vins!

Couple, adieu; je vais voir l'ombre que tu devins.

What happens in *L'Après-midi d'un faune,* and the essential basis
of its structure, may appear more distinctly if we take into account
the typographical division into two parts and then analyze those
parts separately. There are three passages in the text, lines 26–32,
63–74, and 82–92, that are set off from the rest by the use of italics.
Two of these passages are introduced by words in capitals, "CONTEZ"
in line 25 and "SOUVENIRS" in line 62, and these state the function of
the whole part in italics: it recounts or narrates what had happened
on the preceding afternoon as the faun remembers it. This is a
narrative of the events, all the simple and concrete events, that the
faun is able to recall with some clarity. The rest of the text (and it is
by far the larger portion) is devoted to the faun's commentary, or
meditation, or gloss upon these same events as he thinks about them
on this "morning after." The total effect proper to the text results
not only from the combination of these two parts, but also from the
way in which the sections are ordered and interwoven.

These are the events:

> . . . *je coupais ici les creux roseaux domptés*
> *Par le talent . . .*   [27]

As a player upon pipes which he himself fashioned from reeds that
he cut, the faun was engaged (yesterday afternoon) in the cutting of
reeds (*"je coupais ici les creux roseaux"*), and they were those
particular reeds that would serve for his pipes (*"domptés / Par le
talent . . ."*). I might point out that this statement about his activity
gives us a first insight into the nature of the faun. He is not merely
an animal—a two-legged creature with hooves and horns—but a
creature to whose animal nature has been added a modicum of
human quality; this is signified here by the capacity (*"le talent"*) to
cut reeds, make pipes, and play upon them. Yet he is not fully a
man, as many other passages will show, and his feelings and

thoughts and capabilities remain essentially those of a beast. His activity is interrupted by something that he sees:

> . . . quand, sur l'or glauque de lointaines
> Verdures dédiant leur vigne à des fontaines,
> Ondoie une blancheur animale au repos.   [29]

A background description of the landscape—vineyards and springs in the distance—becomes the setting for the introduction of other beings into the narrative. Their nature is not yet clear; but for the faun they are *"une blancheur animale"* and this is their important quality. The visual effects as he recalls them are ones of color and of movement, *"l'or glauque," "Verdures,"* and *"blancheur"* for the colors, *"dédiant leur vigne"* (which I take to describe the hilly "movement" of vineyards toward the streams) and *"Ondoie"* for the sense of undulant motion. Then the significant detail: the white beings are *"au repos,"* resting or sleeping and immobile.

While he has been contemplating this vision, the faun has completed the making of his pipes, and he now plays the first notes upon them:

> Et qu'au prélude lent où naissent les pipeaux . . .   [30]

The pipes come into being as pipes (*"naissent"*) when the faun begins, hesitatingly, to play upon them (*"le prélude lent"*). But his playing has as its immediate effect to arouse the sleeping beings and to scatter them in all directions:

> Ce vol de cygnes, non! de naïades se sauve
> Ou plonge . . .   [32]

The faun describes the episode in the sequence of its occurrence: the awareness first of a flight or fleeing, an initial identification as swans of the beings constituting the *"blancheur animale,"* a correction (through the *"non!"*) and providing of the proper description (*"naïades"*), and the statement of the action itself—*"se sauve"* for those creatures who fled from the spot, *"plonge"* for those who took refuge in the water. *"Vol"* turns out to be ambivalent; it means "flying" as long as the faun thinks that he is seeing swans, it means "fleeing" after he decides that they are naiads. We should observe that (like the faun himself) the naiads are of an ambiguous nature;

they are at least part animal, but are as much woman as the faun is man. We see them, through our mythological associations, as essentially women; and that is the way the faun will think of them.

One part of the true narrative has now been ended. The faun will pause—for commentary—before resuming; when he does, it will be to take up the next episode in the story.

> Mon œil, trouant les joncs, dardait chaque encolure
> Immortelle, qui noie en l'onde sa brûlure
> Avec un cri de rage au ciel de la forêt.   [65]

This is the faun's first real activity relative to the naiads and he thinks of it (in his animalistic way) as more active and efficacious than it really is. What he does, actually, is to look greedily at the females as they plunge into the water. But he thinks of his glances as breaking through the reeds that stand between him and the water (*"trouant les joncs"*) and of each glance as a dart or arrow that reaches and wounds one of the naiads. *"Dardait"* is to be taken as containing the instrument as well as the action, and *"chaque encolure"* is a specification of the *"blancheur animale"* into the separate female forms, seen from behind, as they run away from him or as they swim. If they are *"immortelles,"* it is because he thinks (vaguely) of these beings as goddesses, perhaps also because they are not wholly women or "mortals." Moreover, the faun thinks of his "darts" as wounding the naiads and causing them to cry out in anger; I take this to be the meaning of *"sa brûlure"* and of the *"cri de rage."* *"Noie en l'onde"* repeats the *"plonge"* of line 32, with the added tactile impression of the water that cools (as it covers) the stinging wound; and *"au ciel de la forêt"* points to another feature of the landscape that is variously alluded to in other passages of the poem.

The faun continues his description of what he saw:

> Et le splendide bain de cheveux disparaît
> Dans les clartés et les frissons, ô pierreries!   [67]

The impressions are here all visual—and they are those of the poet who makes the faun speak, not of the faun. The plunging of the naiads into the water is transformed into the *"splendide bain de cheveux,"* where we see only the naiads' hair mingling with the water; and this in turn becomes an impression of the moving water in the sunlight, the *"clartés"* and the *"frissons,"* compared with *"pierreries."* I should add here that the appreciation of the visual image is not entirely outside of the capacities of the faun; for we shall see from other passages that his sensitivities are at times highly artistic and that he is capable of making elaborate comparisons. From active looking, the faun passes to more vigorous activity: *"J'accours"* (line 68). Then he makes a discovery that will determine the rest of the action of the narrative:

> . . . *quand, à mes pieds, s'entrejoignent (meurtries*
> *De la langueur goûtée à ce mal d'être deux)*
> *Des dormeuses parmi leurs seuls bras hasardeux.* [70]

Apparently, his music has failed to awaken two of the sleeping naiads, and he now comes upon them suddenly (*"à mes pieds"*) as he runs forward towards the water.

The attitude in which the faun finds the two naiads is a first witness, within the narrative, to the highly animalistic sexuality that will be expressed again in the central episode. I think it perfectly clear that the naiads are intertwined (*"s'entrejoignent"*) in a lesbian embrace. There is no other way of interpreting the parenthesis *"(meurtries / De la langueur goûtée à ce mal d'être deux)."* They have recently had sexual satisfaction together (*"la langueur goûtée"*); hence their deep sleep. The "mal d'être deux" is, I believe, a reference remotely to the myth of the Androgyne, where the two creatures who had once been one suffer from their division and long to be one again; more immediately, to the common condition of lovers who yearn for the union which will make them one being. The *"mal"* here is that yearning; the *"langueur"* signifies its fulfilment. A further witness to the nature of their embrace is found in the phrase *"parmi leurs seuls bras hasardeux,"* where *"parmi"* describes the intimacy of their embrace and *"hasardeux"* its bold and perhaps indecent character. The fact that the faun finds the two *"dormeuses"* in this attitude will have its importance for him, both as a stimulus to his own erotic urge and as a reason for the way in which the naiads react to it.

As the faun's narrative continues, he tells of his most vigorous action so far:

> Je les ravis, sans les désenlacer . . .   [71]

He continues in the present tense because he is actually seeing, successively, the events as they had occurred. *"Ravis"* has its etymological meaning of "carry away," and we see the faun lifting the two naiads, *"sans les désenlacer"* (which again describes their embrace), and running with them to the *"massif"*:

> . . . et vole
> A ce massif, haï par l'ombrage frivole,
> De roses tarissant tout parfum au soleil,
> Où notre ébat au jour consumé soit pareil.   [74]

The clump of roses described here has essentially one feature: it is completely exposed to the hot sun, without shade, to the extent that the roses no longer give off their perfume. We are supposed to feel the afternoon heat and brightness as something vigorous (hence *"haï par l'ombrage frivole"*), and especially as a proper setting for the faun's intended rape of the naiads. If we give a double, almost punning meaning to *"consumé,"* we may better understand line 74: the "consummation" of our (the faun's and the naiads') pleasure (in this clump of roses) will be similar to and contemporaneous with the ending or the "consuming" of the day. The *"soit"* shows the wish for the future contained in the faun's statement.

The second section of the narrative has now been concluded: after the discovery and arousing of the naiads in the first, the ravishing of the two sleeping naiads in the second. A brief interruption for the faun's comment is followed by the third section, devoted to the actual rape of the naiads by the faun:

> Mon crime, c'est d'avoir, gai de vaincre ces peurs
> Traîtresses, divisé la touffe échevelée
> De baisers que les dieux gardaient si bien mêlée.   [84]

We should wonder, and properly, why the faun calls his action a crime. That will be clarified in other passages of the poem. But here we know this much: that the faun himself considers it as a crime against the gods; for the embrace that he broke had been sanctioned by the gods (*"que les dieux gardaient"*). This is a second reference, within the narrative, to supernatural elements, the first having come in *"chaque encolure / Immortelle"* (lines 63–64). As the faun recounts his act, he gives first his own attitude, *"gai de vaincre,"* and then that of the naiads, *"ces peurs traîtresses."* The naiads have thus wakened and have been frightened by the faun; their fears are *"traîtresses"* from his point of view, since they operate against him and his desires. Then the act: *"d'avoir . . . divisé [par des] baisers la touffe échevelée . . . si bien mêlée. . . ."* That close embrace of the naiads, here stated in terms of their intermingled hair, has thus been destroyed by the faun who came between them with his avid kisses.

Those kisses, however, were merely the "prelude" to the sexual possession of the naiads, both of them. The faun narrates, now, how he accomplished the dual rape, and in terms which leave no doubt, although there is necessarily some ambiguity of statement:

> *Car, à peine j'allais cacher un rire ardent*
> *Sous les replis heureux d'une seule . . .* [86]

Again, the attitudes: the faun's ardor, the receptiveness and the joy of one of the naiads. This is the one he has taken in a normal sexual embrace; for we must consider this to be the meaning of *"cacher un rire ardent / Sous les replis,"* where *"rire ardent"* and *"replis"* are both euphemisms. We note that this embrace is really only incipient, *"à peine j'allais . . ."* Meanwhile, he attempts to communicate ardor and sensual pleasure to the other naiad:

> *. . . (gardant*
> *Par un doigt simple, afin que sa candeur de plume*
> *Se teignît à l'émoi de sa sœur qui s'allume,*
> *La petite, naïve et ne rougissant pas:)* [89]

The general notion is that the sexual excitement of the one naiad, derived from his possession of her, will pass to the other through the intermediacy of his body; or rather, that while he excites the one through his embrace, he will excite the other in another way, *"Par un doigt simple."* *"Gardant . . . la petite"* is again euphemistic, since he wishes to do far more than keep or retain the second naiad.

Once more, he distinguishes between the characters and the reactions of the two; the first is receptive, ready to respond to his caress, *"l'émoi de sa sœur qui s'allume,"* while the second is more innocent (*"sa candeur de plume," "naïve"*) and slower to take fire (*"ne rougissant pas"*). They are differentiated in terms of color, the one thought of as reddening with passion, the other as remaining white from innocence or indifference.

This act of conquest is short-lived, although apparently for the faun it provides part at least of the desired satisfaction. He concludes the narrative with the final episode. We should note that these lines depend upon the *"à peine"* of line 85:

> Que de mes bras, défaits par de vagues trépas,
> Cette proie, à jamais ingrate se délivre
> Sans pitié du sanglot dont j'étais encore ivre.   [92]

His prey escapes. If this is possible, it is because, at the pitch of sexual excitement, his hold upon them is weakened: *"mes bras, défaits par de vagues trépas";* the moment of orgasm is also signified by the *"sanglot dont j'étais encore ivre."* If these are his responses, they are not those of his prey, who escapes (*"se délivre"*) without gratitude to him for what he thinks he has given it (*"à jamais ingrate"*) and without consideration (*"Sans pitié"*) for his own feelings. The narrative is now concluded. It has been told, throughout, in the present tense; but at the very end, in *"dont* j'étais *encore ivre,"* the narrator shows his awareness of the fact that all this has happened in the past.

Such, as he recalls and recounts it, was the "afternoon of the faun." A simple series of events, consisting basically in the discovering of the naiads, the ravishing and enjoyment of two of them by the faun, and their escape. The story is simply told, with only passing references to the characters or the emotions of the participants and to the setting for the events. It is told merely as a sequence of episodes or moments, on a chronological basis that does not attempt to account for what happens next, but only tells it. The narrative is, in every sense, merely a background for what really constitutes the essence of the poem, the meditation that the faun makes, the next morning, upon his afternoon of the preceding day. In the poem called *L'Après-midi d'un faune,* the proper effect results from the morning meditation—reflected, of course, against the story of the afternoon's events and, as the materials are presented, intermingled with it.

That intermingling is the salient device for the creation of the effect. For if the narrative itself is clear and concise, the faun's meditation upon it is anything but that. We shall see, in the analysis, that he has nothing but doubts about the reality and the true nature of the events that he recounts, and his meditation really consists in a speculation upon the very existence of those events. The reader will thus be shifted from unclear commentary to clear event, and because of the sequence in which the shifts take place, will himself end up having doubts similar to the faun's. If he does so, he will experience the special kind of feeling that the poem seeks to produce.

The first line that the faun speaks, in his dramatic eclogue, is a reference "forward" to the other persons involved in his afternoon:

> Ces nymphes, je les veux perpétuer.

The use of "Ces" shows not only that the faun has already been thinking about them, but also that they have a kind of antecedent reality in his mind. Yet the expression of will in "je les *veux* perpétuer" suggests, already, that that reality is not very solid or certain. How, asks the reader who first meets the nymphs here, would one perpetuate them? He must suppose that it would be either by giving them, in some artificial form, an existence beyond their real existence, or, possibly, by endowing them with a real existence that they never had. In any case, the "veux" is a first indication of the fact that the faun will need to make an effort of the will in order to achieve what he wishes. The reasons will come shortly. The following lines are also a preview of the narrative:

> Si clair,
> Leur incarnat léger, qu'il voltige dans l'air
> Assoupi de sommeils touffus.   [3]

Since we have read the narrative, we know that "Si clair, / Leur incarnat léger" refers to the color of the nymphs' skin, to the "blancheur animale." Had we not read it, we would nevertheless get a first impression of rosy-white bodies, those of the nymphs, and of a bright and shimmering color ("qu'il voltige")—just as the faun now recalls it. Another impression of greater complexity is added in the rest of the sentence; the air is heavy with deep sleepiness, in a sense itself asleep as are the sleeping nymphs. A total picture has now been presented: "Ces nymphes . . . Leur incarnat léger . . . sommeils touffus."

A first section of the poem has now concluded. It is made up of the faun's recollection of the sleeping nymphs, of the afternoon air in which he saw them, and of his wish to give them a more substantial form. The quality of his recollection is indicated by the words "léger," "voltige," "Assoupi," and "touffus," which suggest the need for clarification. In the next section (lines 3–7) the faun asks the first of a series of questions about this memory and arrives at the first answer; others will follow in later parts of the poem.

The question, "Aimai-je un rêve?," also supplies new information —the faun's memory of the nymphs includes the notion that he has loved them—along with the reason why he should wish to perpetuate them. The answer will be complex; he will seem not to know whether the nymphs existed only in a dream or in some other way, but he will seem to conclude that he did not actually love them. The causes of his uncertainty appear as an integral part of the answer.

> Mon doute, amas de nuit ancienne, s'achève
> En maint rameau subtil, qui, demeuré les vrais
> Bois mêmes, prouve, hélas! que bien seul je m'offrais
> Pour triomphe la faute idéale de roses. [7]

With "Mon doute," the bare fact of his inability to decide—to know —is stated; he is incapable of a "yes" or "no" answer to the question just asked. But why should he be so incapable? He himself suggests the reason in the phrase, "amas de nuit ancienne." His doubt is an accumulation of doubt; it goes back not only to last night, when the dream might have occurred, but to a very long series of nights preceding, to a very long period of time ("nuit ancienne"); it results, in a word, from the fact that the faun is still a primitive and subhuman being, that his intellectual limitations are those of his kind, that he suffers the incapacity to know that is common to all subrational beasts. This hypothesis with respect to the meaning of "amas de nuit ancienne" is confirmed by the rest of the main clause: "Mon doute . . . s'achève / En maint rameau subtil." We need to see the faun's "doubt" as an activity taking place within his head and moving outward into his horns (the "maint rameau subtil") where it stops before he can reach a resolution of the doubt. Indeed, doubt extends to the point that the faun is unable to distinguish the limits of his own being, to separate himself from the nature of which he is a part. Thus the phrase "qui, demeuré les vrais / Bois mêmes" indicates a confusion between the "branches" on his head and the "branches" of the trees in the woods about him; both "rameau" and "bois" have double meanings. "Rameau" has perhaps a third meaning, that of "ramification," signifying the subtle if ineffectual character of his inquiry. Succeeding sections of the poem will specify the forms taken by the inquiry.

The inconclusiveness of his questioning serves as a proof to the faun ("prouve"), and one that he can only regret ("hélas!"), that he was indeed all alone ("bien seul") on the preceding afternoon, that no nymphs were really present. Therefore the possession of the nymphs ("je m'offrais / Pour triomphe") can only have been imaginary; this explains the meaning of "idéale" as "in idea" or "in imagination," rather than real. With "faute" he for the first time characterizes his act as blameworthy; later he will tell why he thinks of it as a "crime." If he uses the adjectival phrase "de roses," it is because his memory places the act in "ce massif . . . De roses" (72–73). This the reader cannot know until a later point in his reading; but he knows now that the faun believes, consequent upon his first inquiry, that the fault committed yesterday was imaginary and that the nymphs existed only in a dream or in some other insubstantial form.

Since doubt remains, the faun will continue to seek explanations for the memory, or the impression, or the image that he now has of the nymphs and of his relationship with them. "Réfléchissons . . ." expresses his wish to continue the investigation—with such mental powers as he can muster. In the section following, lines 8–22, a second hypothesis is presented and examined: not a dream but rather a translation into the form of the nymphs of sense impressions of a completely different kind. The hypothesis is stated in these lines:

> ou si les femmes dont tu gloses
> Figurent un souhait de tes sens fabuleux!   [9]

We note that "ou si" introduces an alternative possibility, that "les femmes" replaces "Ces nymphes" and emphasizes their quality as females, and that "tu gloses" at once describes the mode of their "perpetuation" and the process by which the faun now comments on yesterday's supposed events. In "Figurent" Mallarmé does what he will do elsewhere in this poem; he gives to a word its basic or etymological meaning, here "to figure forth" or "to give shape or form or figure" to something that does not normally have them. At this point the something is "un souhait de tes sens"; the desire is literally "embodied" in the women. A similar process of language is apparent in "fabuleux"; the faun's senses are not only "fabled" or "fabulous" through their magnitude (going back to his animal nature), but they are "fabling" since they here create the nonexistent beings of whom he speaks.

The faun's "senses" are not specified. But we know that the dominant one at this point is an erotic desire that is "figured" in the nymphs. Alongside this there is a sensation that is alternately auditory, tactile, and visual and that centers in notions of wind and water. As before, vagueness and confusion characterize the faun's apprehension and his identification of these feelings, and the inquiry consists in part in an attempt to clarify. The initial impression relates to one of the two nymphs, "la plus chaste":

> Faune, l'illusion s'échappe des yeux bleus
> Et froids, comme une source en pleurs, de la plus chaste.   [11]

The faun speaks to himself in his effort to reflect. As he evokes the image of "la plus chaste," sensations appropriate to chastity present themselves: "des yeux bleus / Et froids," "pleurs"; and he concludes that these sensations are such that the chaste nymph might well have been an illusion ("l'illusion s'échappe"). That is, they are mild sensations which do not force the opposite conclusion upon him. Two things should be observed about these lines: that the essential image of water in motion ("une source en pleurs") is presented for the first time—it will be extremely important in the rest of the section—and that one of the nymphs is associated with it as a kind of "figuration."

The sensations attached to "l'autre" are opposite in every detail:

> Mais, l'autre tout soupirs, dis-tu qu'elle contraste
> Comme brise du jour chaude dans ta toison?   [13]

Enough of the elements are "contrasted" so that we are justified in completing the missing oppositions; if "brise . . . chaude" stands against "yeux . . . froids" and "soupirs" (they are sighs of sexual satisfaction) against "pleurs," then we may substitute "la moins chaste" for "l'autre." The second nymph is connected with a sensation of warm air in motion, and that sensation, felt by the faun in his "toison," leads him to believe that she did exist. The faun continues the dialogue with himself—this is the form taken by his "reflection" —with a stalemate for the conclusion: one nay against one yea.

The indecision is only momentary, however, for the faun soon finds a simple explanation for both elementary feelings, sound of water and sound of wind. Both had been incorrectly interpreted as witnesses to the presence and nature of the two nymphs; both are now correctly interpreted merely as related to the music-making activities of the faun. With "Que non!" he rejects his error and prepares for the right answer.

>   . . . par l'immobile et lasse pâmoison
> Suffoquant de chaleurs le matin frais s'il lutte,
> Ne murmure point d'eau que ne verse ma flûte
> Au bosquet arrosé d'accords . . .   [17]

The description of the afternoon heat, in lines 14–15, has its antecedents in "l'air / Assoupi de sommeils" and in "brise du jour chaude"; in the faun's memory, it represents the situation of "ce massif, haï par l'ombrage frivole, / De roses tarissant tout parfum au soleil." At the present point, its purpose is to recreate the afternoon setting, to place the faun in it, and to provide circumstances that may lead to the correct explanation. There were, in fact, no "yeux bleus / Et froids," no "source en pleurs," but only the intense heat, the faun, and his flute. Such a phrase as "l'immobile et lasse pâmoison" amplifies the impression of "l'air / Assoupi de sommeils," with the immobility countering any idea of motion and the heat (emphasized in "Suffoquant de chaleurs") countering any idea of cool water. The total effect of "Suffoquant de chaleurs le matin frais s'il lutte" is to expel any notion either of activity or of coolness. The faun now admits only one activity, his playing on the flute, and only one motion, that of the musical notes that spread out over the wood. By a transposition, the notes are made into drops of water; thus it is possible, negating the wrong solution, for him to say "Ne murmure point d'eau," to use the verb "verse" for his playing, and to speak of the "bosquet arrosé d'accords." (The "bosquet," incidentally, explains in part the "vrais / Bois mêmes" of lines 5–6.) By a similar transposition—but excessive and erroneous—he earlier passed from these same notes to the nymph's tears and then to the nymph herself. He now knows, or thinks he knows, that that nymph did not exist.

As for the "other" nymph, previously sensed as the hot breeze, she too was merely a transposition of another part of his music making, his breath as it passed through the pipes, further transposed into the "breath" of inspiration.

> . . . et le seul vent
> Hors des deux tuyaux prompt à s'exhaler avant
> Qu'il disperse le son dans une pluie aride,
> C'est, à l'horizon pas remué d'une ride,
> Le visible et serein souffle artificiel
> De l'inspiration, qui regagne le ciel.

When he says "le seul vent," the faun denies his earlier thought of the "brise . . . chaude." "Hors des deux tuyaux prompt à s'exhaler" in a sense corrects the previous "flûte"; for the faun sends his breath through double pipes of Pan, the instrument that he will later call "Le jonc vaste et jumeau"—and the instrument proper to his nature as a primitive beast and a primitive musician. Once again, motion is ascribed only to this activity; just as a little before he spoke of the sounds "poured out" by his flute and of the "bosquet arrosé d'accords," he now says that the instrument "disperse le son dans une pluie aride." The latter image is really dual, since "le son" picks up "accords" and "une pluie aride" develops "source en pleurs" (11), "eau" and "arrosé"; both nymphs come together in the image as water and wind are combined. Confusion and uncertainty continue; the faun no more distinguishes wind from water than his own horns from the surrounding woods—or his music making from the imaginary nymphs. The final transposition occurs when he identifies his own breath with the heaven-sent artistic inspiration. Once more, the immobile quality of the afternoon is stressed ("l'horizon pas remué d'une ride"); but an audible quality becomes visible and a mobile one motionless in "visible et serein," applied to the "souffle" that has taken the place of the breath inherent in "vent" and "s'exhaler." "Artificiel" etymologizes again; this is the breath that is a "maker of art." The faun sees it as coming to him from heaven, as being breathed in ("inspiration" has something at least of its proper meaning) and then exhaled through his pipes, after which it returns to heaven. This it was that caused the warm wind in his hair, not the presence of the unchaste nymph.

In the whole of the preceding passage (8–22), the faun has projected himself backward into yesterday afternoon; the present tenses of the verbs (beginning with "figurent") indicate that his effort to reflect has taken the form of a projection of himself into the time and place of the events that he is trying to clarify. Some clarification has been achieved, at least temporarily. We can now therefore see the general development of the poem through its first major section, lines 1–22. If, as I suggested earlier, the real action of the poem is constituted by the faun's meditation this morning (rather than by the events of yesterday afternoon), then the dynamics of that action begin to be apparent. The faun starts, on this morning, with an impression or a recollection of an erotic adventure; he supposes that, if it occurred at all, it occurred yesterday afternoon. But being a faun and not a man, he is not sure that the nymphs really existed or that he really possessed them. His wish to discover the truth sets the action going. He makes several successive hypotheses—first, that he merely had a dream, second, that his erotic desires caused him to imagine the nymphs, third, that his unreliable senses transformed his music making into the presence of the nymphs—and for each hypothesis he finds that it is possible to explain the impression or the recollection without concluding that the nymphs really existed. But he still does not know surely, there are still other paths of investigation open to him; these other inquiries will form the subject of the second major division of the poem.

In that second division the faun continues his inquiry and his reflection. He does so, in part at least, through a reconstitution of the afternoon's events in the narrative passages that I have already discussed. To introduce the first of these, he describes the landscape and his relation to it:

> O bords siciliens d'un calme marécage
> Qu'à l'envi de soleils ma vanité saccage,
> Tacite sous les fleurs d'étincelles . . .   [25]

The localization in Sicily is at last precise—and it needs to be for certain later developments in the poem. Other details are similarly useful. The "bords . . . d'un calme marécage" furnish the place where the reeds grow, while "calme" adds to the impression of the motionless landscape. The "fleurs d'étincelles" accentuate the brightness and the intensity of the sun, likened to a pillager who forces an entrance and plunders. The real usefulness of "saccage" lies in its application to the faun, whose searching looks probably have a dual object: the reeds that he will use for his pipes and the answers to his query about the nymphs. "Ma vanité" could thus characterize both his pretensions as a musician and his pride as a lover. Since the marsh has not yet provided any answers, as he questions it this morning, he utters the command, "CONTEZ" (25); what has been "Tacite" must be made to speak, and to speak the words that will confirm or remove his doubt. If now he appeals to the marsh for a solution, it is because this same marsh was the place where, yesterday afternoon, the adventure began. The identity of place is affirmed by "ici" in line 26.

Taken in the context of the meditation that has preceded, the first narrative section now serves to clarify a number of allusions and to complete certain thoughts that had been fragmentary in the faun's mind. Three things become specific: the fashioning of the pipes and the playing of the first notes; the discovery of the nymphs resting in the distance; and the flight of the nymphs when the music arouses them. As far as the reader is concerned (if he reads the poem, as he should, in its proper order), he may now understand at least part of what the faun has been talking about and at the same time he may appreciate the difference between a clear statement of events (real or supposed) and the faun's blurred hypotheses about them.

As he continues his meditation (lines 32–37), the faun reassembles a number of the elements that have already entered into it: the heat of the afternoon, his erotic desires, the playing on the pipes, and the flight of the nymphs. But he does so in ways that are now somewhat more explicit:

> Inerte, tout brûle dans l'heure fauve
> Sans marquer par quel art ensemble détala
> Trop d'hymen souhaité de qui cherche le *la*:
> Alors m'éveillerai-je à la ferveur première,
> Droit et seul, sous un flot antique de lumière,
> Lys! et l'un de vous tous pour l'ingénuité.   [37]

The immobility of the afternoon is restated in "Inerte," the heat of the sun in "tout brûle," the time of day in "l'heure fauve"; the tense of "brûle" indicates that the faun is once again thinking of himself as present in the afternoon setting. Through the epithet "fauve," he calls attention at once to certain visual aspects of the afternoon and to the emotional qualities that he himself contributes to it. Lines 33 and 34 offer a restatement of the flight of the nymphs. The faun characterizes himself as the musician tuning his pipes—"qui cherche le *la*"—and he speaks of his desire for possession of the females, all of them and more than his erotic capabilities could satisfy ("Trop d'hymen souhaité"); "souhaité" is, of course, a reference back to "un souhait de tes sens fabuleux!" (9), which it helps to explain. Afternoon and landscape are insensitive to the faun's desires and to the nymphs' escape; for they provide him with no information ("Sans marquer") about the manner of their flight ("par quel art"). "Art" has a double meaning, referring both to the simple "way" or "fashion" in which the nymphs escaped and to the more complex "art" of the musician that made them flee. To "ensemble" we must give the sense of "all together," "all at once," while "détala" effectively epitomizes the sudden departure of the nymphs.

Whereas in the three lines just studied the faun has continued the narrative (but in the form of a gloss), in the rest of the passage he resumes his meditation, asking what must be the consequences for himself if all the nymphs did indeed escape. The reply is simple: he will awake next morning in his continued state of sexual desire and of virginity. When he says "Alors m'éveillerai-je" (giving to "alors" a logical rather than a temporal sense), he looks forward to a time of awakening that will conclude this night's sleep; but if the whole adventure was merely a dream, then the awakening will bring an even greater conviction of regret. Both meanings are possible for "à la ferveur première," the first heat of the new day and the original sexual ardor; and both are mingled in the image that follows. With "Droit et seul," the faun pictures himself after the awakening, unaccompanied by nymphs and standing upright—not only because he has arisen, but because he stands erect, already something like a man. Yet his constant awareness that he is not yet a man appears in the next phrase, "sous un flot antique de lumière"; the sun may be the new morning sun, but it is also the sun that has been shining since time immemorial. It gives to the Sicilian landscape an ancient, ritualistic, mythological light, and serves the same function in the poem as the "amas de nuit ancienne" with respect to the faun's sense of his ancient origins. The two formulas, "amas de nuit ancienne" and "flot antique de lumière," complete each other and specify the real time of the action. "Lys!" stands in apposition to the "je" of the speaker (35); it combines the notion of "droit" in the preceding line and that of purity contained in "l'ingénuité." When the faun says "l'un de vous tous pour l'ingénuité" he is addressing himself to all other "lilies," declaring himself comparable to them in purity and virginity. He is not boasting of his virginity, however; rather is he deploring it and regretting that the afternoon's adventure did not really mark its end. The faun's comparison of himself to a lily is another witness to his identification of himself with nature and with natural objects.

If, then, the nymphs did not really exist and the adventure did not really take place, the faun will awaken—has awakened—as from a dream. His inquiry and his "consultation" of the marsh have brought him thus far. There are other facts to be explained, though, among them a bite-like mark on his breast. He will, in this time of morning, continue to seek for explanations.

148

> Autre que ce doux rien par leur lèvre ébruité,
> Le baiser, qui tout bas des perfides assure,
> Mon sein, vierge de preuve, atteste une morsure
> Mystérieuse, due à quelque auguste dent.   [41]

Two new items would seem to serve as evidence of the existence of the nymphs, the kiss that he remembers and the mark on his breast that he sees; he thinks of them in that order of conviction, introducing the first by "Autre que" and using for it the verb "assure" while "atteste" describes the witness of the second. The kiss is more tenuous, being a matter of memory; it is "ce doux rien," it is merely "ébruité," its assurance is "tout bas." But to it attaches a sense of pleasure ("ce doux rien"), and it seems to prove the presence of the "perfides"—perfidious both because they left him and because he cannot be sure of their reality. The other is more definite; looking at his breast, the faun sees the mark upon it. If he calls his breast "vierge de preuve," he again suggests two conditions: there are no other marks upon it, and especially there are no marks that might bear witness to other sexual encounters, hence to the loss of his virginity. (The notion of his sexual inexperience will become increasingly an important part of the argument.) The "morsure" upon it is "Mystérieuse" because he is so far unable to explain its origin, although "due à quelque auguste dent" expresses a first hypothesis about that origin. If it is indeed a bite, then the teeth that made it must have been those of some extraordinary creature; the faun's vanity leads him to believe that it must have been a goddess, a nymph, a naiad—somebody who might be called "auguste."

As before, however, the wishful explanation is soon rejected in favor of another that attributes the mark—simply—to his music-making activities:

> Mais, bast! arcane tel élut pour confident
> Le jonc vaste et jumeau dont sous l'azur on joue.   [43]

Impatient with his original supposition ("Mais, bast!"), the faun says to himself, "It was such a secret place as this (my breast) that my pipe chose as its confidant." This means merely that the mark was made by the pipe as he struck his breast with it—a mark much like a bite because it is a "jonc vaste et jumeau." The phrase "dont sous l'azur on joue" returns the faun (and the reader) to the Sicilian afternoon and to the first notes played on his new pipes. Once again, then, a hypothesis involving the nymphs gives way to a more common-sense one involving only the faun and his pipes. The process is very close to that found in lines 14–22, which will be even more directly paralleled in the lines now to follow. In the long passage beginning with "Qui" (which refers to his "jonc"), the faun identifies his confusion of the "line" of his music with the "line" of the nymphs' forms:

> Qui, détournant à soi le trouble de la joue,
> Rêve, dans un solo long, que nous amusions
> La beauté d'alentour par des confusions
> Fausses entre elle-même et notre chant crédule.   [47]

When he says "détournant à soi le trouble de la joue," he is speaking in purely material terms and giving to "trouble" the meaning of "trembling" or "vibration"; his breath, after passing through his swelled mouth, moves into and through the pipes. As it does so, it makes the music; but the making of the music is called by the verb "Rêve" as the faun harks back to "Aimai-je un rêve?," thereby creating another transposition. This is done because the making of the music, as it creates "fabulous" or unreal creatures, substitutes them for real objects or sensations. Here the real object is the "solo long." As he plays it, the faun thinks that he sees the beautiful nymphs in the landscape, "La beauté d'alentour"; but he recognizes now that there is only his song and that he has committed "des confusions / Fausses entre elle-même [i.e., the collective beauty] et notre chant." The song is "crédule" in so far as he—not it—is willing to believe: another transposition. The phrase "que nous amusions / La beauté d'alentour" offers some difficulties. Were we to take it literally, we should actually have to see the nymphs around, think of them as hearing the music; but we know, from the rest, that this cannot be right. Instead, we must give to "amusions" a very special meaning—again, a kind of etymological one. I think that here it means "to create through the activity of the muse"; "as we played, our muse brought into being the beauty around, by a confusion between that beauty and the music we were making." What is important for the development of the "action" of the poem is that the faun, as he proceeds with his meditation, here names the process that he earlier used in lines 14–22. There, he confused his breath and his music with the impressions of wind and water associated with the two nymphs; here, he actually calls "confusion" the transformation of his song into the beautiful bodies of the nymphs.

That same process continues and is clarified in the four verses that conclude the passage:

> Et de faire aussi haut que l'amour se module
> Évanouir du songe ordinaire de dos
> Ou de flanc pur suivis avec mes regards clos,
> Une sonore, vaine et monotone ligne.   [51]

If anything, the "confusion" is now triple. To the "line" of his music and the "line" of the beautiful bodies, the faun adds the "line" of his erotic desires, thus bringing together with the other two notions the idea of "Trop d'hymen souhaité" in line 34. Only one of these is real, he now concludes, and that is the line of his song, "Une sonore, vaine et monotone ligne": "sonore" because it is a musical line made up only of sound (cf. "il disperse le son" 19); "vaine" because it is empty of any other content, especially that of the nymphs' existence; and "monotone" not because the faun plays only one note, but rather because it has only one tonality, that of music. The key to the other verses lies, I believe, in the interpretation of "Évanouir." Let us think of the three "lines" as existing together in a complex and confused state, with the line of music (a sonorous one) coincident with the line of the faun's love (a passionate one) and with the line of the nymphs' bodies (a visible one). Remove the vision and the passion, and only the sound remains. "Évanouir" signifies this removal; "faire . . . évanouir" as introducing "une . . . ligne" means to draw or empty that line out of the others, out of the complex passion-vision-sound, leaving only the sound; perhaps "vaine," belonging to the same root, describes the state of the line after its removal. The faun begins with his passion, transposed into a musical line: "aussi haut que l'amour se module." This in turn is changed into the "songe ordinaire de dos / Ou de flanc pur," where "songe" recalls both uses of "rêve," "ordinaire" may possibly have the meaning of "ordering" or "that gives order to," and "pur" stresses the linearity of the bodies as the faun sees them. He sees them, to be sure, only in his mind's eye, since they are "suivis avec mes regards clos." Once again, only the faun and his music were present in the afternoon landscape; his senses and his imagination supplied the rest; and his inquiry leads him one step farther in the discovery of his error.

In a sense, the faun's discovery is now complete; he knows that the nymphs never existed and that he never possessed them. Yet the dream or the recollection of the afternoon is still both pleasant and satisfying to his vanity. He still wishes to perpetuate the memory, and this he can do in two ways: by recounting the adventure (finishing the narrative already begun) and by continuing his voluptuous meditation upon it. The next section of the poem, down to the conclusion of the narrative at line 92, will pursue this dual purpose. The faun, who has previously apostrophized the "bords siciliens" and himself, now addresses his pipes:

> Tâche donc, instrument des fuites, ô maligne
> Syrinx, de refleurir aux lacs où tu m'attends! [53]

In the appellative "instrument des fuites," we find another etymological usage in "instrument," "that which is instrumental in causing," while the "fuites" are those of the nymphs; they may also be the flights of the faun's fantasy as he plays upon his pipes. Similarly, he characterizes the "Syrinx" (the name is full of ancient connotations) with the epithet "maligne" because it may be considered, through its effects, as both clever and malevolent. The command to the pipe, "Tâche donc . . . de refleurir," must again be taken figuratively. The same pipe can "reflower" only through being played once more; literally, only new reeds out of which new pipes might be made could "flower again" in the marsh. The former meaning is the one intended at this point; for the faun is going to play his pipes once more and call upon them for the recollection, the narrative, and the perpetuation of the nymphs. "Aux lacs où tu m'attends" refers to those same marshes, where the pipe "awaits" him in the sense that he will re-evoke the marsh through his playing—or in the sense that new reeds will grow there on which he will play new adventures. As we move forward in the poem, the suggestion grows that in some indefinite future there may be afternoons and adventures more real and more satisfying than yesterday's.

Meanwhile, the faun will continue to play—and perhaps also to speak—of his nymphs; the perpetuation will continue even if the real nymphs may never have existed:

> Moi, de ma rumeur fier, je vais parler longtemps
> Des déesses; et par d'idolâtres peintures,
> A leur ombre enlever encore des ceintures. [56]

His intention is clearly stated: "je vais parler longtemps / Des déesses." But we note that his "vanité" causes him to speak now of "déesses" rather than of nymphs or naiads. That same vanity is expressed in "de ma rumeur fier," where "rumeur" is sufficiently ambivalent to denote either his playing alone or his playing accompanied by speech; we do not have to interpret "parler," however, as specifically speech—it may mean here any kind of sonorous expression. The "idolâtres" of "par d'idolâtres peintures" carries the idea, I believe, of "image-making" as well as of "image-worshipping"; for his paintings in sound (music or words) will create those same goddesses whom he will adore. Since the faun now recognizes that the nymphs never existed, calling them "ombres," his rape of them in the re-evocation will be similar to that in yesterday's adventure: "A leur ombre enlever encore des ceintures."

There follows now an extended comparison, introducing the next segment of narrative, in which the faun likens his present reconstitution of yesterday afternoon to another habitual activity of his in which, again, he combines memory with regret:

> Ainsi, quand des raisins j'ai sucé la clarté,
> Pour bannir un regret par ma feinte écarté,
> Rieur, j'élève au ciel d'été la grappe vide
> Et, soufflant dans ses peaux lumineuses, avide
> D'ivresse, jusqu'au soir je regarde au travers. [61]

"Ainsi" introduces the second half of the comparison, and we should thus read into what follows as many of the elements in the first half as are apposite. To signify an action already completed the faun uses the image of the grapes that he has emptied of their fleshy white centers ("la clarté"); then he can characterize his feelings once it has been accomplished: "un regret par ma feinte écarté." The regret is real, the succulent part of the grapes is gone; but he pretends to set it aside. The regret and the attempt to ignore it are pertinent to yesterday's adventure, the statement of intention in "Pour bannir" applies equally to his playing and speaking and to what he will now tell about the emptied grapes. He calls himself "Rieur," yet we know that the laughter is feigned and covers a substratum of regret. His gesture of holding the cluster up to the light is simple enough; as he describes it, with the accompanying details, we are bound to recall traditional sculptures of fauns in the same pose; but that affects rather our impression than the faun's representation of himself. The next phrase, "soufflant dans ses peaux lumineuses," has the kind of ambivalence of which I spoke, the tie between this act and the play- ing of the pipes being made by "soufflant." So does "avide d'ivresse," for we need only substitute "amour" for "ivresse" in order to approxi- mate the faun's attitude towards the reconstructing of the afternoon's events. "Ivresse," however, is uniquely appropriate to the eating of the grapes and the gazing at their skins, now filled with the faun's breath. "Jusqu'au soir je regarde au travers": this is the long process of reminiscence that is also wishful thinking, as suitable for the "idolâtres peintures" as for the act to which they are compared.

To introduce the second segment of narrative the faun (now ad- dressing the nymphs) uses the formula: "O nymphes, regonflons des SOUVENIRS divers" (62), in which "regonflons" derives all its rich meaning from the comparison preceding. The narrative to follow will consist in just such a process of filling an empty dream with the stuff of desire; the "souvenirs" are now not that at all, unless one can remember what happened only in desire. This segment of narrative contains the flight of the nymphs, the faun's discovery of the two sleeping nymphs, and his "ravishment" of them to the clump of roses. Whereas the first narrative piece came at a time when the faun was still in doubt with respect to the nature of his adventure and had made only a first conjecture that it was unreal, the second piece follows upon his definite decision that it was not real at all. Yet the faun recounts it in the same tone, using the same vivid details, telling his story in the present tense except (as before) for the initial verb in the imperfect. Conjecture, dream, or fantasy have the same kind of reality for him as his vanity and his pride lead him to fill out the tale that incorporates his erotic desires. For the reader the effect is different, though, as he now sees the faun and his story in a new light. We no longer see the doubting, wondering creature who cannot be sure, but rather the wilful half-beast half-man who is intent upon having his sexual adventure in any way possible—for the moment, only through his imagination. Something has thus been altered in the general development of the action of the poem. The meditation had as its initial purpose to ascertain whether the afternoon's adventure was real or not; the conclusion having been reached that it was unreal, the meditation now goes on to substitute for it an imaginary adventure that will have some, at least, of the satisfactions of a real one. We shall see, as the poem draws toward its conclusion, that this is an intermediate stage leading to the dream of future erotic experiences that will be real.

When he returns from straight narration to his gloss or commentary on the events, the faun displays his feelings with respect to those events—feelings of satisfaction as real as if the events themselves had been real:

> Je t'adore, courroux des vierges, ô délice
> Farouche du sacré fardeau nu qui se glisse
> Pour fuir ma lèvre en feu buvant, comme un éclair
> Tressaille! la frayeur secrète de la chair.   [78]

He "adores" (and we remember the "idolâtres peintures") even the "courroux des vierges," an anger just referred to in the "cri de rage" of line 65; and he now calls them "vierges" rather than using any of the other terms, possibly for two reasons: because he transfers to the nymphs his own quality of "ingénuité," and because he needs to justify the notion of "crime" that will soon appear in his thinking about the imagined adventure. Both qualities of feeling, his own delight and the resentment (and resistance) of the two nymphs, are contained in the formula "ô délice / Farouche." In this part of the gloss, the faun is really continuing the narrative, as he has done before, and the "sacré fardeau nu qui se glisse" refers backward to "Je les ravis" (71) and forward to "Cette proie . . . se délivre" (91), with "sacré" reflecting again the notions contained in "auguste" and "déesses." A new detail of the story, the faun's many ardent kisses, is now added and becomes a part of his possession and of the nymphs' reasons for fleeing. "Ma lèvre en feu" indicates the degree of his ardor, while "buvant, comme un éclair / Tressaille! la frayeur" shows both the rapidity and the intensity of his kissing and the fright of the nymphs—another cause of their abrupt departure. The nymphs' reaction is epitomized in "la frayeur secrète de la chair," where "secrète," I believe, has the special meaning of "deeply internal" or "intimate."

The remaining three lines of the commentary—and they are really the conclusion of the gloss—further describe the faun's kisses and the reactions of the two nymphs, distinguished and characterized as before:

> Des pieds de l'inhumaine au cœur de la timide
> Que délaisse à la fois une innocence, humide
> De larmes folles ou de moins tristes vapeurs.   [81]

These lines depend on "buvant" and tell how thoroughly the faun covered both bodies with his kisses. Or at least he so boasts. Still thinking of the same opposition as previously, he sees one of the nymphs as "la timide," the one who wept and whose "yeux bleus / Et froids, comme une source en pleurs" (11–12) now are the source of her "larmes folles." The other is called "l'inhumaine"; but she is the one who was "tout soupirs" (12), who was likened to the "brise du jour chaude" (13), and who will be spoken of, in the last narrative section, in terms of "heureux," "émoi," "s'allume" (86, 88). Why, then, "l'inhumaine"? I think that the epithet must be seen as equivalent to "ingrate" (91) and that the faun now refers only to the cruelty of the nymph who, in spite of the obvious joy he had given her, chose to escape from him. This is the real source of his regret. He mentions her only briefly, devoting more time and attention to "la timide" who loses her virginity ("Que délaisse . . . une innocence") at the same time as does the other ("à la fois"). "Innocence" equals "ingénuité" equals "vierges," for the nymphs as for himself. The cold, timid one is "humide" not only with the wild tears which have been hers from the start, but also with "de moins tristes vapeurs," by which the faun can mean only the excretions brought on by sexual excitement. To her, too, the faun has given a pleasure which should have merited some gratitude.

After this interruption, the faun returns to his narrative, concluding it as he would have had it finish had it really taken place, with the account of his rape of the two nymphs, of his reaching a sexual climax, and of the escape of the nymphs. The same precision of detail and the same rapidity of event are again present; the faun tells himself a good story. To his appreciation of the passions involved—his own gayety, ardor, and erotic ecstasy, the fears and the diversified responses of the nymphs—he now joins a judgment upon the action. It was a crime, somehow, against the gods, either because he had separated the two nymphs and interrupted their amorous embrace, or because he had taken their virginity. Or, let us say, had he really done all these things, they would have to be considered as a crime and punished appropriately; perhaps their "criminal" nature was the reason why they did not happen in the first place, why he must find as substitutes for them the imaginary story, or the playing of his pipes, or the dream.

With the narrative, the faun's meditation comes to an end. In a first part of it he asked and answered the question about the reality of yesterday afternoon's adventure, in a second part (knowing that it had been unreal) he tried to give it the kind of reality that unreal things may acquire when one caresses the fictions that are substituted for them: "avide / D'ivresse, jusqu'au soir je regarde au travers." Whatever the form of the adventure, it had been and is a manifestation of the faun's very real eroticism. It was an erotic state that led him to imagine the adventure originally, an erotic state that contributed every act and every passion to it, and an erotic state that is maintained by the wilful reconstitution of it. If we substitute "avide d'amour" for the faun's own words we shall have an adequate description of the motives underlying the whole process of "perpetuating" the nymphs. At the point where the narrative and the meditation have both been terminated, the faun still remains in this state; if, again, we say "que je souhaitais toujours" or "que je désirais toujours" instead of his "dont j'étais encore ivre," we may describe his situation at the end of the section I have just analyzed. In fact, we need to do something of the sort if we are to explain and justify the remaining part of the poem, from line 93 to the end. That part is related to the rest essentially through the faun's eroticism; it looks forward to other sexual experiences—real ones—rather than backward to the imaginary afternoon, and makes use of the latter as a kind of exemplar for future loves.

The final section begins with two transitional verses:

> Tant pis! vers le bonheur d'autres m'entraîneront
> Par leur tresse nouée aux cornes de mon front.   [94]

They are transitional in the sense that "Tant pis!" is a commentary on what has just been related (expressing not so much the faun's regret that the nymphs have left him as his regret that the whole adventure did not really happen) and the future tense of "m'entraîneront" indicates what the faun is about to imagine. We know from "vers le bonheur" that this will once more be a sexual adventure, from "d'autres" that he admits the permanent loss of the nymphs and the necessity of finding their real successors. In "m'entraîneront" itself, the faun establishes his character as a willing victim, putting himself (except for the matter of willingness) in a position similar to that of the nymphs. The next verse is made up of reminiscences of earlier details in the poem, with "leur tresse" echoing "la touffe échevelée" (83) and perhaps also the "bain de cheveux" (66) and "aux cornes de mon front" repeating and explaining "maint rameau subtil" (5). (We may note how, as is so frequently the case with Mallarmé, an element at the end of the poem clarifies an ambiguous element at the beginning.) With "nouée" the faun assures himself that the "others" will not escape from him—or he from them.

To convince himself that later satisfactions of his "passion" will be equivalent to and perhaps superior to the imaginary "triomphe" of the afternoon, the faun indulges in a generalization that is addressed specifically to his "passion." In many ways, it is similar in form to the comparison with the emptied cluster of grapes:

> Tu sais, ma passion, que, pourpre et déjà mûre,
> Chaque grenade éclate et d'abeilles murmure:
> Et notre sang, épris de qui le va saisir,
> Coule pour tout l'essaim éternel du désir.   [98]

His "passion" is not only the "désir" with which the passage ends, and which has figured so prominently throughout the poem, but more broadly the whole of his sensitivity, of his capacity for feeling on the level of the passions. It is significant that he should ascribe knowledge ("Tu sais") to this sensitivity. For his comparison, the faun chooses to speak of the pomegranate at that moment in its development which corresponds to his own state of sexual maturity, "déjà mûre." It then bursts and attracts to itself a multitude of bees; their number is emphasized by the verb "murmure." Similarly desire, once ripe, attaches itself to any and all objects that might satisfy it. "Notre sang," through its plural, provides the generalization, assimilating the faun to all others like himself (and, for the reader who is a man, to all other men). With "épris" the faun specifies the kind of love or desire he envisions, placing it solely in the blood, and with "de qui le va saisir" he stresses both the anonymity or the indefiniteness of the object that will be desired and the passive-willing character of the lover (already suggested in "m'entraîne-ront"). Line 98, as it generalizes, comes to have an apophthegmatic ring, enhanced by the notion of "éternel"; yet it remains closely linked to the specifics of the poem, with "essaim" growing out of "abeilles," "tout" harking back to "d'autres" of line 93 (and thereby admitting successors to the nymphs), and "désir" having its origins as far back as the "Aimai-je un rêve?" of line 3. The faun thus reconciles himself to the unreality of yesterday's adventure only because he can foresee many real adventures on many tomorrows.

Habits of tale-spinning and of imagination are too strong in the faun, however, for him to await inactively the coming of real adventures; the whole of what has preceded in the poem makes it probable that he should manifest his eroticism by imagining a new "afternoon." That is precisely what he does in the next six lines of the *Après-midi:*

> A l'heure où ce bois d'or et de cendres se teinte
> Une fête s'exalte en la feuillée éteinte:
> Etna! c'est parmi toi visité de Vénus
> Sur ta lave posant ses talons ingénus,
> Quand tonne un somme triste ou s'épuise la flamme.
> Je tiens la reine!   [104]

As before, he sets the adventure in the afternoon, probably in the late afternoon, "ce bois d'or et de cendres se teinte," and adds to the color of the setting sun the special color coming from Etna in eruption. "Ce bois" is the wood already referred to as "les vrais / Bois mêmes" (5–6) and as the "bosquet" (17), the locale of yesterday's adventure. Into this twilight wood the faun places a "feast" whose components are the eruption of Etna and the presence of Venus. I think that we may see in "s'exalte" both the upward movement of the flames and the ashes issuing from Etna and the "exaltation" of the passions connected with love and with Venus, including the faun's own. The meaning of "en la feuillée éteinte" is clear: since there is no more sunlight in the leaves, the wood is dark. Etna, as its most characteristic feature, completes the Sicilian landscape that had been identified by "O bords siciliens" (23); the exclamation point following its name adds the whole emotional context that the faun associates with the scene. We should note that the faun, who is at all times speaking to somebody or something present or imagined, here speaks to the volcano. He says "parmi toi" to stress the extent to which Etna and the festival of love are interpenetrated; Venus' visit represents love. The nature of the interpenetration appears in the possessive pronouns, "sur *ta* lave posant *ses* talons ingénus." Venus is personified and given the form of the goddess; she is the last of the "déesses" (55) of whom the faun will speak, and of course is the goddess of love. But for the faun she is, like his other goddesses, a virgin, for that is the meaning to be given to "talons ingénus," relating "ingénus" to the lengthy series "ingénuité—innocence—vierge" that has been developed through the poem. In the next line, the images are mixed in a way to refer equally well to Etna, to Venus, and to the faun. Thus "tonne" and "flamme" belong properly to the volcano, but when one says "tonne un somme triste" one makes a figurative application to the faun's sleep, and with "s'épuise la flamme" one designates both the quieting of the volcano and the subsiding of love's ardor. For the faun, nature, love, and his own being are indistinguishable here as they were before.

"Je tiens la reine." Were we to take the sentence in isolation, it would have no identifiable meaning or reference. But in the light of all that has preceded, it comes to be the concluding statement in a long narrative that the faun does not even need to repeat. Venus comes to visit Etna; the faun, again this afternoon, imagines that he pursues her, seizes her, and possesses her; but this time his triumph does not involve a mere nymph or an anonymous goddess. Instead, he imagines himself as in possession of the queen of all goddesses, of the goddess of love herself. In this statement, as in the rest of the passage, the present tense shows that the faun actually considers himself as present in the time of the events imagined. However, this is now a future with respect to the time of the imagining; for the faun still speaks in the morning hours (although noon is approaching), projecting himself forward into this new adventure rather than backward into the old.

In a completely similar way, "O sûr châtiment . . ." is a resumptive formula. Implicit in it is the idea of crime, and therefore it reminds us, first, of the faun's judgment on his supposed rape of the nymphs, "Mon crime, c'est d'avoir . . ." (82). Since it comes where it does, immediately after "Je tiens la reine," it must also lead us to suppose that the faun makes the same judgment on his new act— still in the future—and that he expects some punishment, inevitable but indeterminate. All these concepts are vague (they move through a vague and confused mind) but they succeed in associating premonitions of crime and punishment with the faun's erotic urges, thereby giving to his passion a richness and a complexity that it could not otherwise have.

Reality reasserts itself, necessarily, the faun returns from the future of his amorous imaginings to the present of his actual state, and in a final passage he says what he will do now that it is noon:

> Non, mais l'âme
> De paroles vacante et ce corps alourdi
> Tard succombent au fier silence de midi :
> Sans plus il faut dormir en l'oubli du blasphème,
> Sur le sable altéré gisant et comme j'aime
> Ouvrir ma bouche à l'astre efficace des vins! [109]

With "Non" the faun denies the fantasy that has been occupying him and returns to present reality; and "mais" juxtaposes the real state to the fantastic. The real state is a state of soul, "l'âme," and a state of body, "ce corps"; both are now deprived of that energy they had earlier in the morning (we remember "le matin frais s'il lutte," 15), the soul because it has spent itself in the words of the meditation and the narrative and is now "De paroles vacante," the body because it is "alourdi" by the noonday sun. (We recall the "air / Assoupi" of the previous afternoon.) Body and soul "Tard succombent au fier silence de midi," "Tard" because the meditation and the struggle against the noonday heat have both been long, "succombent" because the faun will stop his playing and simply go to sleep. (We recall the "Suffoquant de chaleurs" of the previous afternoon.) In a word, the faun admits the coming of another afternoon. He will sleep "en l'oubli du blasphème"; "oubli," we should remark, is the very opposite of "perpétuer" and the faun has come full circle from his original statement of intention for the monologue. "Blasphème" says more than "crime," for it indicates that the crime is one against a god; the faun may apply it either to his nymphs or to Venus or to all, since he judges both adventures on an equal basis. His blasphemy will now be forgotten in sleep, and the faun visualizes the position that he will assume: "Sur le sable altéré gisant," where "altéré" may refer not only to the dryness of the sand under the hot sun but also to the faun's thirst ("avide / D'ivresse," 60–61) and where "gisant" strikes both an ancient and an animalistic note. For the last time—just as he did with the bunch of grapes—the faun presents himself as a devotee of wine (as much, perhaps, as of love): "et comme j'aime" again evokes the "Aimai-je un rêve?" of the beginning, "Ouvrir ma bouche" gives a graphic and typical portrayal, and "à l'astre efficace des vins!" as a periphrasis for the sun, ascribes to it its principal virtue as of the moment. "Efficace" is also the last of the etymological usages; one hears the latinism as the sun becomes the maker of wine.

The poem ends with a single verse, addressed this time to the two nymphs (collectively) and reflecting all of the faun's conclusions with respect to yesterday afternoon's adventure.

> Couple, adieu; je vais voir l'ombre que tu devins.　　[110]

The "adieu" spoken to the couple of nymphs (and we should not neglect any of the overtones in the designation) is a definitive one. The faun knows that they never existed, that it is useless to try to endow them with existence through his playing, and that they can in no way supply satisfaction to his erotic desires. As he sleeps he will see them in the only form they ever had, that of a shadow ("l'ombre"); if he says "l'ombre que tu devins," it is because they had had for him—in the dream, or the meditation, or the confusion with his music—a "real" existence, supplanted by their "shadow" existence only when he could no longer by any subterfuge believe in their reality. He therefore begins his meditation by declaring, "Ces nymphes, je les veux perpétuer," but he ends it by bidding them goodbye, by speaking of "l'oubli," and by recognizing that they have become an "ombre." There will be no perpetuation.

It might be possible, indeed, to see the action of the poem as involving a movement from an initial intention to give substance to the nymphs and to the adventure in which they supposedly figured to a final renunciation of any such proposal. So conceived, the action might be stated as follows: The faun, awaking from his night's sleep, recalls an adventure in which he possessed two nymphs, and he attempts to determine whether it really took place; but he becomes increasingly convinced that it did not. Nevertheless, he continues to construct a narrative of the supposed events, and when that fails to satisfy him fully, he goes on to imagine the rape of Venus herself. His meditation concludes with a return to the sleep from which he had emerged. Stating the action in this way, we make of it a succession of thoughts about a central subject, in an order passing from a positive wish, through a succession of hypotheses, to a negative conclusion. The difficulty of such a reading, however, is that it fails to account for certain elements in the poem, especially the final evocation of Etna and the visit of Venus, and that it does not explain why meditation and narrative should be interspersed as they are. For what reason, we might ask, does much of the meditation precede the narrative, some of it follow? Why is the narrative broken up into three segments? Why should not the poem end at roughly mid-point, where the faun seems to conclude that his adventure was purely imaginary?

Let us suppose that Mallarmé had written *L'Après-midi d'un faune* as I have chosen to discuss it, giving the whole of the narrative first and then appending the faun's gloss or commentary. What would have been the consequences for the nature of the faun's meditation, for the character of the faun himself, and for the general effect of the poem upon the reader? I think we may say, first, that the narrative itself would have appeared (much as it did in my own analysis) as a perfectly clear-cut and straight-forward exposition of events that had really taken place. In his turn, the narrator would have been presented simply as a narrator, as one capable of telling a story precisely and vividly—and having no foolish doubts about whether or not the events had occurred. Had the faun's meditation, single and uninterrupted, followed upon such a narrative, it would have been as anomalous as incomprehensible. Too much of a change would have to be posited in the character of the faun: from the knower to the doubter, from the actor to the dreamer, from the rational man to the creature of feeling. The reader would have difficulty in adjusting his responses to so radical a shift; or at least, he would feel that he was in the presence of two poems rather than of one and that each of the two was attempting to produce its own private effect.

Obviously, that is not at all what Mallarmé wished to do with his poem. What he wished to do, he did; and only by looking at the poem as he made it can we discern what those intentions were. As it stands, the poem begins with a lengthy piece of what I have called the meditation (the second longest in the work, in fact) which has a multifold purpose with respect to the construction of the work. It establishes the character of the faun, especially with regard to his capacity for knowledge: his inability to distinguish reality from the dream, his desires from their realization, his own being from the nature that surrounds him. Against this, the faun is endowed with notable positive capabilities: his talent for the making of pipes and of music on them, his strong sensitivity to the physical qualities of objects around him, and above all a powerful sensuality that subjects to its needs all the rest of his natural faculties. If the faun cannot know, he can certainly feel, vigorously and clearly; when his sensuality takes the form of eroticism, it is most dominant of all. These characteristics appear, not in any abstract or analytical way, but as they relate to the faun's particular problem of this morning, his puzzling over yesterday's adventure. Certain details of that adventure, scattered and fragmentary, are introduced by the faun, and as he mulls over them he begins to establish a proper relationship among things: it was his strong sexual desire that caused him, as he played upon his pipes, to imagine the presence of the two distinct nymphs and to suppose that he had raped them. The reader, as he goes through this initial passage, obtains an impression both of the faun's difficulties in knowing and of the confusing object that he is trying to know.

It is at this point that the first part of the story is "recounted": a brief part, involving only the discovery and the flight of the nymphs. As he reads it, the reader is able to correct and clarify certain notions derived from the commentary preceding. He himself composes the beginning of a narrative, and he does so by superimposing the commentary upon the story; he is aware of two levels of meaning, of some contradiction between them, and of the extent to which he himself must reconcile them. His total response is thus a richer and more complex one, and its complexity is enhanced by the sense that he contributes something, himself, to the making of the total meaning. When the faun resumes his meditation in the longest of the non-narrative pieces, the reader hears it against the background of the earlier opposition between a clear statement of events and a confused interpretation of those events. The new commentary expresses further confusion about yesterday afternoon; but it makes more explicit (for us as we read) the kind of formula "eroticism plus music equals nymphs" that accounts for the faun's impression of his adventure. We now know, as the faun seems to know, that there was no adventure but the imaginary one; but we know as men know, while the faun knows as a faun knows.

Except for seven lines separating the last two sections of narrative, the faun's commentary is now concluded. It has brought him to the point where he must decide whether to continue his narrative as a pure fiction or to abandon all thought of the nymphs. His decision for the former course is prompted again by his eroticism; he is still "avide d'amour," and there will be a kind of joy in the "peintures idolâtres." He undertakes, therefore, what he still calls the "souvenirs" of the afternoon, carrying his tale through to the end except for a brief interruption which is in itself part narrative, part gloss. He tells of finding the two nymphs in their embrace, carrying them off to the clump of roses, raping them, and losing them from his weakened grasp; his adventure ends in this way. For us it is now a purely fictitious story, and we are interested in it not as a story whose outcome might fascinate us, but rather as a manifestation of the faun's character, of his imaginative powers, and of his ability to transmute his eroticism into a colorful and convincing recitation. All these qualities will again be apparent in the last part of the poem. With the kind of economy of means that is possible only at the end of a poem, when probabilities have been established for many constitutive elements, the faun will invent another account—a narrative in the future—of another erotic adventure. This time there is neither recollection nor a pretence at recollection, but only a pure creation of the fantasy. The element of music is absent from the formula, which we now see as "eroticism equals the rape of Venus." The faun's state has in a sense been purified by the morning's activities; it has also been exhausted, and when at last he goes to sleep (undoubtedly to dream) it is in order to return, in a passive and receptive way, to the reminiscence of his lost adventure.

Now the constant in the whole development of the poem as I have just described it is not the faun's continued concern with the solution of a problem. Rather, it is his continued state of erotic exaltation, which leads him first to imagine yesterday's adventure as if it had happened, second to reconstruct it even though it did not happen, third to project another such adventure into the future. It is a state of feeling or sensitivity rather than a state of intellectual inquiry. The poem, as it works from beginning to end, proceeds towards a clarification of that state of feeling: from an initial point where creative, musical activity seems to express the dominant feeling, through a phase where creativity, imagination, and eroticism are indistinguishable, to a conclusion in which the eroticism is separated out from the rest of the emotional complex and identified as the basic force in the faun's meditation. If this be the case, then *L'Après-midi d'un faune* is essentially lyrical in its structure, consisting in the presentation of a unifying state of feeling through devices that are appropriate to that state. Here the devices are partly narrative (if in a curious way), partly direct expressions through such approximations and figurations as the poet has at his disposal for representing the emotions.

Since, in Mallarmé's poem, the emotion represented is, by its nature, a vague and intangible one—we might almost say a sub-literal one—the poet was obliged to multiply the means both for representing it and for making it accessible to the reader, for assuring the production of the proper effect. The invention of the faun's character was the principal of these: a character in which mind could be subordinated to animal instincts, in which all the talents could be natural in their origin and in their powers, in which the whole being could feel himself intimately identified with nature. It is thus appropriate (and useful) that the images given to him as he speaks should be "natural" images close to his own nature: the emptied cluster of grapes (which figures for us his love of wine), the pomegranate (which figures for us his love of love), and the final drinking in of the sun. Besides, the insistence, during the first part of the gloss, on the activities of the faun as pipe-maker and pipe-player serves not only to give us an outward representation of his nature, but also to provide him with his principal argument leading to the conclusion that the nymphs were a fiction. Even incidental and passing comparisons—"comme une source en pleurs," "comme un éclair / Tressaille!"—fit at once his experience as a faun and the natural setting in which he lives.

The poet's main device for creating the desired effect is, however, a kind of indefiniteness or ambiguity of expression that leaves the reader constantly in doubt—in intellectual doubt—about what precisely is meant. The meaning itself is clear, and long and careful reading can make it so. But there are two reasons why it should have been obfuscated in the expression: first, the "intellect" and the feelings of the faun (who is speaking) are such that he is incapable of clarity either in thought or in expression; second, if the reader is to sense in a reasonably direct way both the doubts and the states of feeling of the faun, these must be presented in an appropriately vague and inconclusive way. Were they not, the reader would have to be told about their essential nature, rather than having it presented to him in a properly direct, lyrical fashion. That would destroy the effect. The effect that the reader must get—through his direct, intuitive, nonreflective reading, one that precedes any effort at analysis or at reduction to intellectual terms—is that of the basic voluptuousness of the faun's feelings and of the basic vagueness of his thought. These elicit in the reader, not voluptuousness or vagueness (the emotion of the reader, in any poem, is never exactly coincident with that of the speaker or the protagonist), but rather a multiple impression in which are mixed visual impressions of a primitive Sicilian landscape dominated by Etna, auditory impressions of a music that in a way links to this landscape the creatures who inhabit it, and "moral" impressions of these creatures, the lover, the beloved, and the goddess of love. The latter are primary; they subordinate the others, make them contribute to an impression of a kind of animal and mythological love. The emotion? I should find it difficult to state it in any terms other than those of the poem itself. It is not voluptuousness, but a response to voluptuousness on the part of somebody who observes it from outside; not primitive doubt or animalistic confusion, but a sympathetic and understanding reaction to them by a superior person who is capable of understanding and sympathy. These (and the other complex elements of a complex poem) are raised from a sub-human to a human level by the sensitivities of the reader who, as he synthesizes and organizes the subtle suggestions made by the poem, arrives at a total response of great refinement and delicacy.

Were I obliged to attach a label to Mallarmé's technique in *L'Après-midi d'un faune* (and there is always an insistence that we do attach such labels), I think that I should have to call it "impressionism." I should mean by that not merely the attempt to create impressions through poetry (does not all poetry do that?), but rather the use of devices whose central aim is to make the less-than-clear and the less-than-complete statement. This is done in various ways: by designating only a part or an aspect of the object instead of the whole of it; by using allusions to objects that have not yet been identified, or by using unclear allusions; by disturbing normal word order or the normal meanings of words, in the latter case through the use of etymological or metaphorical senses; by collapsing constructions in a way to make a single word or formula have several kinds of reference simultaneously; by interrupting the expression of a thought so that it surrounds and includes another; by creating an almost impenetrable density of formulation. As all these devices are used together or successively in *L'Après-midi d'un faune,* they serve to produce in the reader, rather than clear ideas and well-outlined emotions, the kinds of nuances or *sfumature* of feeling that we associate with impressionism in the arts.

Among the devices that I listed for the production of "impressionism" in this poem (and others might of course be added), I did not include the symbol; and that—obviously—because I do not find any symbols in the poem. If we use the term in any proper and technical sense, we must mean by "symbol" either the incidental use of one object to represent another object, to which it is related through some common feature, or the constant use of a single object (which thereby becomes the object of representation in the poem) to represent throughout the poem another object, unnamed but in some way identified. It is the second of these usages that produces the "symbolist" poem, and it is in such terms that I have discussed the structure of Baudelaire's *Recueillement* and of Rimbaud's *Le Bateau ivre;* and I have tried in each case to show how the symbol itself is constituted as the basic structural element in the poem and how we are led to a discovery of the object symbolized. But I see no such possibilities in reading and interpreting *L'Après-midi d'un faune.* The faun is a faun; he does not represent or stand for anything but himself; he is not a symbol. Indeed, Mallarmé seems everywhere to have insisted on his "faunness," on all those qualities that made of him a particularly apt subject for the adventures and the meditation assigned to him; and in my reading I have tried to show how those particular qualities became an essential part of the structure. At the same time, I might have shown the absence (if absence can be demonstrated) of the kinds of signs or pointers which, in truly symbolist poems, establish the relationship between the symbol and the object symbolized. I find no such signs in this poem.

I am aware, of course, of the fact that other critics have seen in *L'Après-midi d'un faune* a symbolist poem in which the faun was a symbol for a poet. They have used as their principal arguments the fact that the faun plays on pipes and the fact that we have such lines as "Le visible et serein souffle artificiel / De l'inspiration, qui regagne le ciel." The playing on pipes, they say, must stand for the making of poetry, and inspiration must necessarily be poetic inspiration. Both of these are gratuitous assumptions; if they are signs, they are general signs, belonging only to the reader's general conceptions of poetry and to his wish to read the poem as a poem about poets; they have no specific function as particular signs within the poem, and there is no particular justification within the poem for reading them as such. In fact, such a reading by certain critics merely derives from their universal tendency to read all poems as poems about poets. There is practically no important poem in modern times which has not been so read. The tendency, I believe, springs from the dominance of biographical curiosities over properly critical approaches. The poet becomes the thing, not the poem. Some such argument as this is developed: the real object of our interest is the poet; the poem is important only in so far as it tells us things about the poet; our reading of the poem must make of it a useful biographical document; and it will be an even better reading if it makes of the poem a witness to the nature of all poets and all poetry. An argument that is fallacious and unacceptable at every step—if, indeed, we are really concerned with poems.

7

Mallarmé

Le vierge, le vivace et le bel aujourd'hui

If Mallarmé's *L'Après-midi d'un faune* is not a symbolist poem, if it may be fully read and interpreted without reference to a symbolical structure, the same is not true of his sonnet, *Le vierge, le vivace et le bel aujourd'hui*. This is a poem built around the presentation of an argument concerning the swan, and the swan (as several signs in the sonnet indicate) is a symbol for somebody else. The problem in reading it is not so much in determining whether it is a symbolist poem or not, or even in identifying the "somebody else," as it is a problem of discovering the superficial meaning. For this sonnet is a much more "hermetic" poem than any I have discussed so far; we have greater difficulty in finding out what the words and the phrases mean, in "parsing" the sentences on a purely grammatical level. I wish, in the following analysis, to do two things: to show how, in a poem of this kind, one goes about discovering its basic meaning, and to suggest in what ways the poet establishes and brings to realization the poetic probabilities that hold it together structurally.

Le vierge, le vivace et le bel aujourd'hui
Va-t-il nous déchirer avec un coup d'aile ivre
Ce lac dur oublié que hante sous le givre
Le transparent glacier des vols qui n'ont pas fui!   4

Un cygne d'autrefois se souvient que c'est lui
Magnifique mais qui sans espoir se délivre
Pour n'avoir pas chanté la région où vivre
Quand du stérile hiver a resplendi l'ennui.   8

Tout son col secouera cette blanche agonie
Par l'espace infligée à l'oiseau qui le nie,
Mais non l'horreur du sol où le plumage est pris.   11

Fantôme qu'à ce lieu son pur éclat assigne,
Il s'immobilise au songe froid de mépris
Que vêt parmi l'exil inutile le Cygne.   14

A first step toward the understanding of the poem will be made when we perceive that the initial quatrain is composed of a single sentence, interrogative in form, whose subject is "Le . . . aujourd'hui," whose verb is "Va . . . déchirer," whose object is "Ce lac dur." The remaining phrases and modifiers, of course, specify and enrich the meaning; but essentially a simple question is asked: "Will today break (or tear) this hard lake?" The asking of the question sets up the first probability for the later development of the poem: we shall expect an answer, affirmative or negative. Moreover, in this insistence on the possibility that present time might accomplish an action—and the emphatic position of "aujourd'hui" is important—two other times are implicit: a past when the action did not come about, a future that will follow upon its accomplishment or non-accomplishment; the latter is strongly suggested in "Va déchirer." Indeed, the epithets used to qualify "aujourd'hui" suggest that this new day may have qualities lacking on earlier days. Thus "vierge" emphasizes its very newness, with overtones (again) of a future promise of fertility; "vivace" puts the stress on life and liveliness; "bel" means not "beautiful" but "wonderful" and expresses the ardent hope that the action really will be accomplished. We must assume from all three, looking again at the past, that their contradictories or contraries prevailed on former days; neither newness, freshness, nor hope. The question asked in "Va-t-il . . . déchirer" is accompanied by the unexpressed but fervent wish for an affirmative answer, realizing the positive potentialities of this new day.

"Todays," to be sure, do not break the surfaces of hard lakes, and we know from the start that it is some agent capable of performing the action who will perform it on this new day; this agent, rather than the day itself, will be endowed with new potentials that he previously lacked. The first trait that characterizes the agent is found in the second line, "avec un coup d'aile ivre"; the agent is a winged creature. The same formula tells us two other things about him: that the breaking will come about through a stroke of the wing, and that the stroke will have all the qualities already assigned to "aujour-d'hui"; "ivre" summarizes and intensifies those virtues, as it suggests once more the absence of such vitality in the past.

"Nous" (2) is the so-called ethical dative or dative of interest. I shall speak later of its particular use and meaning at this point.

Lines 3 and 4 provide additional specification for the "lac dur"; they also tell us many more things about the agent. In "oublié" we have the first direct reference to past time (thus completing the time sequence present-future-past and solidifying the probabilities); a lake that is forgotten is one that has a past history different from its present state. In the rest of the sentence, "que hante sous le givre / Le transparent glacier des vols qui n'ont pas fui!" there are already some realizations of probabilities introduced earlier as well as some new elements. So "givre" tells us for what reason the lake is "dur"—it is a frozen lake—and "hante" indicates that under the surface ice some object or being from a former time continues its presence beyond the end of its life; "hante" also prepares the way for the presence, later in the poem, of beings who have so survived. For the moment, the object or being is the "transparent glacier des vols qui n'ont pas fui!"; each word here is rich with suggestions about the object that it represents. "Transparent" has, rather than its usual meaning of "which one can see through," the etymological sense of "which appears through," "qui transparaît"; the "glacier" therefore shows through or is visible through the ice. But only as much of it, of course, as is submerged. A glacier is a mass of ice, part of which may appear above the surface, part of which must lie below it. In this case the frozen mass is not one of ice; for it is a glacier of "vols qui n'ont pas fui," hence it is a figurative representation of the bird who, because he has not flown away, is now caught in the ice.

Several other consequences result from the conclusion of the sentence with "des vols qui n'ont pas fui!" The indication in "avec un coup d'aile ivre" that a winged creature was involved is not only confirmed but completed; it is a bird who might have flown and might have escaped. Past time, earlier associated with the lake through "oublié," is connected with the bird through "ont . . . fui"; he has a history, just as the lake does; but it is a history in a sense negative—there is something he has not done, his flights have not taken place. Moreover, bird and lake (in present time) combine to produce a visual image which has, already, all the essential elements that it will have ultimately: the frozen lake, whose whiteness is stated through "givre"; the bird, whose whiteness is seen in "glacier"; a part of the bird that is under the surface of the lake but that shows through it; and a part of the bird that is free of the ice, that wing that is still capable today of the bold stroke. Finally, we should not fail to note the exclamation point at the end of the sentence. Because of the interrogative order, we should have expected a question mark; and indeed the sentence asks a question. Through the exclamation point, though, a different tone is given to the sentence. It is a question; but it is a question to which we wish an affirmative, positive, encouraging answer. All the qualities in the first three epithets, but especially in "bel," arouse hopes that the negativism and the failures of the past—"des vols qui n'ont pas fui" —will not be repeated, that the bird will break loose from the lake, and that he will take flight. The exclamation point epitomizes those hopes.

In the first quatrain, then, a question is asked: Will the bird, caught in the ice of the lake because he did not take flight in the past, be able today to free himself? And the hope of an affirmative answer is aroused. Since a question is asked, an answer must be forthcoming in the rest of the poem, and something at least of its later development is intimated. We do not know yet whether the answer will come through a narrative of the bird's actions on this day, or through a commentary upon them, or through conclusions with respect to them. We do know these things: that the potential for an action has been stated and that somebody other than the agent has stated it. For this is a lyric poem in which the "person" principally involved in the action or argument is not the speaker, but is spoken about. Who, then, is the speaker? He is not yet specifically identified, nor will he be. Yet it is clear that he takes the position of an outside observer or narrator who is not indifferent to the fate of the bird (this is shown by the way in which the affirmative answer is solicited), who knows about the past history of the bird, and who at the same time identifies himself with the readers of the poem. That identification is one of the functions of the "nous" in line 2. If he does so, it is because he also wishes us to be concerned over the outcome of the action and the answer to the question. This is a way of making us participate in the emotion of the poem.

Some answers begin to be given, including the one to the principal question, in the first two lines of the second quatrain:

> Un cygne d'autrefois se souvient que c'est lui
> Magnifique mais qui sans espoir se délivre . . .   [6]

The bird has been named; he has been related to his past history, to what he was, through "d'autrefois"; and his current state of spirit is described. "Se souvient" serves both to link him with his past—he remembers himself as he was—and to suggest that some of the qualities attributed to "today" may formerly have been his. It also serves, in a way, to move us from the thoughts of the outside observer into the thoughts of the swan; and, by so doing, to make it possible that the thoughts contained in the first quatrain may also have been those of the swan. From "que c'est lui / Magnifique" we learn that he now identifies himself with the swan that he was and that the basic quality common to both is that of "magnificence." Besides, the visual image is transformed; the white bird caught in the ice is now specifically a swan and a magnificent one, with only one detail to mar potentially his vision (and ours) of his plastic beauty, the possibility of the "coup d'aile ivre." To understand "mais qui sans espoir se délivre" we must first note that "se délivre" is not to be taken in the sense of "frees himself" or "liberates himself" but rather as a verb emphasizing the effort being made towards liberation, "tries, strives, struggles to free himself." Its present tense shows that we have moved forward in time from the moment of the question, "Va-t-il . . . déchirer," into a moment when the effort is actually being made and when the observer-narrator can see it being made. The effort, however, is "sans espoir"; this is the conclusion both of the swan himself (the phrase goes back ultimately to "se souvient") and of the narrator; and we now have our negative answer to the question asked in the first quatrain.

That answer does not, however, exhaust the probabilities established by the asking of the question. For as it was asked, we were given very good reasons to expect an affirmative answer (the adjectives in line 1) and we were led to hope for such an answer. These expectations need to be satisfied, if only through an explanation of why they were not realized. The next two lines are devoted to making that explanation.

> Pour n'avoir pas chanté la région où vivre
> Quand du stérile hiver a resplendi l'ennui.   [8]

"Pour" at the very outset assures us that the reason will be forthcoming. What is most striking about the way that reason is given, in the formula "n'avoir pas chanté," is its parallelism in construction to "des vols qui n'ont pas fui!" (4). In the first case, it was a failure to act that had accounted for the swan's presence in the frozen lake; now it is his failure to act in the past that makes his present action impossible. Moreover, the two unaccomplished actions are complementary, representing the two activities proper to a bird, his flying and his singing. We need to give to "chanté," however, an additional, figurative meaning; for when its object is added, "la région où vivre," the sense of "chanté" is considerably expanded. If the swan did not "sing of the region where he might live," he did not yearn with sufficient ardor nor act with sufficient vigor, while it was still time, in order to attain that region. His failure was a failure of the will, expressed here in terms appropriate to a bird. The "region" where he might live is obviously not this frozen lake, but some distant place to which he might have flown and fled. As the poetic probabilities work in this sonnet, the statement at this point of the "région où vivre" does several things. It makes of the swan's present position, of the frozen lake, a "région où mourir," and it prepares the way for the whole larger juxtaposition of life and of death in the poem, of activity leading to life and of inactivity leading to death.

The time of the failure was "Quand du stérile hiver a resplendi l'ennui," thus in that same past time as had been represented in "des vols qui n'ont pas fui!" and "Pour n'avoir pas chanté." But it is now more precise, being at the beginning or the approach of this same winter that now holds the swan locked in its frozen lake; it is, in fact, before the freezing. To "a resplendi" we must again give a rather special meaning: not the actual white shining of winter that has arrived and settled in, but a kind of "shining forth" of winter that announces and presages its coming. It is, as it were, a premonition made visible, in which the actual whiteness of the ice (lake and glacier) accounts for the quality of the vision. The other two terms in the line have moral rather than visual associations. The winter itself will be "stérile," that is, unproductive and fruitless—the very opposite of "vierge" and "vivace," the very opposite of "la région où vivre." Once it comes, the swan will enter into a state of "ennui." Now this is neither ordinary boredom nor Baudelairian despair; rather, it is the essence of inactivity, the opposite of life and of all the epithets that had been applied to the hopes of "aujourd'hui."

As the second quatrain answered the question asked in the first, it realized the major probability established previously; and as it clarified the reason why that answer was not the expected and hoped for one, it further developed the argument along anticipated lines. Moreover, it solved many uncertainties: the identity of the bird, the nature of his failure and the explanation of his present state, the time of his fatal decision (which was of course linked to its cause), his essential denial of life through that decision. All these are seen, now in the second quatrain, from two points of view rather than one: from that of the narrator-observer who describes today's action as it takes place, and to a lesser degree from that of the swan himself. This means that the response of the reader will be richer than before, his participation double, especially when at the end of the quatrains the "moral" terms appear that stand opposed to those at the very beginning. Are, then, all the early probabilities brought to realization, and is there no more to be done? Clearly not; instead, they have been enriched and others have been added. The notion of "Magnifique," stating the swan's vision of himself, is general and ambiguous; it is material rather than moral; it needs to be expanded and explained. "La région où vivre" calls both for specification and, in a sense, for its opposite: "la région où mourir." Past time developed into present time demands a development into future time. Above all, the abrupt and final "sans espoir," leaving us unsatisfied as it does, needs to be more fully justified than it has been in lines 7 and 8.

It will be the function of the tercets to realize these various probabilities. The task is divided between them: in the first we will get a full statement of "sans espoir," in the second we will get an explanation of its moral causes.

> Tout son col secouera cette blanche agonie
> Par l'espace infligée à l'oiseau qui le nie,
> Mais non l'horreur du sol où le plumage est pris. [11]

Two elements are now added to the visual image of the divided swan, half submerged and frozen, half free and mobile. The whole of him is white (in "cette blanche agonie" the term for whiteness appears for the first time) and his free half comprises "Tout son col" as well as the wing; the whole upper part of his body, head, neck, back and wings, is above the surface and capable still of mobility, while the lower part, including the legs and the feet, is caught in the ice. "Tout" gives us a triple impression: of the length of his neck, of its curving shape, and of the total strength of the effort that it will make. With "secouera" we have the first proper future tense in the poem, after the "Va . . . déchirer" of line 2. This is important, for it adds to the normal meaning of "secouer" (since the shaking is now actually taking place) a kind of judgment and commentary: all this activity will be in vain, will not bring about the desired effect; therefore, "sans espoir." All this activity is composite, including the fierce beating of the wings as the swan tries to free himself and the violent movement of his head and neck that accompanies, as it tries to aid, that beating. The image is an image of a creature whose free half is in motion, although he remains fixed to the same spot, and it is an image that is therefore anything but "magnifique"; we juxtapose it, now, to the beauty of the swan as he sits or swims on the water of a summer lake.

What is moved through all this effort (without however any change of position) is an "agonie." We understand at once that this is a way of saying that the swan himself is suffering the pains and the tortures of one who is dying, that he is a dying creature. At the same time, his place of dying becomes "la région où mourir"; "sans espoir" is expanded and explained; and the answer to the original question becomes more completely negative. The following line makes of his death a kind of punishment or retribution for his past action (or inaction). The "agonie" is "infligée." If the swan is its patient or its victim, space itself is its agent and the punishment comes to the swan because he has denied space: "Par l'espace infligée à l'oiseau qui le nie." The verb "nier" again makes of the swan's action a negative one, in a sense; for to deny space is not to affirm it. From what has preceded we know in what ways the swan has denied it; both the "vols qui n'ont pas fui" and the song about the "région où vivre" that was not sung result in the "denial" of space, and space itself becomes one of the elements of the "région où vivre." We should note, besides, that the term "oiseau" is used in this line for the only time, in order to give significance to the denial of space by the one creature for whom such denial is unnatural and fatal.

The free part of the swan's body will be shaken by his last effort; but the surface of the "lac dur" will not be broken and the swan will not be freed. As he says this again explicitly in "Mais non l'horreur du sol où le plumage est pris," the observer states a strong opposition between what will happen "today" and what will not happen ("Mais non . . ."). He now calls the surface of the lake the "sol" which, coming as it does so closely after "l'espace," completes a proportional opposition:

$$\text{région où vivre} : [\text{région où mourir}]$$
$$\text{espace} : \text{sol}.$$

Seeing the lake from the point of view of the swan, he speaks of "l'horreur du sol," where "horreur" applies to the place the feelings about the "agonie" that is happening there. In the series of emotions beginning with the epithets of the first line and with "ivre," passing through "sans espoir" and "ennui," an extreme degree is reached with "agonie" and "horreur." Finally, the last words of the tercet, "où le plumage est pris," add one more detail to the image of the swan (using the characteristic "plumage" as a metonymy for the whole body), as they indicate the definitiveness of the swan's plight through "est pris" (another answer to "Va-t-il . . . déchirer").

As I suggested earlier, the function of the final tercet is to explain the moral causes of that plight:

> Fantôme qu'à ce lieu son pur éclat assigne,
> Il s'immobilise au songe froid de mépris
> Que vêt parmi l'exil inutile le Cygne.   [14]

Since these lines conclude the poem, resolving and realizing all the antecedent probabilities, they are dense and rich in meaning. "Fantôme," for example, brings to conclusion all the indications contained in "hante" (3), in the inferred "région où mourir," in "agonie" (9); he is the being who lives on beyond his life, as a spirit, in a world that once was his but is no longer. At the same time, it is surrounded by all the suggestions of whiteness that had appeared earlier. For "qu'à ce lieu son pur éclat assigne," we must note first the parallelism of idea and of construction with lines 9–10, "cette blanche agonie / Par l'espace infligée à l'oiseau." Just as there space itself inflicted upon the bird his agony, so here another agent ("son pur éclat") assigns the phantom to this place. In both cases, the swan is a helpless patient or victim, some other force is the agent; but ultimately the responsibility is his own. There, it was his "negation" of space, with all its implications for his past history; here it is "son pur éclat." To explain the latter, a number of references to antecedents within the poem will be useful. The clearest of these is "Magnifique" which (along with "se souvient" on which it depends) states an attitude of the swan towards himself, essentially the same one as in "son pur éclat." For "éclat" holds ideas of brilliant whiteness, hence of the general visual representation of his whole body, while "pur" emphasizes not only that same whiteness but also the line of his body—especially of the most beautiful parts of it as they are seen above the surface of the water. There is also a moral side to "pur"; for the creature who thinks of himself as "pur" (as well as "magnifique") is unwilling to destroy that purity of line, of plastic beauty, through violent and disruptive action. The "vols," the "chant" would have constituted such action in the past; now the same kind of action—"un coup d'aile ivre," "Tout son col secouera" —comes too late. It was this conception of his pure beauty and his unwillingness to disturb it that "assigned" or doomed him to this place. We already recognize "ce lieu," named now with such disdain and with such a sense of disparagement; it is the "sol," the "lac dur," the "région où mourir."

Another series of actions is brought to conclusion with "Il s'immobilise." It began with "nous déchirer" (supposing the vigorous "coup d'aile"), it continued with "se délivre" in the special sense which we have seen, it reached a climax in "secouera." Since the action is hopeless and since the swan is doomed, he now renounces action and returns to a state of inaction; "s'immobilise" marks the return to that state. It is also the definite answer to the question raised in the first quatrain. I think that if we see "Il s'immobilise" as a cessation of action involving a return to inaction, then "au" in "au songe froid" marks the passage to the new state (which is identical with his old state in the past); it is in this sense that one can "s'immobiliser à quelque chose." The state is called a "songe froid de mépris"; "songe" is not only inactivity, but also time wasted and unreality— the contrary of "vierge, vivace, bel" and of "un coup d'aile ivre"; and "froid" has both physical and moral connotations, physical because the "songe froid" is in a sense the whole frozen winter landscape, moral because the attitudes of the swan, as they are lifeless and sterile, are characterized as death would be. The whole moral bent is epitomized in "mépris," which is a kind of counterpart of "Magnifique": if "Magnifique" is a statement of the way the swan feels about himself, "mépris" is a statement of his attitude not only toward anything that would spoil that beauty but also toward all other beings and forms of being.

Not only that; the "songe froid de mépris" is an attitude that the swan willingly, perhaps wilfully assumes. In "Que vêt parmi l'exil inutile le Cygne," "vêt" is an active verb having "le Cygne" as its subject (and the "songe froid de mépris" as its object). This, at least, is an activity on the part of the swan, just as "nie" was in line 10; both are what we might call negating activities, both assign to the swan a proper moral responsibility. If the death throes have been inflicted upon him by space, it is because he has denied space in a decision that was his own; he might have acted otherwise. If his "pur éclat" has assigned him to this place of dying, it is because he has chosen to have contempt for living and for the actions that would have assured life. He may be passive and a victim, but in the end all is his own fault. It is thus at the very end of the poem that the complete explanation is given of why the important answer should have been a negative one, when the observer passes from purely physical or material causes to properly moral causes. And it is thus that we may begin to see a dénouement to the action of the sonnet. The dénouement also supplies, in "parmi l'exil inutile," a realization of the probabilities with respect to place, which now is seen to be— simultaneously—moral space as well as physical space. The "exil" is the physical place, the region for dying, the frozen lake; and the swan is "parmi l'exil" because he is identified with it, indistinguishable from it, filling it as it fills him; he is the "transparent glacier" now completely solidified and immobilized, an inseparable part of the winter landscape. The "exil" is moral space in so far as it is "inutile"; the swan is exiled to this place, but he is also exiled from something, and what he is exiled from is life with all its positive possibilities. His form of existence is now "inutile" for a creature of his nature, just as the frozen lake was "oublié," the winter was "stérile" and marked by "ennui," the swan himself was "sans espoir." In a word, he has assumed death as the landscape has assumed (and "vêt" might again be used) its wintry guise. All these qualities and conditions are of course the opposites of those posited of "aujourd'hui" and of the "coup d'aile" in the first two lines of the poem: "vierge, vivace, bel, ivre." Another answer.

The capital "C" used for the swan in the last word of the sonnet, "le Cygne," is full of significance for the total interpretation of the poem. It is, indeed, one of the signs that we have before us a symbolist poem and it helps us distinguish the symbol from the thing symbolized. I think that there are only three such signs in this sonnet, and that the last in the order of presentation to us is this capital letter. At line 5 the central creature was presented as "Un cygne"; he was, then, merely a winged creature whose other features as a bird would later be described and who would ultimately be called by the generic name of "oiseau." Now he is "le Cygne," and both the change from the indefinite to the definite article and the use of the capital inform us that he has become something other than a swan. But what? The other two signs give the reply. First, the "nous" of the second verse, as I have pointed out, served to establish a community of interest between the narrator-observer and the reader; we may now say that it also makes the Swan himself one of us—the reader and the observer, as we all enter into a sympathetic relationship with the swan, do so on the basis of common elements that link us all. Second, those common elements are all the moral traits that have been associated with the swan from the beginning: his attitudes, his dispositions, his decisions, his will, his judgments, his hope and his despair. While the swan remains throughout the poem a bird in so far as all his physical attributes are concerned, he is throughout a human (or a humanized) being with respect to all his moral attributes. Swans do not have moral existences, but men do; and a swan in a poem who has a moral existence, if he does not come to be a man, at least comes to represent the moral existence of a man. It is on this basis only that we understand what is happening to him, that he becomes comprehensible to us, and that we succeed in participating in his adventure.

If the swan, then, is a symbol, the thing symbolized is a man—not a man in general (for this is not an allegory), but a man whose moral experience, action, and plight would have corresponded to those assigned to the swan in the poem. We might say, briefly, that it is a man who, having failed to act in the past in a way to assure his life and his happiness, and that because of his conception of himself and an insufficiency of will, is incapable in the present of taking the necessary action; hence he is doomed to a kind of sterile inactivity that is a form of death. Beyond this we cannot go, for we have no specific indications in the text that might lead us to a more particular notion of the thing symbolized. Both symbol and thing symbolized are entirely present within the poem; that is, all the inferences we may make about the man have their source in statements made about the swan. Structurally, the poem works as other symbolist poems work: it is almost entirely devoted, in its overt and literal statements, to the symbol, but there are sufficient signs to permit the identification of the thing symbolized and the transfer to it of all the thoughts and all the emotions originally associated with the symbol. The symbol is the object represented, the action (or its equivalent) concerns the symbol, and the thing symbolized is in a figurative or metaphorical relationship to the symbol.

In the case of the present sonnet, we need to define another element, beside the symbol and what it represents, if we are to arrive at a total appreciation of the effect; that is the nature and the role of the narrator-observer. The swan, to be sure, is the symbol, the object represented. But what happens to the swan is of secondary importance as compared to what happens to the man whom he symbolizes, and even this, in a sense, is subordinate in importance to what happens in the mind of the narrator as he describes and judges the spectacle before him. Essentially, it is in the spirit of the narrator that hope is aroused as "today" dawns; that judgments are made about the swan's chances of success; that questions are raised with respect to the reasons for his failure; that philosophical generalizations about the moral causes of success or failure (hence of life or death) are deduced from the particular case. Really, there are two "actions" taking place in the poem. One is the action in which the swan is the protagonist, in which he struggles to free himself from the plight to which his past acts have brought him, fails, and resigns himself permanently to that plight. The second is the progress of feelings and ideas in the spirit of the narrator: from an initial state of hope that a man in these circumstances may throw off the incubus of his past and make for himself a possible future; to a deduction that such a hope is unfounded; to a final conclusion that the imperfections of character responsible for past and present will of necessity bring about a future no different from past and present. These are not just thoughts, however, and the observer is not merely engaging in a cold and detached argument. Rather, he is emotionally involved in the swan's lot. He feels hope, then despair; something of the horror of the swan's destiny, followed by a modicum of pity that is not unmingled with a sense of condemnation and of moral judgment.

Because of this emotional context, of the persistent interplay of feeling and thought in the narrator, the reader is kept in a state of emotional involvement. The observer is his interpreter, and he espouses the successive states of soul of the observer (rather than of the swan). There are thus four levels of development in the poem: the action and the thoughts of the swan; the successive states of the man whom he represents; the movement in the spirit of the narrator; and the developing effect in the reader as he responds to all three of these but especially to the last. I include the fourth as "in the poem," even though the reader is concerned, on the assumption that what the reader feels has its cause essentially in the poem, and that hence we may discover it by looking within the poem rather than at the reader. Such a multiplicity of concurrent lines in the poem is a witness to its complexity and helps to account for the complexity of the reader's emotion. It also explains the subtlety of that emotion.

Perhaps if we investigate further the idea of "subtlety" of emotional effect we will come to an appreciation of some of the original features of Mallarmé's poetic technique in this sonnet. The simplest and most unsubtle statement of his poem would have been a statement in the form of a simile: A man in such-and-such circumstances is like a swan who. . . . Next in order of directness (or indirectness) would have been a metaphorical statement: The swan, having in his youth failed to do certain things, is now in his maturity incapable. . . . In either of these cases, the emotion attached to the object or the events would have been clear and relatively uncomplicated, and the reader would have had to contribute little in the way of inference. The first real effort of inference and of interpretation would have been elicited by a symbolical statement, even if in that statement a large number of signs permitting a fairly easy inference had been included; for the essence of the symbol is that the reader discover for himself what is the thing symbolized. Such a statement would have taken essentially the same form as we now have: Will today, with all its qualities of vigor, make it possible for the swan . . . ? For, as we have seen, Mallarmé did make such a symbolical statement. However (and this is one of his main devices for subtlety of effect), he reduced the signs to a bare minimum, to those three that I have discussed, thus obliging the reader to make a considerable inference. Even on the purely emotional or instinctive level, the reader must respond to a symbolical situation that is far from clear, he must make fine adaptations of his feelings to those of the swan, the man, and the observer.

Beyond the use of a symbolical structure, Mallarmé adopted a number of other devices with the intention, I think that we may fairly say, of making his poem less immediately accessible both to the intellect and to the emotions. These might mostly be classified as devices for "density." At times they involve the individual word, which is made to have an especially rich meaning through etymological reference, or through the building of the context around it, or through figurative usage. At other times they involve whole series or structures of words which, as they add their concepts one to the other, create an interplay of senses and allusions. The latter is a structuring device, and it is really through the converging of various lines of the structure upon the individual word or the individual phrase that the impression of density is reinforced. We might take "Fantôme" as an example. Its lexical meaning makes only a minimal contribution to its force in line 12—and to the richness of its evocation. When we relate it to "hante" and to "glacier," to the "stérile hiver," to "agonie," to "l'horreur du sol," to all the notions of whiteness presented in the poem, and to the concepts that modify it in the second tercet, we give to the single term (dramatically placed at the beginning of that tercet) a great potential for the production of the emotional effect.

To a large degree, the quality and the intensity of that effect will depend upon the willingness and the capacity of the reader to "give to the term"—and to the whole poem—their full possibility to create the poetic effect. Not that the reader makes the poem: readers do not make poems, they read them. But to the extent to which they read them well they extract from them their maximum power. The art of Mallarmé in this sonnet has as one of its consequences to involve the reader constantly, actively, and deeply in the discovery of the meaning and the emotion of the poem. All the devices of which I have spoken, including the basic symbolical structure, call upon the reader to exert his sensitivity and his intelligence in a refined and controlled way. If he does so (allowing the poem to provide the refinement and the control), he will experience a poetic effect of amazing delicacy and forcefulness at the same time. If the poem is hermetic and difficult, it is so for a purpose, and that purpose is both to assure a certain kind of participation on the part of the reader and to reward him with a kind of aesthetic satisfaction that would not be elicited by a poem of more simple structure.

A note on swan songs

The question is constantly asked, with respect to this sonnet and especially to line 7, "Pour n'avoir pas chanté la région où vivre," as to the role of traditional notions of the "swan song" in this poem. According to those notions, the swan sings only once in his life, and that at the moment of his death. Here, however, the swan does not sing at any time. That is one of the manifestations of his failure. Yet I think that there is a possible presence of the old idea, in a curious and indirect way. The swan who sings only his death does not sing his life, and thus he too may be considered as not having sung "la région où vivre"; the swan in the poem is like others, but a personal rather than a general failing is involved. His failure to sing during life is a moral trait, and were he to sing at the time of his death, a whole change in his character would have to be effected.

8
Mallarmé

Toast funèbre

Taking everywhere, as he wrote his poetry, an experimental stance, Mallarmé did not always of necessity address his creative impulse to the invention or the development of the new poetic form. He did not in every case, that is, pursue such innovations as the "impression-ism" of *L'Après-midi d'un faune* or the peculiar quality of his "symbolism" in *Le vierge, le vivace et le bel aujourd'hui*. At times he was content to work with completely conventional structural devices, within which he sought the personal and the individual note by handling either thought or language in his own special way. That special way was, as we have seen, a useful adjunct to major inventive efforts, resulting in a deepening and enrichment of the poetic effect. Its usefulness was similar in poems whose basic organization was simple and traditional but which became—through this way with thought or language—fresh and striking in the impression that they produced.

Toast funèbre is such a poem. Reducing it to its simplest terms, we may say that its structure consists in an opposition, followed from beginning to end, whose purpose is to declare the superiority of "this" over "that." The subject is the praise of Théophile Gautier on the occasion of his obsequies; hence "this" is the life and the death of the poet while "that" is the life and the death of other men. The basic opposition is developed in every line of the poem and in a great variety of ways. Moreover, the opposition accounts (again in a simple way) for the organization and the division of the poem into its parts. The toast itself, the expression of praise, is contained in line 1; lines 2–15 describe the peculiar quality and meaning of this toast because of the fact that it is addressed to a poet. In lines 16–31, the life and death of other men—and their inferiority—are stated in terms that will make it possible to contrast (in lines 32–47) at each point the life and death of the poet—and their superiority. A final section, lines 48–56, proclaims the real meaning of the poet's burial and of his tomb.

Toast funèbre

O DE NOTRE BONHEUR, toi, le fatal emblème!

Salut de la démence et libation blême,
Ne crois pas qu'au magique espoir du corridor
J'offre ma coupe vide où souffre un monstre d'or!   4
Ton apparition ne va pas me suffire:
Car je t'ai mis, moi-même, en un lieu de porphyre.
Le rite est pour les mains d'éteindre le flambeau
Contre le fer épais des portes du tombeau: 8
Et l'on ignore mal, élu pour notre fête
Très simple de chanter l'absence du poëte,
Que ce beau monument l'enferme tout entier.
Si ce n'est que la gloire ardente du métier,   12
Jusqu'à l'heure commune et vile de la cendre,
Par le carreau qu'allume un soir fier d'y descendre,
Retourne vers les feux du pur soleil mortel!

Magnifique, total et solitaire, tel   16
Tremble de s'exhaler le faux orgueil des hommes.
Cette foule hagarde! elle annonce: Nous sommes
La triste opacité de nos spectres futurs.
Mais le blason des deuils épars sur de vains murs,   20
J'ai méprisé l'horreur lucide d'une larme,
Quand, sourd même à mon vers sacré qui ne l'alarme,
Quelqu'un de ces passants, fier, aveugle et muet,
Hôte de son linceul vague, se transmuait   24
En le vierge héros de l'attente posthume.
Vaste gouffre apporté dans l'amas de la brume
Par l'irascible vent des mots qu'il n'a pas dits,
Le néant à cet Homme aboli de jadis: 28

"Souvenirs d'horizons, qu'est-ce, ô toi, que la Terre?"
Hurle ce songe; et, voix dont la clarté s'altère,
L'espace a pour jouet le cri: "Je ne sais pas!"

Le Maître, par un œil profond, a, sur ses pas,   32
Apaisé de l'éden l'inquiète merveille
Dont le frisson final, dans sa voix seule, éveille
Pour la Rose et le Lys le mystère d'un nom.
Est-il de ce destin rien qui demeure, non?   36
O vous tous, oubliez une croyance sombre.
Le splendide génie éternel n'a pas d'ombre.
Moi, de votre désir soucieux, je veux voir,
A qui s'évanouit, hier, dans le devoir   40
Idéal que nous font les jardins de cet astre,
Survivre pour l'honneur du tranquille désastre
Une agitation solennelle par l'air
De paroles, pourpre ivre et grand calice clair,   44
Que, pluie et diamant, le regard diaphane
Resté là sur ces fleurs dont nulle ne se fane,
Isole parmi l'heure et le rayon du jour!
C'est de nos vrais bosquets déjà tout le séjour,   48
Où le poëte pur a pour geste humble et large
De l'interdire au rêve, ennemi de sa charge:
Afin que le matin de son repos altier,
Quand la mort ancienne est comme pour Gautier   52
De n'ouvrir pas les yeux sacrés et de se taire,
Surgisse, de l'allée ornement tributaire,
Le sépulcre solide où gît tout ce qui nuit,
Et l'avare silence et la massive nuit.   56

Before proceeding to the line-by-line analysis of *Toast funèbre,* to a discovery of its dynamics, I should like to look in a general way at some of the elements which enter into the opposition and which, since they are constant, may be considered as static. "This" is the life and the death of the poet, "that" is the life and the death of other men; and "that" is developed and detailed so that we may better understand and appreciate "this," and give to "this" its proper praise. The life of other men is blind and mute; they neither see nor speak. But the life of the poet is clairvoyant and alive with sound, for he both sees the world as it is and transforms it into words. Thus images of darkness and silence for other men will be contrasted to images of light and sound for the poet. Neither seeing nor speaking, other men will be ignorant; while the poet will gain knowledge as he sees and give it through his words. Whereas other men contribute nothing and belong to the world of the "néant," the poet continues the process of creation as he perpetuates things in words. It is for this reason that other men may be considered as passing and the poet as eternal. Yet because of a false pride, other men believe in an eternal life for themselves after death, as their souls live on; this is opposed to the true humility of the poet, who refuses to accept the assumption of such an afterlife. Reality, however, justifies the poet: the death of other men is a total death, the death of the poet affects only the body. His genius survives in his verses.

Such elements as these (and I think that they are the essential ones) exist simultaneously throughout the poem. They do not have the order I have given them; nor is my order the one in which Mallarmé chose to present them. I have arranged them simply, grouping those which belong to "life" first, then those which belong to "death." In so doing, I have not written (or even re-written) the poem; nor have I paraphrased it. I have merely made a bald statement of the ideas, as ideas, in their basic relationships as groupings on the one hand and as oppositions on the other hand. That statement, while it in no way approximates the effect produced by the poem, does two other things: it shows how the groupings and the oppositions have within them the potential for an argument in praise of the poet, and it suggests that the things said in praise of the poet are such as might arouse the sympathy and the admiration of the reader. Mallarmé does produce an argument, a dynamic development to which all these elements contribute; and he does elicit, through his ways of thought and language, the desired response from his audience.

Mallarmé's solution for providing the dynamics of *Toast funèbre* consists first in inventing a doubly dramatic situation: dramatic in one sense as a set of circumstances—a place, a time, an occasion, an event; dramatic also as a kind of dialogue between the conflicting claims of "this" and "that." The dialogue begins where a dialogue should begin, with the statement of the two positions, proceeds to a development of both cases in the light of implicit criteria, and concludes with a restatement of the winning side and a declaration of the reasons for preferring it. The conclusion involves at the same time a resolution of the circumstantial elements stated at the beginning. This means that the poem works essentially as an argument, but as an argument that is presented in terms of drama and the passions rather than in terms of logic and ideas. Each of the ideas that I listed above is represented by an object or an emotion; and it is perhaps in the necessity of relating each object or emotion to its appropriate idea that the difficulty of reading the poem is found. We may of course feel the basic emotions of the poem without discovering the relationships; but if, besides, we understand those relationships—through the intellectual effort that must be a part of all good reading—our feelings with respect to it will be deepened and intensified.

Both the basic elements of the dramatic situation and the sources of the ensuing argument are contained in the first line of the poem:

O de notre bonheur, toi, le fatal emblème!

This is the toast, addressed (through "toi") to Gautier who will not be named until much later. If it can compress as much as I have claimed into a single line, it is because of ambiguities or ambivalences present in almost every word of the verse. Chief of these is the word "notre." Through it we discover a speaker, who will be present and speaking all during the poem, and we learn that he includes himself in a class which also comprises the "toi" being toasted. He speaks largely in the first person singular and as he does so identifies himself also as a poet: "J'offre ma coupe" (4), "ne va pas me suffire" (5), "je t'ai mis, moi-même" (6), "J'ai méprisé" (21), "mon vers sacré" (22), "Moi . . . je veux voir" (39). The question with respect to the initial "notre" is whether it contains only the "moi" and the "toi" or whether it refers to a broader class; and if so, what class. As we read in the poem, it becomes apparent that "notre" might be applicable to either one of two classes, but not to both; for there are two series of "nous," one for each side of the opposition. In lines 9-10, "élu pour notre fête . . . de chanter l'absence du poëte" indicates that this "notre" adds to the poet speaking all the others with him who also celebrate Gautier in their verses, hence a broader class of poets; and in lines 48–49, "nos vrais bosquets . . . Où le poète" obviously refers to the same class. Against this is the "nous" and "nos" of lines 18–19, spoken now by the members of "Cette foule hagarde!" (18), by the "hommes" (17); this is the class to which belongs the "Homme" of line 28, who speaks for himself in line 31, "Je ne sais pas!" The "notre" of the first line must thus designate the speaker, and Gautier, and the other poets, therefore one group in the opposition; while the other "notre" signifies the other group, that of "other men." (We should not fail to note that at one point the poet speaking addresses the other group, and possibly also his own; this is in the "O vous tous" of line 37.)

The ambiguity of "notre" is resolved before the poem ends; but until it is, the term serves as a source (or a probability) for a dual development, affecting both sides of the fundamental opposition. Until it is, moreover, a similar ambiguity attaches to the "bonheur" that "notre" modifies. We want to know immediately not only whose happiness is meant—the speaker's and Gautier's, or that of a larger if distinct group, or that of all men?—but also what is the relationship between "bonheur" and "fatal," two terms which would seem to be contradictory. If the man who has died and who is being toasted is a "fatal emblème" of our happiness, then is our happiness death or is it life? In so far as these questions arise at the outset, concerning both the "whose" and the "what," the speaker prepares the way for one answer or the other, and we are led to expect that answer. The meaning of "fatal" is equally ambivalent; for in its context we may possibly give it either (or both) of two meanings: since it is applied to a dead man (and we know this from the title of the poem), it may mean that he has been stricken down by the fates; but it may also mean that he was destined or fated to die and to serve as this kind of emblem. We cannot, of course, decide. In the case of "emblème" itself, we know that it means a kind of synoptic or symbolic representation that must be interpreted before it is understood; but what the interpretation should be in this particular case is not indicated. The whole of the poem, indeed, will be devoted to leading us to the interpretation. Thus all four major notions in the first line are susceptible of at least a double construction; it is in this way that they are ambiguous and that they establish the probabilities needed for developing the extended opposition in the rest of the poem.

But the four terms of the first line do not exist in isolation or as abstractions. They form, along with other words of equal importance, an exclamatory sentence. It begins with "O" and ends with an exclamation point, puts the major internal stress (and hence a strong affective emphasis) on "bonheur," isolates and lengthens and accentuates the "toi" for the person addressed, displaces "fatal" before "emblème" as a means to giving it a special quality. The result is a sentence that is "exclamatory" for almost every word, that goes along as a series of strong stresses, and that accumulates a great amount of emotional content. As we read it, we feel the importance and the richness of what is being said, although the meaning itself remains enigmatic. Thus we enter the poem with many questions and expectations, and with an emotional predisposition to participate in the feelings that the speaker is about to express.

The first four lines of the next section, forming a kind of unit, compound rather than solve the difficulties of meaning:

> Salut de la démence et libation blême,
> Ne crois pas qu'au magique espoir du corridor
> J'offre ma coupe vide où souffre un monstre d'or!
> Ton apparition ne va pas me suffire.   [5]

One thing is immediately clear: that the speaker, as he pronounces (or exclaims) his toast, thinks of himself as a celebrant in an ancient (probably Roman) ritual for the commemoration and praise of the dead. The "libation" and the "coupe" used for it, the sculpture in the cup ("où souffre un monstre d'or"), are signs of this association. Later on, with the "rite" and the "flambeau" of line 7, he will confirm it. The "salut" or the toast proper is thus accompanied by a number of acts which, in the aggregate, make up a ritualistic celebration. Another thing that is clear is that the purpose of the rite is not to bring the dead man back to life or to raise his spirit: "Ton apparition ne va pas me suffire" (where "suffire" means, I think, "to correspond to or satisfy my expectations"). This negative expression, of what the rite is not, gives to these four lines their unitary meaning. To propose a toast for this purpose would be to make a "Salut de la démence," an irrational and mad declaration; to pour the wine for this purpose would be to make a "libation blême," one without gayety, color, or hope. The speaker assures Gautier that this is not why he has spoken the words of his toast, "Ne crois pas"; and the "magique espoir du corridor" is a longer and more complete paraphrase of "Ton apparition" (where the "corridor" would be the passage-way from the other world back to this world, the "espoir" the hope for Gautier's return, and "magique" an indication that such a hope would be unreal and supernatural). In terms of later developments in the poem, where the poet disclaims any survival of his soul in an afterlife (leaving that vain hope to other men), it is important that the same disclaimer should be made here by the speaker. Once again, an indispensable element of the total opposition is introduced early in the poem. "J'offre ma coupe vide" goes back to "libation" (just as "Salut" refers to "Toast" in the title and to what has been said in the first line). The description of the sculpture in the cup, "où souffre un monstre d'or," is apparently a transfer to the cup of the kind of representation that frequently appeared on ancient sarcophagi, where the suffering and struggling monster was an "emblem" of the pains of this life on earth.

As they deny any purpose or hope of causing an "apparition" of the dead poet, these lines also evoke an image of an ornate and complex ritual that would correspond to the magic of such an apparition. Only the assignment of such a purpose to the ritual is now denied, not the ritual itself; a subsequent part of this same section will be devoted to the second denial. Meanwhile, the emotion of the very first line is complicated by the addition, to such ideas as "bonheur" and "fatal," of the feelings associated with "démence," "blême," "magique espoir," and "souffre un monstre"—feelings that produce a tortured and unreal impression. These are negated by their context; they will be negated more completely in the line that follows, both through its idea and through the simplicity of its expression:

> Car je t'ai mis, moi-même, en un lieu de porphyre.   [6]

As I suggested earlier, this line, with its "je" and its "moi-même," makes a very personal reference to the role of the speaker in the celebration of the poet. It also states clearly the time of the toast, putting it after the time of the entombment, and it describes the tomb: "un lieu de porphyre." The whole line states why the speaker can expect no return of the dead poet: he himself participated in the burial, and the place of burial was such as to make impossible any issue from it. There is also, in "porphyre," another reference to the image of a Roman funeral.

Another part of the second section, comprised of the five lines following, answers our obvious question: "If that is not the ritual and that is not its purpose, what then is being done and why?"

> Le rite est pour les mains d'éteindre le flambeau
> Contre le fer épais des portes du tombeau:
> Et l'on ignore mal, élu pour notre fête
> Très simple de chanter l'absence du poëte,
> Que ce beau monument l'enferme tout entier.   [11]

Here the "ritual" is reduced to a simple physical act, separated from the actual "fête" which is a spiritual act. The former is "pour les mains" only, and since it consists in the extinction of the torch it once again is related to ancient rituals; the solidity of the tomb is emphasized in "le fer épais des portes," which builds upon and expands the image sketched in "un lieu de porphyre." The latter is "Très simple" (again in contrast to the first suppositions about the ritual) and is devoted exclusively to "chanter l'absence du poëte." The speaker acts in both ways; he has helped in the entombment and has put out the torch, he now (in these verses which are his toast) sings of the absent poet and of the poet's absence. "Absence" stands as a further denial of "apparition." In lines 9 and 10, the "notre" (and the implicit "nous") of the first line begin to be specified. Since this is "notre fête," its celebrants are all those who contribute to singing the praise of Gautier; any one of them is "élu" for the celebration because of his own quality as a poet; and "on" is a generalized way of speaking of all those who are so selected. Now all these poets have special knowledge: they know, with respect to Gautier, that "ce beau monument l'enferme tout entier." This is not, however, stated as positive knowledge; in "l'on ignore mal," we have a negative formulation whose purpose is to say that it would be wrong on the part of these poets not to know this fact—whereas others may well ignore it. The phrase thus prepares for the kinds of knowledge that others may have, opposed to that of the poets. "Ce beau monument," building upon "un lieu de porphyre" and "le fer épais des portes du tombeau," adds the notion of the beauty of the tomb, a necessary notion since the beauty is a part of the tribute to the poet (note, in line 54, the full expression in "de l'allée ornement tributaire"). Once more, "l'enferme" denies the false ideas of "magique espoir du corridor" and "apparition," while it looks forward to the contrasting notion that some part of the poet does escape—a notion that will first be developed in the lines immediately following, then in a major way later in the poem. Similarly, the "tout entier" must at this point be ambiguous; its final clarification will come only in line 55, with the phrase "tout ce qui nuit."

With respect to the progress both of the ideas and the emotions of the poem, the five lines just studied correct erroneous impressions and supply new information. The "rite," they tell us, is a simple one and it consists in the singing of the poet's praises after his burial; it has no other hopes or pretentions; for its celebrants are also poets and they know what the functions and the limitations of the "fête" must be. They have knowledge, also, of what the death of the poet— and hence their own—must mean. It is this association of the celebrants with Gautier celebrated that adds primarily to the exclamatory quality of these lines. Each of them is an "élu," each knows what he does in the double ritual and why he does it; all are responsible for the "beau monument," the action of all is simple, dignified, and pure. Moreover, since "notre fête" is now conjoined with "notre bonheur," we link with both a feeling of joy—of real celebration—as we give to the toast its proper meaning and its proper emotion. False and trivial hopes are cleared away, although we are still uncertain as to how we should feel about "fatal emblème" and we still resist the categorical suggestion of "tout entier."

It will be the role of the next four lines, concluding the second section, to reassure us about the "absence" of the poet and about "tout entier." They do so by separating (clearly and simply again) the poet's spirit from his body, his genius from his mortal remains. The fact that the whole passage is a qualification and a correction of

what has just preceded is indicated by the "Si ce n'est que" which
introduces it:

> Si ce n'est que la gloire ardente du métier,
> Jusqu'à l'heure commune et vile de la cendre,
> Par le carreau qu'allume un soir fier d'y descendre,
> Retourne vers les feux du pur soleil mortel!   [15]

Here the central image represents the idea that the poet's genius,
which has come to him from the heavens, returns to the heavens at
the time when the body dies; thus although the body is sealed
entirely within the tomb by the "porphyre" and the "fer épais des
portes," the poetic spirit—an immaterial spirit—escapes through the
pane of glass that allows light to enter the mausoleum. The image
itself is one of light, coming down from the sun and reflected back
up to it, assimilated to the poet's genius through the phrase "la gloire
ardente du métier"; "la gloire . . . du métier" is metaphorical, signifying at once the poet's inspiration and art (with the emotion that
he himself and others attach to them) and a kind of material representation of them as a "gloire." It is only if we see this second
meaning that we can understand the physical process described in
"la gloire . . . Par le carreau . . . retourne," and that "ardente"
can have its dual meaning of "passionate" and "glowing." "Ardente" seems also to have an active verbal or gerundive meaning,
since upon it depends the whole of the following verse, "Jusqu'à
l'heure commune et vile de la cendre." The poet's art burns bright
until his death.

His death involves essentially the death of his body. Therefore it
comes at the same time as that of other men, "l'heure commune
. . . de la cendre," and it is as trivial and as unimportant, as debas-
ing ("vile") as theirs. "Vile" stands in opposition to "gloire," "cendre" may be taken in relationship to "ardente" as the residuum of
that burning. The oppositions are unequivocally put and by introducing the idea of "l'heure commune" the speaker begins to look
forward to the next major section, where the life and death of "other
men" will be fully estimated. Meanwhile, after the poet's burial, his
spirit returns to its source. If the pane through which it escapes is lit
by "un soir fier d'y descendre," it is because another tribute is being

paid to the poet, this time by the setting sun. The downward motion of the sun's rays, coloring the pane, will be answered by the upward motion of that spirit "vers les feux du pur soleil." The image of moving light is now completed: "ardente," "carreau qu'allume un soir," "feux du pur soleil," along with all the metaphorical implications. "Pur soleil mortel!": because the sun is credited with being the source of the poet's genius (again metaphorically), it may also be the source of the poet's purity; "pur soleil" at this point is explained by "poëte pur" in line 49. The explanation for "mortel" may possibly be the same, with the added figure of the sun's setting at the end of his course (and this is the "soir" of his setting) compared to man's death at the end of his life. The sun would be "pur" like the poet and "mortel" like all men; and the "soleil mortel" begins to have connections with the "fatal emblème" of the first line. The group of four verses has given us the real substitute for the false "apparition," it has told us of a "présence" that will compensate for the "absence" of the poet. In so doing, it has laid the groundwork for the fourth major section (lines 32–47), where the nature and the wonder of that presence will be fully detailed.

The group of four verses has also been an exclamation. For the note of admiration for the poet's spirit, accompanied by the contempt for man's body, demanded an enthusiasm that would continue and complete that of the original toast. In a way, the exclamation that affirms is here a counterpart and a conclusion to the exclamation that negates (lines 2–4). It results in an emotion, on the part of the reader, that corresponds to the feelings associated with "gloire," "fier," "pur," feelings that now belong to the poet and that distinguish him from other men. These are his "bonheur," hence the "bonheur" of those who celebrate him; and positive and almost joyous emotions are appropriate.

Although the third section of *Toast funèbre* will tell of the ways in which other men are inferior to the poet, and therefore of the poet's implicit superiority, its first two lines have the poet as their subject ("tel"). They serve to make the transition from the exclamatory praise of the poet to the exclamatory condemnation of other men, and their first three epithets (16) epitomize what has just been spoken about him.

> Magnifique, total et solitaire, tel
> Tremble de s'exhaler le faux orgueil des hommes.   [17]

"Magnifique" (still full of the note of admiration) goes even beyond the laudatory concepts so far related to the poet; "total" not only restates the idea of "tout entier" (11), but it prepares for the notion of a divided being ascribed to other men a little later in this same section; and "solitaire" is juxtaposed to "commune" in line 13 and to the "foule" of line 18. The net effect is to isolate the poet from all other men and to magnify his stature and his qualities. It also makes more dramatic the statement of the next line: if a man of this kind trembles ("tel / Tremble") to act as other men do, he rejects categorically their mode of action and he demonstrates the superiority of his character to theirs. The extent of the rejection is shown by the way in which the verb is "diminished"; "s'exhaler" implies that the poet would not only hesitate to express in words "le faux orgueil des hommes" but that he would not even wish to breathe it out or to have it come as an emanation from his being. "Le faux orgueil des hommes" will be explained immediately; now we need to note that it stands in close proximity to the "fier" of line 14 (which we must take to be a true pride) and to the "fier" of line 23 (which must be this same false pride). Besides, "des hommes" as a class makes clear the opposition, basic in the poem, to the solitary "tel."

As against the reticence of the poet, the pride of other men will be loudly proclaimed and its subject firmly identified:

> Cette foule hagarde! elle annonce: Nous sommes
> La triste opacité de nos spectres futurs.   [19]

From the outset, a note of depreciation and disdain is connected with "other men." They are called disparagingly "Cette foule" and each man is thereby deprived of any identity or individuality; and with the epithet "hagarde" their moral state is characterized. The epithet is not, I think, without reference to the "libation blême" of the first line; the same forlorn and colorless quality is suggested. The opposition continues with "elle annonce," designating a loud and sure proclamation as against the "Tremble de s'exhaler" for the poet. What is announced is the belief of other men that their present material life is of secondary importance as compared with a future spiritual existence after death; "Nous sommes" and "futurs" make the opposition in time, "opacité" and "spectres" in their forms of being; and "triste" establishes the relative value of this life (as it also differentiates these men from the poet, "Magnifique, total et solitaire"). Other men thus consider their existence and their lives as divided; but the poet, as he should, considers himself as one, putting no false pride in a superior afterlife and no false hope in an "apparition."

To demonstrate the extent to which the hope of other men is a false hope, the speaker now describes their death in a way which recalls, through contrasts explicit and implicit, the death of the poet as described in the preceding section, and which points forward to a new description of the poet's death in the section following. Lines 20–25 have as their function to compare the reality of the death of other men with their conceptions about it:

> Mais le blason des deuils épars sur de vains murs,
> J'ai méprisé l'horreur lucide d'une larme,
> Quand, sourd même à mon vers sacré qui ne l'alarme,
> Quelqu'un de ces passants, fier, aveugle et muet,
> Hôte de son linceul vague, se transmuait
> En le vierge héros de l'attente posthume. [25]

The speaker again speaks as a poet, and as one who, through his special knowledge as a poet, has seen the life and death of other men and who, with his art, has written to them about it. What he has written to them in his "vers sacré" is, we must suppose, the truth about their life and death; that is why his verse is "sacré." But no one of them has listened or heeded his warning ("qui ne l'alarme") and each has approached his death in terms of his former superstitions. I believe that we must see the whole of the "faux orgueil" as a superstition that conforms to normal Christian beliefs about death, and that the speaker is rejecting these beliefs in favor of non-religious concepts of life and death. Sections II and III thus introduce another opposition: on the one hand a notion of life and death that aggrandizes man through the role it assigns to his genius (in this case the poet's), on the other hand a thesis that diminishes man by making his life secondary to his death ("La triste opacité de nos spectres futurs"). In the total structure of the poem this opposition serves the purpose of adding another basis for praising the poet.

Line 20, as it evokes images of Christian commemoration of death, strikingly different from the pagan images just presented, begins with an adversative "Mais" that stands against both the "faux orgueil" and "elle annonce." It is to be constructed, I think, as a kind of ablative absolute that belongs to the whole of the sentence following and that has special reference to "Quand" (22), since it is at the time of death that one sees "le blason des deuils épars sur de vains murs." Two remarks of importance here: "le blason des deuils" is a kind of paraphrase of "le fatal emblème," with an "opposite" reference and intention; and "épars sur de vains murs" begins a note of derogation and irony that will be constant throughout the sentence. Both "épars" and "vains" suggest an insubstantial quality that will be repeated in "linceul vague" and that will differ from the qualities of solidity associated with the poet's tomb. At the same time that the speaker sees these outward signs of death (signs that belong to "triste" rather than to "notre bonheur"), he sees in the eyes of the mourned (and perhaps of the mourning) "l'horreur lucide d'une larme"; it is really the tear that is translucid and that permits him to distinguish, beyond the surface pride and confidence, the real "horreur" in the soul of those who die. And for this horror he has only contempt ("J'ai méprisé"), since it shows him to what extent the pride is false and the confidence in the future illusory. The speaker's negative feelings towards "other men" are even stronger here than they were in "Cette foule hagarde!" and throw into even sharper relief his admiration for the poet.

The man who dies thus is called a "passant" (23), not only because he thinks of himself as in transit to a better existence, but because of the really transitory nature of his life; the real significance of "passants" will be apparent only when we come to "Le splendide génie éternel" in line 38. So, too, will the traits assigned to him, "sourd," "fier," "aveugle," and "muet," have their full import only when the positive traits of which these are the privatives come to be attributed to the poet. We have already seen "fier" as a restatement of "faux orgueil"; but coming now as it does after "sourd même à mon vers sacré qui ne l'alarme," it adds the idea that part of the man's pride is expressed in his unwillingness to listen to the poet. The really important traits are on the one hand "sourd" and "muet," on the other hand "aveugle." For they are the counterparts in other men of the great and distinctive virtues of the poet, his capacity to see—and hence to know—and his capacity to speak what he knows through his verses. (The speaker has done both through his "vers sacré"; but the "passant" has not heeded him.) Blindness and silence will be further developed for other men in the remaining verses of this section; the "œil profond" and the "voix" of the poet (32, 34) will provide the basis for praising him in the next section.

We may now, with the last two verses of the sentence, discover its basic grammatical structure: "J'ai méprisé . . . Quand . . . (le blason des deuils épars) . . . Quelqu'un de ces passants . . . se transmuait / En le vierge héros." This is the death, according to their lights, of other men. Any one of them is the "Hôte de son linceul vague" in two senses: he is during his life, as a passer-by, the guest of his body, which in a way "shrouds" his spirit; and he is, at the time of his death and burial, the guest of a real shroud, "vague" because of a form that is really not that of the body itself and because of the non-durability of its material. The note of depreciation present in the whole phrase continues in "se transmuait," where there is a definite pointing to a supernatural, religious conception of death and the afterlife, a conception which the speaker disdains. The verb is completed by the verse, "En le vierge héros de l'attente posthume"; the last two words summarize the ideas contained in "nos spectres futurs," in "Ton apparition," and in "magique espoir," and as they do so they emphasize the speaker's irony, since he gives to "attente posthume" no more credence than to the other formulas. The passer-by, for him, is "tout entier" in his tomb just as is the poet being celebrated. Similarly, when he calls the dying non-poet a "vierge héros," the speaker is being strongly ironical; we see a hero who will be such only in another life, not in this one, and who will be "virgin" in the sense that he will begin to live only in that other life. If we set up against "attente posthume" some such concept as "actualité vivante" (translating "triste opacité"), then the passer-by is reduced in this living present to nullity with respect both to his capabilities and to his achievements. The opposite, again, of the poet.

It is not without design, surely, that following upon the pagan evocation of the second section and the Christian context of the first part of the third, that third section should end with a kind of parable in which the spirit of the Old Testament is strongly evident. The parable involves a dialogue in which Death asks a question and Man gives an answer:

> Vaste gouffre apporté dans l'amas de la brume
> Par l'irascible vent des mots qu'il n'a pas dits,
> Le néant à cet Homme aboli de jadis:
> "Souvenirs d'horizons, qu'est-ce, ô toi, que la Terre?"
> Hurle ce songe; et, voix dont la clarté s'altère,
> L'espace a pour jouet le cri: "Je ne sais pas!"   [31]

One part of the dialogue is upheld by all the elements of the universe, called largely as they are in Genesis: the "gouffre" and the "néant" (which are synonymous), the "amas de la brume," the "vent," the "horizons," the "Terre," finally "L'espace." Besides, there is throughout a kind of violence of expression that reminds one of the original chaos: "Vaste gouffre," "l'irascible vent," "Hurle ce songe," "L'espace a pour jouet le cri." As a final biblical element, but one which places the episode at a time after the Creation, the man who upholds the other part of the dialogue is Adam himself. It is he who is the "Homme aboli de jadis"; and the garden from which he was banished is twice mentioned later in the poem, at points where creation is in question, in "l'éden" of line 33 and in "les jardins de cet astre" of line 41. There is undoubtedly an etymological connection between them and "Adam" that accounts for the capital letters given to "Homme" and "Terre"; *adam,* in Hebrew, means both "earth" and "man," and this is of course a completely familiar etymology.

A re-establishment of the grammatical order of the sentence once again permits us to see the relationships among its parts: "Le néant, . . . Vaste gouffre, . . . Hurle ce songe: 'Souvenirs d'horizons . . .' à cet Homme; et [par] le cri [il répond]: 'Je ne sais pas!'" One of the advantages, structurally, of having the sentence begin with "Vaste gouffre" (which is in apposition to "Le néant" and like it means death) is that these words are thus brought into immediate proximity with "l'attente posthume"; the speaker denies, by his words, all the hopes contained in the man's formula, and the implicit irony of his statement is augmented. In the dense metaphorical modifier to "Vaste gouffre," only some of the elements are explicitly stated; the rest must be inferred by looking back at preceding parts of the text. Thus if the "mots qu'il n'a pas dits" refer directly to "muet," it is possible that "la brume" may be related to "aveugle" in the same line (23); and the "amas" would add the notion of an accumulation through time. Taken as a whole, "l'amas de la brume" would then mean a concentration of ignorance as well as a long amassing of geological time, and this meaning would be explained only later by reference to the poet's knowledge. We need to see, visually, the "amas de la brume" into which the wind blows a "vaste gouffre," a large but amorphous intrusion; metaphorically, we need to understand that into the mass of ancient ignorance enters death, in the person of the newly dead man, caused by his failure to speak. The wind of unspoken words is "irascible" or angry, if my interpretation be correct, precisely because the man has failed to speak.

He will fail to speak again, or will speak in an unsatisfactory manner, in the dialogue that ensues. But now the man is transformed into Man and Man into Adam through the specific biblical reference: "cet Homme aboli de jadis." Of him the "néant" asks a question; the speaker, however, says "hurle ce songe," since the question is asked angrily with some of the irascibility of the wind (and some of the violence of the biblical context), and since the question is more than simply that. "Ce songe" carries the implication that part of the answer to what is asked will be seen and known unclearly, will represent a reality imperfectly apprehended; and that part is the introduction to the question, "Souvenirs d'horizons." The man addressed, "ô toi," is told something as well as being asked something; he is told that he arrives in death accompanied by these "Souvenirs d'horizons," by memories of vistas that he has seen (if imperfectly) in life and that might help him to answer the question about to be put: "qu'est-ce . . . que la Terre?" Now the answer to so abstract a question ("la Terre" becomes all of the life led on Earth) would require knowledge of a kind that is not possessed by

"other men." Hence when he gives the only answer that he can, "Je
ne sais pas!" the dead man speaks in a voice "dont la clarté s'altère";
he has been, in life, both "aveugle et muet," he is now received into
the "brume," and therefore what clarity there might have been in his
voice is diminished. "Clarté" refers equally well to light and to
sound, to seeing and speaking, and "s'altère" is a kind of ironic
counterpart to "se transmuait"; the change hoped for by the man
does not come about, but only a change for the worse. The man's
despair at what actually does happen is indicated by the exclamation
point following "Je ne sais pas!" The speaker, besides, does not say,
"and the Man answers," but rather "L'espace a pour jouet le cri."
"Le cri," here, expresses fully the man's state of tragic disillusionment—he does not really become "le vierge héros"—and the fact
that his utterance is tossed about by space as a toy further intensifies
that state.

The net effect of the third section is to convince us, through a
series of observations and images and through an increasingly ironical tone, of the extent to which the "faux orgueil" of other men is ill
founded—and false. What happens to them in life and as they die
turns out to be the opposite of what they had pretended: ignorance
rather than knowledge, blindness rather than perception, silence
rather than speech. We are made to feel not only the weakness of
their beliefs but also the inferiority of their beliefs to the beliefs and
the reality of the poet. These are less intellectual conclusions on our
part with respect to them than an emotion of disdain and disparagement that increases in intensity through the section and reaches a
climax with the biblical parable at the end. Something of the wrath
of the speaker against the deaths of "other men" is shared by us, and
becomes the basis for the development of opposing feelings during
the part of the poem that will now follow.

From the very beginning of the following section, devoted to the
essential praise of the poet, it becomes clear that all the things said
about the poet will be contrary to those just said about "other men,"
and that we will hence move into a new range of positive, admiring
emotions. In a sense we are still in the biblical parable, still in the
context of Genesis; but we are now hearing about God rather than

about Man and about creation rather than about destruction. The
first four lines state that the God in question is the poet and that the
creation is his work:

> Le Maître, par un œil profond, a, sur ses pas,
> Apaisé de l'éden l'inquiète merveille
> Dont le frisson final, dans sa voix seule, éveille
> Pour la Rose et le Lys le mystère d'un nom. [35]

If the dignity of a capital letter is given to "Maître," it is in part to
make a parallel to "Homme" in line 29, in part to raise the poet (to
whom it refers) above other men and to make of him a god, a
Creator; and "Maître" will come to have, through the passage, the
meaning of creator. We have a vision of him walking through the
Garden of Eden ("sur ses pas") while the Creation was still incomplete and completing it in two ways: by the looks that he casts
about him ("par un œil profond") and by the giving of names to
the things already created but still nameless (just as Adam did in the
biblical account). These things he can do because of his two primary
gifts, of seeing and of speaking. Through the first of them he has
"Apaisé de l'éden l'inquiète merveille"; "Apaisé" may refer back to
the notions of violence and chaos—in a time before knowledge—and
surely refers forward to "inquiète" and "frisson." The miracle
("merveille") of Creation is thought of as bringing order into the
antecedent chaos through a series of motions or agitations. The
poet, as his eye penetrates the created universe, calms these motions
by bringing knowledge where only ignorance had existed. He
differs from the Man in not being "aveugle." Through his other gift,
opposed to the "muet" for the Man, the poet speaks ("dans sa voix
seule"), and by speaking provides the last motion ("le frisson final")
in the process of creation: "Le Maître . . . éveille / Pour la Rose et
le Lys le mystère d'un nom." We note that "Rose" and "Lys" are
also capitalized, bringing them into the same category of abstractions as "Homme" and "Maître," since they are not only these
particular flowers but all created objects in the universe; and that the
giving of names to things, which thereby completes their creation, is
a "mystère" belonging to the whole "merveille" of Creation itself.
Only the poet is adequate to this final step. Even the force respon-

sible for the rest of creation—and, in the light of what has been said before by the speaker, we do not even have to call upon the concept of God—was not capable of this culminating action. The praise of the poet could go no farther.

Having declared the extent and the powers of the poet's gifts contrasted with those of other men, the speaker now goes back to his original assumptions, the toast and the circumstances surrounding it. In three verses, each constituting a separate sentence, he asks another question and provides an answer, this time a definitive one. In the toast he used the formula, "fatal emblème," implying both a finality and a symbolic value for the death of Gautier. A first interpretation held, then, that the finality, the "fatal," meant the complete disappearance of the poet, his permanent "absence." This hypothesis was in a way strengthened by the claim of other men that they lived on in their "spectres futurs," and that in so doing they became superior to those who did not. But the pride was a false one, and what really happened to other men belied their expectations. Now the speaker, since he has found in the poet strengths that are opposed to the weaknesses of other men, asks whether his original statement about the poet might not have been mistaken:

> Est-il de ce destin rien qui demeure, non?   [36]

What gives to the question its special strength and effectiveness is the "non" at the end; for it completes the "rien" to make an essentially negative question and at the same time it repeats the earlier hypothesis contained in "l'enferme tout entier." The question is answered as it is being asked. "Ce destin" says much more than "cette vie," for example, would say, for it includes the extraordinary circumstances of a man who, by his gifts, is destined to complete the work of creating the universe.

In the next line, addressing all other men and perhaps all other poets, the speaker prepares to answer his question—and answers it in part:

> O vous tous, oubliez une croyance sombre.   [37]

The movement of the line, especially "O vous tous . . . ," recalls that of the very first line, "O . . . toi," and through it we return (after doubts and questions) to the exclamatory note of affirmation. The "croyance sombre" that all are to forget is the belief that the whole of the poet is buried in the porphyry tomb ("l'enferme tout entier"), that after his death "rien ne demeure." It is a "somber" belief because it would make of the poet's life and death something identical with those of other men as the speaker knows them, not as they conceive of them. It would, in a word, confuse the poet with "tous." But, as the speaker will declare in the next line, there is every reason for making a distinction:

Le splendide génie éternel n'a pas d'ombre.   [38]

It is his "génie" that distinguishes the poet from other men, both in life and in death, a genius that has just been described in terms of the "œil profond" and the "Voix." It has been called earlier, in a periphrasis, "la gloire ardente du métier." Since it is "éternel," it must last on beyond the death and burial of the poet; he, for one, is distinct from the "passants." The term "éternel" supposes, moreover, that there is for him no division of time into past, present, and future as there was for other men. The other epithet, applied to his genius, is "splendide," and to it we must give two meanings: as against "ombre," it means bright and shining, resplendent; and as against "foule hagarde" and "triste opacité," it denotes the kind of superiority already suggested by "la gloire ardente du métier" and by the three adjectives of line 16: "Magnifique, total et solitaire." In a word, it continues to make the association of bright light with the poet's peculiar quality (cf. 12–15). The same intention is present in the formula "n'a pas d'ombre." On the one hand, genius is so bright that only its light is visible, and there is no shadow; on the other hand, genius is immaterial, and what is immaterial casts no shadow. Finally, connecting the poet and other men, the poet has no "ombre" in the sense that he has no "apparition," while other men have both the "opacité" of their lives and the "spectres" of their death, which are other kinds of "ombres." As an answer to the question in line 36, "Le splendide génie éternel n'a pas d'ombre" affirms that something does remain of the poet's existence after his death, and that that something is his eternal genius and its products. These are immaterial and bright, in every sense.

The particular form of the survival is described in a long sentence that follows on the three crisp and detached verses and that states, in an involved and subtle way, how the act of creation (33–35) is perpetuated. This is the particular and precise answer to the question, and although the sentence that gives it is complex, the answer is simple enough: "je veux voir . . . Survivre . . . Une agitation . . . De paroles." We thus move forward a step in the general development of the argument: unlike other men, the poet does not die entirely, nor does he survive himself as a spirit or a ghost; instead, not only do his verses assure him a life after death, but they assure the objects of which he writes an eternal existence. Part of the long sentence relates to his verses, part to their objects. But the first line relates to the speaker himself and states that what is to follow is his own conception:

> Moi, de votre désir soucieux, je veux voir . . .   [39]

The "Moi" is that of the speaker, already identified as a poet ("mon vers sacré," 22) and as one of the participants in the celebration, and if he emphasizes it now again it is in order to stress the difference between what he is about to say and what other men think. He further strengthens in this way the "je" that is the subject of the sentence. The verb itself, "veux voir," expresses a strong volition to put upon the realities of the case a personal construction that opposes that of other men; and it is significant that "voir" should be used rather than "say" or "know" since seeing is the poet's particular way of knowing and since all that will now be said will be translated into terms of seeing. Addressing now not Gautier but those who might have had some doubts about his survival—or rather some fear that the poet might not survive—the speaker says: "de votre désir soucieux." "Votre" refers to the "vous tous" of line 37, "désir" to the anticipated negative answer to the question in line 36 (they fear a negative answer, desire an affirmative one), and "soucieux" expresses the speaker's concern with giving an answer that will do justice to the poet and that will satisfy his admirers.

In the condensed version of the sentence that I gave a while back, "Survivre" depended directly upon "je veux voir"; and so it should. But the real subject of "Survivre" is not the poet but a thing, and the poet is "survived by" that thing; hence he is related to the verb through an "à" construction introducing the next two lines:

> A qui s'évanouit, hier, dans le devoir
> Idéal que nous font les jardins de cet astre . . .   [41]

"Qui" designates the poet and "s'évanouit" his death—his death seen both as a kind of temporary loss of his state of existence and (coupled with "dans le devoir") as a result of the burdens of that existence. The time indicated, "hier," is that of his death; it is needed to place in their proper chronology his entombment and the toast or festival of celebration, and also the contemporaneous events in the survival; it is also needed to place in relief the timelessness of the survival. "Le devoir" is the same as the poet's "métier" (12), now elevated to the status of a responsibility—he must complete the work of creation—and imposed upon him from without ("que nous font") by the created universe itself ("les jardins de cet astre"). The last formula generalizes the notion of "l'éden" (33) through the plural of "les jardins," thereby making it include all the material objects resulting from the creation—thus the whole of the physical universe—and it designates in another way the "Terre" of line 29. The poet knows what this Earth is and he is under an obligation to say so. All other poets are equally, the duty is imposed on all; and so the "nous" of line 41. Finally, the duty is said to be "Idéal" because it consists in ideas and words and immaterial things; and it is opposed directly to the "Je ne sais pas!" of other men.

After the interruption of his sentence by the reference to the poet, the speaker completes the main clause with a section of a little more than two verses:

> Survivre pour l'honneur du tranquille désastre
> Une agitation solennelle par l'air
> De paroles . . .   [44]

Once again, there is a wilful confusion of sight and sound, of the seeing of things and the saying of words; for the speaker wishes to "voir . . . Survivre . . . Une agitation . . . De paroles." In this sense, the "agitation" would be a visible movement of the air, the "paroles" causing the movement would be heard; but what is really seen is the object represented by the word, as the speaker will say in subsequent clauses. The movement is "solennelle" because of its importance in the whole process of creation and because of the special quality it gives to the poet. That is also the general import of the phrase, "pour l'honneur du tranquille désastre," where the "désastre" must be the poet's death itself and "tranquille" (taking up again "s'évanouit") refers to the purely material silencing of the poet and the cessation of his physical motion. The survival will do honor to death and to the poet, since it will make of death a passage to the greater glory of the poet, where what is really important remains and only the unimportant passes.

In the verses that conclude the sentence and the section, there is a similar transposition of the words and the objects they represent; thus one may see the words and speak of them in terms of color and form:

> De paroles, pourpre ivre et grand calice clair,
> Que, pluie et diamant, le regard diaphane
> Resté là sur ces fleurs dont nulle ne se fane,
> Isole parmi l'heure et le rayon du jour! [47]

At the beginning of the section the speaker had said that, as his part of the work of creation, the poet had provided "Pour la Rose et le Lys le mystère d'un nom" (35). It is therefore possible for him now to put in apposition with the "paroles" that survive, the phrase, "pourpre ivre et grand calice clair," where the Rose is represented by the first image, the Lily by the second. Both images have overtones of feeling that move towards the final exclamation of the sentence, "pourpre ivre" suggesting warmth and abandon (and possibly the passion of love) and "grand calice clair" suggesting coolness and dignity (and possibly religious sentiments). In the construction of the remaining three lines, "Que" relates to "agitation" as its most conspicuous antecedent, making for the following relationships: "je veux voir . . . Une agitation . . . Que . . . le regard . . . Isole." The glance of those who look, comparable to the "œil profond" of the poet, rests upon the movement of the air, really the movement of the objects in the air. Since this glance penetrates and sees through the objects, it is called "diaphane," and since (at the same time) it rests upon the objects (or flowers) like something which may be seen through, "pluie et diamant" are placed in apposition to it. To the visual images of the rose and the lily is added the glistening and sparkling quality of rain and diamonds that might be standing on them. The penetrating glance, equivalent to the word, separates these objects from the rest of existence and takes them out of time; thus "Isole parmi l'heure et le rayon du jour!" Simultaneously, the glance makes the object eternal like the poet's genius: "le regard . . . Resté là sur ces fleurs dont nulle ne se fane."

The whole of the sentence, contorted and interrupted though it may be, produces an idea and an emotion that are relatively clear. The idea consists in the final justification of the poet through his contribution to the eternity of the objects of which he speaks: the Rose and the Lily, because of the names that he gives them, become everlasting and never fade. The emotion of the speaker as he exclaims upon this feat is one of admiration, accompanied by an optimistic rejection of any feeling that might link sadness or doubt with the poet's death. The reader shares this admiration, which is augmented by the brilliant visual images that he is made to see along with the central concepts presented.

There remains still, after the completion of the basic argument, the task of realizing all the probabilities connected with the original assumption of a toast and of a feast of commemoration. That task is assigned to the concluding verses of the poem. They constitute a final section, shorter than the others (except for the first), and filled with references to earlier parts of the poem; for the difference between the initial description of the "fête" and the final one lies in what has happened during the intervening sections. The "tombeau" of the original setting will reappear as the "sépulcre," transformed now into a tributary monument to the poet's genius; and to it will be added another, less material monument in the form of the poet's achievement. It is the latter that is designated in the opening verses:

> C'est de nos vrais bosquets déjà tout le séjour,
> Où le poëte pur a pour geste humble et large
> De l'interdire au rêve, ennemi de sa charge . . .　　　[50]

The place indicated by the introductory "C'est" is unclear; it might be, if the reference is to what immediately precedes, the "heure" and the "rayon du jour" in which stand the objects eternalized by the poet's words. In a more general way, it might merely be the place where the poet's spirit, as it lives on in his verses, now resides. In any case, "le séjour . . . de nos vrais bosquets" should be read as meaning not "the place where our true woods sojourn," but the "sojourn constituted by our true woods." "Nos vrais bosquets" insists on the "nos" of the poets, as distinguished again from other men, as it refers once more to "les jardins de cet astre" (41) and to "l'éden" (33); but it makes a distinction between them and the gardens which belong only to the poets, those of verbal creation. In this sense, "vrais." For the significance of "déjà," we must recall "hier" (40), time of the poet's death, to realize how quickly is accomplished his passage to an eternal artistic life; the other monument to him will also be raised "le matin de son repos" (51). And "tout le séjour" is clarified by "tout ce qui nuit" in line 55: all the spiritual side of the poet "survives" in his works; all the material side is buried in the sepulchre.

There is perhaps, in "le séjour . . . de nos vrais bosquets," a suggestion of a kind of place where dwell the dead poets, like the Elysian Fields of dead heroes; if so, the pagan milieu of the early lines would once again be recalled. The poet is pictured as present there, "le poète" of line 49 confirming the "nos" of line 48, in a state qualified as "pur." From what follows, "pur" may be taken to mean "immaterial and spiritual only," purified of "tout ce qui nuit" (55). Since the adjective has been used previously in connection with the sun, "du pur soleil mortel," and since there the sun was the source and the final goal of the poet's genius, we have an interplay of ideas associated with "séjour" and with "pur." The poet's supposed activity after death is described: "[il] a pour geste humble et large / De l'interdire au rêve." The antecedent of "l'interdire" is "le séjour," and the poet thereby becomes a guardian or protector of his dwelling place against an enemy, a guarantor of its purity. While the celebrants are accomplishing their ritual, the poet too, in a movement parallel to "Le rite est pour les mains," makes the "geste humble et large"; "humble" contrasts with "le faux orgueil des hommes" (17) and with "fier" for the passer-by (23), while "large" repeats the qualities given to the poet in line 16, especially the

"Magnifique." His act consists in warding off "le rêve," everything that would be vague and unclear, that would be unlike the hardness of line and the precision of image found in the descriptions of the preceding section. In the poet's own domain, he sees with complete clarity and speaks with perfect accuracy. This is his "charge," his "métier" (12) and his "devoir" (40), and the dream would be in every sense an "ennemi de sa charge."

If, in his after-death sojourn, the poet accomplishes well his mission (which is the same that he fulfills during his life), he will be honored on earth by the tribute of his fellow poets, perhaps of all men. The cause-and-effect relationship is indicated by the "Afin que" which introduces the concluding lines of the poem:

> Afin que le matin de son repos altier,
> Quand la mort ancienne est comme pour Gautier
> De n'ouvrir pas les yeux sacrés et de se taire,
> Surgisse, de l'allée ornement tributaire,
> Le sépulcre solide où gît tout ce qui nuit,
> Et l'avare silence et la massive nuit.   [56]

This is the re-evocation of the tomb and the monument. But now it is possible for the speaker to make a distinction that he could not earlier have made: whereas, at the beginning, he had said that "ce beau monument l'enferme tout entier," implying that nothing of the poet survived, he has now pursued his argument to the point where he knows that what is in the tomb is merely "tout ce qui nuit." Something does survive, and this is what the poet has produced through his genius; and to it will be erected the tributary monument. That will occur "le matin de son repos," and we are once again reminded of the sequence of events involved throughout the poem. Besides, we are told that the tribute will follow immediately upon the poet's death. If his death (called a "repos" in contradistinction to the "horreur" of the death of other men) is "altier," it is for other reasons than the ones that explain the pride of other men. There are, as I have pointed out, the two prides: "un soir fier" (14) expresses the pride of the evening—the sun, "cet astre"—in the gifts and the accomplishments of the poet, which is the same noble pride as that attributed to the poet himself in "altier." It differs in every respect from the "faux orgueil" of other men, the "fierté" of the passer-by; for this is based on ignorance, blindness, and deafness linked with silence, while the poet knows, sees, and speaks.

These last six verses make a simple subordinate clause as follows: "Afin que le matin . . . Surgisse . . . Le sépulcre." "Le matin" is modified by the two lines that follow, as is indicated by the "Quand," and these have as their purpose to state what death really means for such as Gautier. Death is said to be "ancienne," in spite of the fact that the time is the morning after the poet's death, because it is now the universal death that has come to all men; it is the death of the "heure commune de la cendre." Its particular quality in this particular case is introduced by the restrictive "comme pour Gautier," where the death of poets is differentiated from that of other men. (The rhyme "altier : Gautier" carries reminiscences of an Old French rhyme with such a form as "Galtier" or "Gualtier.") For such as he, death means only the cessation of those physical faculties that were his special gifts, seeing and speaking. The "œil profond" (32) will no longer see: "De n'ouvrir pas les yeux sacrés"; "sacrés" at once places the poet in an extraordinary position because of his capacity to see and to know, and it relates him to all other poets through the "vers sacré" (22) of the poet-speaker. His special voice, "sa voix seule," the only one capable of giving names to the things of creation, will no longer speak: "et de se taire." These two capacities, possessed by the poet to the exclusion of other men, will no longer be able to contribute to the process of creation; the sacred function will cease.

But in tribute to it, the tributary monument will be raised—or will arise of itself: "Surgisse . . . Le sépulcre." Through "Surgisse," the speaker gives the idea of the sudden materialization of the monument; he also recalls the notion of an "apparition" of line 4, although what "appears" will be essentially different. This suggestion is reinforced by the fact that the monument is called "de l'allée ornement tributaire": in the earlier passage, the "apparition" was related to the "magique espoir du corridor"; now, the monument arises as an "ornement . . . de l'allée." "Ornement" repeats the general feeling of "un soir fier d'y descendre," while "tributaire" summarizes the whole sense of debt that the other poets who are celebrants in the rite—and all men—feel toward the dead Gautier. Furthermore, the quality attributed to the sepulchre, "solide," summarizes the traits originally associated with the tomb: "un lieu de porphyre," "le fer épais des portes." Like the poet's body and his physical faculties, the monument is a purely material object, and as such it may bear permanent witness to the admiration of all men for his talents. The tomb encloses the body only, only that which might have been considered as limiting the realization of his capabilities: "Où gît tout ce qui nuit" (the idea is not without Platonic overtones). All that is harmful, indeed, is the loss of the poet's special gifts: "De n'ouvrir pas les yeux sacrés et de se taire"; and this loss is paraphrased in the closing words of *Toast funèbre:* "Et l'avare silence et la massive nuit." Silence and night as against speech and the seeing that depends upon light. Thus all the images of sound and of light, of speaking or naming and of seeing, that had been associated with the poet in the fourth section of the poem (and that had there been the result of a long anterior development) are reduced to their opposites in the final line. The silence is "avare" in contrast with the creative generosity of the poet's speech, and the night (like "l'amas de la brume") is "massive" because it completely prevents the seeing or the knowing of any object.

There is, in the final section, something that very closely resembles the resolution of a plot in a narrative or a dramatic poem. The argument has long since been terminated: questions have been asked and answered, doubts have been raised and allayed. But alongside the argument, throughout the poem, we have noted a kind of conflict between the two forms of being of the poet, between the body or the material self and the genius or the spiritual self. (It would be improper, for the latter, to say "soul," since that would imply a Christian context that is by no means intended.) In the speaker's first thoughts, the whole of the poet was entombed in the monument, except for the vague return of the "gloire du métier" to its source in the sun. This idea was differentiated from that of other men, who thought of themselves as having a double fate, with the body being interred and the immortal soul passing to another existence. What the speaker ultimately discovers is that the poet, too, has a kind of dual destiny: his words and the special reality that he makes live on, while only his body dies and is buried. Even this partial death is not to be considered as a cause of regret or sadness; for the poet himself, and the speaker, and those who listen to the speaker, add to their admiration a kind of quiet joy in the knowledge that what was really great and wonderful in the poet will survive eternally. This feeling is perhaps enhanced by its juxtaposition to the contempt felt and expressed for the lot of other men. The poet is singled out for a final distinction and a final tribute; and in the concluding section the separation between his two selves is made in a way to direct our feelings toward the happy ending and away from its doleful accompaniments.

We may properly ask whether, in the feelings that are aroused by *Toast funèbre,* there are any that are peculiarly appropriate to Théophile Gautier and to the death of Théophile Gautier; whether the poem might not, with a few minor changes, serve equally well as a tribute to any other poet; or whether there are elements, in the very fabric of the poem, that evoke the special genius and the special art of the author of *Émaux et camées.* From what I have said so far, only Gautier's name in the rhyme at line 52 would explicitly identify the subject of the toast, the celebration, and the argument. The structure of the argument itself and of the dramatic conflict and resolution does not of course reflect any personal reference—structures never do—and remains entirely general. Yet Mallarmé was writing about a poet whom he knew well and admired intensely, for a volume of verses the contributors to which were all admirers of Gautier, and for a public of readers for whom the cult of Gautier was an old and revered habit. Would Mallarmé, in such circumstances, have written a poem in which the only "circumstantial" allusion occurred in the single appearance of a name?

My feeling is that, on the contrary, *Toast funèbre* is rich in witnesses to what we might think of as the presence of Gautier in the poem; and these are such witnesses as would be recognized only by the celebrants in a ritual commemorating an intimate friend. The intimate friend is Gautier's poetry rather than Gautier himself. I do not mean that the poem is full of sources and analogues and parallels to Gautier's poetry, and I have no intention to engage in a frenzied hunt for such passages. Rather, I wish to point to a few properties of

Gautier's poetic work that Mallarmé might have had in mind as he wrote his tribute. Foremost of these is the dominantly visual quality of Gautier's art: not only the innumerable poems in which painters and paintings are the subjects, but Gautier's constant effort to paint with words, to describe and delineate, to transpose from the one art to the other. Perhaps one should speak of the visual arts in general, of enamels and cameos and sculptures as well as of paintings, in connection with Gautier's choice of subject matters and with the kind of hard and brilliant image that he attempted to achieve. This visual quality is not unrelated, I think, to two aspects of *Toast funèbre:* first, that one of the gifts attributed to the poet is the "œil profond," the "yeux sacrés," the "regard diaphane" that make him different from all other men; second, that Mallarmé himself attempts the Gautieresque image at places in the poem where it would have special significance. In line 44, "pourpre ivre et grand calice clair," the paraphrases for the Rose and the Lily are made to stand meta-phorically for the words that Gautier had written; in themselves they create the kind of visual impression that Gautier was fond of, especially when they are followed by "pluie et diamant" and by the idea contained in "Isole parmi l'heure et le rayon du jour."

Another form of reference to Gautier consists in the general con-ception that Mallarmé here presents of the poet and his function. To a degree that conception is inherent in the total subject, in the toast that praises a particular poet and through him all poets. Gautier's work is full of self-conscious glorifications of the poet; in such a poem as "Compensation" (in the *Poésies diverses, 1833–1838*) there are both ideas and words that recur in *Toast funèbre*. I cite the first half of it:

> Il naît sous le soleil de nobles créatures
> Unissant ici-bas tout ce qu'on peut rêver,
> Corps de fer, cœur de flamme, admirables **natures.**
>
> Dieu semble les produire afin de se prouver;
> Il prend, pour les pétrir, une argile plus douce,
> Et souvent passe un siècle à les parachever.
>
> Il met, comme un sculpteur, l'empreinte de son pouce
> Sur leurs fronts rayonnant de la gloire des cieux,
> Et l'ardente auréole en gerbe d'or y pousse.

Ces hommes-là s'en vont, calmes et radieux,
Sans quitter un instant leur pose solennelle,
Avec l'œil immobile et le maintien des dieux.

Leur moindre fantaisie est une œuvre éternelle,
Tout cède devant eux; les sables inconstants
Gardent leurs pas empreints, comme un airain fidèle.

Ne leur donnez qu'un jour ou donnez-leur cent ans,
L'orage ou le repos, la palette ou le glaive:
Ils mèneront à bout leurs destins éclatants.

Another such glorification is found in "La Bonne Journée" of the same collection, from which I cite a few verses:

.   .   .   .

Mon front se lève en haut avec moins de pâleur;
Un sourire d'orgueil sur mes lèvres rayonne,
Et mon souffle pressé plus fortement résonne.
J'ai rempli mon devoir comme un brave ouvrier.

.   .   .   .

J'ai poursuivi mon œuvre avec religion,
L'œuvre de mon amour qui, mort, me fera vivre.

These are, of course, commonplaces in the period; but the fact that they are made to re-echo from Gautier's works in a work about Gautier is perhaps significant.

We might say the same about certain thoughts and expressions of Gautier concerning death and the after-life: our memories are stirred as we rediscover them in *Toast funèbre*. In the collection of the *Poésies, 1830–1832,* the piece called "La Tête de mort" contains these verses:

A présent jeune encor, mais certain que notre âme,
Inexplicable essence, insaisissable flamme,
Une fois exhalée, en nous tout est néant,
Et que rien ne ressort de l'abîme béant
Où vont, tristes jouets du temps, nos destinées.

The following two stanzas are from Section IX of *La Comédie de la Mort:*

Je sors d'entre les mains d'une Mort plus avare
Que celle qui veillait au tombeau de Lazare;
    Elle garde son bien:
Elle lâche le corps, mais elle retient l'âme;
Elle rend le flambeau, mais elle éteint la flamme,
    Et Christ n'y pourrait rien.

Je ne suis plus, hélas! que l'ombre de moi-même,
Que la tombe vivante où gît tout ce que j'aime,
    Et je me survis seul;
Je promène avec moi les dépouilles glacées
De mes illusions, charmantes trépassées
    Dont je suis le linceul.

I cite the whole of a short poem entitled "L'Aveugle," from *Émaux et camées:*

Un aveugle au coin d'une borne,
Hagard comme au jour un hibou,
Sur son flageolet, d'un air morne,
Tâtonne en se trompant de trou,

Et joue un ancien vaudeville
Qu'il fausse imperturbablement;
Son chien le conduit par la ville,
Spectre diurne à l'œil dormant.

Les jours sur lui passent sans luire;
Sombre, il entend le monde obscur
Et la vie invisible bruire
Comme un torrent derrière un mur.

Dieu sait quelles chimères noires
Hantent cet opaque cerveau!
Et quels illisibles grimoires
L'idée écrit en ce caveau!

Ainsi dans les puits de Venise,
Un prisonnier à demi fou,
Pendant sa nuit qui s'éternise,
Grave des mots avec un clou.

Mais peut-être aux heures funèbres,
Quand la mort souffle le flambeau,
L'âme habituée aux ténèbres
Y verra clair dans le tombeau!

Finally, in "Bûchers et tombeaux" (also in *Émaux et camées*), there is an extended comparison of pagan and Christian burial which may be reflected, if slightly, in the organization of the first parts of *Toast funèbre*.

As an additional kind of echoing, I might point to a number of figures and words, of rhymes and sonorities, that seem to link *Toast funèbre* with the poetry of its subject. Some of these are a standard part of the baggage of Gautier's contemporaries, and in themselves they would be of little interest; but in association with the other links that I have mentioned, they may improve the case that I am making for a wilful recalling, on Mallarmé's part, of the corpus of Gautier's poetry. I quoted, earlier, some verses from Section IX of *La Comédie de la Mort;* the same section contains other passages that will have a familiar sound after a reading of Mallarmé's poem:

> Je n'ai pas eu le temps de bâtir la colonne
> Où la Gloire viendra suspendre ma couronne.
> . . . .
> J'ai dit aux belles fleurs, doux honneur du parterre,
> Au lis majestueux ouvrant son blanc cratère,
>   A la tulipe d'or,
> A la rose de mai que le rossignol aime . . .
> . . . .
> Air vierge, air de cristal, eau, principe du monde,
> Terre qui nourris tout, et toi, flamme féconde,
>   Rayon de l'œil de Dieu . . .
> . . . .
>   Vos pleurs de diamant.

The rhyme of "diaphane" and "fane" in "La Rose-thé" (*Émaux et camées*); the fact that in "Inès de las Sierras" we have this image: "D'un long corridor en décombres . . . débusque un fantôme charmant" and that this phantom is later called an "apparition fantasque," are other examples of this sort of tributary quotation.

I speak of these various manifestations of the "presence of Gautier's poetry" in *Toast funèbre* at this particular point, and before I answer certain other questions, because I think it necessary to do so in connection with the effect produced by the poem and with the structure that produces it. For our feelings (or the effect) will depend in some degree on our capacity to relate the poem, or certain parts of it, to Gautier: to make of it a particular celebration of Gautier as well as a general celebration of all poets. If we hear through the lyric certain echoes of Gautier's poetry, then the words and the lines that produce those echoes will have a richer significance for us, a meaning beyond the literal or even the structural meaning. I think it possible that Mallarmé may have wished to add an allusive technique of this kind to the other devices employed in the composition of *Toast funèbre*. This would be quite different from the allusive technique of later poets such as Eliot, since it would propose to bring into the context of the poem images and ideas and feelings derived from the works of a single poet, rather than divers literary texts useful for various reasons at various points in the new poem.

I do not wish to imply, however, that these allusions ever become a predominant element—or that the poem becomes a pastiche of Gautier. Far from it; for the totality of the impression is completely distinct from the one that we get from any poem of Gautier's. Mallarmé's art is of a different order. The sentence that, in Gautier, was simple and direct, becomes in Mallarmé contorted and indirect, interrupted by insertions and prolonged by derivative or associated ideas. The word that, in Gautier, had its normal and even commonplace meaning, in Mallarmé takes on all kinds of special and even obscure senses, determined usually by the structure of the poem into which it is integrated. (We may think, for example, of "diaphane" which, in "La Rose-thé," means "that which is seen through": "Son tissu rose et diaphane"; whereas "le regard diaphane" in *Toast funèbre* gives to it the meaning of "that which sees through.") The simile that, in Gautier, brought into relationship things between which the relationship was obvious, is replaced in Mallarmé by the obscure metaphor—obscure because the continuum between the two objects is not immediately apparent. The reader must participate through his own perception of the bases for the comparison; and in the same way he must discover the special meanings of the words and the proper parsing of the sentences.

Most of all, the reader must either sense or understand the overall development of the poem, its structure. The individual line will make its proper impression only after he has integrated it into the totality of the work. I pointed out, at the beginning, the difficulties involved in the interpretation of the first verse of *Toast funèbre,* the toast itself: "O de notre bonheur, toi, le fatal emblème!" Those problems are not fully resolved until the whole of the poem has been embraced and ordered by the reader's sensitivity. He must realize, as he goes along, that "notre" refers specifically to poets rather than to all men; that "bonheur" has a special meaning as connected with the destiny of poets, which is to die only in the material sense while they live on through the works of their genius, and that part of their destiny and their "bonheur" consists in their possession of extraordinary gifts; that "toi" is to be taken as very particularly relating to the form of those gifts as they existed in Gautier and as they are reflected in his poetry; that Gautier is an "emblème" or a symbol both of the gifts of poets and of their lot; that he is a "fatal emblème" because he is now dead and because the nature of his death distinguishes him from other men just as his gifts and his life distinguished him from other men. The whole of the juxtaposition of the poet to "other men"—and the argument that springs from it— is presupposed in "notre." The unmitigated glory and the "splendide génie éternel" of the poet are announced in "bonheur." "Toi" is not only a form of address, but it is a direct evocation of Gautier who will be indirectly evoked at various points in the poem. The extensive opposition of two concepts of death has its source in "fatal," while the lengthy argument leading to the conclusions about the poet's death and life is a development from the notion of "emblème."

Toast funèbre, seen as a total poetic structure, really offers no new or extraordinary features of organization. It is ordered essentially as an argument, proceeding through successive logical steps to a conclusion. The argument itself necessitates an opposition between the poet and other men, and that opposition is fully exploited. It is accompanied, also, by a kind of dramatic conflict between the body and the spirit of the poet, resolved at the end through the triumph of the spirit. And through all this there are hints that what is being said is equally germane to poets in general and to the specific genius of Théophile Gautier. These various structural elements, all interrelated and intertwined, are of course not visible on the surface of the poem; we know them only as we penetrate, through feeling and knowledge, far below the surface. The surface, instead, presents a series of highly evocative (if sometimes enigmatic) images, of passionate expressions either of admiration or of contempt, of apostrophes to the dead Gautier. Had these been said in a banal or a traditional way, they would undoubtedly have achieved some of the effect and aroused some of the emotions that we do find in the poem. Said as they are in Mallarmé's own special way, with all the subtle allusions and inferences, they produce an incomparably vigorous effect. That effect, moreover, grows increasingly poignant as we work downward from the surface to its foundations, to the meanings and the feelings that we ourselves need to ferret out. If, in such a poem as *Toast funèbre,* Mallarmé makes a contribution to the development of the techniques of modern poetry, it is not by the exploitation of new structural possibilities but rather by the way in which he clothes a traditional structure in devices of language and expression that are both individual and inventive.

9

Mallarmé

Le Tombeau d'Edgar Poe

Like *Toast funèbre,* another of Mallarmé's memorial pieces, *Le Tombeau d'Edgar Poe,* is constructed in a traditional way on the basis of a simple opposition of two concepts. The processes of development and expression of the opposed elements are similar. If anything, the sonnet on Poe is more hermetic than the long lyric on Gautier, more difficult of interpretation, possibly because of its greater density and conciseness. So much meaning in condensed within the restricted limits of the sonnet that each word and each phrase is asked to bear an extraordinarily large share of sense and of suggestiveness. In reading *Le Tombeau d'Edgar Poe,* the critic must strive to clarify its meaning by identifying all of the senses and all of the suggestions; but he must avoid the kind of misreading or of over-reading that consists in forcing into the poem meanings from outside sources that are not justified by the context of the poem itself.

Le Tombeau d'Edgar Poe

Tel qu'en Lui-même enfin l'éternité le change,
Le Poëte suscite avec un glaive nu
Son siècle épouvanté de n'avoir pas connu
Que la mort triomphait dans cette voix étrange!   4

This is a revision of an essay published in *L'Esprit Créateur* (I, 1961, pp. 117–24) under the title "A Suggested Reading of *Le Tombeau d'Edgar Poe.*"

Eux, comme un vil sursaut d'hydre oyant jadis l'ange
Donner un sens plus pur aux mots de la tribu,
Proclamèrent très haut le sortilège bu
Dans le flot sans honneur de quelque noir mélange.   8

Du sol et de la nue hostiles, ô grief!
Si notre idée avec ne sculpte un bas-relief
Dont la tombe de Poe éblouissante s'orne,   11

Calme bloc ici-bas chu d'un désastre obscur,
Que ce granit du moins montre à jamais sa borne
Aux noirs vols du Blasphème épars dans le futur.   14

Perhaps the first attempt to explain publicly the meaning of *Le Tombeau d'Edgar Poe* was made by Jules Lemaître. In an article dated October 18, 1888,[1] he gave the following paraphrase of the recently published sonnets:

> Redevenu vraiment lui-même, tel qu'enfin l'éternité nous le montre, le poète, de l'éclair de son glaive nu, réveille et avertit son siècle, épouvanté de ne s'être pas aperçu que sa voix étrange était la grande voix de la Mort (*ou* que nul n'a dit mieux que lui les choses de la Mort).
>
> La foule, qui d'abord avait sursauté comme une hydre en entendant cet ange donner un sens nouveau et plus pur aux mots du langage vulgaire, proclama très haut que le sortilège qu'il nous jetait, il l'avait puisé dans l'ignoble ivresse des alcools ou des absinthes.
>
> O crime de la terre et du ciel! Si, avec les images qu'il nous a suggérées, nous ne pouvons sculpter un bas-relief dont se pare sa tombe éblouissante,
>
> Que du moins ce granit, calme bloc pareil à l'aérolithe qu'a jeté sur terre quelque désastre mystérieux, marque la borne où les blasphèmes futurs des ennemis du poète viendront briser leur vol noir.

Like Lemaître's paraphrase, the "exegeses" of modern critics (I think of Charles Chassé's "interprétation objective"[2] and of Gardner Davies' "exégèse raisonnée"[3]) have sought primarily to discover a meaning. But whereas Lemaître remained silent on his devices of discovery, the modern critics (we never remain silent!) indicated theirs most specifically: Chassé, his reference to Mallarmé's

[1] *Les Contemporains*, V, 43–48.
[2] "Essai d'une interprétation du *Tombeau d'Edgar Poe*," *Revue de littérature comparée*, XXIII (1949), 97–109.
[3] *Les "Tombeaux" de Mallarmé* (Paris, 1950), 89–114.

own translation of an earlier version; Davies, his use of other passages in Mallarmé to specify the meanings of individual words in the sonnet.

My own intention here is different. I mean to seek the total structure of the poem as the cause of its total effect, and I shall use a different device: that kind of self-definition and self-determination which every well constructed poem provides to the reader who considers it as a self-contained entity.

It seems clear from a reading—multiple readings—of the sonnet that the essential emotion aroused by it is rather one of anger at Poe's times for having misjudged him than of admiration for Poe himself. Not that the latter emotion is not developed in the poem, but it is exploited largely as a means to augmenting and emphasizing the anger. To this end the object of anger must be distinguished, and the reasons for being angry with it must be stated: the object, those people in Poe's day who disdained and condemned him; the reasons, their failure to recognize him for what he really was and their incapacity to do so. This leads to a basic opposition in the poem:

the people : Poe.

But since Poe was in reality and at all times one and the same—himself—and since the people's error was limited by his lifetime, another basic opposition emerges:

the past : the present and future.

The moment that separates the past from the present and future is the moment of Poe's death.

Structurally, the poem consists in an elaboration of the two sides of this opposition, in the attaching to each side of images and epithets and ideas, in a way to state as vigorously and as clearly as possible the nature of the objects. Emotionally, the poem proceeds by attaching to each side of the opposition, in a careful progression, the proper state of feeling: to the past, the basic anger; to the present and future, the admiration that should have been present in the past, whose absence there is the reason for the anger.

The first line, "Tel qu'en Lui-même enfin l'éternité le change," at once states the opposition and establishes a first ingredient of the emotion. If we start with the word "change," we learn of that act of transition from past to present which brought the "Poëte" from a state which was not properly his own (a false opinion about him) to a proper state: "en Lui-même." The agent of this change is Death, "l'éternité." Already, several things have happened with respect to the emotion. Through the capital letter of "Lui-même" the desirable nature of the change has been suggested, and at the same time, the poet has taken on his dual nature as a particular being (Poe) and as a universal being (the Poet). The fact that the agent is "l'éternité"— not yet "la mort"—contributes to this approving and admiring attitude toward the change. This attitude is enhanced by the presence, at the emphatic caesura, of "enfin," indicating that the change had been long desired before it was accomplished. "Tel que" points to the present status and indicates that the whole line is a modifier of "Le Poëte" in the next line. To this point, we are entirely on the "right" side of the opposition, with respect both to the objects and to the emotions:

> : Tel que
> Lui-même
> enfin
> éternité
> change.

The next lines present the poet, as now changed by death, in an act of revenge upon his guilty contemporaries: "Le Poëte suscite avec un glaive nu / Son siècle . . ." Two things should be noted at once: first, that an act performed by the poet after death must be due to an agency other than his mortal, material self; second, that this act, in death, brings life or an awakening to the men of his time. The first accounts both for the fact that the "Poëte" is capitalized (with the meaning already noted) and for the introduction of that supernatural instrument, the "glaive," which will later be associated with that other-essence of the poet, "l'ange." Moreover, the epithet "nu," adding a visual quality to the sword along with an indication of its efficacy, presents half of another opposition to be exploited later: the quality of light (cf., later, "éblouissante") as against that of darkness (cf., later, "noir" and "noirs"). The second element gives us our first qualification of the poet's times:

"suscite" supposes that these men were, before the act, dead or asleep, and "Son siècle" gives to them a finite quality opposed to the "éternité" of the poet. New items are thus added to the opposition, and for the first time some of them are on the "left" side:

Son siècle : Le Poëte
[dead or asleep] : suscite
[a dark object] : glaive nu.

With respect to the emotion, the admiration for "Lui-même" is enhanced by his identification as "Le Poëte" and by his shining arm, as well as by his awakening or life-giving act; and we have the first suggestions of a disapproval of a century that needs to be "suscité."

That disapproval grows with the characterization of the century in the words, ". . . épouvanté de n'avoir pas connu." Present and past are here again juxtaposed (in an order reversed from the preceding) as two attributes are given to the "siècle," that is, present horror at the discovery of past ignorance. "Connu" must here have primarily the meaning of "reconnu," and the awakening takes the form of a recognition. The last line of the quatrain (one of the two really difficult lines of the sonnet) tells us what constituted ignorance and recognition: "Que la mort triomphait dans cette voix étrange!" I think that we can appreciate all the implications of the line only if we consider it strictly in terms of what has gone before in the quatrain, of the oppositions already established. "La mort" has already appeared as "l'éternité" and we know its meaning for the poet; "triomphait" summarizes at once all the activity previously noted, the "change" for the poet, the "suscite" for the century and the horror and the recognition brought to it. The poet, in death, triumphs over the enemy. "Cette voix étrange" is a paraphrase for "Le Poëte," whom it describes as the century had seen him. What the century now recognizes is that the "strange voice," which it had defeated in life, was to triumph in death. (This is a meaning essentially different from Lemaître's.) The opposition of the first quatrain is thus completed—

: la mort
triomphait
cette voix étrange—

in a way to augment the admiration associated with the poet and the disapproval associated with the "siècle."

While the first quatrain is constructed largely as a set of revelations about the poet, with some secondary indications about the "siècle," the proportions are reversed in the second quatrain: it is mostly about the century. Yet, its components are ones that have already been introduced, but are now expanded, clarified, made more vivid. Thus, the first two lines, "Eux, comme un vil sursaut d'hydre oyant jadis l'ange / Donner un sens plus pur aux mots de la tribu," are built entirely upon the original opposition: the "siècle" is resolved into "Eux" and "la tribu," the poet (then as now different from them) becomes "l'ange," and the activity of the poet in his life ("jadis") is such as was to be expected from "cette voix étrange," that is, "donner un sens plus pur aux mots." However, the moving of the whole action from the present into the past accounts for a number of developments, all of them consisting in the reduction of these men to a kind of primitive, prehistoric society, not only by the comparison to the hydra and to the tribe, but by the use of the archaic "oyant" and certain features of the remaining two lines of the quatrain. As for the single problem of syntax here, I am convinced that (were it not for the prosody) there should be a comma after "hydre," making "oyant" depend directly upon "eux" and "comme un vil sursaut d'hydre" a modification of "Eux . . . proclamèrent." The emotional effect of the two lines is again dual: the whole comparison "comme un vil sursaut d'hydre" and the "tribu" disparage the "siècle" to which they are applied, introduce an element of disgust and contempt, whereas the designation of the poet as "l'ange" and the description of his activity as "donner un sens plus pur aux mots" are admiring and approving. Thus:

eux : [Lui-même]
hydre : ange
vil sursaut
mots de la tribu : sens plus pur.

The remainder of the second quatrain, "Proclamèrent très haut le sortilège bu / Dans le flot sans honneur de quelque noir mélange," explains at last the form of the error committed by the poet's contemporaries: failing to understand his achievement and unable to attribute it to any proper cause (which would be beyond their comprehension), they have declared that the spell cast upon them was the result of the poet's drunkenness. Thus, by assimilating the poet's art to a kind of black magic, they have taken all honor from him. But the terms in which their error is expressed represent them as ignorant, superstitious savages and remove instead all honor from them. The emotional effect is to augment the contempt for the hydra-headed multitude while at the same time, by a kind of anticipated rebound, augmenting the admiration for the poet.

The first line of the first tercet, "Du sol et de la nue hostiles, ô grief!" is the most difficult and obscure line in the poem, both because the meanings of the individual words are not clear and because the syntactical relationship to the rest of the sonnet is not readily perceived. The suggestions made by earlier commentators seems to be of little help; but Mallarmé's own translation of an earlier version of the line ("Of the soil and the ether enemies, o struggle!") may contain a useful hint. Again, clearer light may be cast upon the problem if we consider the line in relation to its particular place in the development of the total structural context of the poem. It comes at a transitional point, concluding a section which has dealt largely with the poet's contemporaries, introducing a section which will deal with those who (after his death) will be responsible for a proper estimate of his merits—with "nous." His contemporaries have made an incorrect judgment: we may make either an incorrect or a correct one.

Now if we seek the most obvious syntactical link between this line and the others, we find it in the plural noun "hostiles," which Mallarmé had translated as "enemies." It could stand in apposition either with "eux" or with the "nous" implicit in "notre idée." I think that it applies to both and is thus properly transitional. It means that the poet's contemporaries, in their condemnation of him, were enemies both of the earthly and the heavenly principles that composed his genius, and that this was a lamentable misjudgment! It means, on the other hand, that "we" also will be enemies, and equally wrong, if we do not do certain things about the poet's memory.

The conditional nature of our own judgment is indicated in the

"Si" that introduces the final long sentence of the remainder of the poem. Here again, I must propose a reading which is at variance with those of my predecessors. Perhaps this can best be done by re-establishing what I believe to be the proper syntactical order of the poem's parts: "Si, avec ce granit (calme bloc ici-bas chu d'un désastre obscur) notre idée ne sculpte un bas-relief dont la tombe de Poe éblouissante s'orne, que du moins ce granit montre à jamais sa borne aux noirs vols du Blasphème épars dans le futur." The total meaning of the tercets would be approximately this: We can attempt, through our own opinion and judgment, to give Poe the shining place in man's estimate that he deserves; failing that, we can at least make certain that the blasphemies of the past will never again exist in the future. Into this total meaning, line 9 fits as a modifier of the "nous" implicit in "notre," indicating that we too would err unless we found a solution different from that of the ignorant multitude.

In this reading of the tercets, the idea of the "tombeau" comes to have both a literal and a figurative meaning. So the granite block will mean, on the one hand, the raw material from which the tombstone is carved, on the other hand, the poet himself who will be given a kind of permanent form in the judgment that is made of his work. If this hypothesis be granted, the interpretation of the tercets becomes evident. In the next line, "Si notre idée avec ne sculpte un bas-relief," the "notre" receives the emphasis; it juxtaposes strongly the desirable present and future to the undesirable past, us to the ignorant "siècle," and admiration to condemnation; it effects the turn in the emotions. Hence, "idée," which it modifies, stands against the "n'avoir pas connu" of line 3 and, in a way, is equivalent to "un sens plus pur." The basic opposition develops:

$$\text{siècle : notre}$$
$$\text{n'avoir pas connu : idée}$$

"Avec" as complement to "sculpte" looks forward to "granit," in both its meanings, whereas "un bas-relief" specifies only the literal meaning for the sculpturing, the granite, and the tomb.

Something of the figurative meaning, along with a further development of the emotion, appears in the next line, "Dont la tombe de

Poe éblouissante s'orne." Yet, in the same line comes the first specification of "poet" to "Poe," prepared for earlier only by the specific
nature of the charge of drunkenness brought against him by his
contemporaries. The figurative meaning is suggested by the laudatory phrase "éblouissante s'orne," in which both words carry a feeling of wonderment and admiration: "éblouissante" reintroduces the
notion of shining light earlier contained in "glaive nu"; "s'orne"
falls into the general category of change for the better with which
the poem begins:

$$
\begin{aligned}
&\text{: éternité} \\
&\text{change} \\
&\text{suscite} \\
&\text{triomphait} \\
&\text{sculpte} \\
\text{noir :}\ &\text{éblouissante} \\
\text{vil sursaut :}\ &\text{s'orne.}
\end{aligned}
$$

It should be noted that "tombe" (as contradistinguished from "tombeau" in the title) probably has here only the literal meaning of the
tombstone.

The first line of the final tercet, "Calme bloc ici-bas chu d'un
désastre obscur," modifies "granit." This is in its literal meaning.
But figuratively it also modifies the "Poe" of the preceding line.
What is important is not that the granite block (as Lemaître says)
should have fallen to earth as the result of some mysterious disaster,
but that the poet, now again in his proper form as angel, should
have "fallen" to earth from a better domain. The "calme" is thus a
description of his angelic, imperturbable nature; the "ici-bas" sums
up all the disastrous features of his sojourn on earth (among "us");
"chu" describes the process of birth, with a moral judgment added,
just as "l'éternité le change" had described the process of death; and
the disaster is "obscur" (hence related to "noir") because of the fate
that awaited him on earth.

If this be the metaphorical meaning of the line, given it by its
position after the mention of Poe, then it assumes its proper and
material meaning when we read the next line, which contains the
substantive "granit:" "Que ce granit du moins montre à jamais sa
borne." After one possible meaning for our "tombeau" for Poe,

introduced by the "si" as a "conditional of uncertain achievement," the alternative is now proposed. It is less desirable; hence the "du moins." If it is less desirable, it is because it is both material (rather than spiritual) and neutral (rather than positive). The best "tombeau" would be the kind of judgment that would give to Poe full glory after death; anything less is a "pis aller." Of such a lesser kind is the tombstone which is merely a material object, one which sets a limit. For the future it sets a limit to the kind of blasphemy which in the past had plagued the poet: ". . . sa borne / Aux noirs vols du Blasphème épars dans le futur." Since the limit is a physical one, so the blasphemy will become a material object and its spread will take the form of flights. Through the use of the epithet "vols noirs," they become linked to the "noir mélange" of line 8 and, through it, to the "siècle," to the "hydre" of the poet's contemporaries. The capital letter of "Blasphème," however, once again generalizes and universalizes the situation; the Poet takes the place of Poe; and the "tombeau" becomes a memorial to any poet who might be preserved, by our form of remembrance, from a similar fate. Finally, just as at the beginning we had a moment in the present set off against a period in the past—the period of blasphemy—so at the end we have the moment in the present (moment of the "tombeau") set off against the whole of the future ("à jamais . . . dans le futur") when, if we succeed, the same Blasphemy will be forever prevented.

Through the course of the tercets, several things have happened both to the basic opposition and to the progress of the emotions. Against the "éblouissante s'orne" have been placed the "désastre obscur" and the "noirs vols," against the earlier "vil sursaut" the "calme bloc," against the "Blasphème" the "tombe," and against the past the future:

désastre obscur : éblouissante s'orne
noirs vols : granit, borne
vil sursaut : calme bloc
Blasphème : tombe
past : (present), future.

The opposition is now complete, all the elements stated at the beginning have been clarified and defined, their opposites have been provided. With respect to the emotions elicited, the anger of the earlier sections has been replaced, temporarily, by admiration for the poet and for Poe, an admiration attached to the proper conception of the poet and to the glory of his true "tombeau." But this admiration merely serves, at the very end, to produce an intensified anger against the original blasphemy in the past and at any possible recurrence of it in the future. One is left with a hope for an eternity of good repute for the poet, with a determination that it will come about, and with a hatred for any who would stand in its way.

IO

Mallarmé

Un Coup de dés jamais n'abolira le hasard

For Mallarmé, the writing of *Un Coup de dés jamais n'abolira le hasard* represented a very special effort in the direction of experimenting with the art and the possibility of a striking contribution to French poetry in particular and to poetry in general. It gave him the occasion, besides, of pushing to the extreme those devices of poetic expression that he had been developing and exploiting throughout his career as a poet. We have already seen with what effectiveness some of those devices had been used: the isolated word revivified by a return to etymological meanings, sometimes by a play of senses and sonorities approaching the pun; the syntax of the sentence distorted and contorted for purposes of rendering the meaning more subtle and the emphasis more forceful; the disposition on the page, and especially differences in typography, used to indicate change in speaker, or distinctions of ideas, or prosodic refinements that might otherwise escape the silent reader. All these devices, and others of perhaps lesser prominence, will again be called upon to aid in the making of the new poem.

But the newness of the new poem goes beyond the reassemblage of old devices. Mallarmé himself feared that it might escape even the wary reader; and so, with some misgivings, he wrote a "Préface" that might serve as a guide to the reading of the poem, as a justification of some of the innovations that he had introduced, and as a

236

kind of *art poétique* for the poet of the future. For those who would interpret the poem now, this preface is full of precious suggestions. Hence I shall present a brief commentary on it before going on to a study of the poem.

"J'aimerais qu'on ne lût pas cette Note ou que parcourue, même on l'oubliât . . ." Why, having undertaken to write a prefatory note, should the poet wish us not to read it or, once having read it, that we should set it aside? Part of the reason is in the poet's conviction that his poem should be comprehensible and effective on its own, without notes or commentary or explanatory addenda. And indeed it is. But the note that he writes has as its purpose to aid our comprehension and hence to assure the effectiveness of the poem; once these goals have been achieved, we may indeed forget the preface. ". . . elle apprend, au Lecteur habile, peu de chose situé outre sa pénétration . . .": making a distinction between two kinds of readers, the one who is "habile" and the other who is "ingénu," Mallarmé declares that even for the former something is to be gained from studying the Note; it may be "peu de chose," but it is still a positive quantity. Moreover, he tells us what our goal should be, a "pénétration" into the meaning of the poem, and this is consonant with what he will say at the end of the note about the intellectual quality of the poem—a quality that will emerge progressively during the reading of the poem itself. This part of the first sentence may be taken as an invitation to exercise our intellectual capacities on a work that treats a subject that is of "imagination pure et complexe ou intellect."

The first sentence concludes: "mais, peut troubler l'ingénu devant appliquer un regard aux premiers mots du Poème pour que de suivants, disposés comme ils sont, l'amènent aux derniers, le tout sans nouveauté qu'un espacement de la lecture." For the "habile" as for the "ingénu," this statement is as revelatory as it is important. For we all learn what our "pénétration" will reveal: first, what is traditional or un-new about *Un Coup de dés,* that it presents a continuous statement (we do not know yet whether it is of an idea or a passion or an action) from a "beginning" ("aux premiers mots") through a "middle" ("de suivants") to an "end" ("aux derniers"); second, what is original or new about it, that it makes this presentation in a special order ("disposés comme ils sont") and that the order results in an unexpected or extraordinary "espacement de la lecture." We are thus invited to pursue two avenues of "penetration" into the poem, on the one hand towards the discovery of the essential continuity of the meaning, on the other hand towards the explanation of why that continuity should have been destroyed through a "spacing out" of the statement and of the poetic advantages that accrue from the reconstituted order.

"Les 'blancs' en effet, assument l'importance, frappent d'abord. . . ." The first peculiarity of his poem that seems to Mallarmé to require explanation is the extraordinary arrangement of blacks and whites on the printed page, of the words against the paper. This is what first strikes the eye, hence the attention of the reader, as characterizing the "disposing" of the words and the "spacing out" of the reading. The poet will insist that his procedure is traditional in so far as the proportion of white to black (of empty space to inked words) is concerned, untraditional only in the way that the words are arranged on the page: "la versification en exigea, comme silence alentour, ordinairement, au point qu'un morceau, lyrique ou de peu de pieds, occupe, au milieu, le tiers environ du feuillet. . . ." This is the tradition: when, ordinarily in the past, poets followed the customary practices of versification, they covered with their verses, printed down the middle of the page, about one-third of that page. The "white" or "blank" areas had a function in the reading of verse; they represented a surrounding silence, presumably as compared with the totality of sound that would have been demanded by a fully printed page. If Mallarmé interprets past practice in this way, with this reference to the sounds of the reading, it is because he will wish to give to his own practice in the distribution of blacks and whites a basically musical potential. We thus have another hint for reading and interpretation. ". . . je ne transgresse cette mesure, seulement la disperse." This is the novelty: we should expect to find the usual one-to-two proportion of words to blank spaces, but the central column of words will be broken up and dispersed, with the words falling irregularly upon the page in ways not yet foreseen. As a consequence, sound and silence will be distributed according to a new principle.

The next sentence, a long and complex one, states the new principle: "Le papier intervient chaque fois qu'une image, d'elle-même, cesse ou rentre, acceptant la succession d'autres et, comme il ne s'agit pas, ainsi que toujours, de traits sonores réguliers ou vers—plutôt, de subdivisions prismatiques de l'Idée, l'instant de paraître et que dure leur concours, dans quelque mise en scène spirituelle exacte, c'est à des places variables, près ou loin du fil conducteur latent, en raison de la vraisemblance, que s'impose le texte." Perhaps the best way to understand the sentence—and to profit from its suggestions for the interpretation of the poem—is to follow the distinction that it continues to make between the traditional and the new. In the tradition, says Mallarmé, words were printed or "imposed" on the white page (the sense of "s'impose" is technical) in that central column according to the needs of a prosody, and in that prosody lines or verses were of equal lengths and demanded a vocalization divided into sound units of equal lengths. Besides, the meaning expressed was both continuous and patent; as one read along, following the meaning and the sound from verse to verse, one also followed a clear and apparent "fil conducteur" from beginning through middle to end. It was the prosody, not any special demands of the expression of the idea, that determined spatial relationships of black and white. Mallarmé, against this tradition, will start from an intention to give a discontinuous expression to the idea; the "fil conducteur" will still be present, it will still carry the reader through the poem, but it will be latent and hidden rather than patent and obvious. The idea will be broken up just as a ray of light is broken up in its passage through a prism, and its parts will be distributed or dispersed over the page in a way to represent separations and combinations, junctions and disjunctions of idea or image. The prosody will now be subordinated to and determined by the need to represent at once the presence of the "fil conducteur" and the fragments into which it has been cut.

"Le papier intervient chaque fois qu'une image, d'elle-même, cesse ou rentre . . .": The first principle of arrangement is that the image (used in a broad and indefinite sense) is made into a kind of sub-unit by its separation from other formulas of expression, and that the separation in turn is indicated by blank spaces that precede and follow. Since the image may "return," we should expect both interruptions and resumptions in the statement of a given thought, with other thoughts occupying the intervening space: "acceptant la succession d'autres." The divisions are not, as they were in traditional French prosody, those of a verse pattern: "et, comme il ne s'agit pas, ainsi que toujours, de traits sonores réguliers ou vers" (it is important to note that Mallarmé here stresses the regularity of sound patterns in conventional poetry). ". . . plutôt, de subdivisions prismatiques de l'Idée": rather, they are divisions of the central or organizing idea, "prismatic" in the sense both of a gradation downward from the more general to the more particular, and of a splitting into smaller and smaller elements. If we visualize, in connection with "prismatique," the top-to-bottom division of the lines in a spectrum, we shall be prepared for the top-to-bottom distribution of words or phrases or lines on the double page that constitutes the spatial unit in the book-editions of *Un Coup de dés;* perhaps, even, we may see the differences in height and in blackness as different type faces are used. Moreover, since the lines are not of regular length, not being verses, but rather suit the length of the part of the idea they express; and since they are not, through concerns with convention, arranged in a central column, we may also anticipate the left-to-right disposition across the double page that accompanies (with variations) the top-to-bottom disposition.

This irregularity of length and of position has its basis in the next fragment of the sentence: "l'instant de paraître et que dure leur concours, dans quelque mise en scène spirituelle exacte . . ." The coming together, here, of the two terms, "instant" and "mise en scène," supplies another clue to our reading of the poem. Mallarmé makes a transfer of relationships in time (those of language whether prose or verse) to relationships in space. Any part of the idea will appear at a given time and will last for a given duration of time, but it will be "placed" or "spaced" in the poem at that point which is required by its function in the expression of the total idea. Its "place" will be its "time," its spiritual "setting." This is precise or "exact" because of the tightness with which the whole of the idea is organized and the rigor with which its subdivisions are distributed with relationship one to another. As we read the double page we will be reading "downward" and "across" (the latter with returns and fresh starts) in space; but we will always be reading "forward" in time as the idea develops through all its complexities and refinements. Hence the rest of the sentence: "c'est à des places variables, près ou loin du fil conducteur latent, en raison de la vraisemblance, que s'impose le texte." We must give to "s'impose," at the end, a double meaning; it refers both to the material printing or "spacing" of the text and also to the internal necessity that requires that each part of it be printed exactly where it is printed. Similarly, the principle of "vraisemblance" is an intellectual or spiritual one, establishing the relationship between the part and the whole and the spiritual "distance" ("près ou loin") of the individual part from the central idea. That central idea, the "fil conducteur," may not at all times be visible as overtly expressed; but it will always underlie the expression of any of the parts, however "distant," and is latent in this sense.

What has just been said is clarified and illustrated in the following sentence, where Mallarmé describes the link that he sees between the movement of ideas and the movement of rhythms: "L'avantage, si j'ai droit à le dire, littéraire, de cette distance copiée qui mentalement sépare des groupes de mots ou les mots entre eux, semble d'accélérer tantôt et de ralentir le mouvement, le scandant, l'intimant même selon une vision simultanée de la Page: celle-ci prise pour unité comme l'est autre part le Vers ou ligne parfaite." We are thus invited to look at each double page as a whole (just as, in traditional verse, we looked at the single line); to perceive its spatial relationships; to evaluate, at a glimpse, the way in which the white spaces separating groups of words both horizontally and vertically establish a total rhythm for the page; and to see the correspondence between the spatial structure of the page (which also moves through time) and the structure of the ideas represented by it: their co-ordinations and subordinations, their equivalences and oppositions. We are invited, at the same time, to produce a reading of the text, silently or aloud, that will follow the temporal indications of the printed page.

"La fiction affleurera et se dissipera, vite, d'après la mobilité de l'écrit, autour des arrêts fragmentaires d'une phrase capitale dès le titre introduite et continuée." From considerations of spacing and printing and reading, Mallarmé passes to the matter that is being presented through such devices. He has previously spoken of the connection between the "premiers mots," the "suivants," and the "derniers"; of the "Idée" expressed by them, which he had later called the "fil conducteur." Now he is more specific: the whole poem is to be organized by and around "une phrase capitale dès le titre introduite et continuée." But rather than expressing the central idea as such, with its intellectual or logical ramifications, the central sentence will transform the idea—or some of it—into a fiction, which will appear and disappear ("affleurera et se dissipera" is another way of saying "cesse ou rentre, acceptant la succession d'autres") as a kind of illustration of the idea itself. In other words, the "phrase capitale" will be interrupted and fragmented, and the fiction or image that fills the intervening spaces will serve both to develop and to exemplify what might be called the "Idée capitale." "Tout se passe, par raccourci, en hypothèse; on évite le récit." That is, the "fiction" will not be offered as a continuous narrative, although it will be essentially narrative in nature. Instead, it will be abridged and abbreviated, only such parts of it actually being expressed as will be necessary to give an intimation of what is happening and what this means.

From these divisions and distributions of the thought, from their manner of representation on the page, there results a necessary manner of reading the text aloud: the printed page becomes a score. Working on the basis of a carefully constructed musical analogy, Mallarmé now develops the "sonorous" side of his poem that is concomitant with the "literary" side. "Ajouter que de cet emploi à nu de la pensée avec retraits, prolongements, fuites, ou son dessin même, résulte, pour qui veut lire à haute voix, une partition." By "cet emploi à nu de la pensée" we should understand, I think, the kind of minimal statement referred to in the preceding sentence: the narrative eschewed in favor of the suggestion, ornaments and explanations avoided, the essential idea clearly and openly expressed. With "retraits, prolongements, fuites," Mallarmé again describes the way in which the idea is interrupted and distributed in the poem; but he does so now in metaphorical terms, equally applicable to music and to pictorial representation; so that "dessin," as it follows, has the same kind of double reference. The clue to the whole passage lies in the term "partition"; for with it the whole musical analogy is stated. The remarks that follow are developments of the analogy. "Les différences des caractères d'imprimerie entre le motif prépondérant, un secondaire et d'adjacents, dicte son importance à l'émission orale et la portée, moyenne, en haut, en bas de page, notera que monte ou descend l'intonation." The score that we shall be reading as we read the text will be made up of two elements: first, a notation in a pseudo-musical sense, in which the various voices or melodies, the "motifs," are distinguished from one another by typographical differences which in turn call for differences of intensity in the oral delivery; second, a musical staff upon which the notation is written. The staff is constituted by the parallel lines that cross the double page, and each line, by its relation to a supposed central line, indicates a relative value in pitch or intonation. As we read "across," we shall expect to read with greater or lesser intensity as the type faces direct us to; as we read "downward," we shall expect to read with a falling intonation—or, at places where the page is only partially used, at a level of intonation appropriate to the positions of the lines actually used.

According to the editor of the 1914 edition, the next two sentences were specifically germane to the disposition of the text as it first appeared in *Cosmopolis* in May, 1897. In that periodical publication, the unit was the single page rather than the double page; and since (with few exceptions) the division into pages was identical, with the whole contents of the present double page crowded into the single-page unit, it was necessary to return more often to the left-hand margin in order to combine the movement "downward" with movements "across." As a result, the total movement "downward and across" was less regular than it became in 1914, and the shuttle motion was more apparent. This meant, in effect, that one had a succession of "staffs" on the page rather than something approaching, in most cases, the single musical staff. Yet what Mallarmé says in these two sentences is almost entirely pertinent to the present form of the text, and to exclude it from our study would be to lose much that is important for the total theory underlying *Un Coup de dés*.

"Seules certaines directions très hardies, des empiètements, etc., formant le contre-point de cette prosodie, demeurent dans une œuvre, qui manque de précédents, à l'état élémentaire . . ." In this statement, Mallarmé establishes a kind of parallel between the general movement of the ideas in the poem and the general development of its musical qualities. Just as the "fil conducteur" of the idea is accompanied by secondary or illustrative ideas (of various kinds), so the main system of rhythms and intonations, here called the "prosodie" of the poem, is accompanied by variant movements that constitute a sort of counterpoint. These variant movements are called "certaines directions très hardies," by which we may suppose that they are excepted or exempted from the general "downward and across" and "high and low" directions. They are also called "empiètements," by which is signified again an interruption or complication of the set patterns of arrangement and of reading. Mallarmé declares that this way of handling a poem is new and original, that his work is without precedent, but that he has not been able to go as far as he might have liked to in introducing innovations; the novelties remain "à l'état élémentaire." He explains why in the rest of the sentence.

The reason is to be found, rather than in any unwillingness on his part to push his experiment to its logical limits ("non que j'estime l'opportunité d'essais timides"), in his recognition of the need to reconcile his experiment with the conventions and habits of periodical printing: "mais il ne m'appartient pas, hormis une pagination spéciale ou de volume à moi, dans un Périodique, même valeureux, gracieux et invitant qu'il se montre aux belles lettres, d'agir par trop contrairement à l'usage." When, posthumously, Mallarmé will finally have that volume of his own for *Un Coup de dés,* with the special pagination that was not possible in a literary review, the double page will replace the single page as the unit of presentation and the new arrangements will be fully exploited. It was in the light of the possibility of such a separate publication that Mallarmé made the final revisions to his text. The poem as published in *Cosmopolis,* and for which the prefatory note was written, represents a compromise between his ultimate wishes and traditional restraints. "J'aurai, toutefois, indiqué du Poème ci-joint, mieux que l'esquisse, un 'état' qui ne rompe pas de tous points avec la tradition; poussé sa présentation en maint sens aussi avant qu'elle n'offusque personne: suffisamment, pour ouvrir des yeux." To awaken his readers to the potentialities contained in the new method of presentation; to surprise them through innovation and at the same time to retain their attention and sympathy; to go as far as he could go without discouraging the publisher and alienating the audience: these were Mallarmé's goals in the initial "state" of his poem. In the final "state," he could obviously go much farther.

What follows in the Preface is really more distinctly an *art poétique* for the new kind of poetry than a technical explanation of its workings. As he expresses his hopes for the future of the new poetry, Mallarmé states once again the ways that it is rooted in tradition and in contemporary tendencies. "Aujourd'hui ou sans présumer de l'avenir qui sortira d'ici, rien ou presque un art, reconnaissons aisément que la tentative participe, avec imprévu, de poursuites particulières et chères à notre temps, le vers libre et le poème en prose." As before, he calls attention to matters of prosodic presentation, to the special rhythmical qualities of his poem resulting from an adaptation of free verse, and to the additional liberties of arrangement permitted by the use of prose. These, he freely admits, are practices known to his readers and acceptable by them; yet he has gone beyond their expectations with respect to both devices and developed his own approach. It may, today, contain elements of the "imprévu"; in the future, should his method prove successful and attractive, it may lead to the development of a new and distinctive art of poetry. (I might note that in this sentence the phrase "rien ou presque un art" is a kind of echo of a phrase in the poem itself, "rien n'aura eu lieu que le lieu excepté peut-être une constellation." This is more than a chance similarity. As we shall see later in the analysis of the poem, the thought expressed here is an essential part of the Idea developed in the poem, just as it is fundamental to Mallarmé's thinking about his own art.)

"Leur réunion s'accomplit sous une influence, je sais, étrangère, celle de la Musique entendue au concert; on en retrouve plusieurs moyens m'ayant semblé appartenir aux Lettres, je les reprends." The justification for the musical analogy is now stated clearly: if Mallarmé has joined free verse to prose, if he has combined them according to principles proper to music, if he has spoken of staffs, intonations, and counterpoints, it is because he has wished to achieve in the art of poetry certain effects usually produced by the art of music. Not the whole art of music, however, but rather those more complex forms in which various voices or various themes or various lines of development are exploited simultaneously as well as successively. If one looks only at the "musical" side of his poem, at its prosody, one will discover a multilinear organization from which there derives a complex but unitary effect. If one looks at the properly "literary" side, one will note that the single and central Idea is broken down into components that are expressed, not consecutively in the normal way, but simultaneously by means of the interruptions and the juxtapositions of which I have spoken. There is, however, an important difference between the two arts, and it is this that prevents Mallarmé from founding a totally new art. Musical sounds may actually be produced simultaneously and the resulting complex sound may be completely intelligible; likewise, whole lines of such sounds may be pursued together in a way to create a single composite line which need not anywhere lose its perspicuousness. But were two single words to be pronounced together, neither would be understood; and were two or more lines of thought to be read simultaneously, say in a choral reading, only complete confusion and unintelligibility would result. Hence Mallarmé's system in *Un Coup de dés* never involves simultaneity—except for that kind of simultaneity which only the individual reader can himself achieve by holding one or even several lines of thought in abeyance and suspense while he pursues, separately and now, the thought contained in the words immediately before him. The movement must always be "downward and across," and when one thought is to be presented, all the other surrounding thoughts must be temporarily interrupted. There is analogy only, not identity between a proper musical staff and Mallarmé's stafflike arrangement of words on the page; for there can properly be no chords in poetry. It is for this reason that he surrounds his statement here with reservations, that he speaks of "presque un art" and that he limits his pretensions to "plusieurs moyens."

(Continued after text of *Un Coup de dés*)

The text of *Un Coup de dés jamais n'abolira le hasard* which appears on the following pages is reproduced in photographic reproduction from the 1914 Gallimard edition.

UN COUP DE DÉS

JAMAIS

QUAND BIEN MÊME LANCÉ DANS DES CIRCONSTANCES
ÉTERNELLES

DU FOND D'UN NAUFRAGE

SOIT
   que

          l'Abîme

     blanchi
        étale
          furieux
               sous une inclinaison
                  plane désespérément

                        d'aile

                     la sienne

                          par

avance retombée d'un mal à dresser le vol
et couvrant les jaillissements
coupant au ras les bonds

très à l'intérieur résume

l'ombre enfouie dans la profondeur par cette voile alternative

jusqu'adapter
à l'envergure

sa béante profondeur en tant que la coque

d'un bâtiment

penché de l'un ou l'autre bord

LE MAÎTRE

surgi
    inférant

            de cette conflagration

                    que se

             comme on menace

       l'unique Nombre qui ne peut pas

                             hésite
                     cadavre par le bras

plutôt
      que de jouer
           en maniaque chenu
               la partie
            au nom des flots
                           un

                 naufrage cela

            hors d'anciens calculs
        où la manœuvre avec l'âge oubliée

                jadis il empoignait la barre

à ses pieds
            de l'horizon unanime

prépare
    s'agite et mêle
        au poing qui l'étreindrait
un destin et les vents

être un autre

                Esprit
                    pour le jeter
                            dans la tempête
                    en reployer la division et passer fier

écarté du secret qu'il détient

envahit le chef
coule en barbe soumise

direct de l'homme

        sans nef
            n'importe
                    où vaine

ancestralement à n'ouvrir pas la main

                             crispée
                   par delà l'inutile tête

     legs en la disparition

                à quelqu'un
                      ambigu

        l'ultérieur démon immémorial

ayant
      de contrées nulles
             induit
le vieillard vers cette conjonction suprême avec la probabilité

                celui
                   son ombre puérile
caressée et polie et rendue et lavée
        assouplie par la vague et soustraite
        aux durs os perdus entre les ais

                né
                  d'un ébat
la mer par l'aïeul tentant ou l'aïeul contre la mer
        une chance oiseuse

                                  Fiançailles
dont
      le voile d'illusion rejailli leur hantise
      ainsi que le fantôme d'un geste

             chancellera
             s'affalera

                folie

N'ABOLIRA

COMME SI

                                    Une insinuation

                                        au silence

                              dans quelque proche

                                          voltige

simple

enroulée avec ironie
                    ou
                        le mystère
                                    précipité
                                            hurlé

tourbillon d'hilarité et d'horreur

autour du gouffre
                        sans le joncher
                                    ni fuir

            et en berce le vierge indice

                                        COMME SI

plume solitaire éperdue

sauf

que la rencontre ou l'effleure une toque de minuit
et immobilise
au velours chiffonné par un esclaffement sombre

cette blancheur rigide

dérisoire
en opposition au ciel
trop
pour ne pas marquer
exigûment
quiconque

prince amer de l'écueil

s'en coiffe comme de l'héroïque
irrésistible mais contenu
par sa petite raison virile
en foudre

soucieux
        expiatoire et pubère

                                                    muet

La lucide et seigneuriale aigrette
                au front invisible
    scintille
          puis ombrage
une stature mignonne ténébreuse
    en sa torsion de sirène

par d'impatientes squames ultimes

rire

que

SI

de vertige

debout

le temps
de souffleter
bifurquées

un roc

faux manoir
tout de suite
évaporé en brumes

qui imposa
une borne à l'infini

C'ÉTAIT
issu stellaire

CE SERAIT
pire
                    non
                    davantage ni moins
                                        indifféremment mais autant

LE NOMBRE

EXISTÂT-IL
autrement qu'hallucination éparse d'agonie

COMMENÇÂT-IL ET CESSÂT-IL
sourdant que nié et clos quand apparu
enfin
par quelque profusion répandue en rareté
SE CHIFFRÂT-IL

évidence de la somme pour peu qu'une
ILLUMINÂT-IL

LE HASARD

Choit
    la plume
        rythmique suspens du sinistre
                        s'ensevelir
               aux écumes originelles
naguères d'où sursauta son délire jusqu'à une cime
                 flétrie
        par la neutralité identique du gouffre

RIEN

de la mémorable crise
ou se fût
l'évènement

accompli en vue de tout résultat nul

              humain

        N'AURA EU LIEU
       une élévation ordinaire verse l'absence

                   QUE LE LIEU
inférieur clapotis quelconque comme pour disperser l'acte vide
          abruptement qui sinon
        par son mensonge
          eût fondé
        la perdition

dans ces parages

        du vague

           en quoi toute réalité se dissout

EXCEPTÉ

    à l'altitude

        PEUT-ÊTRE

            aussi loin qu'un endroit

fusionne avec au delà

                    hors l'intérêt
              quant à lui signalé
                                        en général
selon telle obliquité par telle déclivité
                                        de feux

          vers
               ce doit être
                    le Septentrion aussi Nord

                                   UNE CONSTELLATION

               froide d'oubli et de désuétude
                                   pas tant
                              qu'elle n'énumère
                    sur quelque surface vacante et supérieure
                         le heurt successif
                                             sidéralement
                    d'un compte total en formation

veillant
          doutant
                    roulant
                         brillant et méditant

                              avant de s'arrêter
               à quelque point dernier qui le sacre

               Toute Pensée émet un Coup de Dés

We may find a further lesson for the reading of the poem in what I have just said about the musical analogy and the limits to be imposed upon it. Mallarmé's typographical distinctions among the separate components of his Idea indicate more than the matters of hierarchy of thoughts and of differences of volume to which he himself refers. They provide what we might call a visual means for producing that kind of "private" simultaneity which will make it possible for the individual reader to "see" the whole of the Idea, with all its ramifications and subdivisions, at one and the same time. They permit him, in a word, to form a kind of composite "image" (in his mind's eye) that will be comparable to a composite sound that his ear would be fully capable of hearing. Let us say that the reader records an image of a sentence or a part of a sentence that the printed text presents in a given type face. He may then superimpose upon that image another whole or partial sentence printed in another face. The composite or combined image that the memory or the imagination is able to achieve will keep the two faces visually separate; but the two parts of the thought will be merged into a total concept that may resemble simultaneity. The two thoughts could not have been printed as simultaneous, nor could they be read silently or aloud as such; but the mind of the reader may grasp and apprehend them together. The intellectual "chord" is possible, and its achievement is what Mallarmé's method of presentation has as its ultimate goal. As we read, we must use all those resources of our intellect that are susceptible of leading us to the intellectual "chord."

"Le genre, que c'en devienne un comme la symphonie, peu à peu, à côté du chant personnel, laisse intact l'antique vers, auquel je garde un culte et attribue l'empire de la passion et des rêveries. . . ." In the concluding sentence of his Preface, Mallarmé makes a fundamental distinction: his new poetics, with its innovations of prosody and presentation, will be suitable to one category of subject matters, while the traditional art that uses conventional verse forms will continue to treat its usual materials. He therefore speaks of a new genre rather than of a whole new art (perhaps another reason for the "presque un art" in an earlier passage) and he makes tentative claims for the realization of the genre ("que c'en devienne un") just as he had previously been modest about the future of his experiment ("sans présumer de l'avenir"). He states the difference between the two genres in terms of his musical analogy: the new multi-voiced and simultaneous genre will be comparable to the symphony, to the "Musique entendue au concert"; the old mono-voiced and essentially successive genre will be comparable to the song, to the "chant personnel." It is the personal quality of the latter that makes it the ideal instrument for the expression of "l'empire de la passion et des rêveries"; and Mallarmé sees no reason why "l'antique vers" should not continue to be used essentially as it had been in the past. He himself had long been a devotee of that verse.

But for matters that belong to the mind rather than to the heart, the new devices of the new genre should be preferable: "tandis que ce serait le cas de traiter, de préférence (ainsi qu'il suit) tels sujets d'imagination pure et complexe ou intellect: que ne reste aucune raison d'exclure de la Poésie—unique source." The central formula is here unequivocal: "Imagination pure et complexe ou intellect." It relates the present theoretical statement to what Mallarmé had previously said about his own poem when he had spoken of "l'Idée," of "la pensée," and at the same time it identifies specifically the subject of the poem that is now going to follow ("ainsi qu'il suit"). As it establishes synonymity between "intellect" and "imagination pure et complexe," the formula does more than merely distinguish this kind of spiritual activity from the passions and dreamlike meditations; it furnishes the basis, I believe, for the new poetics and the prosodic innovations of *Un Coup de dés*. Because the matter of the poem is an Idea, it may be stated in a central sentence that provides the "fil conducteur"; and because that Idea is complex, the sentence may be modified and extended to contain all the useful subsidiary and contributory ideas. The faculty that produces such an Idea and such a Poem is the pure imagination, the intellectual faculty that organizes and orders the component parts of a concept. The faculty that permits the reader to perceive the complexities and the hierarchy of the organization is also the pure imagination. For this is the faculty—and I think that we do not go beyond Mallarmé's meaning in saying so—that both enables the poet to dissolve his intellectual chord into its constitutive notes, which may then be presented as successive or alternative, and that makes it possible for the reader to restore those same notes to their original simultaneity.

Passion and intellect, between them, supply the matter for the whole art of poetry. Or, to reverse the statement, the art of poetry is sufficiently ample to contain ideas as well as sentiments and dreams. Mallarmé implies that this "single source" has perhaps not always been hospitable to the Idea to the extent to which it might have been. He would enlarge that hospitality, and the technical innovations that he proposes should offer the means of turning Ideas into Poems. *Un Coup de dés jamais n'abolira le hasard* may serve as an initial experiment.

In the 1914 edition, which is supposed to represent Mallarmé's final wishes for the printing of his poem, *Un Coup de dés jamais n'abolira le hasard* occupies eleven double pages which, for convenient reference, I have numbered 1 to 11. (Those numbers appear on the reproduction of the 1914 text included here.) These eleven pages correspond to the nine single pages of the periodical publication in *Cosmopolis* for May, 1897. The discrepancy in number of pages results from the fact that not only are the contents of the single pages spread out over the double pages, but especially that this is not done in a precise one-for-two ratio. At several points we find that one single page of 1897 gives two double pages in 1914; thus page 419 becomes pages 1 and 2, with the left side of both double pages remaining blank (or "white"). Elsewhere, the contents of the single pages have been differently divided and distributed, sometimes covering almost two double pages. The materials on page 423 of 1897 now are spread over all of page 6 and most of page 7 (down to "quiconque"), making, of course, for a lesser concentration of the materials and a greater proportion of blank spaces. The original page 424 now occupies the rest of page 7 and all of page 8, whereas the present page 9 contains all of page 425 and the top of page 426 from "rythmique suspens" down through "gouffre"; the latter change made it possible to give the whole of the italicized passage in uninterrupted form. Again, the rest of page 426 is reproduced on the whole of page 10. I shall speak as I go along about the effect of these rearrangements of the materials.

The most immediate effect is the great prominence and emphasis given to the short sentence that is at once the title of the poem and the principal element of its "fil conducteur": "Un coup de dés jamais n'abolira le hasard." We may gather, from what Mallarmé says in the prefatory Note, that he meant the poem to have no separate title; rather, the reader was to discover the title, intertwined with the rest of the text, as he read along in the poem. The sentence is printed in the largest and boldest type of the text (48-point display capitals) and all its words are given additional prominence by their placing and spacing. "Un coup de dés" appears alone on the right side of the double page 1, at the bottom of the upper quarter of the type page (I shall use this designation for the area which, throughout the book, may be occupied by type, excluding thus the margins); the rest of the right side and the whole of the left side are blank. "Jamais" is centered in the third quarter of the right side of page 2; it is followed by three lines of type in the fourth quarter, and the left side is blank. "N'abolira" is found at the bottom of the otherwise blank right side of page 5, and is juxtaposed to a fairly heavy page of type on the left. "Le hasard" is placed on page 9 right, at the same height as "Jamais," with one cluster of type above it, another below it, and a scattering of words on the opposite left side. Two double pages of text follow the last word of this central sentence. If we picture the whole of the sentence at the back of our mind, we shall see all of its components, in the boldest type, on right sides of the pages, in an arrangement something like this:

UN COUP DE DÉS

    JAMAIS   **LE HASARD**
      N'ABOLIRA

This "vision" of the sentence represents a pattern of "sounds" in which intensity remains the same—and the highest in the poem—and in which intonation falls, then falls again, then rises to the mid-point. Against this basic ground of sight and of sound we shall, as we read, project the rest of the text.

But there is also, and primarily, a basic ground of meaning. What does the sentence mean? Something simple enough, I believe, something like: "A throw of the dice will never alter anything in the course of chance (or fortune)"; or, conversely, "The course of chance (or fortune) will go on unchanged whatever 'game of chance' one may play against it." This is the organizing Idea of the poem, presented baldly and in completely intellectual terms; it will be illustrated, as it is expressed, by the "fiction" or the "image" that constitutes the major part of the text. That illustration will sometimes begin with, sometimes converge upon the words of the central sentence; everywhere, it will convert the pure Idea into a visible situation, or into moral determinations that create an emotional response, or into metaphors that reinforce both the idea and its emotional accompaniments. But for the time being, the "phrase capitale" remains clear and separate, loud and black against the white silence that surrounds it.

The white silence begins to diminish on page 2 where, after "jamais," the first of the modifying developments is introduced. Indeed, "jamais" is placed here in the sentence, rather than after "n'abolira," not only in order to emphasize the negative but also and primarily to permit the first major "interruption" at this point. It must be here in order to prepare for the next one. This section of the text, depending upon and modifying "jamais," is printed in 14-point capitals; hence it is among the most prominent, typographically, of all the parts. If we follow the section through, we get this text: "quand bien même lancé dans des circonstances éternelles du fond d'un naufrage soit le maître existât-il commençât-il et cessât-il se chiffrât-il illuminât-il rien n'aura eu lieu que le lieu excepté une constellation." The way in which the text should be read becomes clear if, on the one hand, we take into account its "espacement" with respect to the words of the major sentence and, on the other hand, we supply the punctuation (or the divisions and subdivisions) that the meaning seems to require. The words "quand bien même lancé dans des circonstances éternelles, du fond d'un naufrage," appear below "jamais" in the fourth quarter of page 2, right side, with "du fond d'un naufrage" separated from what precedes; I indicate this separation by the commas. "Soit" is the next word in the total text, appearing at the top of the left side of page 3 (and itself introducing, as we shall see, a whole dependent development); it concludes the construction of the verb, "quand bien même soit lancé," and hence should be separated from what follows it in this type-face by a semicolon indicating a major break in the meaning.

To this point, the words of the "interruption" depend directly upon "jamais" and are themselves uninterrupted. There is, however, a distortion of the normal syntactical order, for reasons that we shall soon discover. If we restore the normal order and punctuate, we obtain this continuous meaning: "jamais, quand bien même [il, i.e. un coup de dés] soit lancé dans des circonstances éternelles, du fond d'un naufrage." "Quand bien même" indicates the absolute quality of "jamais"; chance will not be changed even if the dice are thrown in the most extraordinary circumstances, "des circonstances éternelles." These last words prepare for two later developments in the poem: the circumstances will be "eternal" both because life and death are involved in the cast and because the constellation will result from it. The phrase "soit lancé du fond d'un naufrage" initiates the narrative element of the poem, the storm at sea, the peril of the ship, and the activity of its master. I shall inquire into these meanings and into the poetic probabilities that result from them as I proceed with the detailed analysis.

Of the next part of this development, "le maître existât-il commençât-il et cessât-il se chiffrât-il illuminât-il," only the subject, "le maître," appears before "n'abolira," the next word of the major sentence; the rest comes immediately before "le hasard." This means that we must read both "le maître . . . n'abolira . . . le hasard" and "illuminât-il le hasard" ("le hasard" thus concludes both the major sentence and two other elements in it, as well as another sentence started at a later point). "Le maître" is printed at the top, right, of the left side of page 4; everything that follows it on page 4 and on the left side of page 5 belongs to it and modifies it. What comes between "le maître" and the five verbs that complete the clause, terminated at the top right of page 9 (between "le nombre" of another sentence and "le hasard"), needs to intervene if we are to understand the meaning of those five verbs. Each of them is modified by interrupting phrases and the whole of the clause is an *incise* of a conditional character, probably depending grammatically upon "quand bien même"; we thus must read it as follows: "quand bien même . . . le maître existât-il, commençât-il et cessât-il, se chiffrât-il, illuminât-il [le hasard]," terminating this segment, like the preceding one, with a semicolon to mark a considerable pause.

Mallarmé, *Un Coup de dés*   253

"Rien n'aura eu lieu que le lieu excepté une constellation" is really a separate sentence; it comes after "le hasard" (from which it is separated by our semicolon) and states a conclusion at a point close to the conclusion of the whole poem. In itself it is broken up by intervening phrases, but it requires no punctuation to clarify its meaning. "Rien" appears alone on the left side of page 10, somewhat in from the right margin in the second quarter; it is followed, farther to the right in the third quarter, by a small group of words. We find "n'aura eu lieu" and "que le lieu" in the third quarter of the right side of page 10, preceded, separated, and followed by other groups of words. "Excepté," "peut-être" and "une constellation" move downward and across from the upper quarter of the left side of page 11 (where the first two are found) to the bottom of the second quarter of the right side of page 11, near the right margin; other words separate the three pieces and the whole ending of the poem follows upon "une constellation" down to the bottom of page 11.

If we recall now that visual representation of the "phrase capitale," the heavy black capitals against much white background, arranged roughly as I have indicated above, we may superimpose on that picture the elements of the long "interruption" just discussed. We shall have to do so in several distinct pieces. Thus between "jamais" and "n'abolira":

JAMAIS   soit   le maître
Quand bien même lancé dans des
circonstances éternelles
   du fond d'un naufrage

                                                                    N'ABOLIRA

And between "n'abolira" and "le hasard":

                        existât-il
               commençât-il et cessât-il
                     se chiffrât-il
                     illuminât-il
                   LE HASARD
N'ABOLIRA

Thus except for the first fragment, printed below "jamais," all the words of the passage so far are printed at or near the top of the pages, and higher than the words of the central sentence. As for the part following "le hasard," the arrangement is somewhat as follows:

> excepté
> > peut-être
>
> rien
>
> > une constellation
>
> LE HASARD
> > n'aura eu lieu
> > que le lieu

I have not tried, of course, to reproduce faithfully the spacings; but these rough approximations should serve to show at what points and in what ways the parts of this passage "interrupt" the main sentence or continue it, and how the intonational pattern—generally "higher" than that of the main sentence—is added to and mingled with the pattern of that sentence. (Here, my reader will have to do what Mallarmé's reader is expected to do: project one total visual image upon another, hear the two patterns of intensity and of intonation superimposed.)

What is important, of course, is that we should understand how the meaning of the main sentence is completed and developed by the so-called "interruption"; after all, the composite picture and the chordal sound exist only as means to showing how meanings are to be combined and interrelated. If we start with the original sentence, "Un coup de dés jamais n'abolira le hasard," we find that the throw of the dice will occur, in the example now to be pursued, in "circonstances éternelles" involving life and death; that the particular circumstances are defined by "du fond d'un naufrage," that the person who will cast the dice is the "master" of the storm-tossed ship. Nevertheless, in spite of the gravity of the extraordinary circumstances, neither the throw of the dice nor the master who throws them will in any way change the course of fortune: the ship will sink or remain afloat as it was destined to do, whether or not the dice are cast. Yet the dice must be cast; for although "nothing will have happened" aside from the casting of the dice in these circumstances ("que le lieu"), it is possible ("peut-être") that something momentous far beyond the saving of the ship may result. That something is here given magnitude and eternal existence in the form of the constellation.

The original bare and purely intellectual sentence has thus been given a concrete and sensible meaning. The act involved in the throwing of the dice has first of all been placed in particular circumstances. Then it has been provided with an agent, the master of the ship. In the part between "n'abolira" and "le hasard," this agent becomes minimally specified: as a man, he is born and dies ("existât-il, commençât-il et cessât-il"); through the cast of the dice he converts himself into a number ("se chiffrât-il") and he may possibly produce the constellation ("illuminât-il"). He will not abolish chance, but he may permanently transform it. These will be the results of his act. The abstract axiom still remains dominant through the poem; we see it as darkest and hear it as loudest. But the modifying phrases that weave around it attain their own prominence through their high pitch (they tend to fall above the words of the main sentence), through their relatively heavy typography, and through their number and grouping. Moreover, they finally come to outweigh the major sentence because of the fact that they become the source or the center of the most considerable developments in the poem.

In a very real sense, the rest of the poem is developed out of elements in the "interruption." "Soit," top left on the left side of page 3, gives rise to the statement of the circumstances that moves down and across the whole of page 3; the statement contains the description of the storm and of the vessel battling the storm. "Le maître," top right on the left side of page 4, is the subject of a long and much-interrupted sentence that shuttles back and forth across and down the whole of double page 4 and the left side of page 5, where it runs into "n'abolira" on the right side of page 5; the sentence traces the life history of the master, describes his hesitations with respect to the act and his final accomplishment of it, and makes a judgment about its effect. So far, the circumstances, the agent, and the act, connecting and surrounding "jamais . . . n'abolira . . . le hasard," with, between "n'abolira" and "le hasard," a part of this auxiliary text that epitomizes the life and the act of the master. (The two major words are also separated by three long metaphors, of which I shall speak later.) The remainder of the auxiliary sentence (it becomes an independent one) is spread over pages 10 and 11, with a movement down and across from "rien" (centered in the second quarter of the left side of page 10) to "n'aura eu lieu" and "que le lieu" (in the third quarter of the right side) and then from "excepté" and "peut-être" (top of left side, page 11) to "une constellation" (center, right, of right side of page 11). Coming after "le hasard," this independent segment expresses a new idea that is related, through the accompanying words, to all that has preceded as well as to the conclusion of the poem. As is the case for the main sentence, the meaning of this "interruption" is apparently complete and self-contained; but all the implications and all the specifications become known only through the further parts of the poem that are subordinated to them.

Indeed, it is through the developments based upon "soit" and upon "le maître" that we pass, in the reading of the poem, from the "Idea" to the "fiction" (which, as Mallarmé indicated in his Preface, "affleurera et se dissipera . . . autour des arrêts fragmentaires d'une phrase capitale"). And it is to the "fiction" that we will attach such emotions and passions as will accompany the understanding of the "Idea."

The word "soit" served to complete a verbal construction in the auxiliary sentence: "quand bien même lancé . . . soit." But as he will do at other places in his poem, Mallarmé uses the word to serve another grammatical function; this is one of the devices for linking the various parts of the poem to one another and to the "phrase capitale." Thus "soit," separated from the preceding words by its position at the extreme upper left of page 3, becomes the first word in a new clause, printed entirely in 14-point lower-case letters (except for the capitals of "sorr" itself and of "l'Abîme") and moving downward and across the whole of page 3. We must see the whole of this clause as in a way "hanging" from "soit" just as "soit" itself concludes a clause that depends upon "Jamais"; and we must hear it as of even intensity, lesser than that of "soit" and far below that of the major sentence, and as of a constantly falling intonation. We are, we might say, at a third level of intensity and, for the first time, in an intonational pattern that moves constantly downward. The text reads as follows (I indicate by diagonals the pieces into which it is divided): "sorr / que / l'Abîme / blanchi / étale / furieux / sous une inclinaison / plane désespérément / d'aile / la sienne / par avance retombée d'un mal à dresser le voile / et couvrant les jaillisse-ments / coupant au ras les bonds / très à l'intérieur résume / l'ombre enfouie dans la profondeur par cette voile alternative / jusqu'adapter / à l'envergure / sa béante profondeur en tant que la coque / d'un bâtiment / penché de l'un ou l'autre bord."

If "soit" divides two parts of a sentence grammatically, finishing one and starting another, it also divides two parts of the poem poetically. I mean by this that it makes the transition from a general statement about "circumstances" to a detailed account of the particular circumstances, in much the same way as "quand bien même" had made the transition from the abstract and proverbial sentence to that general statement. Besides, it passes from the abstract future of "n'abolira" to a kind of double conditional: the past conditional of "lancé . . . soit" and the present conditional of "soit que . . ." In so doing, it denotes the passage to the particular example that will illustrate the truth of the abstract sentence. We should remark also that "soit que . . ." as here used does not lead to another "soit que . . ." for an "either that . . . or that . . ." construction; stand-ing by itself, it means something like "as an example" or "supposing that . . ."

The clause that it introduces is much broken up and its elements are much modified (Mallarmé said, "on évite le récit"). But we may perceive the essential line of the meaning, which is simple enough: the supposition is that in a raging storm a wave of the sea, likened to the sail of a ship, engulfs the shadow of the vessel. We obtain this meaning by omitting a large number of words from the sentence: "soit que l'Abîme . . . étale . . . la sienne [i.e., d'aile] . . . et couvrant les jaillissements . . . résume l'ombre . . . jusqu'adapter à l'envergure sa béante profondeur . . ." If this be the central mean-ing of the statement, then we may go back and explain the sense and the usefulness of the omitted words, and in so doing we may arrive at a total interpretation. "L'Abîme" is used to signify the "sea" or the "deep"; it is capitalized in part to personify it (since it becomes an agent), in part to magnify its importance in the idea that will follow. With "blanchi" we have not only the first visual repre-sentation of the state of the sea, indicating the fury of its motion, but we also have the first basis for the assimilation of the sea's wave to the ship's sail; both are to be white. "Étale," referring to the spreading of the sea's wave, may also describe the spreading of the ship's sail—and, as will be shortly apparent, the spreading of a bird's wing; a third image is superimposed on the other two, and all three will move along together through the sentence. Although "furieux" is an adjective, masculine to agree with "l'Abîme," its real use is adverbial and it qualifies the movement of the wave as it modifies "étale." The phrase "sous une inclinaison" is still more complex in its meanings and associations. First of all it is the angle, and I suppose a fairly sharp one, of the wave and the sail and the wing. But it is also an astronomical-navigational term, the first of a number that will appear throughout the poem, and as such it introduces the heavens and the stars into the vision—the stars almost in an astrological connotation, with all the suggestions of chance and fortune that that carries with it. Hence "*sous* une inclinaison."

After the verb "étale," another verb appears to ascribe action to the abyss, and it does so in terms of the bird who makes up the third part of the image. "Plane désespérément / d'aile" describes an action which is either that of the sea itself or of some object upon or above it; and "aile," as it relates to the bird, provides a complement that can be used only metaphorically for the sea. What happens, then, is that "l'Abîme . . . plane . . . d'aile," in an image that combines sea and bird, hence wave and wing. The adverb "désespérément" builds upon "furieux," adding to it a human emotion and a vision of erratic or frantic flight. "La sienne" refers to the sea's wing, that is, its wave; it is the direct object of "étale" and as a possessive pronoun refers to a noun that had been used in an adverbial phrase as belonging to the bird. The sea and the bird thus come to be inextricably mingled in the metaphor. So they are again in the longish phrase that follows, "par avance retombée d'un mal à dresser le vol." It would be difficult to apply "dresser le vol" to the ship's wave, except in the metaphorical way already suggested; it is easy to make it represent the bird's flight; and it is almost as easy, by extension, to see it as describing the ship's motion over the water. "Un mal à dresser le vol" (and "dresser" would be a correction of "inclinaison") may simultaneously estimate the bird's difficulties in controlling his flight and the crew's difficulties in righting the ship—both because of the fury of the storm. Thus as we move backward to "par avance retombée" we realize that wave or wing or sail would with difficulty be made to resist the "furious" storm, and that the situation for all is "desperate."

Two successive phrases now continue the description, one of them possibly designating the activity of the wave ("et couvrant les jaillissements"), the other more specifically pertinent to the activity of the ship ("coupant au ras les bonds"). The "jaillissements" are sudden spurts or gushes of water, the "bonds" are the more continuous surges of the waves. Any one wave (such as the vast one that will soon appear) might cover the minor "jaillissements"; I suppose that it might also roll over other waves, but the expression "coupant au ras" seems rather to designate the motion of the ship as it "flies" over the waves. For the next phrase, we must again return to the subject, "l'Abîme," to which it supplies another verb and an adverbial modifier: "très à l'intérieur résume." "Résume" has an etymological meaning (a frequent procedure with Mallarmé); what is "resumed" is "taken back into" or "taken in once again," and it is taken deeply into the interior of the wave that covers it. That object is identified in the following long line: "l'ombre enfouie dans la profondeur par cette voile alternative." Some of the words here are explained by what has preceded. Thus "dans la profondeur" is roughly equivalent to "très à l'intérieur," but it adds the more general notion of the sea or the "Abîme" as a whole (the word will be used again in this sense a few lines lower on the page). "Cette voile" is the first direct and proper reference to the ship's sail, although this has been alluded to metaphorically at several previous points. We will know what is meant by "voile alternative" only when we reach the bottom of the page and find the phrase "penché de l'un ou l'autre bord." This completes the visual image: the ship, tossed by the furious sea, leans alternatively from one side to the other; as it does so, its sail casts a shadow upon the water, down into the hollow of the wave; and this shadow is in turn engulfed by the wave that rolls over it. Hence "l'ombre enfouie . . . par cette voile," hence the verb "résume" of which this whole line is the direct object.

To this point, a whole series of verbs have served as predicates to "l'Abîme": three finite forms, "étale," "plane," and "résume," and two present participles, "couvrant" and "coupant." In the next lines an infinitive construction concludes the basic sentence: "jusqu'a-dapter / à l'envergure." All the other actions of the abyss lead to this one: it adjusts or conforms or adapts the size of its wave to the total spread of the ship's shadow. This is the action that links the storm with the ship, puts the ship at the mercy of the storm; for if the shadow is engulfed, the ship could also be engulfed. The ship has not yet been named, but its sail has been spoken of and now its "envergure" is indicated. ("Jusqu'à adapter" is reduced to "jusqu'a-dapter" for purposes of the rhythm and to avoid the hiatus—even the mental one—involved in the full form.) The rest of the page provides the object of "adapter" and introduces specifically the ship and its movement: "jusqu'adapter / à l'envergure / sa béante pro-fondeur en tant que la coque / d'un bâtiment / penché de l'un ou l'autre bord." "Sa béante profondeur" is a paraphrase for the "Abîme" itself, indicated by the possessive "sa"; but it also reinforces the idea of "profondeur" just three lines above, and presents in "béante" a kind of counterpart to "enfouie." The shadow of the ship can be "enfouie" only because the sea is "béante," and the sea is "béante" only because of the height and angle of the great wave. Both "en tant que" and "penché" present problems of interpretation, the first because it has no proper finite verb depending upon it, the second because it is without auxiliary. The solution may lie in interpreting "en tant que" as a kind of adverbial modifier and making of "penché" an adjectival modifier of "bâtiment." This last part of the sentence would then read: "to the point of adapting its gaping depths to the full span, equaling in measure the shell of a vessel leaned over on the one or the other side" (with "bord" as in "babord" and "tribord"). We should note that it is "un bâtiment," not "le bâtiment"; we are still in the realm of supposition and condition.

We therefore have, on page 3, a lengthy development of the conditions under which, "du fond d'un naufrage," the dice might be thrown, conditions of great import involving life and death. The ship that might sink or be wrecked, "le bâtiment," is introduced; its movement over the stormy sea is described; and the sea's great wave is presented in terms that liken it both to the ship's sail and to the wing of a bird. Both comparisons will be of later use in the poem. Since the wave is large enough to engulf the ship's whole shadow, it may menace the ship itself, make of it a "naufrage"; and since shadow or ship may go down into the "profondeur" of the sea, the dice may be thrown upward from the "fond" of the sinking ship (the etymological relationship of the two words is not to be overlooked). The violent motion of the sea is communicated to the ship, added to the ship's own swift flight over the waves. All the necessary circumstances are thus made a part of the supposition. As the clause is arranged and printed on page 3, it is subordinated through its typography to the two preceding sections, and its movement downward and across marks a progressive lowering of the pitch. I think that this cannot be understood too precisely, however, since it would practically be impossible to continue a dropping of the intonation over so long a passage.

Moreover, Mallarmé stated, while he was correcting the proofs of a "definitive" edition that never appeared, that he also had in mind imitative effects of a visual nature. In a letter to André Gide, quoted by Gide in a lecture on Nov. 22, 1913 and later published in *La Vie des lettres* for April, 1914, Mallarmé referred specifically to the visual effect that he desired for this page:

Le vaisseau y donne de la bande, du haut d'une page au bas de l'autre, etc.; car, et c'est là tout le point de vue (qu'il me fallut omettre dans un périodique), le rythme d'une phrase au sujet d'un acte, ou même d'un objet, n'a de sens que s'il les imite, et figuré sur le papier, repris par la lettre à l'estampe originelle, n'en sait rendre, malgré tout, quelque chose. (Quoted in the Pléiade edition, pp. 1575–76.)

We are thus meant to see the vessel moving lower and lower, in a rolling way, at the same time as we hear constantly lower notes as the page is read. This disposition of the typography and the statement about it are curious indeed; for they lead us to infer that, in spite of his theory of orchestration and his concern with rhythmical and intonational patterns, Mallarmé was perhaps primarily concerned with the effect of the poem as seen on the printed page.

Hence the visual effect of the long statement that occupies both sides of page 4 and the left side of page 5 is undoubtedly significant.

Rather than moving regularly downward and across (which is al-most the normal pattern for the poem), the materials of the sentence that develops "LE MAÎTRE" move back and forth on the page. No sequence of words, of course, is to be read "backward"; but the reader goes across a part of the page, returns to a starting point similar to that of the preceding line, goes across again, returns again. This means that for the double page 4 the point of reference is really the center line that divides the two sides (rather than either or both of the margins), while on the single left side of page 5 the lines are divided by a center line that would bisect the page. As a result, in both cases many of the lines cross the dividing line, are split by it (whereas on page 3 only one line moved across from the left side to the right side of the page, and of that line only one word, "par," appeared on the left side). The reason for this arrangement is, I believe, double. On the one hand, it is meant to visualize the move-ment of the vessel from the one to the other "bord"; on the other hand, it represents the hesitations of the master, the "back and forth" movement of his mind, as he prepares to cast the dice.

For the new development (about twice as long as the preceding one) concerns the master of the vessel as agent in the throwing of the dice. It begins with "LE MAÎTRE," a part of the sentence in 14-point capitals, and ends with "N'ABOLIRA" in 48-point display capitals at the bottom of page 5, right side (in the same letter, Mallarmé had written: "Tel mot en gros caractères à lui seul de-mande toute une page de blanc, et je crois être sûr de l'effet"). The intervening text is entirely in 14-point lower case, except for the cap-ital letters of "Nombre," "Esprit," and "Fiançailles." This is the same type as that of the preceding interruption, and it puts the passage at the same level of importance. But whereas the preceding text came to a full stop with "penché de l'un ou l'autre bord," without returning to higher sections of the poem, the present text runs into the "phrase capitale" in two ways: first, as we see the sequence "Le maître . . . n'abolira . . . le hasard," second, as this sentence comes to its own conclusion with "Le maître . . . folie n'abolira."

The sentence itself is extremely complex, with interruptions of the interruptions. Essentially, it confuses and interweaves three separate lines of narration, which need to be separated again if we are to understand what is happening. The first (and major) one relates the activity of the master with respect to the throwing of the dice; we may reduce it to these elements: "LE MAÎTRE, . . . inférant . . . que se prépare . . . au poing . . . l'unique Nombre . . . hésite . . . à n'ouvrir pas la main . . . ; celui . . . tentant . . . une chance oiseuse . . . chancellera, s'affalera, folie N'ABOLIRA . . ." An alternative ending to the sentence would be "chancellera, s'affalera, . . . N'ABOLIRA . . . LE HASARD"; both endings need to be kept in mind as we read the poem, for the meaning is at all points multiple. This is the action of the man placed within the "eternal circumstances" that have just been outlined. In the summation that will come later (page 9, right, above "LE HASARD"), this action will be epitomized by "SE CHIFFRÂT-IL," where it is reduced to the essential act of finding the fateful number through the throw of the dice. The summation also provides, in "EXISTÂT-IL, . . . COMMENÇÂT-IL ET CESSÂT-IL," a résumé of the second line of narration, the one devoted to the existence, the whole life and career of the master and his intimate relationship to the sea and the ship. If the act is to be done, the agent must exist; if it is to be done right, the agent must be one who, through his history and his associations, will be capable of putting chance to a sufficient test. In the second narrative line the narrative order is disturbed, the natural chronology of a man's existence and career is disrupted. We therefore find the elements in the following order: "hors d'anciens calculs . . . la manœuvre avec l'âge oubliée . . . jadis il empoignait la barre . . . cadavre . . . maniaque chenu . . . en barbe soumise . . . ancestralement . . . legs . . . à   quelqu'un / ambigu . . . de contrées nulles . . . le vieillard . . . son ombre puérile / caressée et polie et rendue et lavée / assouplie par la vague et soustraite / aux durs os perdus entre les ais / né / d'un ébat / la mer par l'aïeul . . . ou l'aïeul contre la mer . . . Fiançailles . . ." Were we to restore the natural order, we should find here all the pertinent events in the life and career of the master: his ancestry, the wedding of his parents, his birth, his boyhood, his maturity as master of the ship, his old age, his impending death.

For the third line of narration we also find the summary word, on page 9: "ILLUMINÂT-IL . . . [LE HASARD]"; it refers basically to the results of the master's act in throwing the dice, to the consequences of his trying of chance. Those consequences will be firmly stated in the last part of the poem, in the sentence (also in 14-point capitals): "Rien n'aura eu lieu que le lieu excepté peut-être une constellation." The present statement is less definitive; it is negative rather than affirmative; it is more specifically limited to the throw of the dice, as it juxtaposes winning against losing and suggests what would happen to the master in either case. These are its elements: "comme on menace un destin et les vents . . . l'unique Nombre qui ne peut pas être un autre . . . pour le jeter / dans la tempête / en reployer la division et passer fier . . . par le bras écarté du secret qu'il détient / plutôt / que de jouer . . . la partie / au nom des flots . . . naufrage cela direct de l'homme / sans nef / n'importe / où vaine . . . en la disparition . . . l'ultérieur démon immémorial . . . vers cette conjonction suprême avec la probabilité . . . le voile d'illusion rejailli leur hantise . . ." Moreover, these elements are intertwined with the others in such a way as to give them added meanings and references that they do not have in isolation. After all, the poem is the poem only as it stands in its totality.

If we return to the beginning of this second narrative section, we may see how the three lines of development affect one another and how a total meaning and effect results. "LE MAÎTRE / hors d'anciens calculs / où la manœuvre avec l'âge oubliée / surgi": the sentence begins with its subject, the master, and through a participial clause attributes a first action to him, "surgi." We should note immediately that this action is opposite to the ones described in the preceding section, where ship, sail, and shadow all moved constantly downward; this is an upward movement, the first of several such in the current passage. The master arises out of his calculations; these are "anciens calculs" both because they go back many years in the life of the master and because they are centuries-old among mariners. Their mention relates the master to the tradition of navigational techniques by which men have, through the ages, attempted to dominate the sea by the use of the mind. All these inferences will be exploited later in the passage. As he engages in his calculations, the master withdraws himself from the actual physical maneuvering of the ship, an activity of his younger days: "où la manœuvre avec l'âge oubliée." He has thus, in his lifetime, passed from the action of the body to the action of the spirit—another preparation for later elements in the text.

The next clause is also participial, with its present participle related to "le maître": "inférant / jadis il empoignait la barre / de cette conflagration à ses pieds / de l'horizon unanime / que se prépare / s'agite et mêle / au poing qui l'étreindrait / comme on menace un destin et les vents / l'unique Nombre qui ne peut pas être un autre." As was the case in the preceding clause, the various strains are intermixed: thus "inférant," the next step in the master's activity, is followed immediately by a biographical indication, "jadis il empoignait la barre." Present spiritual action (it will turn out to be not quite that) is juxtaposed to past bodily activity, old age is contrasted with virile maturity, and in a way to sharpen the opposition: "em*poign*ait" is used for the grasping of the tiller with which the master once controlled the ship's direction, *"poing"* will soon be used for the holding of the dice that will determine the ship's fate. The inference is made not only on the basis of astronomical or navigational calculation, but also from observation of visible phenomena. From the "conflagration" at his feet—the term is metaphorical and refers to the raging and seething sea—and from the horizon in which sea and sky are indistinguishable, the master deduces that the critical moment in his destiny has arrived. The first reference to the dice occurs in the phrase "que se prépare, s'agite, et mêle au poing . . . l'unique Nombre." But the number that is to result is not the product of orderly calculation; the three verbs, and especially "s'agite et mêle," signify rather the uncertainty of chance for him as the master shakes the dice in his fist. The reflexives make the master a passive observer in the preparation of the number; chance itself is the agent, the master merely provides the motion, in the "poing qui l'étreindrait," that will permit the dice themselves to "prepare" the number. The verb "étreindrait" in its conditional form gives a meaning parallel to that of "empoignait" but adds the notion of surmise that was introduced with "quand bien même lancé soit."

With "comme on menace un destin et les vents," an interjection within the developing clause, several important ideas appear in the poem. The first three words once more represent an upward motion:

one sees the clutched fist raised towards "destiny" and the winds. "Menace" itself does give agency to the master (even though it is only "comme on menace") since it shows him in the posture of one who opposes both the winds that threaten his ship and the fate that threatens his life. However, his opposition is weak and must be ineffectual, especially since he will now use neither mind nor body but will merely "try his luck." The hopelessness of his effort is verified in what follows: "l'unique Nombre qui ne peut pas être un autre." Since the number that will show when the dice are thrown is predetermined by destiny and can be no other, since it is the "only" number possible, the master is powerless—either through his calculations or through his shaking of the dice—to change it.

As I pointed out earlier, only three words in this passage are capitalized, "Nombre," "Esprit," and "Fiançailles" in that order. The capital letters are there not only to indicate that these words take on the value of abstractions in the poem, but also to establish a relationship among the three. Since "Nombre" is the first, we are not immediately aware of the latter function; we discover immediately and primarily its abstract quality. That discovery is made by a reference back to the initial words, "Un coup de dés," and to the formula "circonstances éternelles" that follows closely after, to "un destin" that immediately precedes; but especially by a reference forward to the text of this same section. A few lines lower on page 4 the "Number" is called "un secret"; and on the next page comes what may be considered as a definition of the abstract significance of "le Nombre," in the phrase: "cette conjonction suprême avec la probabilité." Finally, near the bottom of page 5, left side, we have the phrase to which I have already referred, "tentant . . . une chance oiseuse." From all these passages it becomes clear that "le Nombre" is not only the "number" that will appear when the dice are thrown, but it is also the representation of the precise way—the time, the place, the circumstances—in which the master comes in contact with, in opposition to the forces of destiny that will determine whether, in this crisis, he will live or die. We see the basic opposition in the poem: on the one hand, the master, the man whose fate is at issue; on the other hand, the forces against which he must struggle. Besides, we see in the present passage the means that he has

at his disposal for the struggle: his body, and all the physical potentials he may have to control his destiny; his mind, and all the
"calculations" or intellectual potentials; and the appeal to chance or
luck, which means a surrender of the other two means. What will he
do, and with what results? These actions will constitute the matter
of the "fiction" contained within the poem.

In the next line, and constituting by itself the whole of the line,
comes the second capitalized word, "Esprit." In a very real sense, we
have here the "supreme conjunction" of the poem. After "le Nombre" or the abstraction for the circumstances that will be opposed to
the master, "Esprit" or the master himself, seen in his essentially
human quality as intellect (rather than as body) that makes it
possible for him to oppose those circumstances. The capital "E"
relates the word to "Nombre" just as it again signifies an abstraction.
For "Esprit" we once again have the preceding and following words
that delimit and specify its meaning. The "anciens calculs" and
"inférant" toward the beginning of the passage, "le chef," "l'inutile
tête," and "induit" coming after "Esprit," combine to distinguish
this quality of the master from his mere existence as "l'homme."
Moreover, "Esprit" comes into the passage as an interruption of the
developing sentence, with no proper syntactical relationship to the
rest. It stands in apposition to "Le Maître" at the opening of
the passage and to "celui" at the middle of the next page, emphasizing
by its isolation the special capabilities of intellect belonging to the
master.

The following phrases return to the fiction, continuing the words:
"se prépare . . . l'unique Nombre": "pour le jeter / dans la tempête
/ en reployer la division et passer fier." They thus depend upon the
participle "inférant" and belong to a modifying or "interrupting"
clause. In themselves they are a kind of paraphrase of parts of the
main sentence: "pour le [un coup de dés] jeter [lancé . . . soit]
dans la tempête [dans des circonstances éternelles / du fond d'un
naufrage]." But whereas the main statement has ended with a negative conclusion, "jamais n'abolira le hasard," this sentence concludes
affirmatively with a positive prediction for the outcome of the
throw: "en reployer la division et passer fier." There is, in the
phrase, no subject for the verbs "jeter," "reployer," and "passer fier";

they thus belong to the same impersonal development as "se prépare . . . au poing qui l'étreindrait" and "comme on menace." But their reference to the master is clear: it is he who shakes the dice, he who menaces destiny, and he who would make the throw into the storm for the purpose of overcoming it. "La tempête" summarizes, in a way, all the activity of the storm and the sea that had been fully described on the preceding page, and in so doing it epitomizes the circumstances that are now opposing the master; "la tempête" brings into this section on the master the whole of the preceding section ("soit que . . .") devoted to the storm that threatens the ship. Were the throw of the dice to be successful, were chance to be abolished, the divided sea would again be made smooth, the great waves would be flattened ("en reployer la division"), and the ship would sail safely on ("et passer fier"). This being the case, there is really a different real subject for each of the three infinitives: the master's fist will throw the dice, the resulting number will cause the end of the tempest, and the ship will pass safely onward. Master, ship, and sea are brought into conjunction.

But the mode is still conditional, for there are still and always two alternative results for the throw of the dice: it may save the ship, or it may do nothing at all. The first probability is the one considered by the master so far and the one that leads him to undertake the action. But the second one is always present; should it come about, and should master and ship perish as a result of the throw—we must note that the dice are credited with agency in the saving or losing of the ship—then the master will have brought about his own destruction. Therefore the master hesitates. "Hésite," alone and central on a line (with long white spaces before and after it), is the verb of which "le maître" is the subject; after many interpositions and participial clauses, the finite verb finally appears; many other interruptions will occur before the prepositional clause depending on it will come along, before the "hésite à" construction is completed.

The first interruption following "hésite" is again an appositive to "le maître." It again refers to the conditional nature of the throw: "cadavre par le bras écarté du secret qu'il détient." The first suggestion of the line is a visual image: we see the master (now in the form of a corpse) with his arm stretched upward, the dice in his fist. He is of course still alive, and the image is almost entirely a physical one. The fist ("qu'*il*" refers to "le poing") holds the dice, the dice are the potential for a number, the number is the "secret" held within the fist. Should it be the number that means the master's death, he will pass from the state of man to the state of corpse; therefore, it is the length of his arm that measures the distance, for him, between life and death ("cadavre écarté du secret qu'il détient par le bras," or "cadavre écarté par le bras du secret qu'il [le poing] détient"). In the word "cadavre" we have the final stage in that biographical sequence that I alluded to earlier. The sequence is presented in inverse order, from last to first, and if we wish to reconstruct the proper order, we must go to the bottom of page 5, right margin of left side, and read "upward and back" (rather than the usual "downward and across"). We should then get some such sequence as this: "Fiançailles . . . ébat . . . né . . . puérile . . . homme . . . chenu . . . cadavre," with additions (out of their proper inverse order) of "vieillard," "jadis il empoignait la barre," and "anciens calculs"; there will even be, at a useful point in the sequence, the term "ancestralement." The reasons for the reversal of the biography will be apparent later; but we may suggest that "cadavre" comes where it does, here and first, because the passage to the state of corpse is precisely what is at stake in this critical action of the aging master.

If the master hesitates, it is because of the existence of the second, undesirable alternative, that the sea may be the winner in the throw. That possibility is stated in the next clause, which makes a small concentrated group near the bottom of the left side of page 4: "plutôt / que de jouer / en maniaque chenu / la partie / au nom des flots." "Jouer la partie au nom des flots" obviously means to produce the number that would give the victory to the sea; "jouer la partie" will be restated later in the formula "tenter . . . une chance" and the "flots" are another summation of the stormy sea. The whole idea is the contrary of "pour le jeter / dans la tempête / en reployer la division et passer fier." The master, playing in this way against himself, would be acting (as he himself recognizes) "en maniaque chenu." Both terms are highly important, "maniaque" because it indicates that the master will have surrendered the use of his intellect and acted as if insane ("folie" will be the last word in this section), "chenu" because it identifies the age of the master, makes of him the "vieillard" approaching death.

Like "Esprit" higher on the page, the next phrase, "un envahit le chef / coule en barbe soumise," is an interruption without syntactical connection with the rest. Like "Esprit," also, these words refer to the master, owner of the "chef" and the "barbe." I think that the subject "un" must stand pronominally for "un nombre," since there is no other antecedent that makes satisfactory sense. We should then read: "un nombre envahit [entre dans] le chef [la tête du maître]." At this point in the master's action, while he hesitates to throw the dice that he has been shaking, a number is formed both in his hand and in his mind (hence the parallelism of construction with "Esprit"); presumably this is the number that would signify the sea's victory, the master's defeat, since the phrase comes between "jouer . . . la partie au nom des flots" and "naufrage cela direct." If the number enters the master's head, this does not necessarily mean that he has returned to calculation and intellection; he is still relying on chance to save his life and merely comes to a knowledge of what chance has decided for him—supposing that he throws this number. "Coule en barbe soumise" gives a physical existence and a physical locus to the number, continuing the suggestions of "envahit le chef." In a way the visual image of the hoary head is completed when the beard is "put beneath" it ("soumise"), when "chenu," "chef," and "barbe" are joined in a series. But there is a moral implication as well in "soumise"; the master's body as well as his mind "submits" passively to the decision of destiny which "flows," we may say, from the number in the hand to the head and then to the body.

To submit in this way is to be vanquished: that is the statement that concludes this page. The statement, however, is made in the form of a generalization, of a universal conclusion applicable to all men. Through it we begin to foresee the abstractions that will conclude the poem, that are in a sense its purpose. If we are to read the new clause as complete we must use the "un" again as the article belonging to "naufrage," a usage justified by the position of "un" directly above "naufrage cela" to the left of the central dividing line. The clause then reads: "un . . . naufrage cela direct de l'homme / sans nef / n'importe / où vaine." "Cela" makes the connection with what precedes, referring both to "jouer la partie au nom des flots" and to "un envahit le chef." If one, if anyone ("l'homme") acts in this way, turning his destiny over to chance, he can end only in disaster. "Naufrage" thus takes on a meaning beyond the specific one of "shipwreck," coming to signify in a general manner "failure" or "disaster" or "death." This interpretation is corroborated by the formula "sans nef"; a "naufrage . . . sans nef" (and the play upon the etymological relationship of the words should not be over-looked) is necessarily a general kind of failure. The generality is further reinforced by the substitution of "l'homme" for "le maître." If the shipwreck or failure is "direct," it is because man becomes responsible for it through his own action: there is no intermediation of any other cause. The final words, "n'importe / où vaine," modify "nef" and as they do so they contribute further to the generalization. Were the man in such a situation, anywhere and at any time, to interpose between death and himself such an artificial means of salvation as a ship, he would nevertheless be lost; his effort and its instrument would be vain, since he would already have surrendered his responsibility to fate. "N'importe" is separated from "où" in an extraordinary fashion, probably to emphasize "où"; this once more would point to the conclusion of the poem, where "le lieu" takes on special importance.

The development relative to the master and his action continues on the left side of page 5. But as I pointed out earlier, the shuttle motion is restricted to a single side rather than moving back and forth across a double page. As a result the left side presents the kind of crowded arrangement of words and lines that was characteristic of the whole of the 1897 edition; the spacing here is identical with that of page 422 of the periodical printing except for the fact that the lines there were printed even more closely together in order to allow for the large "N'ABOLIRA" at the bottom of the single page. When the text of page 5 begins with "ancestralement à n'ouvrir pas la main / crispée / par delà l'inutile tête," it rejoins the central sentence, completing the "hésite à" construction. What the master hesitates to do is to throw the dice, to open the hand that holds the secret number. He is presented again in the posture previously described, his hand raised upward and his fist clenching the dice. His hand is

272

"crispée" (not merely "fermée") in witness to the moral and spiritual tension embodied in the physical gesture. He holds it above and beyond the "inutile tête"; the meaning of the adjective is now clear since, as he has abandoned calculation and ceased to operate as an intellect, the master makes no further use of his mental potential. Perhaps "chef" in the preceding passage, as opposed to "tête" here, was intended to signify the purely physical or material part of the body. The verbal phrase "hésite . . . à n'ouvrir" is modified in two ways, by the adverb "ancestralement" and by the negative "ne . . . pas." "Ancestralement" belongs in the series of biographical elements related to the master. If it comes at this point, it is because only now is the verbal complement of "hésite à" to be introduced: the hesitation in surrendering to destiny is an "ancestral" hesitation in so far as it is human. To allow the head to become useless, to negate intellect, is to deny the tradition of the race, and this is what the master now hesitates to do. The negative "ne . . . pas" comes along (against our expectations) to emphasize the hesitation—hence to stress his real wish to retain control of his situation.

For the following phrase, "legs en la disparition / à quelqu'un / ambigu," which is an appositive phrase, the problem is to discover to what it is in apposition; that is, what becomes a legacy? It would seem that the best candidate is "tête," the word immediately preceding. If that were so, the meaning would be that when the master dies ("en la disparition"; cf. "cessât-il") his intellectual capacity ("tête") is passed on to some unknown future member of the race. That future member would be "ambigu" both because unknown and because it would be doubtful, in such situations as this, how he would use that intellectual capacity. The future ambiguity would correspond to the present hesitation, just as the notion of passing something on to posterity is a counterpart to the notion of receiving something from one's ancestry. The master stands at a point between the past and the future.

How he has been brought to this point, to the present crisis, is revealed in the next clause: "l'ultérieur démon immémorial / ayant / de contrées nulles / induit / le vieillard vers cette conjonction suprême avec la probabilité." Once more, the last part of the clause is the clearest. The master in his old age (already seen and now reiterated) has been brought to the moment in his life where its continuation is to be decided. The meeting between man and destiny, the "conjonction," is supreme both in the sense that it is of the highest importance and in the sense that it may be final. "La probabilité" is synonymous with "le hasard" and, on the level of the fiction, with "l'unique Nombre" that will result from the throw of the dice. The first part of the clause may be explained by what has gone before it. Its subject, "l'ultérieur démon immémorial," obviously refers to some supernatural force, some extra-human element such as "un destin" that might have the capacity to lead the master to this time and place. The force is "ultérieur" in that it is beyond and outside man and his volition, "immémorial" in that it goes back infinitely in time (just as does the master through "ancestralement"). Its verb, "ayant induit," will not be used as a participial construction to prepare for another verb, but will instead stand as a kind of ablative absolute, making the whole clause depend from what has preceded rather than leading into anything new. We should note that the verb is "induire" and not "conduire"; the master is "led into" the situation, but he is also an "Esprit" who infers and hence there is a kind of logical "induction" related to his present plight and his action. The inference from the particular to the universal, from the case of the master to the abstraction about destiny, is a part both of the fiction and of the Idea as they develop in the poem. "De contrées nulles" states the place of origin of the master; it is cognate with "vers cette conjonction"; and again it moves back indefinitely in time (continuing thus the series "ancestralement," "immémorial"). The master comes out of unknown times and places antedating the very beginnings of the human race; he is brought to this point by an unknown and secret destiny; and when he dies, his legacy will pass to an equally unknown posterity.

So much time has passed and so many things have happened since the introduction of the subject of this long development that it is now necessary to provide the pronoun "celui" to replace and recall "le maître." The new clause will be short and simple: "celui . . . tentant . . . une chance oiseuse . . . chancellera / s'affalera / folie / N'ABOLIRA"; but it will again be much interrupted and modified and a number of the biographical elements will be contained in it.

The first element—in the established inverse order—is his childhood or young manhood: "celui / son ombre puérile / caressée et polie et rendue et lavée / assouplie par la vague et soustraite / aux durs os perdus entre les ais." In spite of its apparent simplicity, this statement is rich in implications. Just as we have previously been invited to see the figure of the master (still menacing destiny with his clenched fist) transformed into the corpse that he would become were he to die, so we should now see him in another figuration of himself, as a boy or young man at the beginning of his association with the sea. In this sense his "ombre puérile" is presented to us. We discover immediately that this is that form of his upon which the sea will exert its influence, changing it gradually into the present weather-worn figure. We discover also that the terms used to describe the process are precisely the ones that would be used for a ship maintained through the years by a master and a crew: "caressée et polie et rendue et lavée." There is no mention of the elements that would normally be associated with a mariner's body, wrinkles, sunburn, toughness. Master and ship have been completely confused and identified in the description. Moreover, one of the terms, "rendue," is a "terme de marine"; used absolutely in this way, it is applied to a manoeuver of the ship: "Se dit d'une manœuvre, quand elle est arrivée au point de tension qui lui convient" (Littré). The adjective belongs essentially to the ship; but since it applies ostensibly to the master as well, along with the others, it refers back to two previous statements about the master: "la manœuvre avec l'âge oubliée" and "jadis il empoignait la barre" (these represent, in inverse order, two later stages in his career).

In a similar way, the next phrase, "assouplie par la vague," pertains simultaneously to master and ship, perhaps primarily to the latter; in this way, the sea itself becomes an agent in the tempering of the vessel and its master and a first kind of "conjunction" is established. This is an activity of the waves opposite to the one previously attributed to them in the poem, just as the master's menacing of the winds was contrary to his maneuvering of the ship. The concluding words of the development, "et soustraite / aux durs os perdus entre les ais," seem rather to modify "ombre puérile" as properly the figure of the master; for it would be difficult to see "les ais" (the planks) as anything but a part of the ship itself, and one could not well remove it from itself. My conjecture is that the words simply mean "kept alive" for the master, in which the "durs os" would relate to the "cadavre" of the preceding page and "perdus entre les ais" would effect a further identification of the ship with the master (now in the form of the corpse that he would become were he not so kept alive); although I have difficulty at this point in seeing the precise meaning. In any case, I should point out that the identification of ship and master is corroborated by the use, on page 3, of "l'ombre enfouie dans la profondeur" and of "son ombre puérile" in this passage; the simple term "ombre" serves to link the two objects. And perhaps the "enfouie dans la profondeur" of the first use may provide some clue to the meaning of "perdus entre les ais" of the second.

Still regressing in the master's biography, we come now to a short section that treats of his conception and birth: "né / d'un ébat / la mer par l'aïeul tentant ou l'aïeul contre la mer / une chance oiseuse." All this is one or two steps back of the period of "son ombre puérile." It will later be summarized by the formula "COMMENÇÂT-IL" in the same way as the "disparition" and other indications of his death will be epitomized by "CESSÂT-IL." "Né" indicates the actual moment of birth, "d'un ébat" the "conjunction" of his parents in joyful intercourse. I use the term "conjunction" advisedly since, here and elsewhere, master, ship, and sea are inextricably conjoined. In the present passage, "tentant . . . une chance oiseuse" (the words become a group typographically) has two subjects and two meanings. For one, the subject is "le maître" as represented by "celui": "celui . . . tentant une chance oiseuse . . . chancellera" and so forth. For the other, the subject is the master's parents, "l'aïeul" and "la mer"; he is linked to the sea from the beginning through his parentage. But the subject is stated in two separate and distinct ways: "la mer par l'aïeul," in which there is a kind of genealogical indication of dam and sire entering into conjunction; and "l'aïeul contre la mer," in which instead there is an opposition—a physical opposition, first, that places the ancestor against the sea in the amorous act, a moral opposition, second, in which two inimical forces are pitted one against the other just as they will be in the master's present crisis.

Whether they are together or opposed, the act of the progenitors consists in "tentant une chance oiseuse"; what they will beget is unknown and ambiguous (cf. "à quelqu'un / ambigu") and yet it is predetermined and ineluctable. If the master is the subject, the trying of luck is idle and useless ("oiseuse") because nothing in his destiny will be changed by it ("n'abolira le hasard"); if the parents are the subject, the same is true because their act is merely a necessary step in the plan of the "ultérieur démon immémorial." The master's "aïeul" is only one in a long series of his ancestors (and we must return to the implications of "ancestralement") all of whose activity led him to this particular crisis.

Before the actual conjunction of his ancestors, another kind of bringing together signified by the "Fiançailles" that introduces the next phrase: "Fiançailles / dont / le voile d'illusion rejailli leur hantise / ainsi que le fantôme d'un geste." "Fiançailles" is the third of the words in the section distinguished by a capital letter; or if we read "upward and back" in the proper order for this series, the first: "Fiançailles," "Esprit," "Nombre." Perhaps it would not be going too far to add to the series the "Abîme" on page 3. Now we should note that in the 1897 edition none of the three words was capitalized (although "Abîme" was). Mallarmé added the capitals when he prepared the definitive edition, undoubtedly to indicate the connection among the three words, possibly to add them to "Abîme" as a fourth. In fact, they are connected, not only because they make a "downward and across" movement from the top left of page 3 to the bottom right of page 5 (left side, which is treated as a complete page), but because when properly arranged they make a total sense that is the essence of the Idea to this point: the "Fiançailles" are a conjunction of a man of intellect (or "Esprit") with his eternal circumstances ("l'Abîme") in a crisis in which the man calls upon chance ("l'unique Nombre") to find the needed solution. As we superimpose one pattern of words upon another, in that "chordal" picture that Mallarmé wishes us to produce, we must see these four words as set off from the rest in the two developments (concerning the sea and the master) both by their capitals and by their pattern of arrangement. Another connecting line has been added to the visual and the intellectual structure.

The "Fiançailles" in the broad abstract sense are the bringing together of intellect and circumstances; in the specific sense of the fiction they mean "cette conjonction suprême [du vieillard] avec la probabilité"; at this particular point in the retrospective narrative, they are the engagement of the master's ancestors, "la mer" and "l'aïeul." To this latter sense are related the rest of the words in the phrase. "Dont" must here serve as a relative of place, meaning "whence, from where"; as it functions in the phrase "Fiançailles / dont / le voile d'illusion rejailli," it establishes some such meaning as this: "Betrothal out of which [had] sprung up the veil of illusion." Again, as had been the case with "ombre," the terms are drawn from the passage on the sea. "Rejailli" goes back to "couvrant les jaillissements," with the "re-" perhaps indicating a resumption or recovery of the activity; "le voile" (in spite of the difference in gender and meaning) goes back to "cette voile alternative." We should get increasingly accustomed, as we go along in the poem, to this kind of play on sonorities and meanings, for it will be used to an extreme degree later on; similarly, we should note constantly both the recall of words from earlier passages and the prophecy of words in later passages. The "voile d'illusion" that rises up out of the betrothal is probably some kind of hope, illusory and deluded (cf. "tentant une chance oiseuse"), for the offspring of the marriage, for the sea-man who will be produced by this mating of sea and man (hence the pun on "voile").

Throughout both the developments, on sea and on master, there has been a considerable use of metaphors involving the notion of substance and shadow, of object and image. So, on page 3, "cette voile alternative" represented by "l'ombre enfouie"; the "maître" represented both by the vision of his "cadavre" (page 4) and by his "ombre puérile" (page 5); the hopes for the betrothal represented by "le voile d'illusion." These metaphors, I believe, may serve to explain the remainder of the insert: "leur hantise / ainsi que le fantôme d'un geste." The "geste," returning to preceding passages, would be the one accomplished by the master as he prepares to cast the dice, variously represented by "au poing qui l'étreindrait," "comme on menace," and "la main crispée par delà l'inutile tête." It is a pre-vision of this gesture, a "phantom" (and "ombre" and "fantôme" may in one sense be synonymous), that "haunts" or perturbs the master's progenitors as they are brought together. If these hypotheses are correct, there would be, at the very beginning of the series of biographical elements, a prefiguring of the crucial event: man and sea, as they unite for the ultimate engendering of the master, foresee and foretell the "conjonction suprême [du vieillard] avec la probabilité."

Echoings, sonorities, and plays on meanings provide the key to the remaining words of the page as the sentence is finally completed: "celui . . . tentant . . . une chance oiseuse . . . chancellera / s'affalera / folie / N'ABOLIRA . . . [LE HASARD]." The master has taken up the dice, prepared the number in his hand, hesitated, menaced the heavens with his closed fist; the time has come to make the throw. I wish to suggest that the verb "chanceler" is used to indicate the actual trying of luck that is involved in throwing the dice. It is formed on "chance" (several lines above it on the same page); it may go back to the Latin etymon *cadentia,* used properly for the falling of dice; but at the same time it puns on the normal meanings of "chanceler," to hesitate and waver and display weakness. The poet needs a verb that will combine and telescope a large number of meanings. He takes an existing verb and, by context and allusion, both extends and specifies its reference (we have seen Mallarmé doing this in other poems, and he will go even farther in *Un Coup de dés*). A similar process is used in the case of "s'affalera," which properly means "to collapse upon oneself, to fall into a heap." Mallarmé wishes to exploit the notions of downward motion and of moral failure (the reflexive "se" is especially useful here); and by placing "s'affaler" immediately before and almost directly above "folie," he suggests an assimilation to "s'affolera" and a concomitant intellectual collapse—which is precisely what is involved in the throwing of the dice. The whole action so expressed will rather confirm madness than abolish it, and so the sentence ends with "folie n'abolira." The madness of the master's gesture had begun to appear early in the development, had been emphasized by "en maniaque chenu," then by "par delà l'inutile tête"; it is now clinched by the word "folie" itself, which comes to be the single noun standing for the whole of the action.

The single prominent "N'ABOLIRA" at the bottom of the right side of page 5 has a dual function. It concludes the sentence that had begun with "le maître"; but it also is the verb of the main sentence of the poem, "Un coup de dés jamais n'abolira le hasard," and as such it builds upon as much of the sentence as has so far been presented and it leads into the rest. The fact that it also completes the negative "jamais . . . ne" is of special importance, since the whole futility of the "coup de dés" is now categorically asserted, after the intimation of some of the reasons for that futility. In both of the sentences to which it belongs, "abolira" means "to annul, to render inefficacious or inoperative, to alter." Neither will chance, destiny, fortune be changed by the throwing of the dice, nor will the master as he throws them any the less act as a madman.

With "N'ABOLIRA" we reach a kind of turning point or breaking point in the development of the poem—not a true stopping point, since the main sentence is yet to be concluded, but a moment when the major part of the fiction has been completely expressed and when something new and fresh will begin to happen. Much has been accomplished so far. Most of the "phrase capitale" has been stated, "Un coup de dés jamais n'abolira," and the rest, "le hasard," is not too far ahead. We can now see the whole of the sentence, distinguished by its type face and its intonational pattern—and in a position of major prominence through both. Immediately subordinate to the sentence that expresses the Idea, we see the modifying clauses (in a smaller type but still in capitals) that transform the Idea into the fiction: "quand bien même lancé dans des circonstances éternelles / du fond d'un naufrage / soit . . . / le maître . . ." The fiction involves the master of a ship, the ship in danger of shipwreck, and the throwing of the dice by the master. From these clauses "hang" two major developments: that concerning the sea, storm, and ship depending from "SOIT que . . . ," and that concerning the master and his throw of the dice depending from "LE MAÎTRE" and concluding its own private sentence with "folie N'ABOLIRA." These developments are printed in lower-case letters except for four words that establish a connection between them, distinguished by initial capitals. Both of the "hanging" developments proceed, visually, by a "downward and across" movement, although the second complicates this by a shuttle movement that is probably representative of the master's hesitations and by a countermovement (this one both visual and intellectual) that invites us to read "upward and back" through the life and career of the master to this time and place of crisis. We "see" now three kinds of typography that should lead us to "hear" three levels of intensity; we see and hear three descending and rising patterns of intonation, superimposed one on the other; and we "understand"—through many interruptions and modifications and qualifications—as much of the Idea as has been presented through the fiction.

Then the pause, really a kind of major interruption. Both Idea and fiction will now be abandoned in favor of three whole double pages of comparisons and metaphors. The type face will change from 14-point romans to 14-point italics; the new face will be used throughout pages 6, 7, and 8 and for a related section at the bottom of the right side of page 9. We shall thus have to superimpose a fourth typographical unit upon the other three. But the abandonment of Idea and fiction is only apparent; both will reappear as elements in the similes or metaphors. Indeed, the persistence is witnessed even in the typographical treatment: the type size is the same, even though italics have been substituted for romans; the initial words of each development are in capitals, the rest in lower case, just as had been done for the two parts of the "fiction"; and the movement down and across the pages repeats in essence that of pages 3, 4, and 5. Our visual and auditory superimposition will be of two highly similar arrangements which are really devoted to expressing the same things.

If we are to understand the comparisons now to be presented, we must reduce Idea and fiction to a kind of essential statement. The Idea, of course, has already been stated as a quintessence: "Un coup de dés jamais n'abolira le hasard"; were we to abstract it even further, we might get something like: "An appeal to chance will never change the course of destiny." As this becomes the fiction, the situation representing destiny or the "circonstances éternelles" is invented: it consists in the tempest at sea and the peril to the ship; the man who will make the appeal to chance, the ship's master, is introduced and characterized; and the appeal to chance is made through the preparation of the dice, the hesitation to throw them, and (perhaps) the actual throw. We should thus expect to find in the comparisons that follow these three basic elements: a situation, an agent, and an act; something like the storm at sea, somebody like the master, an action like the throwing of the dice.

The first comparison reads as follows: "COMME SI / Une insinuation simple / au silence enroulée avec ironie / ou / le mystère / précipité / hurlé / dans quelque proche tourbillon d'hilarité et d'horreur / voltige autour du gouffre / sans le joncher / ni fuir / et en berce le vierge indice." The "ou" constituting the fourth line probably indicates that there are two separate comparisons; but both subjects lead to the same (singular) verb and elements of the predicate are common to both. In the first part, the equivalent of the situation is found in "au silence," of the agent in that person—otherwise unidentified —who would perform the act "avec ironie," and of the act itself in the rolling of "une insinuation simple" around the silence. What does this mean? In a situation involving a number of silent persons, somebody says a single and simple thing that makes an ironic suggestion about one of the other persons or about the situation in general. Several correspondences with the fiction should be noted: the insinuation is "Une" just as the number was "un"; both insinuation and irony imply an intellectual activity on the part of the agent comparable to the master's inference; and "enroulée au silence" has a kind of symmetrical resemblance to "adapter à l'envergure."

In the second part, the correspondences are somewhat clearer. The situation is described as "quelque proche tourbillon d'hilarité et d'horreur," again a human situation but one that is opposite to the silence of the preceding one. "Tourbillon" suggests eddying water or air, hence a motion both like that of the "insinuation . . . enroulée" and like that of a whirlpool in the stormy sea. "Hilarité" and "horreur" are opposites, representing for the persons involved two contrary moral poles. Into this situation is introduced "le mystère," parallel to the "insinuation simple" and (in the major fiction) to the "coup de dés." It is brought by an unnamed man. The verbs used to describe the act are "précipité" and "hurlé"; the first means to cast or throw downward, and the motion would be the same as for the throwing of the dice. I think that the second may mean the same:

for in addition to the ordinary French sense of a loud shouting (which would thus stand against the "silence" of the preceding comparison and propose a sound related to that of "hilarité"), the verb may be used as if it were English "hurl" to designate a casting or throwing downward. (Mallarmé, in this poem, would be quite capable of such a usage.)

Then comes the verb and its complement, "voltige autour du gouffre." The subject is either the "insinuation," and then the motion is like that of "enroulée," or the "mystère," and then the motion is like that of the "tourbillon." In both cases, "voltige" establishes a comparison with "hésite" as earlier used for the master, and the "gouffre" is simultaneously equivalent to the "Abîme" of the sea, to the "silence," and to the "tourbillon." The comparisons are made to work precisely through this kind of collapsing of meanings and references. Another phrase now modifies the verb: "sans le joncher / ni fuir." The pronoun "le" stands for the "gouffre" and the two verbs denote opposing actions; the insinuation or the silence will neither fall upon the surface of the abyss (as would several scattered dice) nor will either be removed to a greater distance. Perhaps we may see in "joncher" and "fuir" an exhaustive range of downward and upward movements. Between them, the hovering and the hesitation. The same notion of a rocking or vacillating motion is contained in the verb of the final clause: "et en berce le vierge indice." "En" again refers to "le gouffre"; restoring the subjects and solving the pronoun, we obtain the following sentence: "une insinuation / le mystère berce le vierge indice du gouffre." The insinuation or the mystery, hovering above the abyss with an oscillating movement (like that of the sea), rocks the "vierge indice" that has come up from out of the abyss. The "indice" must be some kind of a sign or witness or epitome of the abyss; but it might also be a number produced by the abyss. It would be "vierge" since it would not before have been used or known—hence like the secret number of the dice formed in the master's hand.

What, then, does the whole of the comparison mean? We must see, on the one hand, the master of the ship, in imminent danger of death and destruction, forming and shaking the number that he hesitates to throw downward into the tempest, the number that comes up to him from the destiny contained in the "fond d'un naufrage." On the other hand, a group of people, either silent or loudly laughing, into whose midst somebody introduces a remark or an incomprehensible statement (it may even be horrifying) which elicits from the people some sign or representation of its nature and attitudes. The comparison puts the situation into totally human terms, introduces a range of emotions from irony and hilarity through mystery and horror, and in so doing attaches these emotions to the "circonstances" of the master. It also reinforces our ideas of the various kinds of movement—upward for the clenched fist, downward for the ship and shadow and for the throw of the dice, to and fro for the waves—present in the main fiction. The downward and the backward-and-forward movements are represented by the typography of page 6.

Page 6 does not end with the last phrase of the comparison, however. Instead, we find another "COMME SI" in the lower right-hand corner. Its position there has two effects. With one "COMME SI" isolated in the upper left-hand corner and another "COMME SI" isolated in the lower right-hand corner, both in 14-point italic capitals, the page seems to turn and return upon itself, adding another kind of typographical motion to the two already described. It becomes closed and complete. But at the same time, since the final "COMME SI" introduces the second major comparison (which will occupy all of page 7 and the top of page 8), this page runs on into the next and the first comparison into the second.

The second comparison is more complex, for it adds its own elements both to those of the preceding comparison and to those of the main fiction. It reads: "COMME SI [p. 6] / plume solitaire éperdue / sauf que la rencontre ou l'effleure une toque de minuit / et immobilise / au velours chiffonné par un esclaffement sombre / cette blancheur rigide / dérisoire / en opposition au ciel / trop / pour ne pas marquer / exigüment / quiconque / prince amer de l'écueil / s'en coiffe comme de l'héroïque / irrésistible mais contenu / par sa petite raison virile / en foudre [p. 7] / soucieux / expiatoire et pubère / muet rire [p. 8]." Typographical dispositions are again highly important. The words "plume solitaire éperdue" are almost alone on page 7, left side, centered at the bottom of the upper quarter of the side; it is a lone feather both lost and distraught. The only other word on the page is the "sauf" of the next phrase, and it serves to make the move into the right side. Diagonal and vertical relationships help us to distinguish and follow certain lines of meaning. Thus we pass from "plume" to "cette blancheur rigide" to "en opposition au ciel" to "en foudre"; from "dérisoire" to "trop" (giving "trop . . . dérisoire") to "exigüment" to "sa petite raison virile." Just as on page 5 we discovered a vertical continuity between "tentant" and "une chance oiseuse," so here we read "la rencontre ou l'effleure . . . et immobilise."

Once again, the comparison is of something else to the main fictional situation. What now moves downward into the waiting situation is the feather, single and expressing through the uncertainties of its fall a state of emotional crisis ("éperdue") not unlike that of the master on his ship. It is a white feather ("cette blancheur rigide") and it will be seen both against a very dark object ("une toque de minuit") and against the sky ("en opposition au ciel"); it may even be seen against the sky like a flash of lightning ("en foudre"), in which case the small and apparently inconsequential object would assume "eternal" proportions. Its fall is arrested, not by the "silence" about which it might be "enroulée," nor by the "tourbillon," nor by the "gouffre," but rather by another round thing whose shape recalls theirs. This is the "toque" or round cap, dark blue or black in color ("de minuit"), made of velours, worn by an unidentified person ("quiconque . . . s'en coiffe"). The encounter of feather and cap is fortuitous ("sauf que la rencontre"); but if it does come about, if the feather is so much as touched by the rough fabric ("ou l'effleure"), the fall will be stopped and the feather will come to rest ("et immobilise"). In the same way as a moral or emotional quality had been ascribed to the feather with the adjective "éperdue," the toque is said to be of velours "chiffonné par un esclaffement sombre." There is, in this description, a whole series of double-entendres. "Chiffonné" in the sempstress' language means "fashioned" or "formed"; figuratively, it means "made rough or irregular"; and morally it means something like "annoyed." It must be the last of these qualities that comes to the toque from the man who wears it, from his burst of laughter ("esclaffement") which is as somber as the velours is dark.

The situation, then: the wearer of the toque is like one of those in the "tourbillon d'hilarité" and the somber quality of his laughter recalls the "horreur" there associated with the hilarity. But he is also like the master, as will be indicated when the phrase "quiconque . . . s'en coiffe" is interrupted by "prince amer de l'écueil." As he stands, a falling feather comes to rest on his cap. If we return to the main fiction and equate the wearer of the toque with the master, what falls is the number on the dice and what it falls into is the head that wears the hat: "un envahit le chef." But this is confused, largely through the preceding comparison, with the abyss or the storm itself, bringing about again the conjunction of man and circumstances; "Esprit" and "Abîme," "insinuation" and "silence," "mystère" and "tourbillon," now "plume" and "toque." In the previous cases, man was represented by his intellect, and we may assume that the same is true in the present comparison; but in some of them destiny and circumstances were non-human, in others (as in this one) the situation was specifically human. The new comparison will present these usual elements in a new combination, and we may understand it if we continue to seek the same ratios of comparison.

Thus when we find, in the next lines, the phrase "cette blancheur rigide" and under it "en opposition au ciel," we may assume that our regular "opposition" is being pursued: against the sky or natural forces and circumstances, something that signifies man's struggle and his determination. The fact that his intellect is involved is revealed by the words that modify "cette blancheur rigide": "quiconque . . . s'en coiffe . . . irrésistible mais contenu par sa petite raison virile." And the comparative weakness of that struggle is seen in a group of words that "surround" the phrase "en opposition au ciel": "dérisoire . . . trop / pour ne pas marquer / exigüment / quiconque . . ." As opposing the heavens, the feather (and what it represents) is negligible, perhaps even ridiculous—so much so that whoever would "wear" or assume or use it would be "marked" as insufficient in the struggle. He is restricted, limited, "contenu / par sa petite raison virile"; yet—and this fact will emerge with greater clarity as the poem develops—he is "irrésistible." The power of his reason, no matter how small, is still great enough to assure him a victory in the end.

For the nature and the activities of that man, we need to examine certain other formulas in the comparison. The essential one is "prince amer de l'écueil," since it identifies him with the master of the ship. If he is a "prince" it is because he is, like the master of the ship, in a position where he might dominate and win over his circumstances. If he is "amer" it is because his inference has led him to the discovery of the magnitude of those circumstances opposing him in this "conjonction suprême avec la probabilité," in these "circonstances éternelles." In the main fiction, those circumstances are epitomized in "l'écueil" upon which the ship might be wrecked; more generally, "l'écueil" would be any obstacle that threatened death and destruction. The man, the master has uttered an "esclaffement sombre," related both to the "ironie" of the insinuation and to the "hilarité" of the group of men in the preceding comparison; related also, if we are to continue to develop the parallel, to what is irrational in his action, to the setting aside of reason in favor of the "coup de dés," to the madness of the "maniaque chenu" and the "folie" that he will be unable to avoid. Yet he himself continues to think of himself and of his action as if they were at the level of the circumstances that he is contesting; he wears the feather, he assumes a moral attitude associated with it, "comme de l'héroïque"; his arm is raised "comme on menace un destin et les vents," the result of his action will be to "en reployer la division et passer fier." It is perhaps in this sense that the feather is seen against the sky "en foudre": one monumental force is set opposite another. It is important to note the image of the "plume" or the "foudre" against the sky (the epithet of "cette blancheur rigide" emphasizes the association) since already the idea of a constellation in the heavens is being organized and prepared.

This second comparison "runs on" to the next page, where it is concluded. The final part is in every sense an *enjambement*. If Mallarmé considers the page—the double page—as the unit of versification, comparable to the traditional line or verse, then an extension of a development onto the next page is exactly like the running of one verse into the following. The idea runs on, too, and concludes at the same time both of the comparisons: "soucieux / expiatoire et pubère / muet rire"; and the phrase has its own "downward and across" movement at the top of the double page. It consists of a noun and four adjectives, and with the noun "rire" standing in apposition with "esclaffement," the whole phrase becomes an appositive to that word, having no other grammatical connection with the rest of the comparison. The "rire" is of course a resumption of the "hilarité" of the first comparison and of the "esclaffement" of this one; it is a "muet rire" in recollection of the "insinuation . . . au silence enroulée avec ironie," also in the first comparison. "Soucieux" may return immediately to the "prince amer," then to the "esclaffement sombre," then to the "mystère" and the "horreur" of the first comparison, finally to the long phrase in the main fiction, "hésite / cadavre par le bras écarté du secret qu'il détient." It signifies the gravity of the whole situation, present even along with laughter and madness. "Expiatoire" makes similar allusions. It supposes some crime or fault, and I should judge that this would be the master's act of surrendering to chance that direction of his life which he should have reserved for his intellect. In a sense, the subordination of "Esprit" to "Nombre." It was the awareness of this fault that caused the master to hesitate, that added the ingredient of "horreur" to the "tourbillon" in the preceding comparison, and that led the "prince amer" to conceive of his act as heroic.

In the case of the fourth adjective, "pubère," the connections with what has gone before are even more significant. We find, when we have come to it, that through the two comparisons there has been developing another "biographical" series: in the first, "et en berce le vierge indice," and in the second, both "sa petite raison virile" and "pubère rire." But there are differences. Previously, the biographical series (in its largely inverted order) consisted of the "ages of man," extended backward into the master's ancestry and conception, forward into his death. Now each of the three terms belongs to a different object—"pubère" to the man's laughter, "vierge" to the number or the sign that issues from the abyss, "virile" to the man's reason. The most important of these is the last, since reason or mind or intellect is one of the principal factors in the Idea; and the fact that man's reason, at its most potent state, should still be "petite" and "dérisoire" as compared to the power of destiny, emphasizes the major opposition of the poem. I use the term "potent" advisedly, since the three stages in this series belong to the sexual, or procreative, or simply creative development of man: "vierge," "pubère," "virile." Translated into terms applicable to the reason, these stages would be equivalent to the reason still untried and unused, the reason mature and ready for use, the reason at the time of its greatest potential. As such, the whole group would stand midway in the total biography, in the time between "son ombre puérile" and the "anciens calculs."

The total effect of this second comparison is to augment and extend the notion of the weakness of the master's intellect ("sa petite raison virile") as opposed to his overwhelming circumstances ("en opposition au ciel"). At the same time, it solidifies the relationship between both comparisons and the section devoted to the master (pages 4–5). It clarifies the emotional response of the reader through such phrases as "chiffonné par un esclaffement sombre," "dérisoire," "prince amer de l'écueil," "s'en coiffe comme de l'héroïque / irrésistible mais contenu / par sa petite raison virile," "soucieux / expiatoire et pubère / muet rire." In spite of the fact that these phrases do have an intellectual content and are thus related to the Idea, their main suggestion is made to the emotions; they build upon the feelings already introduced in the first comparison. Several images are presented that will be exploited later in the poem: the falling feather, the white object against a dark background, the small thing transformed into a great force.

To introduce the third comparison, a different formula is used; not "COMME SI" (in 14-point italic capitals) as for the other two, but "que si" ("que" still in 14-point lower case, "SI" in 18-point italic capitals). There are two reasons for this change; first, since the comparison will not be identical in its effect with the other two, the new formula (a commonplace substitution for "comme si" in French style) calls attention to the difference; second, and perhaps more important, the "SI" is the first word of a new sentence that will continue and conclude on page 9 and that will express one of the essential parts of the Idea. "SI" serves two purposes: as a part of the comparative formula, "que si," it relates what is coming to the two preceding comparisons, and it starts another sentence, "Si c'était le nombre ce serait le hasard." The third comparison occupies all of page 8 except for the "run on" phrase from the second. It is disposed again in a shuttle arrangement around the dividing line between the two sides, with vertical and diagonal relationships again important. The total typographical effect is quite distinct from that of the other comparisons, pointing up the difference in meaning and intention; it is more concentrated and square on the left side, thin and stretched out vertically on the right side (Mallarmé might possibly be asking us to see the "plume" or the "aigrette"). The comparison reads: "que si / La lucide et seigneuriale aigrette de vertige / au front invisible / scintille / puis ombrage / une stature mignonne ténébreuse debout / en sa torsion de sirène / le temps / de souffleter / par d'impatientes squames ultimes bifurquées / un roc / faux manoir / tout de suite / évaporé en brumes / qui imposa / une borne à l'infini."

(In the 1897 version, there are several textual variations from the final form. There, the whole of the text was contained between parentheses, before "La" and after "infini"; and one read "un mystère / faux roc / évaporé en brume" instead of "un roc / faux manoir / tout de suite / évaporé en brumes." "Un mystère" was apparently removed when it was added to the first comparison for the definitive version.)

Since the comparison still involves the main fiction, situation and act are now basically the same as they were before. But the figure of a man, the "prince amer de l'écueil," has been replaced by the figure of a siren; her act will be one appropriate to her nature and her milieu, even though its purpose remains that of the master. Because the figure is now a female one, the master's feather or plume becomes the siren's "aigrette"; it is "seigneuriale" in order to insist on the metaphorical identification of the siren with the "prince" and the "maître" (both lordly and dominant men); it is "lucide" because of its whiteness—we must continue to see "cette blancheur rigide"— and, figuratively, to recall the relationship with "Esprit" and "raison." Similarly, "de vertige" makes two suggestions, of a sense of turning (like that of the descending feather and of the other images of spirals) and of a temporary loss of control of the intellectual faculties; both link the comparison to major segments of the text. The words "au front invisible" are printed immediately under "seigneuriale aigrette," hence modify that phrase. There are two ways of understanding them, either as "invisible on the forehead" or "on the invisible forehead"; the latter is preferable, because we do see the aigrette while the siren's forehead might not be visible because of her abundant long hair. We must also think of something as covering the siren's head just as the toque covered the mariner's, and of the aigrette as descending upon it.

So much for the subject; now the verb. It is a double verb, representing two successive actions, "scintille / puis ombrage." "Scintille," as it designates both the whiteness and the motion of the aigrette, also prefigures the light of the stars in the constellation as, at the end of the poem, they will stand in the night sky. "Ombrage" provides a notion of darkness against which the aigrette may be seen more brightly; in its proper sense it tells us that, after a time of spiralling descent, the aigrette casts its shadow upon the siren's form. That form is the direct object of the second verb: "ombrage / une stature mignonne ténébreuse debout / en sa torsion de sirène." Our question as to why the protagonist should, in this comparison, assume the form of a siren, is answered readily enough: just as the master—agent in the main fiction—was a product of man and the sea, "la mer par l'aïeul . . . ou l'aïeul contre la mer," hence a kind of double being never dissociated from the sea, so the siren—agent in this comparison—is a woman born of man and the sea. She has a woman's head, hair, bust, and arms; but her body terminates in a fish's tail and she swims, and in this comparison performs her necessary action, by means of that tail. Her form is described first as "une stature mignonne ténébreuse." The adjective "mignonne" is important both as suggesting femininity and as providing a counterpart to the master's "petite raison virile"; against "petite raison virile" (where "virile" also means "belonging to a man") we are led to infer "mignonne stature féminine," to juxtapose "virilité" and "féminité." More important still, the juxtaposition puts into relief the essential difference between this comparison and the preceding ones; in the other two, it was the mind that was opposed to the forces of nature or destiny; in this one, it will be the body. Perhaps, in this way, the two phases of the master's career, "jadis il empoignait la barre" and "anciens calculs," are paralleled in the comparisons. The siren's form, finally, is "ténébreuse" both with respect to its dark color, enhanced by the shadow cast upon it, and by its uncertain nature as a mixture of woman and fish.

The siren's form is further qualified as "debout / en sa torsion de sirène" (in this formula we have the first identification of the siren). If "debout" stands separate from the rest of the line, beyond the division of the sides, it is in order to call attention to the extraordinary character of this upright posture for the siren; her normal attitude is horizontal, as when swimming. She will be "debout" only briefly, only long enough to accomplish the action that will be described in words that hang vertically under "debout" on the right side of the page—another reason for the separation. As for "sa torsion," two remarks seem necessary. First, the twisting motion of the upper part of her body is immediately associated with the preceding series of turning or revolving objects: "voltige autour du gouffre," "tourbillon," "enroulée," and so forth. Second, it is not unlikely that we are also to see "torse" in "torsion," thus to see the "stature mignonne" essentially in terms of a woman's torso rather than in terms of the fish's tail, the "squames ultimes bifurquées." Her action is stated succinctly: "debout . . . le temps / de souffleter . . . un roc"; all the other elements on the page are modifications of these words. In "le temps / de . . ." we have an indication of the brevity of the time during which the siren remains upright, hence of the brevity of her action. This intention to diminish the magnitude of the action is continued in the verb "souffleter" itself; "souffleter" carries with it, along with the image of striking with a flat surface, some of the lightness contained in "souffle" and "soufflet." That this is the intention is confirmed by the verb's direct object, "un roc." When "souffleter" and "un roc" are brought together, the standard situation is again apparent: on the one hand, a mighty and immovable force, "le ciel," "le destin," "le gouffre"; on the other hand, an action against that force which must necessarily be weak and ineffectual, the falling of a feather, the cast of the dice, a light and hasty slapping. "Roc" evokes all the hardness, size, and durability needed to make the slapping useless, and the very nature of the slapping action, "par d'impatientes squames ultimes bifurquées," completes the idea. "Squames" are scales and "squames ultimes bifurquées" describes the scaly forked tail that terminates the siren's body; the fact that they are "impatientes" emphasizes the rapidity and perhaps also the ill-humor with which the action is executed. We should note that "par d'impatientes squames ultimes" appears directly under "en sa torsion de sirène," thus giving a figuration of the two disparate parts of the siren's body.

The remaining words on the page modify "un roc": "faux manoir / tout de suite / évaporé en brumes / qui imposa / une borne à l'infini." As they do so, they stress once again the uselessness of the siren's action. For what seemed to be a rock, a "manoir" which would itself persist and upon which one might remain (Latin *manet* is strongly present in the usage here), turns out to be as unstable and evanescent as the action against it. In this sense it is a "faux manoir." Its disappearance is as rapid as the action, "tout de suite," and this is because it was really only a wave or a mass of water which, when struck, was "évaporé en brumes." And yet this obstacle seemed, and perhaps really was in effect capable of imposing "une borne à l'infini"; literally, if the sea was infinity, the rock marked a stoppage or limitation to its extent; figuratively, if the action is one against destiny or fate or "eternal circumstances," then the rock—this point in time and space—seemed to represent a place where man might attack and defeat it. Without hope, of course, for no such place can exist within the suppositions of the poem.

In this third comparison, there are three notions which, when brought together, invite us to add a mythological interpretation to the one already given. First, the notion of the siren leads us back to the "tourbillon" or "gouffre" of the first comparison, then to the "écueil" of the second comparison. The combination of the whirlpool (Charybdis), the rock (Scylla), and the Siren gives the essential factors of the Greek myth, and the "prince amer de l'écueil" may then turn the master into a Ulysses-like figure, generalize further his act and his experience. Second, the "roc" or the "faux manoir," associated with the "sirène," alludes to the same myth. Third, "une borne à l'infini" may, by an association of Mediterranean myths, refer to the Pillars of Hercules which stood at the limits of the known world, hence at the limits of experience and infinity. We do not need to seek further for other details or circumstances related to these myths. Mallarmé uses only as much of them as suits his immediate purposes and as contributes to the realm of reference and emotion associated with his own principal fiction.

When the third comparison concludes, a kind of critical point in the poem is reached. So far, our visual image is made up of the very large and dominant "phrase capitale" and, against it, of the secondary sentence from which hang the two main developments relating to the sea and the master; and, against these, the three comparisons in a different type and with varying configurations. The points of junction among these stand out clearly: "soit que" connecting the section on the sea with the secondary sentence, "le maître" connecting the section on the master with the same sentence, the two "comme si's" connecting two comparisons with these developments and with each other, a more prominent "si" bringing a third comparison into the series. Our intellectual vision of the poem has been similarly constructed: over the sentence stating the Idea, another one that makes the transition to the fiction; two subordinate developments that explain the two major elements in the fiction; and three comparisons that clarify the images, the references, and the emotions associated with the basic situation. But neither the visual image nor the understanding of Idea and fiction is, at this point, complete. The main sentence, "Un coup de dés jamais n'abolira . . . ," is without its last words. The secondary sentence barely begins its final phrase: "quand bien même lancé dans des circonstances éternelles, du fond d'un naufrage, soit; le maître . . ." And the prominent "si" on page 8, while it leads into the third comparison, appears also to set under way another conditional construction.

All these statements need to be concluded, the visual and poetic expectations need to be satisfied. Necessarily, the double page on which all this is suddenly done, page 9, will be the most complex of the whole poem. It will be the most complex visually (and hence aurally), typographically, and poetically. Visually, the page is built around "le hasard" which appears just below the middle of the right side, at the right margin. Above "le hasard," top right, a block of words in short lines and in an essentially vertical arrangement, into which leads a single word (with two minute modifiers) on the left side, top at the right margin, looking like a short handle for that block. Below "le hasard," bottom of the right side, a block of words in somewhat longer lines and in a combined downward-and-across and shuttle movement. Finally, opposite "le hasard" and streaming toward it from the left margin of the left side, two large words and their minute modifiers, looking like a long handle. Most of the text is thus concentrated on the right side, with only the long and the short handles occupying the left side; on the left side, the ratio of white to black is exceptionally large. Typographically, the page is even more complex than would be the sum of all the type faces previously used; for two new ones are added. "Le hasard" at the center of the structure is of course in the 48-point display capitals. The conditional sentence that comes from the "si" on the preceding page is in 18-point italic capitals; but its modifiers are in 10-point italics, lower case. The sentence continuing from "le maître" is in the usual 14-point roman capitals, but with modification now in 10-point romans, lower case. The block of words at the bottom of the right side is in the same 14-point italics, lower case with one capital, as had been used for the three comparisons.

"Le hasard" is also at the center of the intellectual structure of page 9. It terminates the main sentence, and it does so at a point where the whole fictional expansion of "un coup de dés" and of its circumstantial accompaniments has been realized. When, then, the major sentence, "Un coup de dés jamais n'abolira le hasard," is here finally completed, the Idea has a firm basis in the illustrative fiction, the image of the master and the conclusion with respect to the futility of his act are both clear, the proper emotions have been added and directed by the intervention of the three comparisons. "Le hasard," in the second place, terminates the conditional sentence that had begun with the "si" on the preceding page: "Si c'était le nombre ce serait le hasard," adding (without its modifiers) another Idea to the first and one that is presented almost completely on this page. Finally, with "le hasard" we come to the end of that segment of the secondary sentence which had begun with "le maître": "le maître existât-il / commençât-il et cessât-il / se chiffrât-il / illuminât-il / le hasard." Indeed, if "le hasard" is withheld for so long a time (rather than following immediately upon "n'abolira"), it is because its total meaning can be clear and forceful only after the other sentences which it terminates have been explained and illustrated by the three comparisons on the one hand, by the whole of the fiction on the other.

Page 9 begins, at the top, with "c'était" (left side) and "le nombre" (right side); if we follow the typographical indications correctly, we will immediately link these words with the "si" in "que sɪ" of the third comparison and with "ce serait" lower on the same left side. We thus discover quickly the full sentence, "Si c'était le nombre ce serait le hasard." The reference in "le nombre" is obviously to "l'unique Nombre," the number that must necessarily result from the master's throw of the dice—necessarily because even games of chance do not escape the laws of destiny. The new sentence confirms the idea of the "phrase capitale": a throw of the dice will never alter chance, for even if the throw were to reveal the efficacious number—the one that corresponded to destiny—that number would itself be a product of chance. Chance would not alter chance, it would merely corroborate itself. As the new sentence develops we find under "c'était," the first word on page 9, the small modifying words, "issu stellaire." In spite of their 10-point italic type, they are extremely important words for several reasons. They call attention to "c'était" itself which, in spite of the fact that it is merely the copula, here properly indicates existence. It has the same significance for the number as "existât-il" will have for the master. As was the case for the master, whose origins and coming into being have been traced (page 5), "issu stellaire" states succinctly where the number comes from. "Ancestralement," "Fiançailles," "né d'un ébat," are paralleled in the simple phrase. "Stellaire" indicates that eternal and unalterable circumstances bring the number into being. It also suggests a downward movement from the heavens to the master's hand, thence to the place where the dice come to rest; an opposite movement will take place when the stars of the constellation rise upward from the dice to their permanent position in the heavens. The constellation will be an "issu stellaire" in a kind of punning way. The smallest words in the poem become the seed of its greatest Idea.

In "si c'était" the condition, in "ce serait" the result. "Ce serait" is also accompanied by a group of words in 10-point italics, leading in a downward-and-across movement into "le hasard": "ce serait / pire / non / davantage ni moins / indifféremment mais autant / le hasard." These modifying words falls into two categories. Some—"davantage," "moins," "autant"—are quantitative; "non davantage . . . ni moins . . . mais autant" denies any difference in quantity between "le nombre" and "le hasard," makes them exactly equivalent. The other two offer two value judgments, "pire," "indifféremment" (it is likely that the "non" applies to "pire" as well as to "davantage," making "non pire"); or rather, they state the uselessness and the inappropriateness of any value judgments bearing on chance. Chance will operate as chance, regardless of the judgments that one may make on its operations; judgments are indifferent. The whole sentence except for the words "issu stellaire" belongs to the Idea; they belong to the fiction. It expands and completes the negativism contained in the words "jamais n'abolira."

The third sentence that ends in "le hasard" is the one that began long ago with "le maître": "le maître . . . existât-il . . . commençât-il et cessât-il . . . se chiffrât-il . . . illuminât-il le hasard." It is really not a sentence at all, but a conditional clause in which the imperfect subjunctives state a group of suppositions with respect to the master: "Even were he to exist . . ." and so forth. As I have pointed out earlier, the suppositions are all related to the life and career and action of the master, either as narrated on pages 4 and 5 or as ultimately justified on the last two pages of the poem. "Existât-il," like "si c'était" for the number, presents the primary supposition with respect to the man who might attempt to abolish chance: he must exist. The word is modified (as will be the other words in the clause) by other words printed under it in 10-point romans: "autrement qu'hallucination éparse d'agonie." To exist, for the master or for any man, is to exist as an "Esprit," not merely as an "ombre" or an "illusion" or a "fantôme." Two forms of existence—or of nonexistence—are discarded as unwanted: the "hallucination" in which the intellect is in abeyance and the unguided senses rule, the "agonie" in which passion is the only active faculty. With respect to the fiction developed for the master, the "hallucination" is the demented state (we recall the "maniaque chenu" and the "folie") which led him to throw the dice and to believe in their efficacy, the "agonie" is the death-passion that characterizes this moment of crisis ("cadavre par le bras écarté du secret qu'il détient"). Both terms have echoes in the comparisons as well as in the fiction, "hallucination" possibly in "mystère" and in "vertige," "agonie" in "horreur," "sombre," "amer," "soucieux," "expiatoire." As for the expression "éparse d'agonie," it gives a kind of material existence to both abstractions, makes it possible for one to be scattered or dispersed over the other; and as it does so it serves as a common term for the dice which will be so scattered over the surface upon which they will fall and the stars of the constellation which will be dispersed against the sky. The number, the master, and the constellation are linked together.

I have previously referred to the life and career of the master, and it is this that is now summarized in the phrase "commençât-il et cessât-il." The reference of the two verbs to the "biography" on pages 4 and 5 is obvious. They are modified, in this passage, by a fairly long group of words: "sourdant que nié et clos quand apparu / enfin / par quelque profusion répandue en rareté." The four participial adjectives are arranged in a chiasmus, with the two that relate to "commençât-il," "sourdant" and "apparu," placed at the extremes, the two that relate to "cessât-il," "nié" and "clos," placed at the mean. "Que" means "aussitôt que" and "quand" (by assimilation) takes on the same meaning: the existence of the master is brief, his end follows almost immediately upon his beginning; and his end is contained in his beginning. The "enfin" of the group is printed under "nié et clos" and its reference is to them; it means "at last" or "as an end," signifies the cessation of the master's existence. It also links the two participles to what follows: "nié et clos . . . enfin / par quelque profusion répandue en rareté." We must understand "profusion" in its etymological sense (*profundere*) as a pouring out, hence an emanation; and the emanation that brings the master's death must be from destiny or fortune itself. Just as "l'ultérieur démon immémorial" had produced, after endless generations, the master's beginning, so another secret influence—let us say from the heavens—now produces his end. The influence is "répandue en rareté"; "répandue" is a kind of double of "profusion," with a closely allied meaning, and the addition of "en rareté" both adds to the notion of the distance from which the influence comes and suggests an image of something spread over a large physical area (hence echoing "éparse").

Two moments in the master's career still remain. The first is the throwing of the dice in the present crisis, and it is epitomized by "se chiffrât-il." This is the only reflexive verb of the series and its force is to make the action turn back upon the agent. The master, as he prepares the dice, produces a number, "l'unique Nombre," but he also transforms and transmutes himself into that number. This is possible, in the poem, because of the extent to which the master has abrogated his intellect and surrendered himself to the hazards of fortune—"un envahit le chef." Master and number are identified in one way just as master and sea are identified in another. "Se chiffrât-il" is also followed by a modifying phrase, "évidence de la somme pour peu qu'une"; but it is placed farther below the verb than in the other cases, in a way to bring it into proximity with the last element in the clause. "Évidence" is again an appositive, signifying the whole of the action contained in "se chiffrât-il" and bringing master and number even closer together. The master's action is a "making visible" of the number, here "la somme." If "la somme" is qualified by "pour peu qu'une," with "une" prominently at the end, it is in order to recall such formulas as "l'unique Nombre qui ne peut pas être un autre" and "un envahit le chef" and, more recently, "si c'était le nombre . . ." The master prepares the number—"nombre," "chiffre" and "somme" are synonymous—and whatever number results (and only one can result) will be the realization of chance. "Pour peu qu'une" also relates this modifier of "se chiffrât-il" to the modifier of "ce serait," "pire / non / davantage ni moins / indifféremment mais autant," since it introduces similar quantitative considerations with respect to the being and the becoming involved in both cases.

So far, the verbs in this clause have summarized the master's existence and action as already displayed in the poem; the remaining verb, "illuminât-il . . . le hasard," is a reference forward to the producing of the constellation that will be described on the last two pages. Chance will be "illuminated" in the sense that the number that comes up will ultimately be changed into the bright stars shining against the sky. Thus as the clause concludes much that has gone before, it also leads into what is still to come; we have not yet reached the end of the poem, even though three important developments have terminated in "le hasard."

In the passage below "le hasard" on page 9, the three comparisons are similarly terminated. In a sense all had been incomplete. The "comme si," "comme si," and "que si" had on the one hand related them to the antecedent narrative, on the other hand introduced "if" clauses for which no "thens" were forthcoming. This would not have been the case if the comparisons had been preceded only by "comme," "comme," and "que." Consequently, on a page which brings to conclusion Idea and fiction (except for an ulterior development that has been suggested), the "then" comes along to complete the conditional sentences. The insinuation in the first comparison had been "enroulée" about the silence, without falling or coming to rest; the mystery was described in these terms, "voltige autour du gouffre / sans le joncher / ni fuir," hence also in a state of suspension. In the second comparison, the "plume solitaire éperdue" had been seen in the act of falling, as "cette blancheur rigide . . . en opposition au ciel," until it reached the master's toque. In the third, the feather was an "aigrette de vertige," its motion contained in "scintille." Now, in a passage printed in the same 14-point italics as the comparisons, the feather ends its fall: "Choit / la plume / rythmique suspens du sinistre / s'ensevelir / aux écumes originelles / naguères d'où sursauta son délire jusqu'à une cime / flétrie / par la neutralité identique du gouffre."

It is clear that the passage not only completes the comparisons, but that it both concludes the fiction of the dice and advances the fiction of the constellation. It does all this through its suggestion of a double movement, one downward, the other upward. Already in the comparisons, it was obvious that the falling objects were to be assimilated to the dice, and just as these objects were still in a state of suspension, so the dice (except for vague hints like the one contained in "chancellera") had not yet been thrown. Through the identification proper to metaphor, the falling of the feather ("Choit / la plume") signifies at last the throwing of the dice. The indication comes after "le hasard" and all the lines of thought that have led into it; for only when the futility of the act has been established will the report of the act have its full effectiveness. The identification of feather and dice is corroborated by the next phrase, "rythmique suspens du sinistre," in which "sinistre" is at once the "naufrage" of the main fiction and the "gouffre" (with all its variants) of the comparisons. "Suspens" is etymologically that which "hangs above"; it is "rythmique" because of the feather's spiralling descent (cf. "voltige," "enroulée," "scintille"), because of the motion involved in the preparation of the dice and the master's hesitation. Besides, the movement of feather and dice corresponds to the movement of the "tourbillon," literal or figurative, over which they are suspended.

In "s'ensevelir / aux écumes originelles" we are returned to the main fiction. All the ideas of "du fond d'un naufrage," of the "Abîme" and the "profondeur" and the "béante profondeur," are recalled, and "s'ensevelir" repeats "jusqu'adapter / à l'envergure," as well as "très à l'intérieur résume." The fact that the waves are the "écumes originelles" calls attention to that upward movement of dice and number originally stated in "lancé . . . du fond d'un naufrage" and the more abstract notion that the abyss itself is the origin of the master, of the circumstances, and of the number that will represent his confrontation with destiny. Origin and upward motion are confirmed in the next phrase, "naguères d'où sursauta son délire jusqu'à une cime." Such notions of time as had been contained in "ancestralement" and "l'ultérieur démon immémorial" are digested in "naguères," and although the time now described is not as long as that for the master's origins and ancestry (and it should not be, since this is a critical moment), yet the archaic flavor of both "Choit" and "naguères" makes for a sense of distant time. The "sur-" of "sursauta," like the "sus-" of "suspens," stresses the upward movement, more violent and rapid here through the basic verb "sauter" and through the past absolute tense. "Son délire" is ambivalent. For the feather rising upward, it means the erratic gyrating of the ascending flight, perhaps also the dizziness of the height reached at the "cime"; for the master, it means that folly long since discovered in such terms as "maniaque chenu," "folie," "hallucination," "comme on menace un destin et les vents." The "cime" is the high point reached by the feather or the number or, later, the constellation; it is the zenith of the upward motion into the heavens, opposed to the nadir of the downward motion into the abyss.

Standing where it does, isolated on the next line, "flétrie" could modify either "cime" or "la plume"; but the phrase that modifies it, "par la neutralité identique du gouffre," favors the latter interpretation. The feather, hurled heavenward, becomes withered and wrinkled as it reaches the heights. The cause is the "neutralité identique du gouffre," that indifference of the milieu through which it passes, whether water for the "gouffre" of the sea or air for the "gouffre" of the heavens. I take it that "identique" serves to make the two abysses identical, as has already been done by the "horizon unanime" of page 4. The raised hand that prepares the dice, "la main / crispée / par delà l'inutile tête," similarly becomes "le fantôme d'un geste"; but here it is because of a moral indifference, because destiny and fortune and chance—whether contained in the one abyss or the other—are unmoved and unaltered by the master's useless gesture. "Flétrie" has its moral sense of "condemned." The condemnation comes at the very end of the fiction and the comparisons—just before the master's act, in the ensuing development, will be completely justified and exalted.

Thus with its heavy massing of materials crowded against the right margin of the right side, page 9 superimposes upon our visual image of the poem a new kind of pattern. It is one which in every way denotes full stop visually, conclusion intellectually. The latter is emphasized by the appearance, finally, of "le hasard." Yet there are on this page, in such formulas as "issu stellaire" and "illuminât-il," indications that the stop is only partial and the conclusion only tentative. Above all, the establishment via a long series of images and ideas of the general principle that downward motions are cognate with upward motions leads us to expect and to wish, now that the throw of the dice has been accomplished, that the cognate and reciprocal event will occur.

That long sentence that had begun on page 2 with "quand bien même . . ." was a conditional sentence (or clause). Its verbs were subjunctives, used in a conditional meaning: "lancé . . . soit," "le maître . . . existât-il," and so forth. As such they depended from "jamais"—never, even if the circumstances were to be such-and-such and the master were to have been so-and-so. But the same subjunctives may be considered as stating the "if" clauses of the conditional construction, in which case we should read: "even if the dice were thrown in such-and-such a way, even if the master were such-and-such a man"; and the "result" clause would be found in the remainder of the sentence: "rien . . . n'aura eu lieu . . . que le lieu . . . excepté . . . peut-être . . . une constellation." This may really be considered also as an independent sentence. It is printed in 14-point roman capitals, like the rest; it stretches downward and across the last two double pages of the poem; and as such it provides the skeleton and the organizing principle of the poem's conclusion. The whole of the sentence is completed within a relatively short space. But the interruptions, of varying length, are highly important, connecting as they do this whole Idea with the fiction that has preceded.

For the first word, "Rien," this is the interruption: "de la mémorable crise / ou se fût / l'évènement accompli en vue de tout résultat nul / humain." The sounds and the spacings, the interruptions of the interruption, suggest that two meanings exist simultaneously in the clause and that we are to give them equal weight as modifiers of "rien." I mean by this that "ou" may also be heard as "où," "se fût" as "ce fut," and "l'évènement" as a clear cross between "événement" and "avènement," while "humain" (isolated at the end) does double duty as modifier both of "évènement" and of "résultat." I dare to propose these two readings: 1) "Rien de la mémorable crise ou ce fut l'avènement, nul en vue de tout résultat humain, n'aura eu lieu"; 2) "rien de la mémorable crise où se fût accompli l'événement humain n'aura eu lieu." We are asked, in this case, to hear at once two intellectual "chords," depending upon two different arrangements of the same words—or at least the same sonorities. The two combine to give a rich if confused meaning to the clause. The effect of "de la mémorable crise" is the same in both; it refers us to the fiction of the master and the tempest, of the impending shipwreck, and of the casting of the dice. If we read next the alternative phrase "ou ce fut l'avènement," two things happen to the meaning. For one, "avènement" adds to the magnitude and the importance of the memorable crisis; for the other, the whole phrase intimates the idea that the crisis may have been extra-naturally originated (as in the "ultérieur démon immémorial"), that purely human causes may have been supplemented by others. (I resist the possibility that there may be here a suggestion of the meaning in the set phrase "l'avènement du Christ," which would be intensified by the prominent "humain"; although others may not wish to do so. The consequences would be far-reaching for the total sense of the poem.) The rest of the sentence, "nul en vue de tout résultat humain," would reduce the master's act —no matter how memorable and important—to the nullity that has already been attached to it in "naufrage cela direct de l'homme sans nef n'importe où vaine"; "humain" here goes back to "de l'homme" there (page 4). No matter what the consequences might have been for nature or for destiny, for the man and for man they would be non-existent, "rien."

In the second reading, "rien de la mémorable crise où se fût accompli l'événement humain n'aura eu lieu," the relative pronoun "où," putting the emphasis on place (and hence foretelling "que le lieu"), tends to locate the "human event" within the general crisis that involved also nature and destiny. The human event would be the throwing of the dice, with all the accompaniments of surrender of the intellect and of bowing to fortune. The conditional "se fût" (equivalent to "se serait") puts the accomplishment of that event in the same area of supposition as has been previously signified by the present and imperfect subjunctives of the secondary sentence, "lancé soit," "existât-il," and so forth. We should note that both in "ou ce fut l'avènement" and in "où se fût accompli l'événement" there is a notion of uncertainty and hypothesis. If indeed the two readings do exist simultaneously in the text, we should, as we follow it along, develop a composite impression in which uncertainty and hypothesis dominate our other ideas. That serves to characterize the master's act.

For "n'aura eu lieu" the modification is relatively brief: "une élévation ordinaire verse l'absence." It gives, in "élévation," the first of a number of astronomical terms that will appear in the concluding pages. This is not, however, unprepared. Already in "l'horizon unanime" on page 4 and in "sous une inclinaison" on page 3, perhaps also in "en opposition au ciel" of the second comparison (page 7), there were terms with proper astronomical or navigational meanings in addition to those employed at the particular point in the text; so that passages preceding "le hasard" one again contained the elements of what would follow it. Since "élévation" means "altitude" or the angular elevation of a celestial object above the horizon, an "élévation ordinaire" would presumably be one that would be insufficient to cause or signify the positive event. Hence "verse l'absence," where "verse" has the special utility of suggesting a downward motion, a pouring down such as that associated, in astronomical and astrological lore, with the influence of the stars. What is poured down is nothing or nullity, "l'absence"; for nothing will have happened.

A first part of the sentence is concluded with "que le lieu"; "rien n'aura eu lieu que le lieu." There is, of course, a play of words here on "lieu"—"nothing but the place will have taken place"—and it is used to magnify the negation ("rien . . . que") and to minimize the efficacy of the action. The "lieu" is the scene of the crisis (as the modifiers will soon show), "aura eu lieu" represents both the master's action and the result of that action—in this case "rien." The encounter, in the storm, of the aged master with destiny will have taken place, but nothing else will have happened. A long modifier specifies both place and taking place: "que le lieu / inférieur clapotis quelconque comme pour disperser l'acte vide / abruptement qui sinon / par son mensonge / eût fondé / la perdition / dans ces parages / du vague / en quoi toute réalité se dissout." The place is designated by "inférieur clapotis" and "dans ces parages du vague" with their complements, the taking place by "l'acte vide" and the whole "qui" clause that follows.

In "inférieur clapotis quelconque" we have a new set of terms to designate the sea, the abyss, the whirlpool, already represented by so many other words. But new ideas are added. "Inférieur," coming so shortly after "élévation," establishes the opposition of sea and sky, of below and above, at the same time as it provides the cognate for "supérieure" on the last page, where the constellation rather than the abyss will be involved. The gulf is now a "clapotis," an irregular and disorderly agitation of the waters, lacking the grandeur and the power of the original storm and approaching the quality of "inférieur" as an evaluative term, of "quelconque" as meaning "nondescript." In its turn, "quelconque" for the storm or the abyss parallels "quiconque" for the master in the second comparison, "pour ne pas marquer . . . quiconque . . . s'en coiffe." Together they aid in the generalizing process that will enable us to pass from the master to man, from the fictionalized Idea to the abstraction contained in the last line of the poem. "Inférieur clapotis quelconque" is of course in apposition to "le lieu," while the next phrase, "comme pour disperser l'acte vide / abruptement," is a curious kind of adjective—"a place such as one that would disperse . . ." The connotation of "disperser" is primarily that related to "éparse," to "répandue," to the notion of the scattering of the dice that will find its equivalent in the dispersion of the stars; but it also carries with it ideas of loss and dissipation. These are found again in "l'acte vide" which is synonymous with "l'évènement . . . humain" and "tout résultat nul" as descriptions of the throwing of the dice. "Abruptement," like "tout de suite / évaporé en brumes," stresses the rapidity of the master's action—after the lengthy hesitation—and hence its inconsequential nature.

To "l'acte vide" is referred also the next clause, "qui sinon par son mensonge eût fondé la perdition." The force of "sinon" is to imply that were it not for the dispersion of the act, i.e. the dice, by the waves, the act would have brought about a more dire result; "eût fondé la perdition"—and we should remark again that the conditional meaning, as in "se fût accompli"—characterizes that dire result. Whereas the verb used to express the effect of the abyss on the act, "disperser," implies weakening and nullification, an opposite impression is given by "fonder" for the supposed result had the act not been so "dispersed." Perdition, the ultimate destruction of the master, "naufrage cela direct de l'homme," would have been established and founded in a durable way. The act would have produced this effect "par son mensonge," by the initial error that led the master to believe that he might substitute the game of chance for the operation of the intellect in the controlling of his destiny. The throwing of the dice, consequence of that belief, might have resulted in his death in the sense that the forces of nature (the abyss, the tempest) would have met with no opposition on his part.

Directly below "inférieur clapotis," at the bottom of the page where it starts a final downward-and-across movement, comes the phrase that makes the final statement about "le lieu": "dans ces parages / du vague / en quoi toute réalité se dissout." The "ces" of "dans ces parages" has a generalizing intention; it makes of "these regions" the antecedent to the rest of the phrase, hence to another abstraction. They are the areas of the "clapotis inférieur," but they are also areas of a moral and metaphysical nature, as the rest of the phrase will show. They are the areas "du vague," of that which is not firmly founded and established. But they are also, through the same kind of wordplay that has been going on throughout the passage, the areas of "la vague" or "les vagues," proper to the abyss and the sea in general. In the more philosophical sense of "du vague"—that which is not clearly explicable—they are equivalent to areas "en quoi toute réalité se dissout." If all reality is dissolved, during the master's act, into vagueness, this is the same as saying that the solid stuff of the intellect, inference or calculation, is replaced by the dementia and the folly of the appeal to chance—just as in this material area the solid mass of the ship will be dissolved into the waters of the waves that will engulf it. Were this to happen, only the "lieu" would remain.

In that same letter to Gide already quoted, Mallarmé had said that, on the printed page, his constellation was to look like a constellation: "La constellation y affectera, d'après des lois exactes, et autant qu'il est permis à un texte imprimé, fatalement une allure de constellation." Yet as we look at page 11 in the 1914 edition (which, to be sure, is not the one of which Mallarmé was speaking), we must use all our imagination and whatever knowledge we may have of constellations to see on it a constellation. The words in 14-point roman capitals, "Excepté . . . peut-être . . . une constellation," are the most visible, hence the brightest stars. They are arranged so that the first two, with their modifiers, stretch across the top of the central part of the double page, making for a kind of Dipper handle; "une constellation" is at the right margin of the right side, slightly above the middle, with over and under it large massings of words in varying arrangements, some blocked vertically, some downward and across, some standing in isolation. The total effect of the right side is indeed one of a clustering about a central prominent word, but it is quite different from the disposition around "le hasard" on page 9 where a similar principle is employed. At the very bottom of the side, and with nothing to distinguish it typographically except a few capital letters, is found a completely independent sentence that is the real conclusion—both poetical and philosophical—of the poem.

The real dramatic value of "excepté . . . peut-être . . . une constellation" resides rather in what it says than in the way it looks. For it says something strikingly different from what had gone before, almost contradictory to the statement of the preceding page, "rien n'aura eu lieu que le lieu," and something that invites us to change radically our interpretation of the master's act and of the ideas associated with it. Nothing, we have been told, will have happened; the act will have been weak and inconclusive; destiny will pursue its course regardlessly, indifferently. Now we are told that something important, splendid, and eternal does result from the master's act, a constellation. The problem in the interpretation of this page, and really of the whole poem, lies in the discovery of how this sudden and surprising change is justified, both poetically and philosophically.

For the first word, "excepté," we need to note that, since it depends upon "que le lieu," it states an exception to an exception: "rien . . . que le lieu . . . excepté une constellation"; this makes the contradiction of the preceding page even more remarkable, for the first exception diminishes while the second augments immeasurably. The modifier "à l'altitude" resumes the navigational language of page 10. But if, there, the "élévation" (or altitude) was "ordinaire," presumably here it is extraordinary; instead of pouring down absence and futility, it is efficacious in bringing up into the heavens a new presence. How it does so will be revealed later on the page. "Peut-être," rather than diminishing the force of the exception, serves as a kind of ironic modifier to "une constellation"; it leads us to expect something lesser, we find something greater. What follows is really a modifier to "l'altitude," assembling the necessary astronomical conditions for the appearance of the constellation: "aussi loin qu'un endroit fusionne avec au delà / hors l'intérêt / quant à lui signalé / en général / selon telle obliquité par telle déclivité / de feux / vers / ce doit être / le Septentrion aussi Nord / une constellation." While "l'altitude" creates (aside from its proper astronomical meaning) an impression of height in the sky, "aussi loin" adds the impression of distance. The upward movement has begun. In the phrase "qu'un endroit fusionne avec au delà," besides the harking back to "l'horizon unanime" and to "la neutralité identique du gouffre," the notion of a horizon is added to that of distance; but the horizon is the juncture of two regions in the heavens, not the meeting of sea and sky, and the distance is as extreme ("au delà") as indeterminate. A kind of "abyss" of the heavens is suggested, at the top or outermost reach of which the constellation will take its place.

Now the astronomical or geographical indications are interrupted to make way for a phrase that is "moral" in reference and that treats the man (formerly the master) rather than the abyss: "hors l'intérêt / quant à lui signalé en général." As soon as "interest" enters, the human quality is present. But "hors" excludes that interest from causality in the creation of the constellation; the "intérêt quant à lui signalé" is the concern of the master with the "inclinaison," with the disposition of the natural elements toward him—a concern inferred from his calculations and from his conclusion that his time of crisis was at hand. It is not a concern of the constellation for the master, for that has already been ruled out and will again be denied in a little while. "En général," at the end of the phrase, once more helps in making the passage from master to man; it evokes "humain" of the preceding page, "l'homme" of page 4, and the other passages that moved towards abstraction.

Directly under "fusionne avec au delà," hence related to it in idea, comes the last set of astronomical directions: "selon telle obliquité par telle déclivité / de feux / vers / ce doit être / le Septentrion aussi Nord." Obliquity is the angle between the planes of the earth's equator and orbit, declivity is the deviation from the horizontal; the latter is thus closely related to "inclinaison." I doubt that we are supposed to make any close technical association with these terms as we read the poem; rather, we are expected to visualize a kind of coordinate juncture, a coming together of the forces that make for the right place—"un endroit fusionne avec au delà." But we should perhaps note that the construction of "selon telle obliquité par telle déclivité" suggests that of "la mer par l'aïeul . . . ou l'aïeul contre la mer" and that both represent the kind of situation described in "induit / le vieillard vers cette conjonction suprême avec la probabilité." In all three cases, the "coordinates" cross at a precise time and at a precise place. The constellation comes into being when the "conjunction" is right. The obliquity and the declivity are now not of wave or sea or sail, but instead of the heavenly bodies—"de feux" —in their relationships to one another. The fixed point by which they are measured and situated is the North. I presume that both "Septentrion" and "Nord" are given with capital letters in order to call attention to their specific astronomical meaning of the Big Dipper and the North Pole; and also that the two terms are given rather than one so that the common, popular, human designation may be added to the scientific and celestial one.

It is, of course, the constellation that takes its place in the heavens "à l'altitude . . . selon telle obliquité par telle déclivité . . . vers ce doit être le Septentrion." It also "takes place," since "excepté" goes back as well to "aura eu lieu": "rien n'aura eu lieu excepté peut-être une constellation." The constellation, through its magnitude, its importance, its eternity, is the direct contrary of "rien"; it is presence not absence, foundation not perdition, utility not futility. Yet it comes into being because of the throw of the dice, the "acte vide." The dice are thrown downward and spread over the surface of the abyss; the stars of the constellation are thrown upward and spread over the surface of the heavens. This causality and this simultaneity of motion are characterized in the words that come just below "une constellation" on page 11. These are divided into two groups. The first one, largely in a vertical, block arrangement, reads as follows: "une constellation / froide d'oubli et de désuétude / pas tant / qu'elle n'énumère/ sur quelque surface vacante et supérieure / le heurt successif / sidéralement / d'un compte total en formation."

As is proper in the ending of a poem, the elements of which this group is compounded all relate to things that have gone before, to the master, the sea, and the dice. The first modifier of "une constellation," "froide d'oubli et de désuétude," is a clear reference to the first passage describing the master's state, "hors d'anciens calculs / où la manœuvre avec l'âge oubliée . . . jadis il empoignait la barre" (page 4). "Oubli" is repeated and the notion of disuse, "désuétude," summarizes the master's practice of his arts. Even the idea of "froide" may be likened to the master's age. But all these terms, which make sense when applied to the master, would make little sense if used to characterize the state of a constellation; rather we must see in them attitudes on the part of men toward the constellation. They would be connected with the earlier phrase, "hors l'intérêt / quant à lui signalé / en général." If the master no longer calculates by the stars, no longer maneuvers his ship according to those calculations, then the stars are forgotten and neglected by him; the constellation may be said, by extension, to be "froide" because of this neglect—as well as because of its location in the extremes of stellar space.

Nevertheless, these attitudes are not of sufficient force to prevent the constellation's coming into being. "Pas tant que" states that it comes into being anyway, and "elle n'énumère" that it comes into being as a number. Just as the dice, when thrown, compose a number, so do the stars of the constellation, albeit a number of a different kind. And while the dice do so on the lowest surface of the abyss, the stars are scattered "sur quelque surface vacante et supérieure." The "surface . . . supérieure" of the heavens is juxtaposed to the "inférieur clapotis" of the sea into which the dice were thrown; both "inférieur" and "supérieur" have special meanings in astronomy that are alluded to here, in order to reinforce the context of technical terms. The "surface vacante" may be reminiscent of the surface of the abyss in the first comparison—"sans le joncher / ni fuir"—and it may also provide a counterpart to the "acte vide" of page 10. The object of "énumère" is "le heurt successif . . . d'un compte total en formation," where the general sense is that the constellation "numbers out, or makes a number out of, the successive striking (upon the surface of the heavens) of the individual numbers which, as they come together, combine into a single sum." We should see, simultaneously, each die with its number strike the surface of the sea and each star (metaphorically a number) strike the "surface" of the sky;

the process of the successive striking is the "formation," the end result is the "compte total." For the dice, the sum (and "somme" was used on page 9 in "évidence de la somme pour peu qu'une") is the number, "l'unique Nombre qui ne peut pas être un autre." For the stars, the sum is the constellation. Each act, like the master's act, has resulted in the formation of a number, and the verb "se chiffrât-il" applies equally well to any one of the three. But the stars are the only agents that accomplish the act "sidéralement," in the way of stars. The adverb recalls, through its sound and its prominent position, the "ancestralement" applied to the master's act. And since the way of stars is the way of brilliant light, the "illuminât-il" in the description of the master's career is now explained by the making of the star-number, "sidéralement."

It is essential to observe, here, that in the last analysis it is the master who has made the constellation. He has thrown the dice, apparently—as far as his own destiny was concerned—an "acte vide." But as the dice struck the bottom of the abyss, in the same way as the feather from the "écumes originelles . . . sursauta . . . jusqu'à une cime" (page 9), the stars rose from the bottom of one abyss to the top of another. Had the dice not been thrown, nothing would have happened; but they were thrown, and a constellation takes place. The first block of words under "une constellation" has told how that was accomplished. The second group gives what we may think of as the moral or metaphysical consequences: "veillant / doutant / roulant / brillant et méditant / avant de s'arrêter / à quelque point dernier qui le sacre." The arrangement is a kind of imitation of the whole upper part of the page with its "constellation" form. The series of verbs, separated in a downward-and-across motion, looks like the handle at the top of the page; the rest hangs from it in a much smaller block, of course, but one that has related shapes.

The five verbs that constitute the series are so chosen as to be applicable almost equally well to both master and constellation, and taken in the ensemble they also evoke the dice. The first, "veillant," describes properly the attitude and the activity of the master as he watches over his ship; it may, by extension, apply to the stars of the constellation as they "watch over" the destinies of men. "Doutant" is a direct reference to "hésite" as applied to the master, epitomizing his doubts about the throwing of the dice and the consequent denial of his intellect. "Roulant" would seem to refer specifically to the dice as they come to rest, but as well to the stars as they move toward their appointed positions in the sky and to the master as he moves with his storm-tossed ship. The pair "brillant et méditant" effects a final collapse of constellation and master; for the "brillant" belongs properly to the stars, only figuratively to the master as in "illuminât-il une constellation," while "méditant" is proper to the calculations and the intellectual activities of the master. It may be used only metaphorically of the constellation, just as "veillant" was. Through the whole of the series we have again a conflation of the three essential elements, master, dice, and constellation, and we are obliged to think of them not only simultaneously, but as materially and morally interrelated.

The activity ascribed to the stars of the constellation lasts only until the formation is complete. It is now so restricted by the phrase "avant de s'arrêter," which both limits the activity and states its termination. The coming to rest of a moving object, the completion of an activity, has been anticipated at various points in the poem, perhaps as early as the "jusqu'adapter à l'envergure sa béante profondeur" on page 3. "Immobilise" as applied to the feather in the second comparison belongs in the series, as does perhaps "le temps de souffleter . . . un roc . . . tout de suite évaporé en brumes." These terminations are examples comparable to the ending of the master's life, described in "cessât-il" and in "nié et clos . . . enfin." When, however, the constellation comes to rest, it does so as an object that will last for all time and that will be visible to all men, perhaps useful for all men. It is this that "consecrates" it and that justifies the final line in the group: "à quelque point dernier qui le sacre." Like "quiconque" and "quelconque" earlier, "quelque" in this phrase tends to generalize the situation and the act, to move from this particular case to others like it. The "point dernier" (and "point" is another astronomical term that is used as well in navigation) is the "endroit," the "surface" upon which the constellation is formed, and it is "dernier" in the sense that it marks the end of the movement. It is also the last point to be reached in the triple development of the poem; master, dice, and constellation conclude their motion here. Because this is true, the point of arrival renders sacred the "compte total," the constellation, consecrates it by marking its "altitude" and its "infinitude." This is the point where infinity has no limits and where every place merges with the beyond.

There is still one more line in the poem, at the very bottom of page 11. It is a simple declarative sentence, for once uninterrupted and unmodified. It reads: "Toute Pensée émet un Coup de Dés" and is printed in 14-point capitals and lower case letters. Although it seems to complete the circle of the poem by repeating at the end the words used at the beginning, "un Coup de Dés," and although it is an independent sentence just as was the first one, yet it says something new that was not said before. Indeed, it seems again to contradict what had gone before, just as was the case in the clause beginning with "excepté." It returns to the throw of the dice, rather than continuing with the constellation, and it affirms vigorously rather than negating. We might have expected something like "Tout Coup de Dés émet une Constellation," since that would be a direct development of the preceding narrative. Yet it is precisely because, on this same page, dice and constellation had been merged into a single concept that the sentence may say what it does—and make sense. Through the identity of dice and constellation, "Toute Pensée émet un Coup de Dés" is equivalent to "Toute Pensée émet une Constellation"; hence the thought, any thought and every thought of any man and every man, is capable of becoming permanent and sacred through its mere existence. "Toute Pensée" is justified and comprehensible in the poem because of such antecedent ideas as "anciens calculs," "inférant," "Esprit," and others which, as they related to the master or to the persons like him in the comparisons, attributed thought to the only objects in the poem susceptible of thought, men. "Émet" is the kind of verb that might serve equally well for a "throwing downward" or a "throwing upward," for "pour le jeter dans la tempête" or "précipité hurlé" or "quelque profusion répandue en rareté." The more immediate notions of "d'où sursauta son délire jusqu'à une cime" and "s'arrêter à quelque point dernier" are also contained in it. In a general way, it comes to mean the production of an effect by the exteriorization of some potential within the agent. The "Pensée" is the force within, the "Constellation" (or the "Coup de Dés") is the effect emitted and externalized.

How does this come about? I think that we cannot and should not hope to know. We are reading, after all, a lyric poem and not a philosophical demonstration; we are in the realm of the fiction and the example, not the syllogism and the proof. The spiritual progress that we are to make through the poem is something like the following: We are told a fiction, a story in which a master of a ship, in peril of shipwreck and of his life, renounces the use of reason and turns to a game of chance to save ship and life. This is an "acte vide," for fortune and destiny will not be altered by such a turning: "Un coup de dés jamais n'abolira le hasard." We are invited to see the dice thrown into the tempest, the number formed, and we are told that the master will die or live as he had been destined to, regardless of what that number might be. The number itself will be a product of fortune. Yet at the same time that we see the dice thrown into the abyss, we see rising from the abyss a whole constellation of stars that takes its place for all time in the highest heavens. The two visual images are similar and complementary and they realize an extended imagery of "downward" and "upward" motions that has been built progressively throughout the poem. It is for us to infer, from the congruity of the two images, that a single cause underlies both motions; that is, the master as he acts throws the dice and creates the constellation. But it is not his mere material act that produces the latter effect; for it is "toute pensée" that is the efficient cause. The material act is an "acte vide"; the spiritual act that determines it, the use of "Esprit" in calculation and inference, the determination itself that leads to action, is the real source of the constellation.

This is a poem about the greatness and the efficacy of the intellect. Man, when he acts in defiance of intellect or without intellect, acts as a madman—or not as a man at all. But the mere fact that he does possess mind and that any action of his is the result of an intellectual determination, consecrates his action and makes it admirable.

The structural principle upon which *Un Coup de dés jamais n'abolira le hasard* is built is relatively simple. It consists basically in three organizing elements. The first of these is what Mallarmé calls the Idea, the abstraction or generalization that is to be propounded and exemplified. Like many other lyrics, the poem is thus one of thought, centered about an idea rather than about a passion or a character or an action. In spite of the title, however, the Idea is multiple; we need to add to "un coup de dés jamais n'abolira le hasard" at least three other ideas. For one, the idea that even what seems to be the work of chance is the work of destiny: "si c'était le nombre ce serait le hasard." For another, the idea that however empty the act, if only it result from mind it will have great and noble consequences: "rien n'aura eu lieu que le lieu excepté peut-être une constellation." Finally, the idea that it is the thought involved in the act that produces this result: "toute pensée émet un coup de dés." All four of these fundamental ideas—and the first three lead toward and culminate in the last—are stated explicitly in the text; we do not need to infer or deduce them. Moreover, they are stated as a series, one after the other, except for the fact that the two that end with "le hasard" must overlap to a slight degree; the second is introduced just about when the first is to conclude. This serial arrangement provides a skeleton for a part of the temporal organization of the poem.

The second organizing element is the "fiction" that the poet invents to illustrate and to support his Idea. Although Mallarmé declares that "on évite le récit," there is a narrative constantly present; it is "avoided" only in the sense that it is made discontinuous and fragmentary. Every one of the usual components of a narrative is present: an agent, the master, with enough character to bring him to the required action; a situation requiring action, the storm at sea imperiling the master and his ship; and the action itself, broken down into successive acts—the inference with respect to the danger, the decision to throw the dice, the preparation and casting of the dice, the making of the constellation. Here, again, the true narrative order is followed, with statements and events chronologically arranged from the beginning through the middle to the end. Yet the timing of statement and event is neither independent nor self-generating; rather it is subordinated to the necessary order of the ideas. Fictional elements can be introduced only at those moments when the ideas that they illustrate have reached the proper point of expression. This is, of course, one way of avoiding the narrative, by subordinating it to the architectonic component of the Idea. The fiction is the most extensive part of the poem, occupying considerably more space than the four ideas and even more space than the comparisons. This is, we may say, a correct proportion, for it is through the fiction that the Idea is made clear, visible, and both dramatically and emotionally effective.

Finally, the third organizing element is the set of three comparisons along with the passage under "le hasard" that brings all three to a single conclusion. I call these an organizing element because they supply the structure for a large number of images and terms that are needed if the Idea is to be completely exploited. But they themselves are "organized" by the fiction; in so far as they are comparisons, they compare something to something, and the something-to-which-compared is the throwing of the dice in the fiction. The insinuation or the mystery, the feather falling upon the toque, the siren (with her feather) beating against the impermanent rock, are all metaphors for the basic event in the action, seen in one light or another. At the same time, they introduce details and images that will be useful for the conversion of the dice into the constellation. A hierarchical order is thus established: at the top, the Idea; below it, the fiction; below it, the comparisons—with "below" used in the sense of "subordinated to." As I hope to have shown in the lengthy analysis, every object and every word of the poem is intimately connected with one or several of the organizing elements, and so is justified as a part of the total structure.

I should insist here that neither the use of a fiction nor the invention of the metaphors makes of *Un Coup de dés* a symbolist poem. The master of the ship is a master of a ship and his act is directly and overtly described; he does not stand for anything but himself and his act, while it may be representative, is not symbolical. He and his act are given as examples of man and human action; but they are so named ("naufrage cela direct de l'homme," "l'évènement accompli en vue de tout résultat nul humain") and that feature so essential to the constitution of a true symbol, the suppression of one of the ratios in a proportional metaphor, is entirely lacking. If man and action are abstracted into a generalization, it is because they were meant from the start to serve as examples of an Idea in itself abstract and general. The same may be said of the objects entering into the comparisons. Since both the something-compared and the something-to-which-compared are fully and clearly present, we have merely the standard metaphorical relationship between them. The mere fact that we are obliged to use our imaginations in order to discern the analogies and to put one and one together does not in any way change the nature of that relationship. The appeal to our discernment and our participation is one of the devices by which the modern poet involves us more intimately and more completely in the poem than did his more literalist predecessor.

I cannot be so sure about the constellation itself. It is clear that the constellation is not merely itself, nor can we abstract from it to something greater and more general in the same category. Such abstraction as we make from it is to moral and intellectual qualities that are certainly not a part of its own essence; these are perceptible through such phrases as "supérieure," "veillant / doutant / roulant / brillant et méditant / . . . qui le sacre," but they are not otherwise directly connected with it. To attach qualities of this kind to a purely material object is to work in the way of the symbol, and to express them as they are here expressed is to provide the kind of "signs" that lead to the identification of the object symbolized. If there is a symbolic meaning to be attached to the constellation, however, it is only at one point in the poem; the symbol is of the "incidental" or "occasional" type that I have distinguished, not of the "structuring" type that would make of this a symbolist poem.

In its basic structure, then, *Un Coup de dés* is entirely traditional: an idea, a fiction to materialize it, a group of comparisons to extend and clarify the fiction. The order is a compromise between the intellectual order required by the idea and the narrative order required by the fiction, with the former dominant and subordinating. Mallarmé's hope that from his new genre might spring "rien ou presque un art" ("rien n'aura eu lieu . . . excepté peut-être une constellation") must thus have been based upon something other than the organizing principles found in a unifying subject matter and in its disposition. Primary among his innovations was, of course, the typography and its arrangement on the printed double page: "le tout sans nouveauté qu'un espacement de la lecture." He had already experimented, for example in *L'Après-midi d'un faune,* with typography, alternating passages in italics with others in romans, using capital letters for certain words, breaking the line as in dramatic dialogue. In *Un Coup de dés* he went much farther. At least eight separate type-faces are used (more if we count certain mixings), a heavy emphasis is placed on the proportion of white spaces to black print, the double page replaces the single verse as the prosodic unit, lines of type are divided into small pieces arranged according to standard patterns—downward-and-across motions, vertical arrangements, blocks of words or words in isolation. Besides, there is a patent intention to create picture-grams or *calligrammes;* Mallarmé identifies two of them for us, the rolling of the ship on the waves, on page 3, and the constellation, on page 11. Others may also be found, such as the shape of the feather (or perhaps of the siren herself) on page 8. All these are visual devices aimed at producing visual impressions in the imagination.

But the extension of visual devices is not a goal in itself. Mallarmé has other aims in mind. He wishes to use typography as a corrective for the fragmentation of ideas, of fictions, of images. If a single sentence is broken into pieces and scattered through the poem—for structural purposes that have already become evident—how make sure that the reader will put the pieces together properly and reconstruct the sentence? The solution is simple: one uses a single typeface for the whole of the sentence and the reader is guided to a correct reading. Even larger bodies of material may be spotted in the same way, for example the connection of the block of materials below "le hasard" with the three comparisons to which it belongs. Visual imagination becomes an aid to understanding. It also becomes a guide to the establishment of a scale of importance for the various parts of the poem. The larger the type, the more important the sentence or the clause or the passage printed in it; hence the "phrase capitale dès le titre introduite et continuée" is printed in the largest and blackest capitals of all, the next size is reserved for the short sentence, "Si c'était le nombre ce serait le hasard," and so progressively downward in size of type and significance of idea. There are, however, some exceptions to this general principle, lest the pattern become routine and mechanical. Three of the four sentences that express the Idea are given in capital letters exclusively; yet the fourth, which is perhaps the most weighty, is printed inconspicuously in 14-point lower case with a few capitals. Under "c'était" on page 9, a key word in the development, appears the modifier "issu stellaire" in 10-point lower-case italics, the smallest face of the whole poem; yet these words constitute a kind of crux in the passage from the dice to the constellation ("issu stellaire" in the case of the number means "an issuing from the stars," in the case of the constellation "an issuing of stars," and thus the transition is made). Mallarmé is simply emphasizing through understatement.

If typographical-visual devices need to be used to reassemble the scattered parts of a passage, there must have been a major necessity for effecting the original scattering. We have seen one reason for it in the requirements of timing—in the need, for example, to bring three separate lines of sense together in "le hasard." In a true chordal structure such as one may have in music, it would be possible to run the three "sentences" together, simultaneously, and have them end in a chord of resolution. Since this is impossible with ideas, Mallarmé does the next best thing by achieving an interposition or staggering of the parts of the dismantled sentences and by ending with a single concept. Similarly, if he wished to introduce for each word the total modification of that word before going on to others, he had to detach the word, delay those following, interrupt and interpolate. Striking examples of this procedure are found in the cases of "soit" (after which the full body of circumstances is inserted) and "le maître" (after which comes the lengthy history and characterization of the principal agent). If we follow the same sentence, we find under each of its words printed on page 9 the appropriate modifiers; and on pages 10 and 11 the whole of the poem's conclusion comes as a gloss on the remaining words of the sentence. The new "prosodie," as Mallarmé names it, has a full poetic and intellectual justification.

Ultimately, desires with respect to the effect to be achieved dictated both fragmentation and reassemblage. Mallarmé did not wish to be clear. His hermeticism, however, was neither capricious nor snobbish. It was calculated to involve the reader in the poem in very special ways, subtly and intimately, by leading him to discover many things in the poem for himself, through inference and association. A certain number of his most salient practices in the poem are accounted for by this purpose. Some of them we have seen in his other poems, a few of them are invented especially for this one. Such a word as "évènement," wilfully incorrect in order to induce us to see in it both "événement" and "avènement," goes beyond his typical puns and etymological usages. It requires of us an act of intelligence and sensitivity; once we have done it, the entire passage in which the word appears turns out to be equally ambivalent; but we must make both the first step and the ones following. "Se chiffrât-il," in so far as it means "to turn himself into a number," is a neologism; or at least it is semantically fresh and forceful. It achieves these qualities only through the fact that, associating it with many passages before it and after it in the poem, we see in it—suddenly—a résumé of the whole life, career, action, and glorification of the master. Through its particular context in this poem, the word becomes something that it had never been before, and it is our perception that makes it so. The process is, of course, a universal one with poets who are intent upon enlivening the vocabulary that tradition has given them; but Mallarmé goes to his own private extremes in applying the process, and from it derives some of his most characteristic effects. The pun, the play on words, the double-entendre, the etymological reference, the crossing with other languages, are all instruments to insure the serious involvement of the reader in the poem.

Is mere brain-cudgeling, coupled with the satisfaction of discovery and understanding, the effect at which Mallarmé aimed? I think not —not at all. If we would appreciate what is accomplished by these various devices, we need only compare in our minds a simple, direct, declarative statement of the Idea with the complex, indirect, intimative and suggestive statement that Mallarmé gives us, or a straightforward and continuous recitation of the fiction with his tortured, broken, and overlapping account. In either case, the first would be largely devoid of emotional accompaniment—or it would have only such emotional overtones as might be found inherently in the Idea and in the object. The second, what Mallarmé does with both Idea and fiction in *Un Coup de dés,* is infinitely rich in potentials for poetic effect. Our involvement will be both intellectual and passionate, and that simultaneously because of the way in which Idea and fiction are merged. A first enrichment. Each part of the Idea will become visible, palpable, sensible (as well as intelligible) through its translation into the fiction; and each part of the fiction will be transcendentalized as we pass from it to the particular idea, then to the general idea, ultimately to the universal abstraction. The universals, in the poem, have a kind of sensual beauty with which Mallarmé endows them through his art, and hence the emotions are stirred by them. The devices of fragmentation and juncture, of interruption and commentary, of mingling and confusion, of ambiguity and ambivalence, of visual image and visual sonority, of pattern and arrangement, are all used to complicate exceedingly the total emotional effect of the poem. From which the cold light of the intellect is never absent.

I I

Valéry

Le Cimetière marin

In the discussion centering about Paul Valéry's *Le Cimetière marin* since its appearance in 1920, there have been two essential issues: the "translation" of the poem and its philosophical implications. Two questions have been raised consistently: "What does the poem say?" —how might one translate it into simple, unmetaphorical French? —and "What does the poem mean?"—what are its philosophical arguments and conclusions? Both of these resolve themselves into a consideration of meaning. To answer the first question, one studies the syntax, the connotations of words, the allusions, the figures of speech, and one arrives at a kind of paraphrase or prosification of the work. What might be called the "grammatical" meaning is discovered. To answer the second question, one turns the images into ideas, studies the relationship and the sequence of those ideas, discerns the argument and the conclusion. What might be called the "logical" meaning is apprehended.

If debate upon both of these issues is possible, it is because clear and unequivocal answers are apparently not contained in the poem itself. On the one hand, the language is not literal but metaphorical; objects are not called by their own names, but by substitutes; adjectives attribute physical characteristics when abstract qualities are meant; verbs are used in a derived rather than in a primary sense. In the translation of these non-literal terms into literal terms there is

This essay was first printed under the title "An interpretation of Valéry's *Le Cimetière marin*" in *The Romanic Review*, April, 1947, pp. 133–58.

much room for hesitation and difference of opinion. On the other hand, once literal meaning has been discerned, there still remains the problem of finding the ideas for which the objects identified are supposed to stand. For this is an essentially metaphorical poem in the sense that the objects and actions described are themselves merely the representatives of abstract meanings. In the search for these ulterior meanings there is again occasion for much uncertainty and variety of approach. The task is admittedly a difficult one. In spite of its difficulty, much light has been thrown on the poem by its commentators and much has been contributed to its understanding and enjoyment.

To these discussions in general, we may offer two objections. First, they have not been relevant to the analysis of the poem as a poem; second, they have furnished no basis for the evaluation of the poem as a poem.

A poetic structure differs from any other—from a logical or a rhetorical structure—in the nature of its internal organization. It uses words that represent objects so organized (if it be a good poem) that there is an internal "poetic" justification for the presence and the place of every word. It has a principle of unity which determines how every word belongs in the total structure and it has a principle of order which determines where every word belongs in the total structure. Both of these principles are internal; they are self-contained rather than imposed from without, they are unique and germane only to a given poem rather than general or universal. If the poem is narrative or dramatic, both of these principles are derived from the plot (taken in the broadest sense); anything present in the poem gains entry because of its relevance to one of the elements constituting the plot; its place in the work is determined by its belonging to the beginning of the plot (that part in which the conflicting situations and characters are stated), or to the middle (that part in which the conflict is developed), or to the end (that part in which the conflict is resolved). If the poem is not narrative or dramatic and there is no plot strictly speaking, something analogous to a plot contributes the internal principles of unity and order. With respect to evaluation, esthetic judgments on the beauty of the poem may derive from an analysis of its unity and its order and may be, in large part, in terms of the degree of achievement of these internal relationships.

In the discussions of *Le Cimetière marin,* critics have so closely applied themselves to the two kinds of meaning already mentioned that they have largely neglected its nature and its worth as a poem. On the "grammatical" side, in the search for the literal interpretation of the language, they have proceeded largely by a process of fragmentation. They have singled out the individual simile, the isolated allusion, the difficult phrase, for study and analysis; when they made reference to context, it was merely to repetitions of word or phrase by a kind of cross-reference which might support or deny a given interpretation. They made little if any attempt to understand the phrase in terms of the total poetic structure—or the total poetic structure in terms of the phrase. On the "logical" side, in the search for the symbolical interpretation of the work, critics have proceeded to study the argument of the poem, its premises and its conclusions, just as if it were not a poem at all but some philosophical demonstration. Argument has been treated independently of poetic structure; that is, the critic (*e.g.* Jean de Latour) has tended to rearrange the ideas of the poem into a logical sequence which might or might not be related to the sequence and to the structural workings of the poem. In a word, these critics have not always made a distinction between the logical relationships of ideas and the esthetic development of poetic elements.

Obviously, neither of these approaches could be productive of evaluative conclusions with respect to the poem. If one proceeds by fragmentation, the relationships which make for unity and order are destroyed rather than made patent, and there is no way of telling if and to what extent they have been achieved. Hence the basis for evaluation is lost. If one proceeds to apply philosophical criteria to the argument, one may indeed arrive at evaluations; but they will not necessarily be evaluations of the goodness or the beauty of the poem as a work of art. They may indeed be so considered in a critical system in which esthetic criteria are indistinguishable from other criteria, ethical or metaphysical or political. But they could not be considered as valid in a critical system in which a work of art, approached from different points of view, is judged by separate and individual criteria for each point of view.

In the present essay I shall attempt to supplement these earlier studies by another, in which attention will be focussed specifically on the discovery of internal structural relationships in the poem. I shall be using a critical approach in which just one aspect of the poem, its form or structure, will be considered, and in which only criteria pertinent to that single aspect will be applied. Once these relationships have been discovered and clarified, I shall try to derive whatever evaluative conclusions seem to be justified by the analysis. Any such reading and judgment of the poem is merely a hypothesis—an interpretation which can be valid only so long as it confirms the reactions or the intuitions of the sensitive reader, only so long as it illuminates the work for the sensitive reader and makes it at once more understandable and more beautiful for him. If it fails to do this, it must be discarded as an interpretation. Any such failure may be imputed either to the error or the insufficiency of the analyst or to the fault of the method of analysis employed, or to both.

In *Le Cimetière marin,* the unifying structural element is an extended metaphor to which all words in the poem are related. The principle of order is contained in the development of that same metaphor from a situation of apparent but unreal balance at the beginning, through a middle in which that balance becomes manifestly untenable and is disturbed, to an end in which the false balance is totally destroyed and a harmonious relationship within the metaphor is achieved.

The metaphor establishes a parallelism or equivalence among three separate elements: the sea, the cemetery, and the spectator. It is thus more complex than the usual metaphorical relationship in which only two elements are juxtaposed. The reason for this is that one of the three elements, the cemetery, differs from the other two in a fundamental—but not immediately apparent—way. In this difference lies the disturbing element in the initial balance, and hence the source of the whole "action" is introduced.

Each of the elements in this tripartite metaphor has in itself two aspects, a superficial one and an internal one. The sea has its calm, unbroken surface upon which shines the high sun of noon; but it also has the turbulent waters beneath its surface, waters held in check—for a time at least—by the immobile exterior. The spectator displays an attitude or appearance of philosophical disdain for all the concerns and functions of life; but he also has beneath this exterior a living organism contained—if only temporarily—by this attitude of detachment. The cemetery has the gleaming tombstones and the pines; but these cover—this time, eternally—the remains of the spectator's ancestors.

A metaphorical relationship is thus established: the surface of the sea is like the attitude of the spectator, and the surface of the cemetery is like both of these. Therefore, whatever is said of one of these may apply, metaphorically, to the other two; any expression will be capable of a triple interpretation. Similarly, beneath each of these exteriors there lies something hidden or suppressed, and the ratio *surface* : *subsurface* may also be used metaphorically. But there the perfect parallelism ends. If a complete state of balance existed among all elements of the metaphor, we should be able to extend to all three "subsurface" elements the same comparison, the same terms and the same interchangeability of expression. This is not possible. For while that which is contained beneath the surface of the sea is turbulent and is only temporarily subdued, and while that which is hidden by the disdain of the spectator is alive and is only temporarily subjugated, what lies beneath the stones and the pines of the cemetery is forever dead. The third element of the metaphor, the cemetery, contains a factor which cannot be made to fit in with the others. The balance is not genuine. There is a basis for change and for development, similar to that which produces the conflict in a narrative or dramatic plot.

In the poem, indeed, there is a disturbance of this balance and the final achievement of a situation in which a new balance is brought about. This change is what determines the order of the poem. In the beginning, all three "surface" aspects are placed in relationship; their similarity is emphasized, and there is only the slightest intimation of what lies beneath each of these surfaces. The spectator is like the immobile sun, the still water, the pines and the monuments, and he is happy. In the middle, however, the "subsurface" elements become increasingly prominent, and the one discordant character-istic is brought into play. The spectator discovers that although he is alive and the sea is alive, the cemetery covers only death. To be like the cemetery is to be entirely dead, and perhaps disdain is equivalent to such a death. But to be like the cemetery is also impossible for him so long as he is alive; for he is like the sea. In the end, the spectator casts off his disdain and becomes thoroughly alive, just as the sea, ruffled by the wind, becomes entirely mobile. A new metaphor, in which sea and spectator are completely assimilable, is established. From it the dead stones and their dead men are excluded.

If now the parts of the poem be translated into a philosophical argument, its meaning becomes patent. At the beginning, the specta-tor states a case for philosophical detachment from life itself, for stoicism. In the middle, he discovers that to affect such stoicism is to be like the dead, and is in the nature of things an impossibility. In the end, he determines to live the life of the living. This "argument" is at the same time a part of the poem *qua* poem and something extraneous to it. It is a part of the poem since it is implicit in the language, the metaphors, the arrangement of the poem; but it is extraneous in the sense that the statement of the argument involves the use of other language and of another structure: it is not some-thing explicitly stated in the poem itself.

Thus the unity of the poem—what belongs and what does not belong,—the order—where things belong,—and the meaning—what things mean,—are all contained within the single structural device of a metaphor. The degree of integration is high. Let us see how, in the detail, this integration is achieved, before going on to a few evaluative statements on *Le Cimetière marin*.

Le Cimetière marin[1]

I

Ce toit tranquille, où marchent des colombes,
Entre les pins palpite, entre les tombes;
Midi le juste y compose de feux
La mer, la mer, toujours recommencée!

[1] Text of the *Œuvres de Paul Valéry,* Paris, Editions de la N. R. F., 1933, III, 157–163.

> O récompense après une pensée
> Qu'un long regard sur le calme des dieux!   [6]

In the first stanza, all three elements are clearly introduced: in line 1, the "toit tranquille" of the sea, in line 2 the "pins" and the "tombes" of the cemetery, in line 6 the "long regard" of the man. To the first belong the rest of line 1 (referring to the sails upon the water), line 3, line 4, and the second half of line 6; to the last belongs the "récompense" of line 5. The adjectives and verbs referring to all three are of the same general sense: "tranquille," "juste," "compose" (to be taken in the sense of "calms, smoothes"), "le calme des dieux." That is, we are here dealing in each case with the surface or visible aspect of the object: the impression is one of balance, calm, eternity, divinity. But already, as needs must be, something at least of the instability is intimated; the "toit" is only part of an edifice, covers what is beneath; high noon ("Midi le juste") is but a momentary state; the normal condition of the sea is one of movement ("toujours recommencée"). In line 5, "O récompense *après une pensée*," there is a definite indication that something else lies before and beneath the "long regard." Note that these "subsurface" indications all refer to the sea and to the spectator; this will generally be the case in the first part of the poem. The way is thus prepared for later developments.

II

> Quel pur travail de fins éclairs consume
> Maint diamant d'imperceptible écume,
> Et quelle paix semble se concevoir!
> Quand sur l'abîme un soleil se repose,
> Ouvrages purs d'une éternelle cause,
> Le Temps scintille et le Songe est savoir.   [12]

III

> Stable trésor, temple simple à Minerve,
> Masse de calme, et visible réserve,
> Eau sourcilleuse, Œil qui gardes en toi
> Tant de sommeil sous un voile de flamme,
> O mon silence! . . . Édifice dans l'âme,
> Mais comble d'or aux mille tuiles, Toit!   [18]

In the second and third stanzas, significantly, the cemetery does not enter; the attention is still on similarity rather than on dissimilarity. The lines are spent largely in describing the process by which the sea is calmed by the noonday sun, and the resultant static condition. Again, the same descriptive impressions are produced: "pur, fins, paix, purs, éternelle, stable, simple, calme." But a more complete suggestion of the substructure is given in such phrases as "Quand sur l'abîme," "qui gardes en toi tant de sommeil"; in the word "semble" (line 9); and even in the intimation that Time and Dreams, here momentarily transformed, do have a more real form and existence. Moreover, in line 17 comes a specific statement to the effect that the soul does exist beneath the surface; it is the "Édifice dans l'âme" lying beneath the personified "Toit." One should note here, finally, that the metaphor of the temple—dedicated to the symbol of divine wisdom—which is introduced at this point is given extensive development later on.

IV

Temple du Temps, qu'un seul soupir résume,
A ce point pur je monte et m'accoutume,
Tout entouré de mon regard marin;
Et comme aux dieux mon offrande suprême,
La scintillation sereine sème
Sur l'altitude un dédain souverain.   [24]

If the cemetery was omitted in the preceding two stanzas, it is given full attention in the fourth. It is the "point pur," the "Temple du Temps" (note how the term changes in reference), the "altitude." The sea enters in the "scintillation sereine," the man in the other lines. Just as previously the sea was in a state of *becoming* calm, serene, and so forth, so is the man here *becoming* disdainful: "je monte et m'accoutume"; the serenity to which he attains is like an offering to the same gods already mentioned in line 6—a kind of similarity with them. Nevertheless, the phrase "qu'un seul soupir résume" again reminds one of the living flesh thus subjugated.

V

Comme le fruit se fond en jouissance,
Comme en délice il change son absence
Dans une bouche où sa forme se meurt,
Je hume ici ma future fumée,
Et le ciel chante à l'âme consumée
Le changement des rives en rumeur.   [30]

In the fifth stanza, those suggestions of change previously scattered are brought together in a compact metaphor, and made to refer specifically to the man: just as a fruit, losing its form, disappearing, dying, is changed into pleasure and delight, so the man—his soul consumed—is transformed into nothing more than a pleasurable smoke. The pleasure is denoted in the phrase "je hume," the fact of change in the verb "change" of line 26 and in the "future" of line 28 (also, metaphorically, in the "changement" of line 30). That so sensuous an image should be used is in many ways appropriate: sensuality is one of the things being discarded in favor of the "sovereign disdain," and it is the refusal of this sensuality to be so discarded which leads the man to his ultimate conclusion (cf. Stanza XVI, especially). It should be noted, moreover, that this transformation is a kind of death for the fruit ("où sa forme se meurt"), and that for the man the word "future" gives the same implication—an implication of primary importance for the subsequent progress of the poem. In the last two lines, the metaphor of the sea and the heavens is again introduced.

VI

Beau ciel, vrai ciel, regarde-moi qui change!
Après tant d'orgueil, après tant d'étrange
Oisiveté, mais pleine de pouvoir,
Je m'abandonne à ce brillant espace,
Sur les maisons des morts mon ombre passe
Qui m'apprivoise à son frêle mouvoir.   [36]

The two elements, man and sea, are again combined in the sixth stanza. The heavens, now apostrophized, have their old attributes, "beau, vrai," the sea is still "ce brillant espace." But for the man, although the element of change is still stressed ("regarde-moi qui change," "je m'abandonne"), the emphasis is upon a notion earlier suggested—*from* what the change is being made. It is from an abundance of "orgueil," of "étrange oisiveté," from human weaknesses. For both of these a kind of defense is offered in the phrase "mais pleine de pouvoir"; after all, they are the soul within, which is to be the successful protagonist in this action. But they are changed, now, into a shadow ("mon ombre passe"), their power into a "frêle mouvoir"; and even this frailty still can keep the changed man in subjection. It is even possible that a secondary meaning of "ombre" (ghost) is intended here, and that the implication is already made that the man is as one dead. Finally, the third element enters with the "maisons des morts," lying beneath the tombs, over which this shadow moves.

VII

L'âme exposée aux torches du solstice,
Je te soutiens, admirable justice
De la lumière aux armes sans pitié!
Je te rends pure à ta place première:
Regarde-toi! . . . Mais rendre la lumière
Suppose d'ombre une morne moitié.   [42]

The image of the shadow, suggested in the sixth stanza, forms the basis for the seventh stanza and for the revolution which it contains: the ellipsis in line 41 marks the end of a first section of the poem. The phrase "L'âme exposée" continues line 34 ("Je m'abandonne à ce brillant espace"), emphasizing now the fact that it is the soul that is thus delivered over. "Torches du solstice" is, in the same way, a reference to the "Midi le juste" of line 3; as in that line "juste" was used in the etymological sense of "equally spaced between two extremes" (hence, high noon), so here the word "solstice" has its original meaning of the standing still of the sun. Both refer to the state of arrest of the sun—a state to which the man has now abandoned himself. In the next two lines, the same image is restated in "admirable justice / De la lumière aux armes sans pitié." The "je te soutiens" contrasts with verbs previously employed in that it represents, instead of the earlier state of becoming, a state of being: man and heavens are now identified, man now can withstand the pitiless gaze of the sun, and the image which he reflects back to the sun is the sun itself. "Regarde-toi!" This is the culmination of all the ideas previously expressed, and at the same time a kind of partial resolution of the metaphor: man and sun—human and deity—have been merged.

But all is not so resolved. Beneath the heavens and the surface of the sea still lie the mysterious waters, beneath the disdain the conquered passions of the man. Against the "toi" still stands the "moi" of the spectator (cf. line 31, "Regarde-moi qui change"), the "moi" which will be so fully treated in the next section of the poem. Finally, the shadow of the substantial man still lies beneath the gleaming, divine figure. The "ombre" of line 35 is recalled, and with it the realization expressed in the lines "Mais rendre la lumière / Suppose d'ombre une morne moitié." The dreary half is what man was and what—it is soon to be discovered—he must always continue to be. A second phase of the argument is reached through the subtle turning about of an image.

VIII
O pour moi seul, à moi seul, en moi-même,
Auprès d'un cœur, aux sources du poème,
Entre le vide et l'événement pur,
J'attends l'écho de ma grandeur interne,
Amère, sombre et sonore citerne,
Sonnant dans l'âme un creux toujours futur!   [48]

Iterated and reiterated, the "moi" in the first line of the next stanza is brought into sharp contrast with the "toi" already mentioned; so the argument veers as the development of the metaphor continues. Now, in detail, will come a description of the man hidden by this assumed disdain. Of what does this "moi" consist? Of physical love ("Auprès d'un cœur"), of intellectual creation ("aux sources du poème"), of all those acts of begetting between the nonentity ("le vide") preceding birth on the one hand and death ("l'événement pur") on the other. These are the things opposed to the immortal and eternal "toi." But in these things there still and always remains a flaw; their realization is always in the future. The "grandeur interne" sounds only as an echo, and does not ring true. It lacks the perfection of death, of the "événement pur." Hence we are still at a point in the poem where the man prefers disdain to this kind of living—where it is still possible to establish, metaphorically, a parallelism between the "abîme" (line 10) of the sea and the "citerne" of the internal man, and to apply to the latter a group of adjectives ("amère, sombre, sonore") in direct contrast to those earlier applied to the surface of the sea.

IX
Sais-tu, fausse captive des feuillages,
Golfe mangeur de ces maigres grillages,

Sur mes yeux clos, secrets éblouissants,
Quel corps me traîne à sa fin paresseuse,
Quel front l'attire à cette terre osseuse?
Une étincelle y pense à mes absents.   [54]

Stanza IX reassembles all three elements of the metaphor, the sea ("captive, golfe mangeur"), the cemetery ("feuillages, maigres grillages, terre osseuse"), and the disdainful spectator ("mes yeux clos, me traîne, sa fin paresseuse"). Once again, the potentially turbulent character of the sea is suggested in the words "fausse captive." But the emphasis is still on the living man, on the body which brings him and the mind which attracts him to this place. Body and mind are the dazzling secrets; they are related to the ideas suggested in the "Auprès d'un cœur, aux sources du poème" of the preceding stanza; they contain the spark which remembers the spectator's "absents"— his dead ancestors as well as his unrealized present desires. Here, once more, the introduction of the dead ancestors works toward the upsetting of the metaphorical balance.

We might note, at this point, that that balance has not as yet been disturbed. Suggestions of the possible basis for disruption have been made; in some cases, even, those suggestions have been developed. This merely means that the beginning of the poem contains the sources for the development in the middle and even for the end. The next four stanzas, X to XIII, will complete the presentation of this metaphorical balance; they differ from the preceding stanzas in their concentration on the cemetery, "surface" and "subsurface."

X

Fermé, sacré, plein d'un feu sans matière,
Fragment terrestre offert à la lumière,
Ce lieu me plaît, dominé de flambeaux,
Composé d'or, de pierre et d'arbres sombres,
Où tant de marbre est tremblant sur tant d'ombres;
La mer fidèle y dort sur mes tombeaux!   [60]

The "surface" elements predominate in the tenth stanza, where they receive the same attributes as those given sea and sky in the first lines of the poem. The place itself is indicated in a variety of phrases —"fragment terrestre, ce lieu, pierre et . . . arbres sombres, tant de marbre"; the attributes are "fermé, sans matière, offert à la lumière."

Again, the characteristics are all divine, immortal. Note that in the line "Fragment terrestre offert à la lumière" there is a parallelism, in idea and in phrase, to the spectator's offering of himself to the gods (cf. line 22); in a sense, he himself is such a fragment, whose terrestrial nature prevents the realization of the offer. Sea and sun enter in the phrases "à la lumière, dominé de flambeaux, composé d'or, la mer fidèle y dort." The spectator figures only in the words "me plaît" and "mes tombeaux." Finally, two "subsurface" elements are contained in "sur tant d'ombres" (a repetition of the "ombre" in lines 35 and 42, but now having still another meaning) and "sur mes tombeaux."

XI

Chienne splendide, écarte l'idolâtre!
Quand solitaire au sourire de pâtre,
Je pais longtemps, moutons mystérieux,
Le blanc troupeau de mes tranquilles tombes,
Éloignes-en les prudentes colombes,
Les songes vains, les anges curieux! [66]

If in the first part of the poem the spectator had identified himself with the sea and the sky, had assimilated at least a part of himself to their extra-human and eternal aspects, in the next group of stanzas he relates himself more directly to the third element of the complex metaphor, the cemetery. Stanza XI begins with an apostrophe to the sea; the image of the "chienne splendide" harks back to the "mer fidèle y dort" of the preceding line. The same image is made operative for the whole of the tripartite metaphor: the sea is the watchdog, the spectator the shepherd, the tombs are the sheep. Even in such auxiliary figures, the principal structural relationships of the whole poem are implicit. The verbs "écarte" and "éloigne(s)" refer to the sea; line 62 and the first half of line 63 to the spectator; the rest of line 63 and line 64 to the "surface" aspects of the cemetery. Once more, note the adjectives; the sea is "splendide," the spectator is "solitaire" and smiling; the tombs are "mystérieux, blanc, tranquilles." In the last two lines, the "prudentes colombes," the "songes vains," the "anges curieux" are objects which might disturb the balance. The latter two are human attributes; the "colombes" are those same sails which, in line 1, moved upon the sea and might approach the cemetery. But now, through the adjective "prudentes," they too acquire a human and disturbing trait. They are such living qualities as might spoil the distant contemplation. The interchangeability of all elements and terms in this metaphor is at work.

XII

Ici venu, l'avenir est paresse.
L'insecte net gratte la sécheresse;
Tout est brûlé, défait, reçu dans l'air
A je ne sais quelle sévère essence . . .
La vie est vaste, étant ivre d'absence,
Et l'amertume est douce, et l'esprit clair.   [72]

XIII

Les morts cachés sont bien dans cette terre
Qui les réchauffe et sèche leur mystère.
Midi là-haut, Midi sans mouvement
En soi se pense et convient à soi-même . . .
Tête complète et parfait diadème,
Je suis en toi le secret changement.   [78]

Stanza XII and the first four lines of Stanza XIII summarize and epitomize the state of false balance which has been developed since the first lines of the poem; they are the last expression of this balance. All of the assimilable elements are here assimilated: the spectator's disdain, the "surface" elements of sea and cemetery, and the dead beneath the tombstones. The non-assimilable elements, the turbulent sea waters and the living spectator, are omitted. In line 67, "Ici venu" refers to the spectator, "l'avenir est paresse" to his attitude of contentment with the present. The immobility of time stressed earlier ("Midi le juste," line 3; "Le Temps scintille," line 12) is again emphasized. Lines 68 and 69 relate to the cemetery; such words as "sécheresse, brûlé, défait, reçu dans l'air" contribute to the idea of lifelessness associated not only with the cemetery but with all the other elements metaphorically related to it. Line 70, "A je ne sais quelle sévère essence," belongs specifically to the sea-sky element; but by implication it extends to all parts of the metaphor, as does the "tout" of the preceding line. The "sévère essence," once more, is a repetition of the "pur travail," the "ouvrages purs," the "feu sans matière" of earlier lines. Similarly, the last two lines of the stanza are general in application; but the spectator is more especially envisaged.

That which is absent from life is life itself, since living qualities (such as "amertume") are reduced to their opposites ("douce") and the troubled spirit is clear.

Such a setting is appropriate for the dead—"Les morts cachés sont bien dans cette terre" (line 73); "surface" and "subsurface" are in accord. Their mystery—life—is warmed and dried (note the parallelism to "sécheresse" and "brûlé" in lines 68–69, a parallelism which makes "surface" and "subsurface" elements identical). Finally, the sun, responsible for the sea's calm and the cemetery's stillness, symbolical of the spectator's disdain, is introduced as the culminating and epitomizing element. "Midi là-haut, Midi sans mouvement" revives the idea and construction of "Midi le juste" in the first stanza (giving, incidentally, the meaning to be attached to "juste"). The line "En soi se pense et convient à soi-même" contains the whole philosophy of the preceding stanzas—the self-sufficiency of the immortal sun, of the marble cemetery, of the dead, and of the disdainful spectator. The "soi" and "soi-même" of this line replace the "toi" used in the earlier apostrophe and in subsequent lines, and stand in juxtaposition to the "moi" of line 43 and the strong "Je" of the concluding line in this stanza. They bring to an end the first main division of the poem.

For with the next two lines (77–78), a new development is begun. The balance of the metaphor is broken; "surface" and "subsurface" are separated. Line 77, "Tête complète et parfait diadème," recapitulates the preceding section, refers to the perfect and complete externals involved. Line 78, "Je suis en toi le secret changement," introduces the theme of the new section. It is significant that the change is within ("en toi"), that it is "secret"—hence "subsurface" and hidden; the word "changement" itself is the opposite of all that was immobile, immortal, eternal and dead in the description of the "surface" elements.

Three stanzas now follow in which two contrasting ideas are developed. First, the living human traits which differentiate the spectator from his surroundings are enumerated; these have already been intimated in the first section, they are now made more explicit. Second, the fact that these traits belong only to the living—that the dead possess them no longer—is clarified. This second notion, too, had been earlier suggested (cf. lines 71, 74) and is now completely developed.

XIV

Tu n'as que moi pour contenir tes craintes!
Mes repentirs, mes doutes, mes contraintes
Sont le défaut de ton grand diamant . . .
Mais dans leur nuit toute lourde de marbres,
Un peuple vague aux racines des arbres
A pris déjà ton parti lentement.   [84]

Stanza XIV definitely states the disparity between the spectator and the dead, so definitely breaks the balance of the metaphor. The "que moi" of line 79 once and for all divorces the spectator from the elements with which he had previously identified himself. He is separated from them by the "craintes, repentirs, doutes, contraintes," human characteristics which had previously been subjugated under his disdain. These are the things which constitute the flaw in the picture of perfection previously elaborated. They introduce the mortal, the evanescent, the imperfect into a set of relationships where previously the immortal, the eternal, and the perfect had dominated. The word "diamant" (cf. "diadème" of line 77) epitomizes these "surface" elements, just as the word "défaut" (which is a kind of antonym to "parfait") summarizes all the newly discovered "subsurface" elements. Throughout, the "moi" and "mes" against the "ton" and "tes" serve to sharpen the contrast. Lines 82–84 now proceed to separate further—and definitively—what lies beneath the poet's disdain from what lies beneath the tombstones. The surface elements are restated: "toute lourde de marbres, des arbres." But what lies beneath, "un peuple vague," has become the same as that which covers them (line 84). It should be noted that these "subsurface" elements are described in terms related to the "ombre" of lines 35, 42, 59: "leur nuit, vague." The last line, at the same time that it describes the fate of the dead, parallels the activity of the man when he was *becoming* like the other elements ("je monte et m'accoutume, regarde-moi qui change, je m'abandonne"). With the dead the activity has resulted in complete identification; with the spectator, the process of identification still continued during the first part of the poem. The "déjà" marks the distinction; for the dead it is too late, but for the spectator there is still time.

XV

Ils ont fondu dans une absence épaisse,
L'argile rouge a bu la blanche espèce,
Le don de vivre a passé dans les fleurs!
Où sont des morts les phrases familières,
L'art personnel, les âmes singulières?
La larve file où se formaient des pleurs.   [90]

For an understanding of the role of Stanza XV, reference must again be made to the first part, to Stanza V. The first line, "Ils ont fondu dans une absence épaisse," condenses the idea and the phrasing of lines 25 and 26:

Comme le fruit se fond en jouissance,
Comme en délice il change son absence . . .

But the application is now to the dead, and the tense of the verbs is past; in the earlier stanza, the reference was to the changing spectator and the verbs were present. The definite use of "absence" in the sense of death is the same as that earlier implied in lines 26, 54, 71. Finally, the adjective "épaisse" (like the "lourde" of line 82) is in contradiction to the notion of "fumée" (line 28); the spectator's anticipation of an immortal, incorporeal future is belied by the reality of the material corpses. The second line, "L'argile rouge a bu la blanche espèce," repeats line 27 of the earlier stanza, "Dans une bouche où sa forme se meurt," with the notion of drinking now substituted for that of eating, the red clay for the mouth, and the living flesh for the fruit. The process of dying in "se meurt" is replaced by the completed act of disintegration in "a bu"; again, the verb tenses change with the passage from the first to the second part of the poem. In line 87, "Le don de vivre" is the key phrase for this whole group of stanzas. It will be explained and developed in the next nine lines. It summarizes all those qualities which, so long as they are present in the spectator, differentiate him from the "surface" aspects of the metaphor and whose absence from the dead makes the dead completely assimilable to those "surface" elements.

The second hemistich, "a passé dans les fleurs," describes the process by which that assimilation has been achieved. Four of these living qualities are indicated in the *Ubi sunt* question and in its answer: "les phrases familières, l'art personnel, les âmes singulières, les pleurs." All three adjectives have as their function to individualize, personalize, particularize these qualities, and thus to contrast them with the divine, impersonal aspects of the spectator's disdain. It is the absence of these traits from the dead that makes them more like the "surface" elements of the metaphor than like the "subsurface"; it is their presence in the spectator—which he is about to discover— that makes his original alignment in the metaphor untenable.

XVI

Les cris aigus des filles chatouillées,
Les yeux, les dents, les paupières mouillées,
Le sein charmant qui joue avec le feu,
Le sang qui brille aux lèvres qui se rendent,
Les derniers dons, les doigts qui les défendent,
Tout va sous terre et rentre dans le jeu! [96]

Taking up the "auprès d'un cœur" of the first part (line 44), the next five lines (comprising most of Stanza XVI) offer sensuous love as an additional example of these living qualities. The description is given in terms of parts of the body exclusively, and there is no intimation that the love involved is anything but sensuous. Again, there are reasons in the nature of the total pattern for the choice of such an example. In the early stanzas the spectator's attitude, in keeping with the immaterial elements with which it is identified, is one of detached contemplation in which no corporeal consideration is allowed to enter. The "tête" alone comes into play. But in the transitional passages (cf. Stanza IX), where the "subsurface" elements begin to receive greater prominence, the body appears as one of those elements—"Quel corps me traîne à sa fin paresseuse" (line 52). Now, in a series of stanzas which definitely establish the character of the living man hidden (temporarily) beneath the surface, this description of physical love is given in terms of the body only—"cris aigus, chatouillées, yeux, dents, paupières mouillées, sein, sang, lèvres, dons, doigts." But these things—since an answer is still being supplied to the "Où sont" of the preceding paragraph—are lost when life is lost. That is the meaning of the last line of the stanza, "Tout va sous terre et rentre dans le jeu." The first hemistich of this line is another of the many allusions to "subsurface" elements: "les maisons des morts" (line 35), "cette terre osseuse" (line 53), "Les morts cachés sont bien dans cette terre" (line 73), "dans leur nuit" (line 82). The second hemistich, "et rentre dans le jeu," in a sense destroys the original metaphorical balance; the "jeu" is the whole composite of unliving things, the non-human and eternal movement and substance of the universe. In so far as the dead enter into this mechanism they become like the sun, the surface of the sea and of the cemetery, and the attitude of the spectator, who himself has taken on the qualities of the others. They cease to be true "subsurface" elements.

Since the metaphor breaks down in this one respect, the whole of it must disintegrate. If one "subsurface" element, the dead, is unlike the others, the living sea and the living man, the proportion is destroyed. The next five stanzas, completing this second part of the poem, have as their function to emphasize the disparity. This is done solely in terms of the spectator, concluding with a statement of his dissatisfaction with the initial situation in the poem. Stanza XVII indicates the difference between the soul and the other "surface" elements. Stanza XVIII stresses this difference, rejecting the immortal qualities previously accepted as a solution. In Stanza XIX, the spectator is differentiated from the "subsurface" dead, life providing the distinguishing characteristic. The nature of that living quality, and its domination of the spectator's life, are emphasized in Stanza XX. Stanza XXI, finally, gives a definitive statement (resulting from the four preceding stanzas) of the unacceptability of the original metaphorical arrangement in the poem.

XVII

Et vous, grande âme, espérez-vous un songe
Qui n'aura plus ces couleurs de mensonge
Qu'aux yeux de chair l'onde et l'or font ici?
Chanterez-vous quand serez vaporeuse?
Allez! Tout fuit! Ma présence est poreuse,
La sainte impatience meurt aussi!

[102]

To return to Stanza XVII: The first line serves two purposes. In the address to the "grande âme" there is at once a contrast to the body, treated in the preceding stanzas, and a reintroduction of the "surface" element predominant in the early part of the poem. Compare line 17, "édifice dans l'âme"; line 29, "l'âme consumée"; line 37, "l'âme exposée"; line 45, "sonnant dans l'âme." The aim will now be to show that the soul, like the body, is mortal, human, passing—hence unlike the elements to which the spectator had at first assimilated it. It will be noted that (consistent with the metaphorical character of the whole treatment) the sea is also addressed in the same apostrophe; this becomes apparent in line 100. The "songe" of the first line is also a repetition of the first part (cf. line 12, "et le Songe est savoir"). In both cases, the repetition is for purposes of denial. That denial is contained in the next line, "ces couleurs de mensonge"; the original metaphorical balance of the poem is a lie. If it is a lie, it is because the body will not enter into the proportion, cannot accept the assimilation ("qu'aux yeux de chair"). "L'onde et l'or," the "colors" of the lie, are a summation of the whole pictorial situation in the early stanzas; they are roughly equivalent to sea and sun. Line 100, "Chanterez-vous quand serez vaporeuse," is addressed at once to the sea and to the soul, directly and by implication. The "chanterez-vous" refers to the sound of the sea "toujours recommencée," to the "changement des rives en rumeur" (line 30) as well as to the singing of the sky to the exalted soul ("le ciel chante à l'âme consumée," line 29). The "quand serez vaporeuse" applies equally to the evaporation of the sea ("consume / Maint diamant d'imperceptible écume," lines 7–8) and to the death of the soul. The word "Allez!" provides the negative answer to the preceding question; it is the single word of denial. "Tout fuit!" negates the whole notion of stability and immobility and immortality implicit in the initial metaphor. The remaining words of the stanza make direct application of the denial to the spectator himself. Again, both body and soul are involved; "Ma présence est poreuse" indicates the passing of the body, "La sainte impatience meurt aussi" the death of the soul. It is significant that the latter should be described in the words "la sainte impatience," in marked contradistinction to the "dédain souverain" of the original alignment. The impatient soul can never accept the immobility of high noon.

XVIII

Maigre immortalité noire et dorée,
Consolatrice affreusement laurée,
Qui de la mort fais un sein maternel,
Le beau mensonge et la pieuse ruse!
Qui ne connaît, et qui ne les refuse,
Ce crâne vide et ce rire éternel!   [108]

Nor can the soul accept any notion of immortality as a consolation. Stanza XVIII contains another denial. The original metaphor is assimilated—and subordinated—to a group of classical and medieval (and religious) symbols of immortality, the "maigre immortalité noire," the "consolatrice . . . laurée," the "crâne vide," the "rire éternel." Of the original "surface" elements, only the word "dorée" remains, along with the secondary suggestions contained in "éternel." The denial of this immortality is expressed indirectly in "affreusement" and all of lines 105 and 106, and directly in line 107, "Qui ne connaît et qui ne les refuse." Both a life of immobile, sovereign disdain and a death considered as accompanied by immortality of the soul are rejected.

XIX

Pères profonds, têtes inhabitées,
Qui sous le poids de tant de pelletées,
Etes la terre et confondez nos pas,
Le vrai rongeur, le ver irréfutable
N'est point pour vous qui dormez sous la table,
Il vit de vie, il ne me quitte pas!   [114]

In this stanza (XIX) the old metaphor is reintroduced, but only to be gainsaid. Again, as in several stanzas of this section of the poem, sea and sky are omitted, only the cemetery and the spectator remain; this is so that dissimilarity may be emphasized. The "surface" of the cemetery reappears: "sous le poids de tant de pelletées," "sous la table." The "subsurface" dead, "Pères profonds, têtes inhabitées" (cf. the "crâne vide" of the preceding line), are apostrophized. But the deadness of the dead ("Qui . . . Etes la terre," "vous qui dormez") is contrasted strongly with the living character of the spectator ("Il vit de vie, il ne me quitte pas"). In the development of the meta-phor, the worm which inhabited the dead body ("La larve file où se formaient des pleurs") now becomes the living principle which inhabits the living spectator: "Le vrai rongeur, le ver irréfutable." The phrase "N'est point pour vous" once more punctuates the irre-concilable difference between the dead dead and the living living, hence the fallacy of the original metaphor in which "subsurface" dead and "subsurface" spectator were presumed to be similar.

XX

Amour, peut-être, ou de moi-même haine?
Sa dent secrète est de moi si prochaine
Que tous les noms lui peuvent convenir!
Qu'importe! Il voit, il veut, il songe, il touche!
Ma chair lui plaît, et jusque sur ma couche,
A ce vivant je vis d'appartenir!   [120]

The attributes of the worm—of life—so frequently intimated in earlier passages of the poem (cf. line 32, "orgueil," line 33, "oi-siveté," line 66, "Les songes vains, les anges curieux," lines 79 ff., "craintes, doutes," etc.) are again investigated in Stanza XX. As be-fore, the answer is tentative and incomplete. Self-love and self-hate are both suggested (line 115). But no definitive solution results—"Sa dent secrète"; cf. "leur mystère" of line 74. The one thing certain is that he (or it) is fully identified with the spectator (lines 116–117). He posses-ses the activity of the body ("Il voit, il touche") and that of the mind ("il veut, il songe"), just as the spectator in earlier lines was moved by both impulses ("Quel corps me traîne, quel front l'attire," lines 52–53, *e.g.*). The hemistich, "Ma chair lui plaît," throws into relief that part of life which receives the emphasis—since it forces the conclusion—in these latter stanzas of the poem. It is equivalent to the "blanche espèce" of line 86, repeats the "yeux de chair" of line 99. The last line and a half of the stanza state, decisively, the identifica-tion of the spectator with his "rongeur"; they imply, indirectly, the impropriety and the inadequacy of a situation in which the man, forsaking the body for the intellect, would also forsake life for a divine disdain. The final statement of that inadequacy and that impropriety comes in the next stanza.

XXI

Zénon! Cruel Zénon! Zénon d'Élée!
M'as-tu percé de cette flèche ailée
Qui vibre, vole, et qui ne vole pas!
Le son m'enfante et la flèche me tue!
Ah! le soleil . . . Quelle ombre de tortue
Pour l'âme, Achille immobile à grands pas!   [126]

Zeno of Elea's appearance, in the next stanza, with two of his famous paradoxes, seems like the interjection of a new and unprepared element. Yet the makings of this metaphor are so closely assimilated to the components of the major metaphorical structure of the work as to contribute to, rather than detract from, the effectiveness of a culminating moment in the development of that structure. For Stanza XXI concludes (except for the "Non, non!" of line 127) the rejection of the original sea-cemetery-spectator relationship, and the consequent rejection of the philosophy of immobility which it symbolized. If Zeno's paradoxes are introduced at this point rather than earlier, it is because they represent practical impossibilities, although they may have an intellectual probability. The attitude of divine disdain is here abandoned as a practical impossibility for a living man. The first line identifies Zeno, makes him responsible—and at the same time blames him ("Cruel Zénon!")—for the paradox in which the spectator finds himself. Lines 122–124 exploit the paradox of the arrow which, since it is at rest at every moment of its flight, must be at rest during all of its flight, and hence cannot move at all. The relationship to the symbols of immobility at the beginning of the poem is apparent. But the arrow ("cette flèche ailée") itself comes to represent the same living qualities, the same life, already so frequently characterized. Like the worm, it possesses the spectator himself ("M'as-tu percé"); in the same way, it is alive and gives life ("Qui vibre, vole . . . ," "Le son m'enfante"). But in so far as it is held motionless ("qui ne vole pas") as in the paradox, it takes life away ("la flèche me tue!") as in the static disdain of the spectator at the outset. The last two lines, alluding to the paradox of Achilles and the tortoise, do so in terms derived almost exclusively from the first part of the poem. The phrase "Ah! le soleil . . ." has two functions. It recalls the initial situation (cf. lines 3, 10, 37, 56, 75) of the sun arrested at high noon. At the same time it forms the basis (as it had before on several occasions) for the substance-and-shadow image about to be evoked. The substance is the motionless Achilles—the spectator himself, again—who stands exposed to the sun's rays (cf. lines 37 ff.). But the shadow is a tortoise's shadow, unrecognizable as belonging to the substance casting it. The shadow image, again, is a recurrent one in the poem (cf. lines 42, 59). It is this disparity between substance and shadow which makes the situation producing it untenable to the soul ("Pour l'âme"). For the soul does move—"à grands pas!"—and a tortoise's slow shadow is entirely irreconcilable with it.

The final section of the poem, consisting of the three remaining stanzas, provides a positive solution in place of the unsatisfactory one just definitively rejected. That solution, again, is found in the original metaphor and is expressed in terms still derived from that metaphor, constitutes a continuation of it. For in the original relationship (to repeat) the one element which did not "belong" with the others was the "subsurface" cemetery element—the fact that the dead beneath the tombstones were unlike the living sea beneath the calm surface, unlike the living man beneath the disdainful attitude. The section of the poem just preceding has stressed that unlikeness, disowned any parallelism that might exist between the spectator and the dead as a result of the metaphorical analogies. The last section will salvage four elements from among the original six, "surface" and "subsurface" sea, "surface" and "subsurface" spectator. The dead cemetery will be excluded. What remains is entirely comparable. Moreover, since during the denial it was the existence of the body, of the living principle, which brought about the disturbance of the original balance, that living principle must now be dominant in the final solution. Hence the metaphor will be finally resolved with all four persisting elements in a state of motion, of life.

XXII
Non, non! . . . Debout! Dans l'ère successive!
Brisez, mon corps, cette forme pensive!
Buvez, mon sein, la naissance du vent!

Une fraîcheur, de la mer exhalée,
Me rend mon âme . . . O puissance salée!
Courons à l'onde en rejaillir vivant!   [132]

By way of transition, the first two words of Stanza XXII are a summary of all the foregoing negation: "Non, non!" But the next word, "Debout!" is the single word of affirmation, contrasted to the denial contained in the deprecatory use of "Allez!" in line 101. It is the first call from contemplation to action. Now, one by one, the various components of the original static situation will be replaced by their contradictories. Thus "Dans l'ère successive!" stands on the one hand as a departure from the immobility of the opening situation (cf. line 12, "Le temps scintille") and on the other hand as a substitute for the invalid future of later passages (cf. line 67, "Ici venu, l'avenir est paresse"). In the next line, "cette forme pensive" is an epitome of the original attitude of the spectator; this attitude is now to be destroyed ("Brisez . . .") and, as one might have guessed, it is the body ("mon corps," the receptacle of the living principle) which is the agent of destruction. The imperative "Buvez" makes another call to physical action, and is again addressed to a part of the body. But the remainder of the line, "la naissance du vent!" shifts to the second element of the reconstituted metaphor, the sea. And because of the metaphorical relationship now prevailing, the birth of the wind (to be juxtaposed both to the previous motionless condition of the sea and to the long prevalence of death in the poem) also means the rebirth of the spectator. These two elements, sea and spectator, will now appear alternately in the second half of the stanza. "Une fraîcheur" is synonymous with the "vent" of the preceding line; but it provides the additional notion of coolness, and hence another contrast with the dazzling brightness of the beginning. Similarly, "exhalée" joins to the idea of "naissance" the further factor of movement. The hemistich "Me rend mon âme" contains the last of a long series of references to the soul. In the others, however, the emphasis was on separation ("Edifice dans l'âme, / Mais . . . ," lines 17-18, and "L'âme exposée . . . ," line 37), on disappointment ("Sonnant dans l'âme un creux toujours futur!" line 48), on differentiation from the body (lines 97-99), on the unsatisfactoriness of the whole original assumption ("Quelle ombre de tortue / Pour l'âme," lines 125–126). Now, in the new life where body and soul are brought into harmony, all the former states are corrected; that is the significance of "me rend." The next address to the sea, "O puissance salée!" continues the process of contrast; what was a "Masse de calme, et visible réserve" (line 14) is now a "puissance," and the word "salée" brings in the peculiar characteristic which symbolizes the "life" of the sea. Line 132 again identifies spectator and sea, making a physical contact of the two through two verbs of motion ("Courons, rejaillir"), and communicating to the spectator in the word "vivant" the quality of life already attributed to the sea in the three preceding lines. In terms of the general development of the metaphor, then, this stanza serves to establish the new relationship between sea and spectator, one in which "surface" and "subsurface" elements are both alive and in motion and in which therefore a complete parallelism obtains.

XXIII

Oui! Grande mer de délires douée,
Peau de panthère et chlamyde trouée
De mille et mille idoles du soleil,
Hydre absolue, ivre de ta chair bleue,
Qui te remords l'étincelante queue
Dans un tumulte au silence pareil . . .　　　　　　[138]

Stanza XXIII is devoted to a recharacterization of the sea in terms of movement and life, and with no difference between "surface" and "subsurface." The two elements persist, but are now similar. Indeed, there is a kind of reversal by which each of the aspects of the old, immobile sea is redescribed in contrasting terms. "Oui!" at the beginning is thus juxtaposed to the "Non, non!" opening the preceding stanza. The phrase "de délires douée" stands in opposition to such expressions as "le calme des dieux!" (line 6), "Stable trésor" (line 13), "Masse de calme" (line 14), "La mer fidèle y dort" (line 60). These "délires" are the stuff of life of the sea and are comparable to the various traits ascribed to the living man throughout the poem; it should be noted that they constitute an immoderate and uncontrollable quality. There follow now three comparisons of the sea to other objects. In the first two, "Peau de panthère et chlamyde trouée / De mille et mille idoles du soleil," the comparisons are used to describe the appearance of the sea's surface. In both cases, the image is one of a spotted surface; in the second, the spots are the "idoles" or reflections of the sun. But furthermore the surface—unlike the static "toit"—is one which in each case reveals, rather than obscures, a lithe, muscular, moving and living body. This is the case of the panther's skin. This is also the case of the chlamys, clothing the Greek athlete or rider or ephebus. Both images refer back to the scintillating surface of the first stanzas; in "mille et mille idoles" there is a direct reprise of the "mille tuiles" of line 18, with the same meaning. Moreover, there is at least a suggestion of the whole religious terminology, from the "temple" of lines 13 and 19 to the "idolâtre" of line 61, and beyond. The third comparison adds to the description the movement of the sea, the incessant succession of waves. These waves are at once the heads and the tails of the beast; hence the "Hydre . . . Qui te remords l'étincelante queue." "Absolue," used in the sense of complete or self-sufficient, is explained in the rest of this line and the following one. In "ivre de ta chair bleue," "ivre" amplifies the idea contained in "délires" above, while "chair" supplies another reference to the "body" of the sea consonant with the new role of the spectator's body—"Brisez, mon corps, cette forme pensive!" That sense of repetition found, very early, in line 4, "La mer, la mer toujours recommencée," is enhanced by the next line, 137, which also contains in "étincelante" a repetition of the earlier "scintille" (line 12) and "scintillation" (line 23) and the notions related to them. The "tumulte" of the last line augments the indication "changement des rives en rumeur" (line 30). But whereas in the first part of the poem the dominating effect was one of silence ("quelle paix semble se concevoir," line 9; "O mon silence!" line 17), in this last part the effect of noise has become so constant as to be like silence itself. Thus the twenty-third stanza, recharacterizing one element of the new metaphor, the sea, does so through a tissue of echoes and repetitions of the original characterization; but all of these are now so turned as to create an opposite effect, one of movement, of noise, of force and life. Such treatment would have been impossible in the original arrangement of the metaphor; now it is almost made necessary by the intervening development.

XXIV

Le vent se lève! . . . Il faut tenter de vivre!
L'air immense ouvre et referme mon livre,
La vague en poudre ose jaillir des rocs!
Envolez-vous, pages tout éblouies!
Rompez, vagues! Rompez d'eaux réjouies
Ce toit tranquille où picoraient des focs!   [144]

By way of conclusion the poem recombines, in the last stanza, the two remaining elements of the metaphor. The stress will still be on the vision of the sea, just as it was in the opening stanzas. Yet the ratio of *sea : spectator* will be clearly stated at times and implicit throughout. The first hemistich, "Le vent se lève!" completes the long apostrophe left incomplete in the preceding stanza. It reiterates the phrases "la naissance du vent" (line 129) and "Une fraîcheur, de la mer exhalée" (line 130); in so doing, it provides the cause for the activity just described. The rest of the line, "Il faut tenter de vivre!" makes the application—now patent—of the same moving spirit to the spectator. "Vivre" is the key word; it represents the activity of the reunited body and spirit, of their common movement into the future. In the next line, "L'air immense ouvre et referme mon livre," another secondary metaphor is compounded of old elements. "L'air immense" goes back to the recent references to the wind; "ouvre et referme" gives a description of the waves similar to that in lines 136–137. However, the waves are now likened to the pages of a book, one in which the spectator reads ("un long regard sur le calme des dieux," line 6) only to discover new truth. Line 141 again has its echoes and its new meanings. The phrase "ose jaillir" expresses the same determination to movement as does the key phrase "Il faut tenter de vivre"; but it also realizes a possibility established long before in the "fausse captive" of line 49. Finally, a series of imperatives—parallel to those addressed by the spectator to himself (lines 127–132)—is now directed at the sea: "Envolez-vous," "Rompez, vagues," "Rompez d'eaux . . ." The "pages" are once more the waves; if they are "tout éblouies" it is at once because of their own sparkling in the sunlight and because of the wonderment which the spectator has derived from gazing upon them. If they are "réjouies," it is at once because of their own movement and because of the joy which the spectator has found in discovering their lesson. In the last line, "Ce toit tranquille où picoraient des focs," the very first line of the poem is repeated practically without change, with "picoraient" being synonymous with "marchent" and "focs" with "colombes." But one fundamental change has been introduced—the tense of the verb. For the wind has brought the waves, the waves have destroyed the smooth roof of the sea, the sails have been scattered. The static condition of the beginning of the poem has been replaced by a new dynamic relationship; "surface" and "subsurface" sea, "surface" and "subsurface" spectator have been completely identified in living movement. The new metaphorical relationship has been established, with no conflicting or disparate elements, and hence the development of the poem and its structure are complete.

The broad general lines of that structure and its merits are now apparent. Consistently and without ever deviating from his plan, Valéry has translated the "idea" of his poem and all mutations of that idea into a single metaphor and the development of that metaphor. Even in its original statement, the metaphor includes certain features which make it imperfect; those features come into increasing prominence with the progress of the poem, making for a growing disturbance of the original apparent harmony; they must finally be excluded in the end to make way for a new metaphor which is really valid. This development is not a plot, but it is analogous to a plot: the initial metaphor is like an expository situation with characters and circumstances in conflict; the development of that metaphor is like the tying or knotting of an action in which the conflict finally reaches a critical point; the realignment at the end is like a denouement which brings a final solution or resolution of the conflict. But this is all only an analogy. The structure has its own internal principle, which is neither narrative nor dramatic, and which is contained in the special character of the components and the internal relationships of the metaphor. It has its own kind of necessity, which is again not narrative or dramatic, but which depends upon the exploitation and unfolding—to the utmost—of all those meanings and implications contained in the original statement. The internal principle and the internal necessity are lyric in character.

Nor is the basis of development a logical one. True, one may resolve the poem into an argument, into a set of premises and conclusions, into a syllogistic form. But then it ceases to be the poem. It is the poem only so long as it remains the metaphor. What happens from stanza to stanza or from sentence to sentence is not a matter of logical necessity—of the needs of an argument—but rather of poetic necessity—of the needs of a lyrical statement. The poem is not a "good" poem to the extent that it makes a valid or successful argument for a given point of view, but to the extent to which it satisfies or exploits the conditions of that lyrical statement.

With respect to the argument, it is also apparent that from the incidental symbols and images of the poem there emerges a set of philosophical statements which make for a total philosophical meaning (but how commonplace when thus abstracted!). In the beginning, the spectator believes that by divorcing himself from the processes and preoccupations of life, by becoming divinely disdainful, he may achieve the happiness which has so far escaped him. But he discovers, in the middle portion, that so to divorce himself is to be like the dead, whereas so long as he has a body, so long as he remains alive and corporeal, such a divorce is as much impossible as it is undesirable. Hence he concludes, in the end, that only by exploiting life to the fullest can he attain the joy which hitherto has been absent from his life. In this sense, *Le Cimetière marin* becomes a kind of commentary on the quotation from Pindar which serves as its epigraph: "Μή, φίλα ψυχά, βίον ἀθάνατον σπεῦδε, ταν δ' ἔμπρακτον ἄντλει μαχανάν," "Do not, dear soul, strive for an immortal life, but rather exploit the possible." The philosophical meaning of the poem is indistinguishable from the metaphor, so that a single structural analysis of the poem discovers both aspects.

That structure is very tightly compounded. The unifying element is the metaphor, to which all parts of the poem are intimately related. A more searching reading of the poem than that given above would probably reveal a structural justification for every significant word. Even in so cursory an analysis as that presented, it is clear to what a degree all hinges upon the central metaphor. Such secondary metaphors as that of the eaten fruit, of the shepherd, of Zeno's paradoxes, are allied to the main metaphor either as they make a similar relationship or juxtaposition of elements or as they use the same words. They are not in any sense random images, but ones which grow out of the basic conditions of the poem. The principal metaphor at the same time provides the ordering principle of the poem. The meanings to be attached to words, the kinds of secondary metaphors used, the images, the very tenses of verbs depend for their character upon the place in the metaphor at which they appear. Adjectives and epithets useful at the beginning would be less appropriate in the middle, entirely inadequate at the end. The metaphor of the "chienne splendide" would be just as out of place at the end of the work as that of the "pages éblouies" at the beginning. Perhaps the most striking—and the most obvious—of such cases is the contrast between the first and the last lines. This merely means that there is a definite progression in the poem, that the progression works in every detail, and is inseparable from the development of the metaphor itself.

All of these—the fact that there is a unifying element, that there is an ordering element (and that they are the same), that metaphor and symbols and meaning are inseparable—are presumed to be virtues in a poem. It is good that there should be a reason and a justification for the presence of every word. It is good that there should be a recognizable cause for the particular place of every word or image or metaphor. It is presumed to be a virtue of the composition, moreover, that a wide variety of images and secondary metaphors is brought to reinforce the basic metaphor, contributing to it an additional richness; the possibilities inherent in the original lyric statement are fully exploited. It is an excellence, in a word, that the poem should present itself to the reader as a consistent, consecutive, and unified whole.

12

Valéry

Les Grenades

Les Grenades is the last of the sonnets that I shall be treating in the present group of studies. I have chosen to include it, along with the others, as an illustration of the persistence of a traditional prosodic form that houses a variety of innovatory techniques. Baudelaire's *Recueillement* was taken as an example of a fully achieved symbolist poem, joining to the poet's habitual methods the essential features that were to distinguish the new school. In Mallarmé's *Le vierge, le vivace et le bel aujourd'hui,* those features were exploited almost to a maximum, through the reduction in the number of the "signs" used to suggest the identity of the object symbolized. The same poet's *Le Tombeau d'Edgar Poe,* a non-symbolist sonnet, used the form in more conventional ways, developing a basic opposition of concepts complicated by several auxiliary metaphors and expressed in hermetic language. Valéry's *Les Grenades* is more conventional still, operating as it does on the basis of a simple comparison—simple, but highly complex in its implications and in its potential for a refined emotional effect.

Les Grenades

Dures grenades entr'ouvertes
Cédant à l'excès de vos grains,
Je crois voir des fronts souverains
Éclatés de leurs découvertes!

4

353

Si les soleils par vous subis,
O grenades entre-bâillées,
Vous ont fait d'orgueil travaillées
Craquer les cloisons de rubis,   8

Et que si l'or sec de l'écorce
A la demande d'une force
Crève en gemmes rouges de jus,   11

Cette lumineuse rupture
Fait rêver une âme que j'eus
De sa secrète architecture.   14

One of the objects entering into the simple comparison is the pomegranates (always plural and general), the other is the soul, expressed first in the plural and general form of the "fronts souverains," finally as singular and particular in the phrase "une âme que j'eus." In a strange way, the comparison is never stated explicitly as such; there is no "comme." Instead, formulas indicating that the speaker himself is bringing the two objects together, namely "Je crois voir" (3) and "Fait rêver" (13), are substituted for the customary adverb. As a consequence, the comparison is neither a straightforward simile nor a metaphor; but this unusual kind of juxtaposition makes it possible to work, throughout the poem, on the supposition of a similarity without excluding the possibility— so essential for concluding the poem—of a dissimilarity.

The very mention of the two objects compared, "grenades" and "fronts" (or "âme"), raises the question about the basis on which they have been brought together. How are they alike? It is a question that arises in any discussion of simile or metaphor, just as the question of the middle term needs to be asked in any discussion of a syllogism. Indeed, the analogy of the middle term is useful for an understanding of how a poetic structure of this kind is achieved: just as the middle term is present in the major and minor propositions and serves to "mediate" between them, to connect them, so there is in any comparative or metaphorical structure a poetic "middle." It consists of those elements that are common to both of the objects compared. It may be a material resemblance, a shape or a form; or a state of feeling that attaches equally well to the two objects; or an idea that grows out of both of them. In the case of *Les Grenades,* what relates "grenades" to "fronts" is the dual concept of a container and what it contains; they are different kinds of objects but the functions are comparable. For the pomegranates, the container is the hard rind, what is contained is the seeds; for the "foreheads," or the "soul," the container is the head itself, with its hard and resistant bony structure, whereas what is contained is the intellectual activity within the head. In the light of this last identification, it would perhaps be more useful, for the pomegranates, to define the "contained" also as an activity, as the growth and expansion of the seeds and pulp within. The two objects would thus become more closely parallel: a hard container outside, inside an activity that tends to burst (literally or figuratively) that container. That tendency really establishes the important similarity between the objects; and where there is difference, as at the end of the poem, it will lie in the domain of the activity, of the contained, rather than in that of the container.

Since the important "middle" between the two objects compared is an activity, we should expect to find a temporal element within the poem, marking the beginning, the duration, and the end of the activity. We should also look for the bases both of similarity and dissimilarity in the same activity; for while the activity may be the same in the two objects, the occasional lack of it in one member of one of the classes involved, or variations in the mode of its accomplishment, may constitute the vital dissimilarity that accounts for the "surprise" turn of the denouement.

As he builds his poem—and he does so with amazing brevity and concision—Valéry selects carefully the traits that will represent the essential nature of each object and that will prepare, all at once, for the development of resemblance and difference and for the development in time. He begins with the "object to which compared," the pomegranates, and he specifies (in "Dures grenades") the characteristic that will make them withstand, up to a certain point, the force of the internal activity. The very hardness of the rind calls attention to the remarkable vigor of that activity, so that the addition of "entr'ouvertes" to the first two words gives a dramatic quality to the short first line: "Dures grenades entr'ouvertes." A time sequence is implicit in the juxtaposition of "Dures" and "entr'ouvertes": from a time when the hard rind resisted the pressures of the internal force to a time when the force prevailed and the rind cracked open. The same sequence is more clearly indicated in the second line, "Cédant à l'excès de vos grains"—the moment of triumph for internal force in "Cédant," the whole process of activity within the pomegranate, of passage from the "containable" to the "no-longer-containable" quantity of seeds in "à l'excès de vos grains." It is the gradual growth from the first to the final stage that makes up the internal activity of which I have been speaking; and the use of the generic term "excès" prepares the transition to a non-material or spiritual growth within the "object compared."

After the first two lines, addressed by the speaker to the pomegranates, the quatrain is completed with the introduction of the other object entering into the comparison:

> Je crois voir des fronts souverains
> Éclatés de leurs découvertes!

One should complete the phrase "Je crois voir" by the addition of some such formula as "en vous"; the speaker, speaking to the pomegranates, tells them of an association that they bring to his mind. (The "en vous" would serve to express in a way the absent "comme," to link the two objects.) The extent to which the speaker makes a wilful connection between "grenades" and "fronts" is shown by the use of "Je crois voir" rather than "Je vois," and at the same time some doubt with respect to the absolute comparability of the two objects is suggested. In "des fronts," there is a minimum of visual suggestiveness, as there must be; for on the one hand too close a parallelism would be distasteful or ridiculous, on the other hand the speaker wishes to allude to a non-material or "moral" activity in an object that is, as he conceives it, non-material. The adjective "souverains" establishes a category of "heads" or "minds" as it separates those of which he speaks from ordinary, unproductive, undistinguished minds; he is interested only in those which are "Éclatés de leurs découvertes."

In this last line, the physical resemblance is stated by "Éclatés," which is parallel to "entr'ouvertes" and which comes to contain all the implicit allusions to a resistant external form, to a progressive internal development, and to a final yielding. But there is also, in "Éclatés," a spiritual connotation, the one required by "découvertes." Since discoveries are immaterial, the activity that produces them is a spiritual one, and they "burst forth" as intellectual triumphs. There is neither physical rupture nor visual presence—except through the analogy to the pomegranates. We should note, in the first quatrain, the presence of three "persons": the "vos" and the implicit "vous" of the apostrophe to the pomegranates; the "leurs" used ro refer to the foreheads; and the "je" of the speaker. The fact that the last is dissociated from either of the others, and especially from the "fronts souverains," will provide the basis for the ultimate turn in the meaning of the sonnet.

The first quatrain, comprising one of the two complete sentences in the poem, sets up the basic comparison. As it does so, it adds to the similarities which make the comparison possible and intelligible two fundamental differences: an intellectual activity is opposed to a physical activity, and "some" minds are opposed to "all" pomegranates. The latter is accomplished through the epithet "souverains" attached to "fronts," to which is added the disjunction of "je" from "leurs." Perhaps that separation is emphasized and clarified by the exclamation point at the end of the quatrain. The speaker does not merely see a likeness. He admires and wonders at the discoveries and at the minds that produce them, he may even intimate a sense of envy.

Three separate segments, divided syntactically as they are prosodically, make up the other sentence of *Les Grenades*. It is a conditional sentence in which the first "if" clause (introduced by "Si . . .") constitutes the remaining quatrain, the second "if" clause (presented through the coordinate "Et que si . . .") makes up the first tercet, and the result clause is found in the second tercet. But if the division among these three parts is approximately equal, the amount of space devoted to the pomegranates is much greater than that devoted to the other element of the comparison. I have not said "to the 'fronts souverains' " simply because they do not recur; they are replaced, in the final two lines, by the speaker's own soul ("une âme que j'eus"). The speaker continues to address the pomegranates (twice using the "vous" that was earlier implied) and therefore he speaks, throughout the next eight lines, in terms of physical characteristics, of the material activity and of its visible product. Yet there are moral overtones everywhere in these lines—more so, indeed, than in the last two verses referring to his soul.

Line 5, "Si les soleils par vous subis," resumes the temporal reference already suggested relative to the growth and maturation of the seeds. By pluralizing "les soleils," the poet both extends the time of the activity—one sees many successive days—and creates the impression of light that will be so important for the coming notions of color. Already, merely in the mention of "grenades" and "vos grains," some elementary tones of color have been introduced; they will be specified shortly. The phrase "par vous subis" again makes the pomegranates passive, just as they were in "Cédant à l'excès"; but whereas there the active principle had been internal, here it is external and distant. Not entirely, though, for the effect of the sunshine is to augment the growth of the seeds, hence to intensify the internal activity. When the speaker says "O grenades entre-bâillées," he all but repeats the opening line. "Entre-bâillées" is practically synonymous with "entr'ouvertes" (I doubt that any shade of difference is intended here). Yet the initial "O" adds to the admirative note contained in the exclamation point, and the "grenades" at this point are richer in significance than before. They possess now the qualities designated since the original apostrophe and they bear an overlay of the comparison to the "fronts souverains." All poetry, of course, works in this way; simple repetition is practically non-existent.

Following upon the "Si" of line 5, the next two lines complete the clause by providing a verb and its objects:

> Vous ont fait d'orgueil travaillées
> Craquer les cloisons de rubis.   [8]

The clause thus reads "Si les soleils . . . Vous ont fait . . . Craquer les cloisons . . ." Once again, the pomegranates are both passive and active—passive as they undergo the influence of the sun, active as one part of them exerts its force upon another ("ont fait . . . Craquer"). "Craquer" is a more vigorous verb than "Cédant," adding as well an auditive component that emphasizes the violence of the action, hence the extent of the force. All three verbs in the series

"Cédant," "Éclatés," and "Craquer" are at the beginning of lines. This is a prosodic device that serves both to accentuate the activity that all three represent and to establish firmly the relationship between the two elements entering into the comparison. Then the two modifiers that interrupt the "if" clause: "d'orgueil travaillées" modifies "grenades" by providing a cause for the activity ("d[e]" means "par," "by"). "Orgueil" makes of it a moral cause (once more facilitating the passage to "fronts souverains" and "âme"); but it is a moral cause for a physical activity. From without, the pomegranates are influenced by the sun; from within, they are "travaillées d'orgueil," impelled or stimulated or troubled by a moral quality that leads first to the internal growth or maturation, then to the bursting of the outer rind. The "cloisons" are that outer rind, pluralized as were the "soleils"; they may also include the internal membranes of the pomegranate, although these would be less apt to crack open. In "de rubis," the "de" again has the meaning of "by," pointing to the agency of the ruby-red complex of seeds and pulp that brings about the final bursting. With this phrase, the internal color of the pomegranate becomes precise.

The first tercet contains the second "if" clause:

> Et que si l'or sec de l'écorce
> A la demande d'une force
> Crève en gemmes rouges de jus . . .   [11]

In the initial phrase, the "que" has the effect of augmenting the conditional: "If this is true, and especially if that is true . . ." "Ecorce" is the technical term for the pomegranate's rind, just referred to metaphorically as "les cloisons." It, too, now has a specific color ("l'or sec"), complementary to the red of the interior. It also has a quality of dryness that will make possible the visible and audible cracking: the physical features of the "container" are now completely stated, its hardness, its dryness, its color. The physical-moral activity of the "contained" will be summarized in the next line, "A la demande d'une force," which again makes the interior into an active principle operating against the passivity of the external walls. This is the "force" (the term is sufficiently general to be both moral and physical), and it is exerted wilfully ("à la demande").

Line 11 completes the clause, "si . . . l'écorce . . . crève," placing once again the verb for the bursting, "Crève," in the initial position in the line—the fourth of the series so to be placed. There may be an augmentative order in the three verbs referring to the pomegranates, from "Cédant" (which is relatively mild), to "Craquer," to "Crève" (where the action is most vigorous of all). Besides, the form "Crève en . . ." suggests not only a bursting but a sudden bursting out or bursting forth of what had been inside; in this way, a kind of physical "discovery" takes place. The "grains" of line 2 are resumed as the "gemmes," surrounded by the juicy pulp and having the same color as before ("de rubis, rouges de jus"). That color, as well as something of the shape, is made more striking through the use of the cognate "rubis" and "gemmes."

Color and light, the cracking and the bursting out, are all epitomized in "Cette lumineuse rupture," which serves as subject for the result clause of the conditional sentence. As such, it provides the passage from the "grenades" (the object-to-which-compared) to the "âme" (the object compared). "Cette" shows the extent to which it is a summation of all that precedes; "lumineuse" reduces to a single adjective the notions of light and color previously expressed (while repeating the note of wonderment contained in "Éclatés"); and "rupture" supplies a single noun to replace the four verbs describing the bursting. As a noun, it is more readily relatable to "découvertes." Thus the speaker says to the pomegranates that, as he contemplates what happens to them, he thinks—not about what has happened to himself, but of what might have happened to himself. The negative quality of the comparison is effected by two disjunctions: the separation of the "je" from both the "vous" of the pomegranates and the "fronts souverains," and the difference in time between the present universally used for the pomegranates (and the "fronts souverains") and the past absolute that appears in "une âme que j'eus." To state this difference in time more clearly, the bursting of the pomegranates and the discoveries of the "sovereign minds"—both in the present—are both the result of a long process of development that has led into the present from a starting point in the past. But the speaker's soul remains in the past; there is no parallel growth into the present, and "j'eus" is past definite and definitive past.

361 Valéry, *Les Grenades*

Something of the speaker's disjunction from the other objects and persons brought into comparison is also contained in the formula "Fait rêver une âme." As in "Je crois voir," the statement of the comparison is vague and indistinct, merely because the speaker is seeing at once similarities and differences. He is also passive as were the pomegranates in such phrases as "Cédant à . . . ," "d'orgueil travaillées," "A la demande d'une force." But whereas the pomegranates were acted upon by a powerful force that resulted in their yielding in a violent way, his own activity (induced in him from without by the vision of the pomegranates) is mild and tentative. It involves a spiritual return to the past ("Fait rêver") by a part of himself that also belongs to the past ("une âme que j'eus"). By saying "une âme que . . ." rather than "mon âme," he separates himself (in the present) from this vital part of himself (that remains in the past). The comparison is now reduced to the contained element, to that which, within himself, was like what had been within the pomegranates. The "container," for himself the "front" or merely the corporeal housing of his soul, is present implicitly but it is not stated explicitly; this is as it must be, since there has been and will be for him no rupturing or bursting of the external container. A juxtaposition of "âme" to "fronts souverains" shows the striking absence of any epithet for "âme" comparable to "souverains" and again sets the speaker aside from those others whose spiritual lives he has seemed to penetrate through his vision of the pomegranates.

The disjunction might be graphically represented as follows:

grenades : rupture
fronts souverains : découvertes

but

une âme que j'eus :　　?

To this point (through line 13) there is no explanation of the nature of the difference; hence the question mark, hence the lack of a resolution to the opposing "probabilities" of the poem. Answer and resolution come in the final verse, which condenses into a few words the difficult function of concluding the sonnet. We should note that the initial "De" makes a construction "Fait rêver . . . De," essentially different in its meaning from the more usual "fait rêver à"; the latter would mean, here, something unemphatic like "directs its reverie toward," while the expression that we do have means "causes it to meditate upon." What his soul meditates upon is its own "secrète architecture." The central word is the last word of the poem, "architecture," for it contains the whole notion of a structure, of an organization of parts within by an external form. It is equally applicable to the pomegranates and to the sovereign minds—for their outer form, to the "écorce" and the "fronts," for their inner form, to the "grains" and the "orgueil" (the inner form of a mind is of course a moral form). The speaker's soul is distinguished from both "grenades" and "fronts" by the fact that, whereas their inward activity has brought about an outward explosion, the "entr'ouvertes" and the "découvertes," whatever activity may have occurred in his soul has remained without outward manifestation. Its architecture is still and now "secrète."

That one adjective replaces the question mark in the tabular opposition that I indicated above, and it states the essence of the disjunction. All the elements of obscurity and uncertainty that had carried through the "if" clauses of the long conditional sentence are suddenly identified and explained in this single word of the result clause. At the same time, a certain number of implicit oppositions, not before clearly stated, now become apparent. "Secrète" suggests elements of darkness contrary to the "lumineuse rupture"; it denies the kinds of disclosure implied by "entre-bâillées" and "Crève en gemmes rouges de jus." Its noun "architecture," through the use of this adjective, comes to be a striking opposite to the series of verbs that I have already cited several times, "Cédant," "Éclatés," "Craquer," "Crève"; and whereas they always occupy the prominent position at the beginning of verses, "architecture" is the last word of the poem at the end of the last line. It is most emphatic of all. Indeed it should be, for an "architecture" is a permanent, solid, immovable form of containment; it is unchanging and inanimate. The speaker's soul has either not grown and matured as had the seeds of the pomegranate or the discoveries of other, sovereign minds, or if it has, that growth has not led to the kind of externalization common to those objects. A final disjunction results from the comparison of his soul, not to the pomegranates, but to the souls of other men; those which have produced the discoveries were "sovereign" minds, his is not, was not. We know this by inference, but a direct statement is unnecessary.

One might restate the structural principle of *Les Grenades* in this way: Valéry establishes a basic comparison between two classes of objects, pomegranates and minds, and he discovers the ground for comparing them in the "architectural" notion of a container and what it contains. Such a comparison would be static and would lead to no possibility of a poetic development if the two objects were alike on all points. In order to provide the foundation for a dynamic movement within the poem, the poet divides the second class, the human minds, into two groups. The first of these, made up of the "fronts souverains," is like the pomegranates in so far as it, too, comprises objects in which an intense internal activity leads to the bursting of the containing shape. But the second, made up of the single speaker's soul, is like the pomegranates only in the relationship *outside : inside;* it is unlike both pomegranates and sovereign minds in the absence of any bursting of the outer walls, attributable undoubtedly to the absence or the insufficiency of the internal activity. This, in turn, is to be explained by the simple inference that the speaker's is not a "sovereign" mind. The possibility of a forward movement, leading to the conclusion of the poem, is found in this differentiation of the two kinds of minds, the first of which is described and fully presented as "like" from the very beginning, the second of which is found to be "unlike" only at the very end. The dramatic quality of the sonnet results from the slow preparation and the ultimate revelation of this essential disparity.

All these procedures are completely traditional, and Valéry does not, in this poem, employ any of the new devices that his predecessors and his contemporaries had been developing. Nevertheless, *Les Grenades* is a distinguished poem. Through the inference that it demands of the reader, if he would apprehend correctly the speaker's state of feeling and the meaning of what is said, it achieves the kind of participation by the reader that the symbolists and the impressionists were also seeking. Especially, it exploits in an extraordinary fashion that peculiar capacity of a comparative or metaphorical structure to transfer from one element to the other a set of meanings and feelings that are fully expressed only in connection with the one. In the present poem, this potentiality is further enriched by the simultaneous presence of comparison and opposition, of likeness and difference; so that while one set of expectations is being constructed on an apparent or superficial level, another set—in a way contradictory—is being prepared for the final turn or reversal of the last tercet. I think it not improper to speak of a "reversal" here, even though a proper action is not involved, merely because what happens in the lyric structure of *Les Grenades* is quite comparable to what happens in a narrative or a dramatic action. There is a set of initial circumstances, some of which are immediately realized after their statement, others of which must await the end of the poem for their full actualization. All this happens, here, in the compressed compass of the sonnet (compressed even more through its reduction to the octosyllable), and this is possible only because of the establishment of multiple connotations for almost every word and because of the tightness of the comparative relationship. The prosodic devices to which I have occasionally referred are auxiliary means to the achievement of the intense architecture of the poem.

13

Saint-John Perse

Anabase

Anyone who would undertake to analyze a poem such as Saint-John Perse's *Anabase* is faced with a multitude of problems. Least of these is the fact that it is a poem in prose. For, prose or verse, the essential form of the poem remains the same, its innermost meaning does not change, the poetic genre to which it belongs may be discovered by an identical procedure. One thing only changes; the ultimate effect upon the reader's sensitivity will be different if it is written in prose than if it is written in verse. Different, but not necessarily inferior. Perse's artful prose is just as capable of producing the particular effects that he seeks as would be the serried verses of a Baudelaire.

The analyst's problems center, instead, around other considerations. What, really, is the ultimate effect that the poem tries to obtain? What is the emotion that it wishes to arouse, to develop, ultimately to appease within the reader as he experiences the poem? In fact, there would be several ways of determining this; but none would be as certain as looking for the answer within the text. Unfortunately, looking for answers in a text is an extremely arduous process. What questions do we ask of the text? In literary analysis, as in judicial interrogation, one gets the answers only to the questions that he knows how to ask. If one puts his questions in terms of language and style, he will get answers pertinent only to these

The essay appeared in French, July, 1960, in *Saggi e ricerche di letteratura francese,* edited by Arnaldo Pizzorusso (Milan: Feltrinelli), and in English, in my own translation, in the *Chicago Review,* III (1962), 75–124.

365

secondary aspects of poetry. The effects that he will succeed in explaining will be equally limited, equally minor. But the deeper he enters, by means of his examination, into the total structure of the work, the better will he be able to distinguish the totality of the effect in its essential aspects. It is therefore necessary to ask those questions that will enable one to penetrate, in order, the fundamental organization of the work.

Now for a poem like *Anabase,* this is no easy task. At least superficially, it is a poem whose structure is equivocal in the sense that we hesitate between two temptations: to call it a narrative structure, to call it a lyric structure. Perhaps there are even other possibilities; in art, the alternatives are always multiple, and the apparent form of *Anabase* is sufficiently rich to justify several hypotheses. But as long as we remain undecided on this matter, we shall be unable to interrogate the text itself, either with respect to its ends or with respect to its means. It is imperative that we decide.

Our first inquiry must then bear on the kind of internal organization that we discover in the poem—on its structure, on its form. I hardly dare say "genre," so outmoded has the term become; but that is really what I mean. Perhaps the term "genre" would be more acceptable if I indicated that in using it I did not at all wish to indicate a collection of rules, conventions, and literary traditions irrevocably associated with a given "kind" of poem. The idea of the "rules" is dead—and properly so; if it were alive, poetry itself would die, since new possibilities for the future would be denied. However, it is possible to think of poetic genre in a more viable way. We may see in the term a designation of a kind of internal form which, by particular means, produces its own proper effect. Such would be the difference between the dramatic and the narrative genres, between mimetic and didactic poetry. The important thing is not to say that a poem belongs to such-and-such a genre, but rather, within a framework that includes all the possibilities, to distinguish its general form in order, later, to distinguish its particular form. Everything depends upon the individual analysis of the poem. Attempts at description and classification are merely elementary and preliminary means of arriving at the questions we must ask about the work that is the object of analysis.

For *Anabase,* the first problem is to overcome our hesitation, to decide about the genre, to discover in advance whether it is a narrative or a lyric poem. I shall consider only these two hypotheses; for the first is the one that has been most commonly proposed, the second the one that I should like to propose in its stead.

Anabase has almost always been discussed as if it were a narrative poem. Thus Valery Larbaud, in his preface for the Russian edition of 1926, while he points to the "lyrical penetration," describes the poem in this way: *"Anabase* is the history of an ascent from the shore of the sea up to the deserts of central Asia"; and again, "with *Anabase,* it is the conquest of Asia and of that vast roof of the world." [1] In a similar way Hugo von Hofmannsthal, in his preface to a German edition that never appeared (1929), speaks of a "narrative . . . free of any historical, ideological, or social allusions"; but he recognizes the difficulties of seeing in it only a narrative: "The wilful hardness of the transitions, the abrupt and repeated breaks, the capriciousness of an Oriental evocation, all make for a reading that is at once accessible and elusive." [2] In the preface to his own English translation of *Anabase* (1930), T. S. Eliot (borrowing the outline from an article of Lucien Fabre in the *Nouvelles littéraires*) gives an essentially narrative scenario for the ten cantos of the poem:

    I. Arrival of the Conqueror at the site of the city which he is about to build.
    II. Tracing the plan of the city.
    III. Consultation of augurs.
    IV. Foundation of the city.
    V. Restlessness towards further explorations and conquests.
    VI. Schemes for foundation and conquest.
    VII. Decision to fare forth.
    VIII. March through the desert.
    IX. Arrival at the threshold of a great new country.
    X. Acclamation, festivities, repose. Yet the urge towards another departure, this time with the mariner.

But along with Fabre he points to the obscurity of the poem when one reads it in this way, and he speaks not so much of a sequence of events or episodes as of a "sequence of images and of ideas." [3]

---

[1] I cite this preface in the text reprinted with the edition of the poem published in New York: Brentano's, 1945; the pages are not numbered.

[2] Same volume; the translation was published for the first time in *Commerce,* XX (1929).

[3] Same volume.

Since the days of these earliest suggestions, critics and interpreters of the poem have tended to adopt them, even when they amplified or corrected them. In an article of 1948, Renato Poggioli suggests a variant on the Fabre-Eliot scenario:

    I. Arrival of the conqueror at the site of the future city.
   II. Transition: impure desires.
  III. Canto of the first morbid intoxications, of physical and spiritual crises, of dissatisfaction and impatience.
  IV. Founding of the city.
   V. Dissension, nostalgia.
  VI. Invitation to adventure.
 VII. Decision to depart.
VIII. Desert march.
  IX. The new country.
   X. Canto of conquest.[4]

Alain Bosquet seems less certain about the usefulness of reducing the poem to a "simple narrative, in the form of a poem, of a military and civilizing expedition into the heart of a continent, preferably Asia." He would like to enlarge the framework and the sense. But when, in his volume on *Saint-John Perse* in the series of the "Poètes d'Aujourd'hui," he studies *Anabase,* he traces its "epic unfolding" in terms of a central action accomplished by a protagonist.[5]

Now the analytical consequences of an interpretation that makes of *Anabase* a narrative poem are extremely important. If we interpret it thus, we must see in it, as its organizing principle, a central action—an action that is made up of a series of episodes or events interrelated through a chain of causality that explains simultaneously their individual character and their collective order. Our interest as readers is attached to this action, to its development and its denouement; the action holds us in suspense. We must see in it also a central personage, a protagonist who does this action and around whom the other actors turn. It is because of his character, his passions, his loves and his hates, that the action is done; it is because reasons are brought to him, because he finds arguments, that he decides to do what he does. In so far as he attracts our sympathy or

---

[4] "The Poetry of St.-J. Perse," *Yale French Studies,* I (1948), 5–33.
[5] *Saint-John Perse,* Paris: Seghers, 1956, pp. 32–43.

our admiration, we come to share his passions; he it is who moves us.[6] Finally, we must see in it the whole complex of situations that put this personage into relationship with his circumstances; the whole interplay of speeches and reasonings that influence the actors; all the elements of setting that have a similar influence. For these direct and regulate the exact quality of our emotions through the narrative. In a word, the totality of poetic effect depends upon a totality of elements in the poem, all of them—according to this hypothesis—organized around the central narrative.

What remains to be seen is whether this is the case in *Anabase*. In an effort to see what goes on in the general structure of this poem, I am going to analyze each one of its sections, seeking to determine for each one what it contains, the character of its individual effect, and the nature of its relationships with the other sections.

Chanson. The scenarios cited earlier do not even mention the two "Chansons" that open and close the volume. Barely does Alain Bosquet, speaking of the first one, say of it in passing: "At the threshold of 'Anabase' a 'Chanson,' a stele that sounds the call of great distances, serves to establish the ambition to reach them."[7] Poggioli goes so far as to assert the independence of the two songs: "Beginning and ending with two independent poems, *Anabase* is divided into ten distinct units."[8] Nothing could be farther from the truth than this statement. For, stated very simply, the two songs constitute the beginning and the end of the whole poem; without them, it does not exist in its totality—or if it exists, it is in an incomplete and truncated form. Moreover, the songs are so completely intermingled with the rest, by their subjects and by their language, that no definition of objects or of terms is possible if they are not taken into account.

---

[6] I do not overlook two other possibilities: that the protagonist may be a "collective protagonist"—a people, a nation, a race; that the protagonist may be an abstraction. But the first does not seem to me to be probable for *Anabase,* given the "single" character of the adventurer who speaks; and the second would have a metaphorical rather than a literal truth. We shall see later in what sense one may "generalize" the adventure. Even generalized in this way, it does not constitute an action and the person who accomplishes it does not become a protagonist.

[7] *Op. cit.,* p. 34.

[8] *Op. cit.,* p. 14.

Let us take the first sentence of this first "Chanson." [9] "Il naissait un poulain sous les feuilles de bronze." The foal will reappear, in a sentence remarkably different from this one, at the beginning of the third paragraph of this same song: "Il naquit un poulain sous les feuilles de bronze" (CH I, 146); in Chant V, "et le poulain poisseux met son menton barbu dans la main de l'enfant" (V, 167); in Chant VI, "le poulain qui nous est né dans les bagages de l'armée" (VI, 173); in Chant X, p. 188, "des sacrifices de poulains sur des tombes d'enfants." A first link, then, between this Chanson and the rest of the poem. But just as there was progression in time between "Il *naissait* un poulain" and "Il *naquit* un poulain," there will be progression in time between the foal and the horse. For one of the meanings of the Greek ἀνάβασις is "the action of riding a horse," and in *Anabase* we shall find numerous cavalcades. Horses and horsemen appear everywhere: "A nos chevaux livrée la terre sans amandes" (I, 149), "les prestations de cavalerie" (IV, 162), "Les cavaliers au fil des caps" (VI, 170), "cavaliers démontés" (VI, 171), "nos chevaux sobres et rapides" (VI, 171), "bâtiments pour la cavalerie" (VI, 173), "mon âme tout enténébrée d'un parfum de cheval" (VII, 177), and so forth. This development makes it possible for the poet to end his poem with a final Chanson, exactly parallel in construction with the first, beginning with the phrase "Mon cheval arrêté sous l'arbre plein de tourterelles," repeated later as "Mon cheval arrêté sous l'arbre qui roucoule" (CH II, 199, 200). The foal born at the beginning, as a necessary prelude to the future cavalcades, will at the end become the horse brought to a stop.

That foal was born "sous les feuilles de bronze." In the same paragraph, the tree bearing these leaves is called "le plus grand des arbres de l'année" (CH I, 145), a little later "un arbre de bronze" (CH I, 146). The process employed to treat this last element of the first sentence—the tree and its leaves—will be the same as the one we have just described: constant repetition throughout the poem, variations in the object, changes in the object through time. (Note that I

---

[9] All passages from *Anabase* are cited from the edition of the *Œuvre poétique*, Volume I, Paris: Gallimard, 1959. The first Chanson is indicated by CH I, the final Chanson by CH II, the various cantos by I, II, III, etc. For each quotation, the number of the section is followed by the page number in the Gallimard edition.

am speaking of the object, not of the word; it is the permanence of the object, along with the changes in its form, that is important.) The bronze tree becomes "un arbre de fer" (VI, 170); a little later we read of "l'éponge verte d'un seul arbre" (VII, 175); at VII, 177, "l'arbre jujubier fait éclater l'assise des tombeaux"; at VIII, 181, an arrival "au lieu dit de l'Arbre Sec"; at IX, 184, somebody announces "la félicité des feuilles dans nos songes." Thus in the final Chanson we discover that not only has the tree become "l'arbre plein de tourterelles" and "l'arbre qui roucoule," but that the "Feuilles vivantes au matin sont à l'image de la gloire" (CH II, 199). We see immediately that there is a clear opposition between "feuilles de bronze" and "feuilles vivantes," that there is a progression from the metallic trees to the living trees, that "félicité" and "gloire" are associated with the living leaves. Moreover, there seems to be a historical and human order in this progression: iron follows bronze in the order of the geological ages, we pass from a state in which life is lacking (the beginning) to a state that is completely alive (the end); and glory is attached to the latter.

From this first sentence, then, there are immediate conclusions to be drawn: that one and the same object, present throughout the poem, undergoes changes that are related to the total progression of the poem; that the exact form given to the object at any particular point depends precisely upon its place in relationship to the whole evolution; that the meaning and the emotion associated with the object display a similar movement. These conclusions may serve as guides to the reading of the rest of *Anabase*.

The first Chanson continues thus: "Un homme mit des baies amères dans nos mains. Étranger. Qui passait." In the following paragraph, these last elements are changed to "Étranger. Qui riait." In the third paragraph, the original formula returns with a single change: "Un homme mit ces baies amères dans nos mains. Étranger. Qui passait." Here it is not the bitter berries that count (they will never reappear), but rather the passing of this man, this Stranger, under the tree and his meeting with the others who are there. Toward the end of the tenth Chant, the situation will be summarized thus: "les conversations muettes de deux hommes sous un arbre" (X, 194), and in the final Chanson, thus: "dans le commerce d'un vieil arbre" (CH II, 199–200). What is the nature of this encounter and what is its meaning? First, the berries: we should note that in the second paragraph, after "qui riait," comes the phrase "Et nous parle d'une herbe." In both contexts, the gift of the bitter berries and the mention of the herbs constitute the "commerce" between the Stranger and the others; they establish the links and they communicate the message. But the herbs and grains will continue to appear throughout the poem: I, 150, "Maître du grain"; II, 154, "pays de hautes pentes à mélisses"; III, 156, "Qu'on les nourrisse de mon grain!"; III, 159, "louant la terre sous l'herbage"; IV, 161, "Des arrivages de farines!"; V, 168, "la terre en ses graines ailées"; VII, 175, "la terre aux herbes s'allumant"; VII, 176, "Pas une graine pure"; VIII, 180, "Homme, pèse ton poids calculé en froment," "ce mouvement d'herbes"; VIII, 181, "un grand pays d'herbages," "et la graine, dis-tu, du cocculus indien possède, qu'on la broie! des vertus enivrantes"; X, 189, "la ventilation d'herbages"; X, 190, " la fabrication d'un beau pain d'orge et de sésame; ou bien d'épeautre"; X, 195, "beaucoup de graines en voyage." This is neither a list nor a collection; it is a group of objects and of uses of these objects that make, taken together, a total sense. The herbs-grains-seeds are found in every country, old or new; they characterize its culture; they have human uses and values. In this first Chanson, especially, they are exotic herbs, coming from a distance (such as the Indian cocculus). Like the bitter berries, they are brought in to amaze and to tempt those who receive them.

This explains why the Chanson continues with "Et voici qu'il est bruit d'autres provinces à mon gré." Bitter berries and herbs speak "of other provinces," of other distant lands; and what they say is pleasant to the listener ("à mon gré"). Therefore in the parallel movement of the second paragraph the idea will be expressed so: "Ah! tant de souffles aux provinces!"; and in the third paragraph, so: "Et voici d'un grand bruit dans un arbre de bronze." In a word, by means of the berries and the herbs these far provinces will make themselves heard in the tree by those who are under it. Now if we consider together these three elements—the report, the breath, the provinces—we see that they explain one another. The report, coming from a distant time or place, speaks always of what is distant: III,

159, "ce bruit d'un autre âge"; IV, 161, "Au grand bruit frais de l'autre rive." It speaks also of what is different, "autre." But sometimes also the same word signifies a great emotional disturbance: "mon âme veille à grand bruit aux portes de la mort" (III, 159). The function of the breath is similar; it comes from afar, it has something to tell "us": I, 152, "ce souffle d'autres rives"; VII, 177, "Fumées qu'un souffle nous dispute!"; VII, 177–78, "ô routes vaines qu'échevèle un souffle jusqu'à nous!" However, the direction whence it comes is specified repeatedly: I, 151 (close to the beginning), "confesseurs de souffles en Ouest"; VI, 170 (in the middle), "Puis ce fut une année de souffles en Ouest." And it is toward the West that the adventure will move: IX, 183 (near the end): "Depuis un si long temps que nous allions en Ouest." The text also suggests other meanings; at two points in the sixth Chant we find the term in another context: VI, 169, "avec nos filles parfumées qui se vêtaient d'un souffle, ces tissus," and VI, 173, "vers nos filles parfumées, qui nous apaiseront d'un souffle, ces tissus." Might we suppose that there are also "breaths" of pleasure and of appeasement? Might we think, in the final Chanson, that there is a variation or a transformation of the "souffle" in the formula, "je siffle un sifflement si pur," "je siffle un sifflement plus pur"? The general methods of the poet in *Anabase* might justify us in so thinking.

As for the provinces (the "pays" frequently alternate with them), they usually become the distant and new lands in which the adventure takes place: VI, 170, "les provinces mises à prix"; VI, 173, "les provinces maritimes." But they are related to the breath through the formula "ces provinces en Ouest" (thus completing the series "souffles en Ouest," "nous allions en Ouest," "provinces en Ouest") at VIII, 181, and they take on a metaphorical value in the phrase "L'œil recule d'un siècle aux provinces de l'âme" which—as needs must be—is found in the last Chant (X, 188). This metaphorical value will be of great importance in the total interpretation of the poem.

But who is this man, this Stranger who passes and who, laughing, brings news of far-away provinces? Since he is a mysterious person, a stranger with a capital letter, it will be necessary to consult a large number of indications in the poem in order to identify him. To begin with, this is one of the actors in the poem: a man who speaks, who acts, and who is spoken of by other actors. We thus start with three sources of information. In this first Chanson, after the gift of the bitter berries, the Stranger performs another action: "l'Étranger a mis son doigt dans la bouche des morts"—an action that is explained by two later passages in the text. First (I, 151), in a passage in which the Stranger himself must be speaking, he says: "J'aviverai du sel les bouches mortes du désir"; later (V, 166), another passage describes an essentially similar gesture, even though certain of the elements are different: "qu'un doigt de miel longe les lèvres du prodigue." In both cases, a substance is put into the mouth in order to "quicken" desire; only, in the first case it is salt in the mouth of the dead, in the second, honey in the mouth of the living. We shall find the explanation of this difference if we pursue the two substances through the text, especially the salt.

Most of the allusions to salt are concentrated in the first Chant; but there are many meanings to be assigned to the term. In a first passage (I, 150), immediately after the formula "Maître du grain," the narrator calls himself as well "maître du sel"; grain and salt are essential products for life, and he who is master of them assures the stability of his society ("et la chose publique sur de justes balances!"). A little later (I, 150), however, in the phrase "et l'idée pure comme un sel tient ses assises dans le jour," the sense is metaphorical and the ratio *idée* : *sel* is established, along with the added notion of purity. This ratio is developed through the following section, where the Stranger is speaking; in general, he tells men of the nature of his invitation and the reasons why they should accept it. Thus he says to them, "Au délice du sel sont toutes lances de l'esprit!" (I, 151), where "sel" is connected with "esprit" and where the invitation, addressed to the mind, promises it the only joys possible. The following sentence, "J'aviverai du sel les bouches mortes du désir," clarifies the sense of this invitation and explains the meaning of what follows: "Qui n'a, louant la soif, bu l'eau des sables dans un casque, je lui fais peu crédit au commerce de l'âme." We thus know that salt arouses thirst, that it is a thirst of the soul, and that the man who refuses this invitation is hardly worthy of being considered a man. Contrariwise, the Stranger says to all men, in a long paragraph following (I, 151–52)—he calls them "ô chercheurs, ô trouveurs de raisons pour s'en aller ailleurs"—that those who accept the invitation take part in the most important adventure of all:

> vous ne trafiquez pas d'un sel plus fort quand, au matin, dans un présage de royaumes et d'eaux mortes hautement suspendues sur les fumées du monde, les tambours de l'exil éveillent aux frontières
> l'éternité qui bâille sur les sables. (I, 152)

Once again the "trafic du sel" (cf. the "commerce de l'âme") signifies the desire of the soul for the adventure, and the adventure itself is generalized in time and in space. It is this last idea that is found at the end of the Chant, where the narrator (replying to the Stranger) speaks of the "Mathématiques suspendues aux banquises du sel!" (I, 152). The "mathématiques" are explained by two earlier formulas, "la chose publique sur de justes balances!" (I, 150) and "l'éclat d'un siècle sur sa pointe au fléau des balances . . ." (I, 152). The "mathématiques suspendues" would thus be a state of stability, a high point of society which would nevertheless be menaced by the whole great mass of desire contained in the "banquises du sel."

Two other passages suggest variants for the meaning of "sel." At III, 159 we find the phrase, "Et des morts sous le sable et l'urine et le sel de la terre"; at VII, 178, "tout le sel de la terre tressaille dans les songes." The formula "le sel de la terre" reappears in both passages, thus generalizing still more the application of the term. Besides, the association on the one hand with dreams, on the other with elements such as sand and urine (which will be explained later), confirms our judgment that the salt stands for the desires of the soul, of the spirit, at the same time as it designates a permanent and essential element of life.

The case for the honey is less clear; but if we study closely the contexts of the three places where it appears, we may find some explanation. In the first (VI, 173), it is found in a list of the "choses de la paix": "les confitures de roses à miel"; in the second, in an enumeration of "choses immortelles": "Couleur de soufre, de miel, couleur de choses immortelles" (VII, 175); in the third, among the "choses périssables" of which the young woman sings: "Je t'annonce les temps d'une grande faveur et la félicité des sources dans nos songes. / Ouvre ma bouche dans la lumière, ainsi qu'un lieu de miel entre les roches . . ." (IX, 185–86). We should note that the honey is everywhere connected with lists of "choses," and that in the last of these passages it is linked with "bouche" and with "songes," exactly as is the salt. The "choses de la paix" and the "choses périssables" would lead us to suppose that, just as the salt kindles desire, so does the honey give recompense in the form of pleasure.

The action of the Étranger, so far, is thus double: he gives the invitation, he suggests vaguely a promise of reward. In connection with Perse's poetic method, what we should note especially is the interlinking of objects and of terms throughout the text. In order to understand the Stranger's first action, we have had to pursue the notions of "doigt, bouche, sel, miel," with their many meanings that explain one another. So, everywhere, we shall have to seek explanations within the text itself, consulting the whole to understand each part.

Still within the first Chanson, another phrase, "et l'Étranger à ses façons par les chemins de toute la terre" (CH I, 146), informs us at once that he is different from other men ("à ses façons") and that his activity is extended and in a way universal. The first of these formulas recalls a phrase that comes a little earlier in the same Chanson: "Mon âme, grande fille, vous aviez vos façons qui ne sont pas les nôtres." I shall return presently to that phrase. The difference between the Étranger and other men becomes clearer in the fifth Chant: "Et l'Étranger tout habillé / de ses pensées nouvelles, se fait encore des partisans dans les voies du silence: son œil est plein d'une salive, / il n'y a plus en lui substance d'homme" (V, 167–68). All the essential activity of the Stranger is there: "pensées nouvelles," the act of attracting partisans, the diminution (through thought) of the "substance d'homme." It is an activity that is closely tied to the one we have already seen. The expression "le commerce d'un vieil arbre" (CH II, 199–200) has already been cited as summarizing the action, under the tree, of giving the berries and mentioning the herbs. The Stranger himself speaks of the "pur commerce de mon âme" (I, 150) and, rejecting any man who cannot be aroused by the salt, he says: "Qui n'a, louant la soif, bu l'eau des sables dans un casque, / je lui fais peu crédit au commerce de l'âme" (I, 151). In a passage that is quite similar, those who do not accept the invitation are once again rejected: "Ceux-là qui en naissant n'ont point flairé de telle braise, qu'ont-ils à faire parmi nous? et se peut-il qu'ils aient commerce de vivants?" (VI, 170–71). The Stranger's activity is thus an activity of the soul, and the voyage to which he invites is a voyage of the soul: "O Voyageur dans le vent jaune, goût de l'âme!" (VIII, 181). Thus it will be possible to say, fairly late in the poem and by way of summarizing its actions, "beaucoup de choses entreprises sur les ténèbres de l'esprit—beaucoup de choses à loisir sur les frontières de l'esprit" (VIII, 180).

Almost the whole of the Stranger's activity is thus reduced to his invitation, given and repeated at various places on the earth, an invitation given in the name of the soul for a voyage of the spirit. There is one single exception. In Chant IX, where the woman is speaking to men, she says of him: "Mais l'Étranger vit sous sa tente, honoré de laitages, de fruits." She speaks of his relations with women, and concludes: "(Je ne sais quelles sont ses façons d'être avec les femmes)." It would seem that, just as he is associated with the departure and the voyage, so he will be associated with that principle of pleasure of which we have already seen a trace in the "miel."

His other function in the poem is to speak: "Et nous parle d'une herbe" (CH I, 146). At several places, we hear his own words; at others, he is quoted indirectly. But for him as for the other personages, it is sometimes difficult to identify the person speaking; there are never any direct identifications, and one is obliged to reconstruct on the basis of the context and of what is said in the speech itself. Thus in Chant I, context and content suggest an attribution to the Stranger (I, 150–52). Chant III begins thus: "A la moisson des orges l'homme sort. Je ne sais qui de fort a parlé sur mon toit." Might we suppose that the one who, through his words, causes man to set out, is the Stranger? It is possible, merely because of the nature of this action. If this is true, it is also probable that the Stranger is the one who speaks the "propos" of Chant VI, 170: "Puis ce fut une année de souffles en Ouest et, sur nos toits lestés de pierres noires, tout un propos de toiles vives adonnées au délice du large"; the invitation, this time, would be for a voyage by sea. In Chant V several speeches (anonymous at first) are finally attributed to the Étranger, in a passage we have already seen: "Et l'Étranger tout habillé de ses pensées nouvelles," and so forth. The "pensées nouvelles" appear at the beginning of the Chant. After an introductory phrase, "Pour mon âme mêlée aux affaires lointaines . . . ," and after an exclamation "Solitude! . . . ," he says: "Je n'ai dit à personne d'attendre . . . Je vous hais tous avec douceur . . ."; the formula recurs near the end of the Chant: "Solitude! Je n'ai dit à personne d'attendre . . . Je m'en irai par là quand je voudrai . . ." (V, 167). It is possible that the other two speeches of this Chant, "Fruit de la femme, ô Sabéenne! . . ." (166) and "Aurore, vous contiez . . ." (167), should also be attributed to the Étranger; they will be examined later. There may even be other speeches, here and there in the poem, that belong to the Étranger; but even from the few that I have just studied, it is clear that his speeches correspond to his actions, that he speaks always of the repeated invitation, of the adventure and of its rewards.

This discussion of speeches and of the difficulty of attributing them accurately leads us back to the first Chanson where, in fact, there are three speeches of the kind. At the end of the first paragraph: "Je vous salue, ma fille, sous le plus grand des arbres de l'année"; at the end of the second, "Mon âme, grande fille, vous aviez vos façons qui ne sont pas les nôtres"; and at the end of the third, "Je vous salue, ma fille, sous la plus belle robe de l'année." Who is speaking, and to whom? This time it is not the Stranger but rather the narrator, the one who received the invitation; and he is speaking not only for himself as an individual, but for all those who will participate in the adventure. "Ma fille" is "mon âme" (see the second citation, "Mon âme, grande fille") and the narrator speaks to that part of himself in which the Stranger had been interested. Thus it becomes more and more evident that the adventure proposed by the Stranger is an adventure of thought, of the spirit, of the soul. When the narrator says to his soul, "vous aviez vos façons qui ne sont pas les nôtres," he distinguishes it from all that part of man which is not his soul, just as the Stranger "à ses façons" is distinguished from the rest of men. As for the two parallel formulas, "sous le plus grand des arbres de l'année" and "sous la plus belle robe de l'année," I believe that the first is literal, alluding to the tree under which takes place the meeting of the Étranger and of the narrator, and calling it "grand" because of the importance of this encounter; and that the second is metaphorical, saying approximately the same thing. But the second, through the image of the dress, relates this Chanson to all the women's dresses that appear in the poem; and both of them, through the reference to the year, relate it to the whole dialectic of the seasons that gives its chronology to *Anabase*.

The same chronology explains the presence, at the beginning of the second paragraph of the Chanson, of the formula "Car le soleil entre au Lion"; it is summer, and the invitation is given around July 23rd. Thus Chant I will begin with the phrase, "Sur trois grandes saisons m'établissant avec honneur . . ."; in Chant VII will be found the sentence, "L'Été plus vaste que l'Empire suspend aux tables de l'espace plusieurs étages de climats" (VII, 175); in Chant VIII one hears of "l'année sans liens et sans anniversaires" (VIII, 181). The adventure will begin at the right moment; it will be pursued through time and through space—with a broader meaning given to time and to space, progressively, as the poem develops.

We still need to explain, in the first Chanson, two parallel movements. In the second paragraph, after the phrase "Ah! tant de souffles aux provinces!" the narrator says: "Qu'il est d'aisance dans nos voies! que la trompette m'est délice et la plume savante au scandale de l'aile! . . ." In the third paragraph, after "Et voici d'un grand bruit dans un arbre de bronze," he says: "Bitume et roses, don du chant! Tonnerre et flûtes dans les chambres! Ah! tant d'aisance dans nos voies, ha! tant d'histoires à l'année. . . ." Once again, the rest of the poem will supply the explanations. Both passages say essentially the same thing: that the invitation is accepted joyfully, not only because of the promise of pleasure that will accompany the adventure, but also because of the two chronicles that will immortalize it, the historian's and the poet's. "Nos voies" are the roads and the routes of the adventure, the "chemins de toute la terre" traveled by the Étranger (CH I, 146), the "Chemins du monde" (VIII, 181); they are "les routes où s'en aillent les gens de toute race" (III, 158)— but they are neither the "routes nocturnes" of dreams (I, 150) nor the "routes vaines" of death's inactivity (VII, 177); they are the "voies du silence" (V, 167), the "voies immortelles" (VI, 172). We may thus speak, in generalizing the adventure, of "toutes sortes d'hommes dans leurs voies et façons" (X, 190), and, indicating its immortal nature, of the "cavaleries de bronze vert sur de vastes chaussées" (VII, 178). The "aisance dans nos voies" of the first Chanson might designate at once the easy life of the adventurer (ease of movement and of "façons") and his feeling of ease. The narrator, hearing in advance the "grand bruit" of this adventure, may thus say that "la trompette m'est délice" and that the adventure is announced by "Tonnerre et flûtes dans les chambres!" One aspect of this joy, of this "délice," appears in the formula "Bitume et roses"; for everywhere roses represent life and pleasure. Thus in Chant III, 158, the adventurer says: ". . . Roses, pourpre délice: la terre vaste à mon désir . . ."; in Chant VI, 170, "l'odeur solennelle des roses" constitutes the "braise" which attracts the adventurer, and later (173) the "confitures de roses à miel" appear in the "pays de grand loisir." In Chant X, 188, the enumeration of "choses vivantes" includes "des purifications de veuves dans les roses." The meaning of the rose is less clear in the question asked towards the end of Chant II (155): "Eh quoi! n'est-il plus grâce au monde sous la rose sauvage?" As for the bitumen, the only reference that clarifies it—V, 166: "Âme jointe en silence au bitume des Mortes"—would lead us to believe that it represents death. Thus life and death are foreseen in the invitation and in what will result from it.

The formula that completes this same sentence, "don du chant!" constitutes the first mention, in *Anabase,* of the poet's activity; besides relating and commenting upon the adventure, he will frequently admit that he himself is doing the relating and the commenting. Usually, these admissions come at the end of a canto; so for Chant I: "Au point sensible de mon front où le poème s'établit, j'inscris ce chant de tout un peuple, le plus ivre, / à nos chantiers tirant d'immortelles carènes!"; for Chant V, "Et la terre en ses graines ailées, comme un poète en ses propos, voyage . . ."; for the final Chanson, "Mais de mon frère le poète on a eu des nouvelles. Il a écrit encore une chose très douce. Et quelques-uns en eurent connaissance. . . ." These words conclude the poem. However, at one single place the Étranger himself addresses the poet: ". . . Et qu'est-ce à dire de ce chant que vous tirez de nous? . . ." (V, 165); and this passage especially helps us understand the "don du chant" of the first Chanson. It also suggests the meaning to be given to the formula (in the same Chanson), "la plume savante au scandale de l'aile"; the feather-pen might be the poet's and the chronicler's (in which case it would be "savante"), the instrument that will give immortality to the adventure.

We may now attempt to specify the nature of this first Chanson. It is a song sung by the narrator of the adventure that will follow, having a lyric form divided into three strophes, each of which ends with an apostrophe that serves as a refrain. Its content, too, is lyrical. Underlying this content there is an episode, an event: the Étranger meets with men under the tree, speaks to them of distant lands. However, what is expressed above all is the emotion of the narrator as he thinks of this meeting: his joy in the promise of the adventure, in his own participation in it, in the immortality that will come to him through it; his exaltation in knowing that the best part of himself, his soul, will achieve thereby its finest expression. Joy and exaltation are such as belong to the beginning of the adventure; and so each element in the song, each object mentioned, also represents a beginning. Each element will be known and explained through the rest of the poem; some of them will be fully known only when we reach the final Chanson.

Chant 1. Lucien Fabre is the source of the tradition which holds that the first Chant has as its subject the "arrival of the Conqueror at the site of the city which he is about to build." I believe that this is not at all the case, and that the incorrect interpretation comes from the fact that the first part of the Chant has been badly read. In fact, the Chant is divided into three sections; in the first, it is the narrator who speaks (the one who has spoken in the first Chanson); in the second, the Étranger answers him; in the third, it is the narrator again—with, at the end, a few sentences added by the poet himself. Now this alternation of speakers supposes a dialogue and this dialogue concerns the invitation proffered in the first Chanson. The question is asked: Should the Stranger's invitation be accepted or rejected? At first the narrator gives a negative answer; he does not wish to leave. But the Stranger (instead of giving berries and mentioning exotic plants) presents a series of convincing arguments. At this point in the discussion, the narrator accepts; and it is at this same point that the poet, who intervenes directly for the first time, can begin his narrative. Let us see in detail how the three sections of the Chant are constituted.

At the very beginning of Chant I the narrator says: "Sur trois grandes saisons m'établissant avec honneur, j'augure bien du sol où j'ai fondé ma loi." Rather than speaking of the new city to be founded, he speaks of the one, founded long ago, that he hesitates to leave. The "trois grandes saisons" are the ones preceding, as they have prepared, the fourth and present season—the season of accomplishment, of stability, of honor. The soil on which he has "fondé sa loi" is the soil that has been inhabited for a long time, that promises a continuation of happiness. If the suggestion that I am here making is valid, then the phrase that follows in the text should be read with a tone of concession, if not of irony: "[You may well tell me that] Les armes au matin sont belles et la mer," to be understood as saying "This argument about their beauty does not persuade me." We should note, however, that even this refusal is expressed through certain elements that will be characteristic of the future adventure: the morning, time of the departure; the sea, one of the routes of travel; arms, a necessary accompaniment. We might read in a similar way—as expressing contentment with the status quo—what follows: "A nos chevaux livrée [in an old adventure completed in a distant past] la terre sans amandes [as a primitive and uncultivated desert] nous vaut [now, as a reward for past sufferings] ce ciel incorruptible [which is dear to us for its present purity]."

We may thus suppose that it is because he is content to remain that the narrator says, a little farther along (I shall return shortly to the passages skipped), that he has made his decision to remain "Pour une année encore parmi vous" (I, 150); here, "une année" signifies the total cycle of the seasons, and "parmi vous" indicates all other men, those to whom the narrator is speaking. So it is that the narrator, here the chief of the civil adventure as he will later be the chief of the military adventure—"Maître du grain, maître du sel . . ."—refuses to leave: "Je ne hélerai point les gens d'une autre rive. Je ne tracerai point de grands quartiers de villes . . . Mais j'ai dessein de vivre parmi vous." The following sentence will then bear the same tone of concession; but in addition it will juxtapose the temptations of departure to the advantages in remaining: "Au seuil des tentes toute gloire! ma force parmi vous!" The tents will appear later in the various "anabases"; as for the narrator's "force," three other passages in the same section are related to it.

The first paragraph (or should I say "first strophe"?) ends with these words: "Et le soleil n'est point nommé, mais sa puissance est parmi nous / et la mer au matin comme une présomption de l'esprit." I believe that the sun (personified) represents here, as elsewhere, a principle of stability; even if he is not named directly, he speaks to men of the heat and the light of the road—convincing reasons for remaining—and thus his power is among them. Later (III, 156), after the departure, his words will be given their proper value: "Va! nous nous étonnons de toi, Soleil! Tu nous as dit de tels mensonges! . . ." For man will find (III, 157) that his experience of the road contradicts the sun's prophecies: "Mon cœur a pépié de joie sous les magnificences de la chaux. . . ." When he says, then, at the beginning of the second paragraph of this section, "Puissance, tu chantais sur nos routes nocturnes! . . . ," he indicates one of the reasons for the hesitation; the "routes nocturnes" are not those of the adventure, but rather the roads of inactivity, roads of the dream that takes place during this night that precedes the morning of the departure.

For the man who hesitates in the night, the sea (one of the routes of the voyage) is "comme une présomption de l'esprit"—of the mind that is to be the principal adventurer and that should not therefore presume to leave. This is why, at the beginning of the second paragraph, the narrator says: "Aux ides pures du matin que savons-nous du songe, notre aînesse?" and at the end of the same paragraph, "et l'idée pure comme un sel tient ses assises dans le jour." Morning and day should here be opposed to night ("nocturnes"), the dream should be opposed to the pure idea (belonging to the mind); the "ides pures" are a culminating point of the morning, time of the departure, just as the salt is the expression of the desire that causes one to depart. He who remains in the night is willing to permit the idea to establish itself ("tient ses assises") in the day.

The Stranger replies, in the section following, to all the points of the narrator's argument. While the man was dreaming in his city, the Stranger came to speak to his soul: ". . . Or je hantais la ville de vos songes et j'arrêtais sur les marchés déserts ce pur commerce de mon âme, parmi vous / invisible et fréquente ainsi qu'un feu d'épines en plein vent." What he is talking about, in fact, is the meeting under the tree and the invitation that is tendered there. We should note that the Stranger, like the narrator, will use the expression "parmi vous"; but whereas the narrator identifies himself with men in general, the Stranger considers himself as different from them. Different, but never absent; for the soul is "invisible et fréquente." The comparison of the soul to a "feu d'épines en plein vent" is full of promise for the rest of the poem; at IV, 160 (where the founding of the city is really at issue), "Des feux de ronces à l'aurore / mirent à nu ces grandes / pierres vertes . . ." (hence a preparation for the buildings), and at X, 190, the founding of another city is accompanied by "les feux de ronces et d'épines aux lieux souillés de mort." The soul, in its adventure, will clear its ground before it builds. When in the second section, then, the Stranger says "Puissance, tu chantais sur nos routes splendides," the change in the last word ("nocturnes" becomes "splendides") gives to the phrase a meaning exactly opposite to the one it had in the narrator's mouth. For the Stranger who invites, the sun's power makes the roads splendid: an argument in favor of the departure. Afterwards he speaks, in a passage already studied, of the joy in the salt, of the desire (and hence of the thirst) that it awakens, of those who have credit in the commerce of the soul. At the end of this development, in parentheses, we find again one of the narrator's phrases: "(Et le soleil n'est point nommé, mais sa puissance est parmi nous)"; this is, I think, a repetition by the narrator, in this dialogue, of one of his arguments.

The Stranger answers, completing his own argument, with another long development that occupies the rest of this second section of the first Chant. He speaks to all those who listen and who will set forth: "Hommes, gens de poussière et de toutes façons," and so on (I, 151–52). He tells them that no other adventure equals this one; for they are going to found kingdoms ("dans un présage de royaumes"), they are going to ascend from the sea to the highest lands (this is the anabasis), they are going to introduce life where it had not existed previously, and they are going to achieve immortality for themselves. I think that both of these last ideas are contained in the single formula "les tambours de l'exil éveillent aux frontières / l'éternité qui bâille sur les sables." He does not fail to recognize that the drums that sound the joy of departure also sound the sadness of exile; but no matter.

This whole development is full of allusions to the rest of the poem. By its general form—the enumeration of a great number of kinds of men—it prepares the way for all the other enumerations of the same sort: of the "gens de toute race" (III, 158), of the men who found the city (IV, 162), of "toutes sortes d'hommes dans leurs voies et façons" (X, 190). But here, although these men come from everywhere, they all go on the same adventure. If he calls them "gens de peu de poids dans la mémoire de ces lieux," it is because the individual, the people, the country will lose their identity in an adventure that will encompass the whole of the human race and the entire Earth. The "flaireurs de signes, de semences" are those who recognize the call to adventure; the "confesseurs de souffles en Ouest" are those who listen to the invitation that speaks to them of distant lands. As for the "leveurs de campements dans le petit vent de l'aube," they are not only the men who abandon their tents when their cities are ready ("Au seuil des tentes toute gloire!"), but they are also those who depart again for an infinite series of adventures. Compare IV, 161: "Les campements s'annulent aux collines!"; IV, 164: "ceux qui veillaient aux crêtes des collines replièrent leurs toiles"; X, 194: "les campements levés sur des nouvelles qui m'échappent." In a similar way, we shall later find the meaning for the "chercheurs de points d'eau sur l'écorce du monde." All these men, in a general way, are the ones who accept the invitation: "ô chercheurs, ô trouveurs de raisons pour s'en aller ailleurs"; they are, in sum, what the narrator will soon become.

The third section of this first Chant is devoted to the narrator's reply. It is a double reply. At first he repeats his refusal. "En robe pure parmi vous," a formula combining a group of ideas already used, means that he considers his sojourn among his fellow-men as a form of purity, hence justifiable; the "robe" comes from the first Chanson ("sous la plus belle robe de l'année") and will reappear frequently in what follows; the word "pure" refers to the "ides pures" and "l'idée pure"; the "parmi vous" comes from this same Chant. Because he is repeating his idea, the narrator uses again the two sentences that follow: "Pour une année encore parmi vous. 'Ma gloire est sur les mers, ma force est parmi vous.' " But in the next short paragraph there is a reversal. The sentence comprising it is very complex. "A nos destins promis," he says, "ce souffle d'autres rives," suggesting that this invitation, "ce souffle d'autres rives" (and we must think back to his "Je ne hélerai point les gens d'une autre rive"), cannot be refused because it is a part of man's destiny. The sentence continues: "et, portant au delà les semences du temps, l'éclat d'un siècle sur sa pointe au fléau des balances. . . ." We should, I think, interpret thus: This breath, like the bursting of a century, is promised to our destinies. The "éclat" is the true action of bursting; for the century, through a metaphor, becomes a plant at its maximum point of maturity, at its "pointe," at the moment when the flail that beats it disperses its seeds. Since it is a "century-plant," its seeds will be "les semences du temps," carried beyond into the future. But why the "fléau des balances"? For two reasons, I think. First, because the narrator has spoken, at the beginning of the same Chant, of "la chose publique sur de justes balances!"; the decision to leave will destroy this stability. Then, because that same decision, when the two possibilities are well weighed (action or inaction), will mark the passage from one epoch to another, from the past to the future. The "pointe," it may be, represents the maturity of an epoch in the sense that man, having attained the maximum in one form of his soul's activity—civilization—finds it necessary, through his "destin," to set out again on the future adventure.

At this moment of decision, when man recognizes this truth, the poet himself enters and terminates the first Chant. In a first sentence, "Mathématiques suspendues aux banquises du sel," he gives his commentary on the narrator's general situation; the "mathématiques suspendues," taking up again the notion of the scales, represent at once the narrator's hesitation and the crisis, the "pointe," of the century. And the "banquises du sel" epitomize the vast desire of the man (awakened by the Stranger) in a form proper to all the marine images that will follow. The poet continues: "Au point sensible de mon front où le poème s'établit [giving to his thought, through the words 'point sensible,' the same appearance of crisis that we have just seen for the narrator and for the century], j'inscris ce chant de tout un peuple." The poem thus founded, like the city that is established, is to be the chronicle of the whole human race, not merely of the narrator and his people; the tendency to generalize the adventure begins here. This song, being the one that immortalizes the most important adventure possible, will thus be "le plus ivre," while the people who accomplish it may be described as follows (and the poet ends his first Chant): "à nos chantiers tirant d'immortelles carènes." The "chantiers" as shipyards belong to that image of the sea that we have already seen; the people draws there the hulls of the boats that it will use for its adventure. But by a kind of play on words, the "chantiers" are also workshops for songs, and the poet will there make the song that will immortalize the people, the hulls, and the adventure.

The first Chant, in the context of the whole poem, is a direct continuation of the first Chanson; the conversation between the narrator and the Stranger, begun under the tree, continues here; the narrator and the Stranger discuss the invitation, the poet comments. If there is an event or an episode, it is constituted by the fact that the narrator reaches his decision. But, once more, it is not the event that counts. We are held, moved, carried along by the conflict of two emotions in the actors: by the contentment and hence the hesitation of the narrator, by the eloquent promise of joy and of immortality coming from the Stranger. We are moved even more by the kind of resolution that we discover at the end, when the narrator, persuaded by the eloquence of the Stranger, changes his mind. Joy and wonderment, suggested in the first Chanson, are increased and refined throughout the first Chant.

Chant II. The second Chant is very short. It has the form of a song (a technique that we shall find again in several other Chants); the same repetition of phrases and of movements, the same development of refrains. Partly, its content is difficult to determine; I do not know whether it is a first description of the departure (a solution that appeals to me only slightly) or whether it is rather the narrator's vision of this same departure. Whatever the case may be, the Chant seems to belong to the narrator's decision; if, in the preceding Chant, he has renounced the "chose publique" as a part of his former life, so here he renounces woman, the symbol of his pleasure in that same life. Everywhere, in *Anabase,* woman figures as a source of pleasure for man; man will leave her each time that he starts out on a new adventure, he will send for her each time that he establishes a new civilization. In this passage, he is about to leave an old civilization.

The Chant begins with an evocation of lands where there is as yet no human habitation: "Aux pays fréquentés sont les plus grands silences, aux pays fréquentés de criquets à midi." The initial formula will be picked up twice in Chant VI, but in speaking of lands of an entirely different kind: at VI, 171, "Aux pays épuisés où les coutumes sont à reprendre"; at VI, 172, "aux pays infestés de bien-être une odeur de forum et de femmes nubiles." We should note that this last example refers to a country quite similar to the one that the narrator is about to leave, hence the exact opposite of the one that he envisions. The locusts that inhabit it will reappear in Chant IX (the one in which woman speaks of the pleasure that she gives to man): "et le criquet s'envole sur son aile bleue" (IX, 185). Similarly, the "grands silences" will everywhere characterize the new lands to be discovered; we may compare Chant V, 167, "les voies du silence," VII, 176, "les essaims du silence aux ruches de lumière," and "qu'elles cheminent en silence," VII, 178, "levez des pierres au silence," IX, 184, "le soin du silence." These details help us to identify more clearly the lands spoken of at the beginning of Chant II.

The narrator continues: "Je marche, vous marchez dans un pays de hautes pentes à mélisses, où l'on met à sécher la lessive des Grands." Several questions, here. Is he speaking of the new country, or of the one in which he has lived for a long time? I am inclined to think that it is the latter, not only because of the human habitation, but also because of the special nature of the washing that hangs there; they are the garments of the Queen and of Her daughter, of the women being left behind. And why the capitals for "Grands,"

"Reine," and "Sa fille"? I do not know. Perhaps he wishes to indicate the importance of these persons for him who leaves; or perhaps he wants to suggest certain political or social hierarchies. In the following two paragraphs (marked by the parallelism typical of lyric strophes), those who are about to leave speak of women: "Nous enjambons la robe de la Reine [. . . de sa fille]"; "Nous" summarizes the "Je, vous" of the preceding paragraph. The two dresses are identical, except that the Queen's is of "couleur bise," Her daughter's of "couleur vive"—I suppose because of the difference in age. I suppose also that they "step over them" because they go beyond, because they leave them behind. However, the reflections that conclude the two strophes are opposite to one another; the first states a principle of life, the second a principle of death. I interpret in this way the two opposed parentheses: "(ah! que l'acide corps de femme sait tacher une robe à l'endroit de l'aisselle!)" and "(ah! que la langue du lézard sait cueillir les fourmis à l'endroit de l'aisselle!)." After all, women are among the "choses mortelles," the "choses périssables" (cf. IX, 183) which hold man back at the beginning of the adventure, just as they reward him at its conclusion.

The narrator sees this desire of man for woman as a permanent part of his life—whether he leaves or not: "Et peut-être le jour ne s'écoule-t-il point qu'un même homme n'ait brûlé pour une femme et pour sa fille." Enjoy them then, but leave anyway! In the following sentence, speaking to the dead who know everything and who laugh at it—"Rire savant des morts . . ."—the narrator declares that he will seize upon this pleasure: "qu'on nous pèle ces fruits! . . ." But this will not prevent him from finding others in lands now desert: "Eh quoi! n'est-il plus grâce au monde sous la rose sauvage?"; if, as we have seen, the rose represents pleasure, the wild rose must mean new pleasures to be discovered. The paragraph ending Chant II therefore repeats the decision to leave. The invitation is repeated, but in the form of an evil because of the resistance to the departure: "Il vient, de ce côté du monde, un grand mal violet sur les eaux." (Remember "la mer au matin comme une présomption de l'esprit.") The decision to leave is made: "Le vent se lève. Vent de mer." This whole passage and what precedes it will be understood better if we compare another passage in Chant VI, a canto in which are celebrated the "choses de la paix," the "filles parfumées": "Mais au soir, une odeur de violettes et d'argile, aux mains des filles de nos femmes, nous visitait dans nos projets d'établissement et de fortune / et les vents calmes hébergeaient au fond des golfes désertiques" (VI, 174). I hardly need insist on the presence here of the same elements, used for an opposite end. Chant II ends with "Et la lessive part! comme un prêtre mis en pièces . . ." The women's dresses disappear, and with them all traces of the old civilization; for the priest, as we shall later see, is always one of the first signs of the establishment of a society.

In its lyrical form, then, Chant II continues the work of the preceding Chant. But the Étranger is now absent, and instead of a dialogue we have a simple song. The narrator uses it to proceed further in his deliberations, to decide even upon renouncing the main pleasures of his past life in order to obtain the ones promised by the Stranger. By means of this hesitation, of these regrets, and of this final decision, the feeling of admiration and of joy that accompanies the adventure will be augmented. Slowly and subtly, the feelings of the reader will be directed toward the final joy of the last cantos.

Chant III. In Chant II we could point to no event in the development of the narrative; in Chant III, we have the first great episode: the departure. Perhaps we should say: the departure and the first stage of the anabasis. For this Chant is devoted to a first ride, a first voyage across unknown countries, a first meeting with unknown and savage peoples. The narrator discovers them all; but he discovers especially that he was right in leaving, that he did well not to listen to the sun, and his joy increases as a result. After so many hesitations, this joy bursts forth many times in this Chant. The six long paragraphs of which it is made are richly interwoven with references to other parts of *Anabase;* nevertheless, there is an internal structure proper to this Chant, a structure that is lyrical in its essence and eminently suited to the expression of joy.

The first paragraph begins with these two sentences, summarizing the departure and the invitation that led up to it: "A la moisson des orges l'homme sort. Je ne sais qui de fort a parlé sur mon toit." The same sentences are found again in the sixth paragraph (giving once more the lyrical tone): "A la moisson des orges l'homme sort. Je ne sais qui de fort a marché sur mes pas." The barley recalls the importance of grains throughout the poem, as well as the season of the departure. The formula "sur mon toit" will have more varied meanings; at V, 166 we find the phrase, "Les Rois Confédérés du ciel mènent la guerre sur mon toit . . . ," where clearly celestial bodies are involved; at VI, 170, a sentence cited earlier: "Puis ce fut une année de souffles en Ouest et, sur nos toits lestés de pierres noires, tout un propos de toiles vives adonnées au délice du large," where the winds "speak" of another adventure. Here, it is possible that "je ne sais qui de fort" refers to the breath itself, a secondary way of indicating the invitation. In the rest of the paragraph, other capitalized personages appear: the Kings, the Ambassador, the Inspector of weights and measures. These are persons encountered along the road, representatives of indigenous societies in a primitive state; note the turgid rivers, the debris of insects, the "fétus de paille dans la barbe." The narrator says: "(Qu'on les nourrisse de mon grain!)"; is he proposing already to share with them the fruits of his spirit, of his soul?

In the following paragraph the sun (who in Chant I was not named at all) is named and challenged. The narrator accuses him of having told lies; for he now knows that the sun exaggerated the dangers of the road: "Va! nous nous étonnons de toi, Soleil! Tu nous as dit de tels mensonges! . . ." He will not fail, later on, to attribute the same character to the sun: at VI, 170, "de grands pays vendus à la criée sous l'inflation solaire," and at VIII, 180, "les prévarications du ciel contre la terre." Now, the narrator defies him to shed his light: "fais éclater l'amande de mon œil!"; for in spite of "les magnificences de la chaux," the narrator's "cœur a pépié de joie." The rest of the paragraph gives the reasons for this joy: "l'oiseau chante: 'ô vieillesse! . . .' [we should read: you should not have counseled us to remain], les fleuves sont sur leurs lits comme des cris de femmes [this is the pleasure in woman; cf. VII, 178, 'les fleuves dans leurs noces'] et ce monde est plus beau / qu'une peau de bélier peinte en rouge!" The last image makes us think, once again, of a prehistoric age of man; it places the adventure in geological eras.

In the third paragraph, the new world is reduced to its foliage, to "l'eau plus pure . . . ," to the powerful odor. But the narrator's spirit vacillates among three possible attitudes towards this world: "la réalité des choses" and the story told about them, the dream and the lie, and doubt. "Ha! plus ample l'histoire de ces feuillages . . ." We thus witness the first of "tant d'histoires à l'année" (CH I, 146). The narrator's joy results from the fact that he has before him realities and not dreams. But he confuses dreams and lies ("songe" and "mensonge"), the sun's eloquence is not forgotten: "Mon âme est pleine de mensonge, comme la mer agile et forte sous la vocation de l'éloquence." One thing only is certain: the man who resists the temptation of the adventure, who refuses joy to conserve his sadness, is not worthy of being a man: "mon avis est qu'on le tue" (to be compared with I, 151, "je lui fais peu crédit au commerce de l'âme . . .").

Reproaches to the sun continue in the fourth paragraph; his eloquence had been entirely mendacious: "Mieux dit: nous t'avisons, Rhéteur! de nos profits incalculables." He is, moreover, a poor judge. Fortunately, he has not prevented the man's enthusiasm, then the joy which is expressed thus: "Roses, pourpre délice: la terre vaste à mon désir, et qui en posera les limites ce soir?" This last idea, equating the man's unlimited desire with the unlimited expanse of the earth—the ambition and the adventure—will be applied in Chant VII to his heart: "Tant de douceur au cœur de l'homme, se peut-il qu'elle faille à trouver sa mesure?" and again in Chant VIII: "(A la mesure de nos cœurs fut tant d'absence consommée!)." It will be repeated also in the next sentence in this same paragraph, applied now to the adventurer's violence: "la violence au cœur du sage, et qui en posera les limites ce soir? . . ."; once more, we must refer to other cantos, to VI, 171, "nos habitudes de violence," and to the end of Chant VIII: "Un grand principe de violence commandait à nos mœurs." The paragraph concludes with an idea, once more a source of joy, that will be constant in *Anabase,* the idea that any man whatsoever may lead his fellows to the adventure: "Et un tel, fils d'un tel, homme pauvre, / vient au pouvoir des signes et des songes." The same idea is found again at the end of Chant IV: "Et un homme s'avança à l'entrée du Désert—profession de son père: marchand de flacons."

The opposition continues: just as the narrator said, in Chant I, "Je ne tracerai point de grands quartiers de villes . . . ," so he says in the fifth paragraph of this Chant III: "Tracez les routes où s'en aillent les gens de toute race, montrant cette couleur jaune du talon. . . ." With "les gens de toute race" (and he will even make here a short enumeration) the narrator generalizes the adventure, as he will tend to do increasingly; "cette couleur jaune" is everywhere the color of the march across the deserts (compare V, 167: "la lumière jaune," VII, 175: "ces terres jaunes, notre délice," X, 192: "mon plaisir, dit-il, est dans cette couleur jaune"). Having enumerated briefly the adventurers, he gives a small list of men who, without being truly adventurers, accompany the expedition: the priest, the grammarian, the tailor; their activity foretells the founding of the city. The joy of the true adventurer increases when he compares himself (at the end of the paragraph) to "l'homme atteint de gonorrhée," to the "malingre."

Certain ideas already exploited in this Chant, plus a few new ones, make up the last paragraph. "L'eau plus pure qu'en des songes" (of the third paragraph) here becomes "l'eau plus pure qu'en Jabal," where the biblical allusion (Gen. IV, 7) recalls a nomadic existence in ancient times. That is the meaning, I think, of "ce bruit d'un autre âge," along with all the noises that announce and that accompany the adventure. The time of this anabasis becomes "le plus long jour de l'année chauve" (compare, in the first Chanson, "le plus grand des arbres de l'année" and "la plus belle robe de l'année"). "Chauve" is juxtaposed to "la terre sous l'herbage," the desert to cultivated lands. This assertion of a principle of life brings the negation of the opposite principle: the dead are scorned, just as the counsels of the sun and the weakness of the malingerer have been rejected: "Et des morts sous le sable et l'urine et le sel de la terre [elements of the adventure, of life, of desire], voici qu'il en est fait comme de la bale dont le grain fut donné aux oiseaux." For the soul and life win out: "Et mon âme, mon âme veille à grand bruit aux portes de la mort" (for "à grand bruit," compare CH I, 146: "et voici d'un grand bruit"). However, death will necessarily be found at the end of the road; the foal will become the dead horse: "à bout de lance parmi nous / ce crâne de cheval."

Perhaps we could say that in this third Chant two methods are used for the expression of joy, a positive method and a negative method; a positive method, in so far as objects are evoked—all related to the adventure—that are capable of satisfying the desires, the ambitions, the hopes of man; a negative method, in so far as everything that might be opposed to the adventure is named, denied, rejected. The poetic emotion, aware of the obstacles that have been overcome, turns more completely to the joy that constitutes the basic emotion of the whole poem.

Chant IV. In the fourth Chant, finally, we find the capital event that completes and crowns the first stage of the adventure: the founding of the city. This founding is not in itself a simple source of a simple joy. Rather, the narrator's joy is complicated by the addition of other passions: by the desire and the expectation of sexual pleasure and of the other pleasures that make up material well-being; by the hope of ploughing and building; by the knowledge that one brings to less advanced peoples all the fruits of one's soul; by the ambition, finally, of leaving again for the next adventure. Through this fourth Chant will come, one by one, all those objects and all those thoughts that are capable of arousing these divers emotions.

In fact, at the very beginning, the founding itself is described as a fairly natural and ordinary episode: "C'est là le train du monde et je n'ai que du bien à en dire.—Fondation de la ville"; a little later (IV, 161), "Ainsi la ville fut fondée. . . ." But the feeling is entirely different when one passes from the state of nomad to the state of city-dweller: "Les campements s'annulent aux collines!" (we remember the "leveurs de campements," I, 151). The adventurers are now in a new world where happiness will soon be theirs: "tête nue et pieds nus dans la fraîcheur du monde, / qu'avons-nous donc à rire, mais qu'avons-nous à rire, sur nos sièges, pour un débarquement de filles et de mules?" Soon they will use these mules; the image will be rich and beautiful: "O mules . . . quatre têtes rétives au nœud du poing font un vivant corymbe sur l'azur" (162); soon, also, the girls will settle in: "la ville jaune, casquée d'ombre, avec ses caleçons de filles aux fenêtres" (163). A similar joy accompanies another sign of civilization: "et qu'est-ce à dire, depuis l'aube, de tout ce peuple sous les voiles?—Des arrivages de farines! . . ." (161).

Greater still, however, is the joy of having changed the desert into fertile soil and of having offered civilization to primitive peoples. Right from the beginning of the Chant we note changes in the aspect of the land: "le navigateur en mer atteint de nos fumées vit que la terre, jusqu'au faîte, avait changé d'image (de grands éco-buages [the "feux de ronces à l'aurore" of a few lines earlier] vus du large et ces travaux de captation d'eaux vives en montagne)." In the next paragraph, the announcement of similar works that remain to be done: "les vaisseaux . . . , ayant franchi la barre, s'arrêtaient / en ce point mort où flotte un âne mort. (Il s'agit d'arbitrer ce fleuve pâle, sans destin, d'une couleur de sauterelles écrasées dans leur sève.)" And toward the end, a generalization on the arrival of man in this desert: ". . . Solitude! l'œuf bleu que pond un grand oiseau de mer, et les baies au matin tout encombrées de citrons d'or!—C'était hier! L'oiseau s'en fut! / Demain les fêtes. . . ." The passage begin-ning with "Solitude!" prepares the lyrical form of the following Chant, where it will be repeated three times; it also prepares that canto's general idea.

For the meeting with the indigenous peoples, we must return once more to the sentence in Chant I: "Je ne hélerai point les gens d'une autre rive." Here, in Chant IV, the opposition is completed; they have indeed arrived at the other shore: "Au grand bruit frais de l'autre rive" (161; we recall "la fraîcheur du monde" just above); and they go far beyond "hailing" these people, they ally themselves with them: "Et ce n'est point le lieu de vous conter nos alliances avec les gens de l'autre rive; l'eau offerte dans des outres, les prestations de cavalerie pour les travaux du port et les princes payés en monnaie de poissons" (162–63). Other alliances of the same kind will take place later; at VI, 170: "les alliances par les femmes au sein des peuples dissolus," at X, 194: "les cavaliers porteurs de lettres d'al-liances." Perhaps it would not be an exaggeration to say that the arrival of these men drives out death, introduces life. In any event, numerous images of death are associated, in this Chant, with the land and the indigenous people. We have already seen, in the river, "ce point mort où flotte un âne mort"; we see, a little later, the "(Crépitements d'insectes à jamais dans ce quartier au détritus!)," and this reminds us of the "pays fréquentés de criquets à midi" (II, 154); later, "Un enfant triste comme la mort des singes"; finally, "les services de voierie emportant à l'aurore de grands morceaux de palmes mortes, débris d'ailes géantes. . . ." In a way, this is the end of the reign of nature, the beginning of the reign of man; this means that the "mort des singes" may be considered as the "sœur aînée d'une grande beauté" (IV, 163), that is, as the predecessor of man's death.

As for the men who found the city, they bring with them all of civilization: not only the products and the processes but also the most refined institutions, the asylums, the libraries, the "constructions très fraîches pour les produits pharmaceutiques," the banks. Even religion: "Et déjà par les rues un homme chantait seul, de ceux qui peignent sur leur front le chiffre de leur Dieu." Festivals, mobs, "les avenues plantées d'arbres à gousses," "les élections de magistrats du port, les vocalises aux banlieues."

Nevertheless—for there must be a poetic preparation for the future departures and for the perpetual continuation of the anabasis—the man thinks already of a new adventure. There is, at the end of Chant IV, a short section separated from the rest in which a new departure takes place. Camp is struck "à la troisième lunaison"; in a mythological rite "On fit brûler un corps de femme dans les sables" ("l'acide corps de femme," II, 154); an unknown man becomes head of the expedition: "Et un homme s'avança à l'entrée du Désert—profession de son père: marchand de flacons."

By means of this last section, the event recounted in Chant IV is split into two: founding of the city, departure. But as in the preceding cantos, the event itself is the least important element. What is important is the accumulation of objects and of actions that constitute the event, and the slow development through the canto of the central emotion. In Chant IV, that emotion is enriched and diversified. It is no longer either the "pépiement de joie" or the vast enthusiasm of the preceding canto, but rather a sober and civilized joy in which one part, at least, is the sense of a humanitarian and civilizing mission—a mission of the soul.

Chant V. Like the second Chant, the fifth is a song. It is composed of some twenty short paragraphs, of about equal length, having a very strong and very complex rhythmical movement. No event at all; but that does not mean that the poem makes no progress through this Chant. On the contrary, one of the essential steps for the total conception of *Anabase* is made here: we pass from the single adventure, the narrator's first, to a multitude of adventures that will constitute the history of the whole human race. To bring about this passage, Chant V will reintroduce the three main persons —the Étranger, the narrator, and the poet—and it will repeat, in a general form, a large number of ideas entering into the series: invitation, hesitation, departure, anabasis, city. Likewise, the geography will be generalized; the whole Earth will become the territory of the adventure, the cities will be multiplied, celestial bodies will be added to our own planet.

The narrator himself makes this multiplication in his first sentence: "Pour mon âme mêlée aux affaires lointaines, cent feux de villes avivés par l'aboiement des chiens . . ." (the woman, in Chant IX, will speak of "l'aboiement des chiens" and of "l'aboiement des chiens de toute la terre," IX, 185, 186). The second sentence begins with "Solitude," referring to the preceding canto; it speaks again of "nos façons" and makes the fundamental revelation: "mais nos pensées déjà campaient sous d'autres murs." Then the Stranger intervenes, with his invitation that is at the same time a reproach: "Je n'ai dit à personne d'attendre . . . Je vous hais tous avec douceur . . ."; and he scolds the poet in a passage that we have already seen. Then the narrator, seeing himself as another Moses, accepts the responsibility, not without wondering how they will pass from the state of dream to the state of action. In the following three sentences (of which the first begins again with "Solitude!"), all the stars of heaven present their arguments to the narrator, repeating in this way the invitation. But the narrator remains in a state of inactivity: the eighth sentence, at the beginning, recognizes this state: "Ame jointe en silence au bitume des Mortes!"; and it even praises that same state: "cousues d'aiguilles nos paupières! louée l'attente sous nos cils!" The sentence makes a double allusion; it refers to the fourth sentence of the same Chant, "où trouver l'eau nocturne qui lavera nos yeux?" and it prepares two passages of Chant VII: VII, 176, "De la fissure des paupières au fil des cimes m'unissant" and VII, 177, "l'homme clôt ses paupières." The praise of what will soon be called "l'activité du songe" continues: the milk and honey of the dream and of the pleasure in woman: "Fruit de la femme, ô Sabéenne! . . ."

Then comes the reversal, as in the first cantos. The narrator, in his thought, rebels against the dreams—"les pures pestilences de la nuit," 166—and decides to depart (in the morning, as usual): "je m'en irai avec les oies sauvages, dans l'odeur fade du matin! . . ." The following two sentences (twelfth and thirteenth) pick up numerous allusions: "Ha! quand l'étoile s'anuitait au quartier des servantes [cf. the fifth sentence], savions-nous que déjà [cf. I, 150: 'Aux ides pures du matin que savons-nous du songe, notre aînesse?'] tant de lances nouvelles [cf. I, 151: 'toutes lances de l'esprit'] poursuivaient au désert [cf. IV, 164] les silicates de l'Eté?" We note, in the last formula, the silicates (containing salt) and the summer (normal season of the departures). The following words, "Aurore, vous contiez . . . ," recall the promise of morning (opposed to that of night), "Les armes au matin sont belles et la mer" (I, 149), whereas the "Ablutions aux rives des Mers Mortes" finally produce "l'eau nocturne qui lavera nos yeux" (V, 165). They can now leave. Therefore all arise: "Le vieillard bouge des paupières dans la lumière jaune"; the woman arises; and as he must for the departure, the foal reappears: "le poulain poisseux met son menton barbu dans la main de l'enfant." We know that they are still in a time of innocence, for the child "ne rêve pas encore de lui crever un œil. . . ."

The final movement of the Chant, composed of three sentences, belongs to the Stranger and the poet. The Stranger repeats his formula: "Solitude! Je n'ai dit à personne d'attendre" and he declares his intention to depart: "Je m'en irai par là quand je voudrai. . . ." Through the thought expressed in his invitation he "se fait encore des partisans dans les voies du silence"; and through this victory of soul he becomes such that "il n'y a plus en lui substance d'homme." The Chant ends with the notion of the voyage generalized to the utmost and with that of the poet who relates it: "Et la terre en ses graines ailées comme un poète en ses propos, voyage. . . ."

The fifth Chant recounts anew, then, the contents of the preceding cantos. Because of its many allusions to those cantos, it can be brief and concise; and through its lyrical form, it can contain all the emotion appropriate to this vast content. But there are no repetitions, since the single departure of the initial anabasis is transformed, in this Chant, into a multiplicity of departures; the anabasis becomes the Anabasis, the "chant de tout un peuple, le plus ivre." Our emotion, as we read it, is transformed and generalized accordingly.

Chant VI. Through its narrative content the sixth Chant follows directly upon the fifth; the multiple adventures terminate in the founding of numerous cities. All the elements that contributed to the establishment of the single city—works, alliances, pleasure—will enter into these new establishments, including man's tendency forever to start out again, never to be still and satisfied. We find here an element of repetition, of insistence, which has as its aim to deepen and to solidify the emotion of joy; for this joy will dominate more and more.

At the very beginning, various elements are combined; power passes from the sun to man, the city becomes plural, man is established on the heights, the perfumed girls arrive. Hence happiness: "nous établîmes en haut lieu nos pièges au bonheur. / Abondance et bien-être, bonheur!" The marks of luxury appear: ice in the glasses, golden plates, servant girls; the narrator says that they "fauchaient l'ennui des sables aux limites du monde," thus indicating the extent of the adventure. "Puis ce fut une année de souffles en Ouest," and the invitation is made once more. This time it is for an adventure by sea: "toiles vives adonnées au délice du large," "cavaliers au fil des caps," "publiaient sur les mers." The "ardente chronique" published over these seas is at once the history and the song announced in the first Chanson; and, in fact, this whole sentence (VI, 170) is modeled after the first Chanson: "Certes! une histoire pour les hommes, un chant de force pour les hommes, comme un frémissement du large dans un arbre de fer." The iron age after the bronze age. The alliances with the "others" come afterwards: "lois données sur d'autres rives, et les alliances par les femmes au sein des peuples dissolus." With the "hauts plateaux pacifiés," we hear once more about what these civilized men bring to indigenous peoples.

As he has already done twice before (I, 151 and III, 157), the narrator expresses here his contempt for the man who has not dared to set out (the man he almost was himself!): "Ceux-là qui en naissant n'ont point flairé de telle braise ['l'odeur solennelle des roses,' 170], qu'ont-ils à faire parmi nous? et se peut-il qu'ils aient commerce de vivants?" The Stranger rejects him also: "C'est votre affaire et non la mienne de régner sur l'absence. . . ." The true adventurers, however, have done "extraordinary" things and have found the joy that they sought: "et nous portant dans nos actions à la limite de nos forces, notre joie parmi vous fut une très grande joie."

In a long speech that occupies almost half of Chant VI, the Stranger says to men what he must always say to them: he repeats the invitation, he promises happiness through pleasure and through the civilizing mission. (I think that it is the Stranger who is speaking here, although he identifies himself with the others by the use of "nous.") He speaks to the others in a moment of halt: "Je connais cette race établie sur les pentes: cavaliers démontés dans les cultures vivrières"; but it is in order to speak to them again of the renewed departure: "un immense péril à courir avec nous! des actions sans nombre et sans mesure." It is only through new adventures, he says, that men will attain the maximum of their human capacity: "des volontés puissantes et dissipatrices et le pouvoir de l'homme consommé comme la grappe dans la vigne." An echo, here, of the "limits" of human desire (III, 158) and of the "measure" of the human heart (VIII, 179). And he mentions the joys of the voyage itself, "nos façons d'agir," and the role of the civilizers: "assembleurs de nations sous de vastes hangars." In a second paragraph, this a short one, he emphasizes "l'histoire de leur goût," noting once more that these unknown men become immortal—"les capitaines pauvres dans les voies immortelles"—and that barbarian peoples ally themselves with them. With respect to the generalization that takes place in this Chant, we should note that whereas in Chant III the adventurers received the Kings, the Ambassador, and the Inspector of weights and measures, here it is the turn of the "notables en foule venus pour nous saluer." The Stranger recounts finally "les choses de la paix: aux pays infestés de bien-être"; a long enumeration includes women, spices, alliances ("les traités d'amitié et de délimitation"), river dams (we remember Chant IV: "Il s'agit d'arbitrer ce fleuve pâle"), all kinds of constructions and institutions. The "homme enthousiasmé" of III, 158 becomes "les pays enthousiasmés"; the "poulain" is born once more; and they envision—a promise of happiness—"la descente, un soir, dans les provinces maritimes, vers nos pays de grand loisir et vers nos filles / parfumées, qui nous apaiseront d'un souffle, ces tissus. . . ."

It is the narrator who, in a final section, speaks of his "singulier destin." His adventure, the activity belonging to the day and the march towards the west, brings him immortality: "de ce côté du monde, le plus vaste, où le pouvoir s'exile chaque soir, [that is to say, where the sun sets] tout un veuvage de lauriers!" His respite, the activity of evening, comes in his cities, with his women: "et les vents calmes [to be contrasted with II, 155: 'Le vent se lève'] hébergeaient au fond des golfes désertiques [to be contrasted with VI, 170, the 'toiles vives adonnées au délice du large']."

Chant VII. The progression towards the universal anabasis, already noted, reaches its climax in the seventh Chant. The dimension of time, earlier suggested by the ages of man, is now added explicitly to the dimension of space, and both time and space receive their greatest development. Time is not only human time, where the generations of men follow until the end of all time, but it is also astronomical time, the infinite succession of centuries. Similarly, space comes to include not only this earth but the whole universe beyond. In spite of this expansion, the anabasis itself does not lose its human dimension; it remains within the "measure" of man, since the problems, the activities, and the results of the adventure are the same as they always were. For it is only in this way that joy (tempered here by a note of sadness) can continue to make itself felt. The universal anabasis will thus contain, essentially, the same elements as the particular anabasis.

"Nous n'habiterons pas toujours ces terres jaunes, notre délice . . ." They will leave these conquered lands not in order to conquer others, but because they will die. The narrator, recognizing this truth, foresees a whole succession of human generations which will assume the responsibility of the anabasis after his own death. This vision is expressed, throughout Chant VII, by images of repetition and succession; so the "tables de l'espace" and the "étages de climats" in the following sentence: "L'Été plus vaste que l'Empire suspend aux tables de l'espace plusieurs étages de climats." So the "pans de siècles en voyage" (176), the "Cavaleries du songe" (177), the "peuple de miroirs," the "suite des siècles," and the "cavaleries de bronze" (178). These images enlarge the framework of the general action, and this effect is enhanced also by the use of certain words ("vaste," for example) and certain conceptions. The following sentence, "La terre vaste sur son aire roule à pleins bords sa braise pâle sous les cendres," is completed farther along by a complementary idea, "toute la terre aux herbes s'allumant aux pailles de l'autre hiver," still farther by the indication of the place "où les peuples s'abolissent aux poudres mortes de la terre."

But in addition to these images, what contributes above all to the strong emotion of this Chant is the order of the ideas presented. We have already seen the first sentences: recognition of the approach of death, description of the movement of Earth through space. The second paragraph adds the notion of the yellow color ("couleur de choses immortelles") and of the vegetation that is renewed with the seasons. Immediately afterward comes a passage in which the relationship between man and the earth is established—the earth that is essentially inert and impure, man who purifies through knowledge and feeling. We saw in Chant V that man's eyelids, closed in his state of inertia, were opened by the ablutions of the departure; now, sight attaches man to the earth: "De la fissure des paupières au fil des cimes m'unissant, je sais la pierre tachée d'ouies. . . ." Likewise, his heart attaches him to everything living: "et mon cœur prend souci d'une famille d'acridiens. . . ." The whole earth becomes the object of his tenderness, which he expresses by personifying—or rather "animalizing"—the hills: "Chamelles douces sous la tonte"; for the earth nourishes man (compare the "ciel agraire" and the "bleuissements de vignes") and is the theater of his activity. In order to respond to this affection, the earth seems to participate in the adventure: "et [les collines] s'agenouillent à la fin, dans la fumée des songes [a little later it will be 'ces fumées de sable'], là où les peuples s'abolissent aux poudres mortes de la terre."

To the paean of man and of the earth that opens the Chant there now succeeds a kind of chant for the dead: "A voix plus basse pour les morts, à voix plus basse dans le jour." The narrator characterizes the whole complex of these feelings: "Tant de douceur au cœur de l'homme, se peut-il qu'elle faille à trouver sa mesure? . . ." Once more, man's destiny consists in finding the full realization of his spiritual capacities. Therefore the narrator returns to one of the formulas of the first Chanson: "Je vous parle, mon âme!—mon âme tout enténébrée d'un parfum de cheval!" This last expression is now completely clear; the soul's mission is so fully linked to the horse who helps the adventurer make his adventure that it takes on some of the qualities of the horse. The last phrase in the paragraph recalls the constant direction of the adventure—"quelques grands oiseaux de terre, naviguant en Ouest." Contrariwise, it is in the east that the whole anabasis (in the next paragraph) is prepared; this is the holy place, with its pale sky, its motionless clouds—features that must be opposed to the brilliant light of the desert and the "violettes de l'orage" (176). This is the place whence comes, we might say, the earth's movement: "où tournent les cancers du camphre et de la corne. . . ." In this last expression, the Tropics of Cancer and of Capricorn (astronomical indications) are transformed into human and terrestrial elements; there may even be, as in the "linges de l'aveugle," an allusion here to the impurity of the earth. Finally, the still clouds become "fumées" which the winds struggle to take from man; and as a result of all this preparation in the east, "la terre enfante des merveilles! . . ."

The rest of Chant VII is devoted to man's death and to his immortality through the anabasis. When, at noon (thus between "matin" and "soir" with their special meanings in this poem), "l'homme clôt ses paupières et rafraîchit sa nuque dans les âges," he joins the dead who have been so frequently mentioned. All his marches are marches toward death: "Cavaleries du songe au lieu des poudres mortes." And just as at the moment of halt the narrator asked, "où trouver l'eau nocturne qui lavera nos yeux?" (V, 165), so at the moment of death he must ask whence will come his successors: "où trouver, où trouver les guerriers qui garderont les fleuves dans leurs noces?" Note that these rivers are to be juxtaposed to the "fleuves morts" (176), as the new generations to the dead generations, and that everywhere in *Anabase* rivers and waters are objects of search and marks of the adventure. So the "grand bruit" of this adventure is called, immediately afterward, the "bruit des grandes eaux en marche sur la terre" (at VIII, 179 the adventurer will speak of the "clepsydres en marche sur la terre") and the salt of desire awakens men of the future: "tout le sel de la terre tressaille dans les songes." These are dreams, however, which will be dissipated by the call to the anabasis: "Et soudain, ha! soudain que nous veulent ces voix?" It is then that the narrator predicts the rebirth of rivers in the future (the poet exploits once more his images of repetition): "Levez un peuple de miroirs sur l'ossuaire des fleuves, qu'ils interjettent appel dans la suite des siècles!" For himself, he predicts the perpetuation of his memory in monuments of stone and bronze: "Levez des pierres à ma gloire, levez des pierres au silence, et à la garde de ces lieux les cavaleries de bronze vert sur de vastes chaussées! . . ."

A final sentence for the Chant: "(L'ombre d'un grand oiseau me passe sur la face)." A return, thus, to the "grands oiseaux de terre" and to "nos oiseaux de mer"; a return, also, of the "grand oiseau de mer" which "s'en fut" upon man's arrival (IV, 163), of the "oies sauvages" which fly away (V, 166), of the "aigles lumineuses" (VI, 170). In a word, the renewal of the adventure is here represented by the passage of the bird. And just as the narrator's soul can be "enténébrée" by the smell of the horse, his face can here receive the "ombre" of the bird; these are creatures that accompany the anabasis.

The emotion of joy of this seventh Chant is augmented by the addition of such elements as man's softness, his tenderness toward the earth and toward all forms of life, his pity for the dead, his knowledge of his own death, his assurance that posterity will thank him for his adventure. There is, also, the nobility of the spirit which, at the moment of its demise, passes on its mission and its responsibility to its successors. We have seen a similar increase and diversification of the emotion in the sixth Chant, by means of still other elements. As a result of the general movement in this direction, the poem is never static in its effects, just as it is always dynamic in its narrative basis.

Chant VIII. Although it is very brief, the eighth Chant is very complex in structure; it is made up of five distinct sections, each of which has a separate aim. It is, in general, the canto of the consummation of promises, of the satisfaction of desires. This is different from the founding of cities and the conquest of countries: the satisfactions are those of the soul. We thus begin to enter into the "denouement" of the emotion, into the production of a joy that is to some degree calmed, tempered, purified.

Without wishing to be too systematic, I believe that each one of the five sections designates another kind of consummation. In the first, speaking for all men, the narrator continues the story of the anabasis. At the halts, cities are founded and laws are established— including those pertaining to horses: "Lois sur la vente des juments. Lois errantes. Et nous-mêmes." Just as in the preceding Chant he gave to the earth the "couleur des choses immortelles," so here he gives to this adventure the "(Couleur d'hommes)." Then, borrowing elements from the same Chant, and especially from "l'orage" (VII, 176), he associates natural phenomena with man's marches: "Nos compagnons ces hautes trombes en voyage [cf. VII, 176: 'des pans de siècles en voyage'], clepsydres [the march of time, calculated by water] en marche sur la terre [cf. VII, 178: 'grandes eaux en marche sur la terre'], / et les averses solennelles, d'une substance merveilleuse [cf. VII, 177: 'la terre enfante des merveilles!'], tissées de poudres [cf. VII, 176, 177] et d'insectes [cf. VII, 177], qui poursuivaient nos peuples dans les sables [cf. VII, 176: 'là où les peuples s'abolissent'] comme l'impôt de capitation." (If I give so many cross-references, it is in order to show how fully this Chant depends upon the preceding one—and, at the same time, to emphasize how Perse composes on the basis of a limited number of poetic ingredients.) Then comes the consummation: "(A la mesure de nos cœurs fut tant d'absence consommée!); the "mesure de nos cœurs" refers to VII, 177, "Tant de douceur, etc." and "l'absence" to VI, 171: "C'est votre affaire et non la mienne de régner sur l'absence." The consummation, here, is the heart's, rewarded for its softness and its tenderness.

In the second section the narrator finds his satisfaction in the halts, the stages, that concluded the marches: "Non que l'étape fût stérile. . . ." Now it is the consummation of the soul, of the spirit: "beaucoup de choses entreprises sur les ténèbres de l'esprit—beaucoup de choses à loisir sur les frontières de l'esprit." Note that the mention of the "ténèbres" follows immediately upon that of the horses ("mon âme enténébrée, etc.") and that leisure is always associated with the cities (cf. VI, 173). The composition and the meaning of the rest of this sentence—"grandes histoires séleucides au sifflement des frondes et la terre livrée aux explications . . ."—are extremely complicated. The "grandes histoires" clearly take up the idea of the histories and the chronicles that are to immortalize the adventure. But what about "séleucides"? I think that the meaning is double: turning backward toward "histoires," "Séleucides" takes its capital letter and refers to the ancient kings and people of that name; but looking forward to "frondes" it designates the bird of the same name—a bird that accompanies or marks the anabasis. It is the mind that gives the "explications" of the halts—hence something different from the summary of the earlier marches in the first Chant: "A nos chevaux livrée la terre . . ." (I, 149).

This consummation, being human, cannot however be either perfect or complete; man is only man. The fact is recognized by the narrator in a second paragraph of this section, and he says so by collecting together the constant elements of the poem: "Autre chose: ces ombres—les prévarications du ciel contre la terre. . . ." If light is perfection, shadow is imperfection—a lie of the heavens like those of Chant III. Then, assuming the role of the rider ("Cavaliers . . . lèverons-nous le fouet . . . mots hongres"), he speaks of the hatred that spoils the happiness of "telles familles humaines" (cf. VI, 171: "tant de familles à composer"). The answer to his question is negative: no, man must not punish anything that belongs to his nature as man. He must admit that his measure is human: "Homme, pèse ton poids calculé en froment"; and that certain things are outside the range of his possibilities: "Un pays-ci n'est point le mien. Que m'a donné le monde que ce mouvement d'herbes? . . ."

The third section continues the anabasis of the second and brings it to its final conclusion: "Jusqu'au lieu dit de l'Arbre Sec" (this may be the "arbre jujubier" of VII, 177, the rendezvous of death). The adventure begun under the "arbre de bronze" ends under the dry tree, for we have here the consummation of death. Thus the halt in the "provinces en Ouest," fixed by the "éclair famélique" (which belongs to the storm), is only the penultimate halt; the last one takes place in the land of death: "Mais au delà sont les plus grands loisirs, et dans un grand / pays d'herbages sans mémoire. . . ." There, time is eternal and indivisible: "l'année sans liens et sans anniversaires, assaisonnée [i.e., having as seasons] d'aurores et de feux." The departure for those lands is announced, as are the other departures, by a sacrifice: "(Sacrifice au matin d'un cœur de mouton noir)."

The consummation of the promise of "une herbe" is found in the fourth section; remembering the "chemins de toute la terre" of the first Chanson, the narrator says: "Chemins du monde, l'un vous suit." And recalling the poor man who has come "au pouvoir des signes et des songes" (III, 158), he speaks of his own "Autorité sur tous les signes de la terre." Then, having identified the voyage as that of the soul—"O Voyageur dans le vent jaune, goût de l'âme! . . ."—he notes the "vertus enivrantes" of the herb that has been found at last: "et la graine, dis-tu, du cocculus indien possède, qu'on la broie! des vertus enivrantes."

One single sentence makes up the fifth section: "Un grand principe de violence commandait à nos mœurs." It marks, I think, another of the limits reached, especially if we relate it to III, 158: "la violence au cœur du sage, et qui en posera les limites ce soir? . . ." and to VI, 171: "nos habitudes de violence." This is the consummation of that principle of activity which, contrary to that of the dream and of inactivity, makes the anabasis possible.

Chant IX. There remained, however, another consummation to be made, that of pleasure and of love. The narrator's hesitations at the beginning had come in part from his desire to remain with woman, and his decision to leave brought with it, in a way, the abandonment of woman ("la Reine" and "Sa fille"). But so that this abandonment might not be permanent (a thing beyond the "measure" of man), woman had to reappear at each stage; this explains the "débarque-ment de filles" and "nos filles parfumées." It was necessary, more-over, if the generations were to succeed one another, that love should take the place of pleasure, that women should take the place of girls. That is what happens in the ninth Chant. The woman who appears there, however, is not merely the companion of man; she is also a prophetess, a kind of sibyl who predicts man's future because she knows all of his past and all the details of his adventure. The Chant begins with a short speech by the narrator, followed by a long prophecy by the woman; another sentence by the narrator ends it.

At first, the narrator summarizes his whole adventure: "Depuis un si long temps que nous allions en Ouest"; and, alluding indi-rectly to the "choses immortelles" of Chant VII, he characterizes it: "que savions-nous des choses périssables?" After the march, the halt: "et soudain à nos pieds les premières fumées," and at the halt, woman: "—Jeunes femmes! et la nature d'un pays s'en trouve toute parfumée." This last phrase is an important variant on the formula used in Chant VI.

It is then that the prophetess begins to speak. She will make four predictions, using a single formula to introduce all of them: "Je t'annonce les temps d'une grande chaleur . . . ," but alternating in it "chaleur" with "faveur." The order will be "chaleur," "faveur," "chaleur," "faveur" (with two uses of "faveur" in the last predic-tion). In the first prediction she announces (along with the "grande chaleur") "les veuves criardes sur la dissipation des morts"; this is the reproach that woman makes to man for having left her, for having preferred the adventure. The same preference is contained in several expressions of the following sentence: "l'usage et le soin du silence," "assis sur les hauteurs," "considèrent les sables / et la célébrité du jour." The "rades foraines" represent the departure and the absence. But the woman insists that there is another pleasure, one really preferable: "mais le plaisir au flanc des femmes se com-pose"; it is as strong as the pleasure of the adventure: "et dans nos corps de femmes [cf. 'acide corps de femme,' II, 154] il y a comme un ferment de raisin noir [cf. 'homme enthousiasmé d'un vin,' III, 158]."

In the second prediction she announces (along with the "grande faveur") "la félicité des feuilles dans nos songes." "Félicité" is "plaisir" augmented. The "songes" being the activity of evening and night, and the "feuilles" signifying the tree of the invitation, what the woman promises here is a pleasure (with her) comparable to that of the anabasis. Since those who had been, at the beginning, the "chercheurs de points d'eau sur l'écorce du monde" (I, 152) have become, as a result of the adventure, "ceux qui savent les sources"; and since woman is now with them "dans cet exil" (cf. I, 152, "les tambours de l'exil"), they can consummate the promise of sexual pleasure and of generation. Pleasure is expressed in the formula "sous quelles mains pressant la vigne de nos flancs," a formula that goes back to "un ferment de raisin noir" as well as to another consummation: "le pouvoir de l'homme consommé comme la grappe dans la vigne" (VI, 171). Generation is expressed in what follows—not only in the words "nos corps s'emplissent d'une salive," but also in the flight of the locust; if the presence of the locust ("aux pays fréquentés de criquets à midi," II, 154) means the absence of human life, its departure may well announce the arrival of human life.

The third prediction is really not a prediction at all. The woman is going to speak to the Étranger, and since "il n'y a plus en lui substance d'homme," she cannot foresee exactly his ways in love. What are the "amours" of the mind and of the soul? Having located the pleasure of life in the "soir" (184), the prophetess now situates it in the night, transforming night into a lover: "et pareillement la nuit, sous l'aboiement des chiens, trait son plaisir au flanc des femmes." The Stranger, at night, lives alone: "Mais l'Étranger vit sous sa tente, honoré de laitages, de fruits." Even his ablutions are made in solitude: "On lui apporte de l'eau fraîche / pour y laver sa bouche, son visage et son sexe." His loves, also, are brought to him: "On lui mène à la nuit de grandes femmes bréhaignes (ha! plus nocturnes dans le jour!)"; the sterility of these women gives a special character to the Stranger's love, just as the use of a term proper to mares makes us think of "l'âme enténébrée d'un parfum de cheval." But why should these women be "plus nocturnes dans le jour"? We may suggest the hypothesis that, being sterile, they carry even into the day their "nocturnal" principle of inactivity. The prophetess adds a "peut-être" to her only prediction in this passage: "Et peut-être aussi de moi tirera-t-il son plaisir"; and adapting to the present situation the formula of the first Chanson, "l'Étranger à ses façons," she concludes: "(Je ne sais quelles sont ses façons d'être avec les femmes)."

Her last prediction develops the possibility that she herself might be acceptable to the Étranger. The initial sentence promises, along with the "grande faveur," "la félicité des sources dans nos songes." Then she offers herself for examination, in terms which suggest— albeit vaguely and delicately—the way in which one examines a horse: "Ouvre ma bouche dans la lumière . . . , et si l'on trouve faute en moi, que je sois congédiée!" The intercalation of the phrase "ainsi qu'un lieu de miel entre les roches" insists again upon the pleasure. If she is acceptable, she will go "sous la tente, . . . près de la cruche [the jug of cold water, 186]"—these details identify the Stranger—to offer herself to him. There is in her offer something extraordinary, supernatural; the Stranger will become for her the "compagnon de l'angle du tombeau"—the idea of death intervenes— and she herself will remain mute (whereas she said, earlier, "et de répit avec nous-mêmes il n'en est point," 184). She sees herself as composed of two elements that were prominent in the first Chanson, as she describes "l'arbre-fille de mes veines"—all of which, in the first Chanson, is clearly connected with the soul. She puts, in the tent, "un lit d'instances" (to be taken, I suppose, figuratively) and "l'étoile verte dans la cruche"; does she thereby associate with this episode all the celestial bodies that had already figured in *Anabase*? And she sees herself there as absolutely alone with the Stranger. Even in her "façons d'être" with him, she is different from other women; silent, she will leave "avant le jour sans éveiller l'étoile verte"; she will not conceive, leaving "le criquet sur le seuil"; her silent departure will prevent "l'aboiement des chiens de toute la terre." In a word, she identifies herself fully with silence, with night, with the soul, with all the qualities proper to the Stranger and to his invitation. (Note that "l'aboiement des chiens de toute la terre" repeats the phrase of V, 165, "cent feux de villes avivés par l'aboiement des chiens . . . ," a passage which in turn refers to one halt in the adventure.) At the very end of this prediction, the woman promises "la félicité du soir sur nos paupières périssables," uniting the notions (heretofore separate) of "paupières" and of "périssables"; then, in a sudden turn, she realizes the futility of her offer: "mais pour l'instant encore c'est le jour!"

This permits the narrator to complete his sentence, left unfinished when the woman began to speak. For him, too, it is day: "—et debout sur la tranche éclatante du jour"; it is the moment of the arrival: "au seuil d'un grand pays"; in a land that does not yet know love: "plus chaste que la mort." The woman's place is again taken by the girls, in a primitive society: "les filles urinaient en écartant la toile peinte de leur robe." And this image is opposed, once again, to what the narrator said at the end of the first Chanson: "Je vous salue, ma fille, sous la plus belle robe de l'année."

The joy that one feels in this ninth Chant is a mixed and limited joy; for on the one hand there are the reproaches and the sadness of the women widowed by the adventure, on the other hand there is the solitude and the isolation of the Stranger. Nevertheless, the adventurer (now multiple) finds the pleasure and the love that he had abandoned on leaving, and they constitute his last consummation, hence his last joy. As is the case for the Chants that immediately precede it, this one produces an emotion enriched and deepened by the intermixture of feelings related to the dominant one.

Chant X. The last Chant, the longest of all, is in many ways the simplest. The narrator's story, as a historical account, and the narrator himself disappear for the time being. He is replaced by the poet, who speaks to us directly—to us, men of the present; for we are in the present, and the poet invites us to consider and to judge the whole adventure that has just been told. We will judge it by what it has produced through the centuries, by objects, institutions, men, those that remain as well as those that have disappeared. The poet will therefore present to us a very long enumeration of these productions; the art of enumeration, practiced in several earlier Chants, will here be pushed to the maximum. The list will occupy the greater part of this tenth Chant. We must not, however, consider ourselves as strangers, as men who look at the anabasis from outside. Rather, we are the most recent generation—but not the last—of adventurers, and we judge the past in order better to prepare the future.

First, the observation post that we are to select and the attitude that we are to adopt: on one of the heights reached by the anabasis, a large hat on our heads: "Fais choix d'un grand chapeau dont on séduit le bord. . . . Par la porte de craie vive on voit les choses de la plaine." "On" rather than "je" or "nous," since it is no longer the narrator who speaks. From this height, we look far into time as well as far into space: "L'œil recule d'un siècle aux provinces de l'âme"; and I hardly need repeat that this adventure of the soul has made conquests for the soul. From this height we see—not the "choses immortelles" of Chant VII, nor the "choses périssables" of Chant IX —but the "choses vivantes, ô choses excellentes!" The formula will be repeated a little later: "beaucoup de choses sur la terre à entendre et à voir, choses vivantes parmi nous!" It is proper that *Anabase* should end on a note of "choses vivantes," if by this we mean the life of the spirit; for the whole adventure has taken place, literally and figuratively, in order to replace dead things, inert matter, inactivity, by the things of life. These are the only truly "excellent" ones.

The first short list of these things carries us back in time, to fairly primitive epochs. (Perhaps we should see in the "oiseaux verts dans les cours en l'honneur des vieillards" a harking back to III, 157: "l'oiseau chante: 'ô vieillesse! . . .'") The second list, concerning civilizations almost as ancient, also refers to phenomena noted throughout the adventure. Thus the "célébrations de fêtes" (189) refers to IV, 163: "Demain les fêtes"; and the "dédicaces de pierres noires" to VI, 170: "nos toits lestés de pierres noires." A third list, introduced by the formula "bien d'autres choses encore à hauteur de nos tempes," presents things that are more closely linked to the spirit, more civilized: habits, customs, institutions. Here, still more references to what has gone before. The "herbages" (189) recall not only the long presence of "herbes" throughout the poem (and their great importance), but above all the passage in VIII, 181: "pays d'herbages sans mémoire." The "enceintes de terre cuite et rose" and the "galeries" seem to split into two the building of IV, 162: "les galeries de latérite," whereas the "fondations d'hospices" are like the "fondateurs d'asiles" of IV, 162. Toward the end of the passage we find a formula, "les feux de ronces et d'épines" (190), which again combines two earlier expressions, I, 151: "ainsi qu'un feu d'épines" and IV, 160, "Des feux de ronces à l'aurore." The bread made of divers grains accomplishes another "consummation." The list is summarized in a final phrase: "et la fumée des hommes en tous lieux. . . ."

All these references, and many others that I have not pointed out, are essential for the structure of the poem. By means of them this retrospective Chant is linked to all the others, and the "things" that it mentions are at least in part known things. This is a way, also, of causing a part of the emotion that remains attached to these objects to pass over into the last Chant; therefore the continuity and the unity of the effect are assured.

From things the poet passes to men, taking as his point of departure the phrase "et la fumée des hommes en tous lieux." He continues: "ha! toutes sortes d'hommes dans leurs voies et façons," a formula that he repeats twice in the course of this long enumeration of categories of men, at X, 192, "tel homme et tel dans ses façons," and at X, 193 (identical with the first), "ha! toutes sortes d'hommes dans leurs voies et façons." The categories themselves are of the most varied: "mangeurs, . . . porteurs" (190), the professions and "l'homme de nul métier," "bien mieux, celui qui ne fait rien . . . et tant d'autres encore!" (192). Among these categories, the most useful men are the least important; the poet wishes to insist rather on those activities of the soul that bear with them their own aim, and, in second place, on those that have a humanitarian aim. We thus find an abundance of verbs and expressions like "tire son plaisir" (cf. IX, 185: "de moi tirera-t-il son plaisir"), "pour son plaisir," "s'y couche et repose," "pense à des dessins," "a fait des voyages et songe à repartir," "a vécu," "joue," "a des vues," "la plume est donnée, non vendue," "mon plaisir . . . est dans cette couleur jaune" (a yellow color, necessarily), "aime," "rêve," "épie le parfum de génie," "pense au corps de femme," "voit son âme," "versé dans les sciences," "fait un don," "bols . . . pour la soif," "ceux qui descendent de cheval pour ramasser des choses," "ceux qui peignent," "l'homme au bâton d'ivoire"—and many others. This is the whole spiritual, intellectual, artistic side of the human soul. The extraordinary quality, the strangeness of certain of these activities is introduced in order to add to the wonderment which, frequently in *Anabase,* accompanies the feeling of joy.

In the last category of men must necessarily figure the poet, companion of the adventurer since the beginning of the poem. The enumeration of men thus ends with "et soudain! apparu dans ses vêtements du soir et tranchant à la ronde toutes questions de préséance, le Conteur qui prend place au pied du térébinthe." There is, here, no self-glorification. Since the first Chanson, the "don du chant" and the vision of the "histoires" have made possible the existence, throughout the poem, of the poet and the historian, the two chroniclers who will bring immortality to the adventurers. The "Conteur," either poet or historian, will merit (through what he does) his priority over all other men. Thus at the beginning of the following paragraph it is he who tells stories: "O généalogiste sur la place! combien d'histoires de familles et de filiations?" The stories he tells are merely the stories lived by the adventurers; III, 157: "Ha! plus ample l'histoire de ces feuillages . . . ," VI, 170: "Certes! une histoire pour les hommes," VIII, 180: "grandes histoires séleucides." Another enumeration, devoted to these histories, follows in the text. It is divided into two lists; the "conteur" guarantees, first, the truth of his observations and the correctness of his judgments: "si je n'ai vu toute chose dans son ombre et le mérite de son âge"; then he recounts the things he was not able to see: "et par delà le cirque de mon œil, beaucoup d'actions secrètes en chemin." The things seen and the things guessed bear the usual relationship to the elements used earlier in the poem. We should point out especially, among the "devinées," events such as the "campements levés," "les cavaliers porteurs de lettres d'alliance," and—remembering the very beginning of *Anabase*—"les conversations muettes de deux hommes sous un arbre. . . ."

The general plan of *Anabase* makes it necessary for certain sequences of events to be observed at all times: march-halt-harvest-invitation-march, or adventure-founding-consummation-invitation-adventure. And this series must be constantly renewed and continued. That is why, in this last Chant, the retrospective glance is accompanied by signs of the next adventure. The poet summarizes and judges: "mais par dessus les actions des hommes sur la terre [this is the whole past], beaucoup de signes en voyage, beaucoup de graines en voyage ['signes' and 'graines' contain the invitation], et sous l'azyme du beau temps, dans un grand souffle de la terre ['souffles en Ouest' generalized], toute la plume des moissons! . . ." As always, this activity will continue until evening, will terminate in the purity of celestial heights: "jusqu'à l'heure du soir où l'étoile femelle, chose pure et gagée dans les hauteurs du ciel. . . ." A final paragraph presents the poet's last judgment; every element in it is meaningful. In "Terre arable du songe!" the poet transforms even the inactivity of the dream into activity; in "Qui parle de bâtir?" he prefers the departure to the founding. Then, continuing the vision of the seventh Chant, he says: "J'ai vu la terre distribuée en de vastes espaces," and he recognizes man's own responsibility and glory: "et ma pensée n'est point distraite du navigateur."

In this tenth and last Chant, the joy that one feels is the sum of all the other joys. It results especially from the immense satisfaction at seeing the adventure accomplished and completed, at discovering the great variety of purely human activities, at knowing that the activities of the soul predominate, at foreseeing the continuation of all these activities into an indefinite future. All extraneous elements are removed from the emotion, and by a kind of poetic purification, we are led into the final Chanson.

Chanson. Composed of three strophes, the final Chanson is in every way parallel, in its structure, to the first Chanson. It makes use also of certain elements introduced in the preceding canto. The parallelism is conscious: for what the first Chanson had begun, the final Chanson must end. Beginning and end of the poem, in a word. In the Chanson at the beginning, we discovered the invitation to the adventure; in the one at the end, we shall discover the last halt. But since, according to the organizing principles of *Anabase,* there can be no "last halt," the one that we have here represents rather a pause, a resting-place in the emotion created throughout the poem. Joy, here, reaches its maximum point.

The first part of the first sentence brings to conclusion two ideas introduced in the other Chanson; "Mon cheval arrêté" realizes all the possibilities contained in "Il naissait un poulain," and "sous l'arbre plein de tourterelles" presents the exact opposite of what we had in "sous les feuilles de bronze." I have already indicated the importance of this passage from inert matter to life. When the narrator says, next, "je siffle un sifflement si pur," he gives to his own narrative, to his attitude toward what he has done, the same purity that he has everywhere accorded to ideas, to the sky, to the waters, and so forth. Purity corresponds to perfection, to consummation. The rest of the sentence, "qu'il n'est promesses à leurs rives que tiennent tous ces fleuves," is explained by its allusions to Chant I. Since the banks of the rivers are the habitation of other peoples (cf. I, 150) and hence the place whence comes the breath of the invitation (cf. I, 152), what they "promise" is the departure, the march, the civilizing halt. Therefore I think that we must complete this sentence somewhat as follows: ". . . that would be capable of tempting me hereafter"; the purity of the whistling would, moreover, be an argument in favor of this interpretation. The allusions to Chant I continue in the parenthesis that completes the first strophe: "(Feuilles vivantes au matin sont à l'image de la gloire). . . ." These living leaves are the turtle-doves in the tree. Looking at them in the morning (cf. I, 149, 152), the normal time for the departure, the narrator finds that his "glory" (cf. I, 150, 152) is already completely realized in them; hence there is no need to depart.

The second strophe shows the cause of this "sifflement pur," of this joy: it is the contemplation of what has been accomplished, represented by the purity and the movement of the heavenly bodies. It contains also, as it must, a slight indication of the human limits set upon this joy: "Et ce n'est point qu'un homme ne soit triste [cf. III, 157]." But—"mais se levant avant le jour [hence, putting an end to the dreams of the night] et se tenant avec prudence [the adventurer is a 'sage,' III, 158] dans le commerce d'un vieil arbre [a formula that summarizes the encounter between the Stranger and the adventurer], appuyé du menton à la dernière étoile [it is toward morning, hence the opposite of X, 195: 'jusqu'à l'heure du soir où l'étoile femelle'], il voit au fond du ciel à jeun de grandes choses pures [cf. III, 158: 'ceux qui ont fait de grandes choses,' and X, 195: 'chose pure et gagée dans les hauteurs du ciel . . .'] qui tournent au plaisir. . . ." The last part of the sentence, repeating certain formulas of Chant VII (especially p. 177), establishes the identity of the "grandes choses" done by man and the "choses pures" that turn in the heavens; the "pleasure" is thus double, but it denotes a purity equally applicable to the two kinds of perfection.

Three elements contribute to the formation of the last strophe. First, the repetition of the initial formula of the Chanson, with (as in the case of the first Chanson) a change in a single word: "Mon cheval arrêté sous l'arbre qui roucoule, je siffle un sifflement plus pur. . . ." The "plus" that precedes "pur," now, weighs and evaluates man's accomplishment—a step in the direction of a greater purity. Then, recalling that on three occasions (I, 151; III, 157; IV, 161) he condemned those who had not participated in the adventure, the narrator pardons them; for they have been unable to feel the joy that he experiences in this moment: "Et paix à ceux, s'ils vont mourir, qui n'ont point vu ce jour." Finally, he speaks of the third personage of the poem, the poet who (since the first Chanson) has always been associated in the adventure as one of those who recount it. And it is of the poet's chronicle, now written, that the narrator offers a judgment: "Mais de mon frère le poète on a eu des nouvelles. Il a écrit encore une chose très douce." This judgment is favorable because the thing recounted in the chronicle is good. The last sentence of the Chanson (and this is parallel to what we saw in Chant X, 193) describes the poet's consummation, similar to the narrator's: "Et quelques-uns en eurent connaissance. . . ." In truth, it is only because we have been able to "know" the "thing" written by the poet that the narrator has been able to achieve his immortality.

The results of my inquiry into the general structure of *Anabase* should now be fairly evident. If we must decide between a narrative form and a lyric form, the solution is easy: the form is essentially lyrical. Of course, certain elements of plot, of action, enter into it; one could even summarize briefly this action: "An adventurer, having received an invitation to an adventure and having overcome his own hesitation, departs for the conquest of new lands; he conquers them and accomplishes his civilizing mission; but he is not content with his repose, and the cycle invitation-departure-march-halt is constantly renewed." It would also be possible, passing to the metaphorical level, to propose a parallel summary for the action of the human soul: "The human soul, having been awakened by the promise of fruitful activity and having overcome its habits of inactivity, undertakes new human conquests; she accomplishes them and reaches intellectual and spiritual heights hitherto unknown; but far from being content to remain there, she sets forth again (after periods of repose) toward a superior ideal." In equally metaphorical terms, we might call *Anabase* "an epic of the human soul." But there would also be a third "action" to be traced, the one concerning the emotion of joy from its creation, through its development, to its final abatement: "The possibility that the soul might attain an ever better expression arouses, in the reader, the emotion of joy; at each new realization of this possibility, that joy is augmented; and in spite of the intermixture of other emotions, it establishes itself within him in a pure and definitive form."

How can we know which of these summaries represents the true structure of *Anabase?* In a sense, they are all true. For there is, in fact, a narrative thread: we can follow a protagonist through a series of episodes that occur in time and that are linked together by cause-and-effect relationships. But this action is only a skeleton; the episodes are rather repetitions of one single action than different, successive events; the protagonist is really not the one who does the action and his character is not its main cause; and the order is determined rather by a "principle" or a "thesis" than by any internal necessity. What, then, is the use of this skeleton? It serves to support, to justify, and to order a certain number of objects and ideas which, by their very nature, are capable of creating and developing the emotion of joy. The principal idea is that of a constantly renewed progress of the human soul toward a better expression; this is what gives order to the action. All the fundamental proportions of the poem—*inert matter : living matter, death : life, lack of civilization : civilization, impurity : purity, privation : pleasure*—are variants on this same idea. In a word, it is this idea that gives its form to our second summary. As for the objects, their role is to concretize an abstract idea and to present it, in an effective form, to our sensitivity. The earth and the heavenly bodies, the rivers and their banks, the yellow deserts, the plains and the heights, tents and buildings, all are chosen and organized in a way to make our emotion pass from an initial state to a final state. We should note also that they are chosen, for the most part, in a way that will make the *anabasis* possible: the passage from the coast to the interior, from the plain to the heights—and then to heights that are still higher.

The third summary is merely the effect of which the second is the cause. This means that the presence and the organization of certain objects and certain ideas within the poem produce, outside the poem, a movement within the reader that is properly aesthetic. The anabasis produces joy, not only in the adventurer and the Stranger and the poet, but also in the reader. Obviously, all poems function in the same way: intrinsic qualities of the poem are responsible for its effect. But whereas in narrative and dramatic poetry—genres that are based on action—the effect is produced by the particular way in which this action is developed, in lyric poetry—which has no action properly speaking—the effect comes from other elements. It may come from objects presented and exploited, from acts or speeches attributed to a personage, from arguments or ideas pursued from their first presentation up to their full realization. All kinds of combinations of these elements are possible, including the one that is found in *Anabase:* a narrative basis (but of secondary importance) which serves to present a fundamental idea (of primary impor-tance) by means of a group of objects capable of arousing the essential emotion. In its sources, rather than in its particular quality, this emotion is lyrical. In the case of *Anabase,* a prosodic lyricism—the constant use of the song form—is added to the fundamental lyricism of the organizing conception.

Appendix

The Limits of Hermeticism, or Hermeticism and Intelligibility

My subject presupposes a certain number of theoretical and philosophical assumptions that I shall have to clarify before going farther. To speak of "limits" and "hermeticism" and "intelligibility" is to introduce terms and concepts whose mutual relationship and interdependence can be explained only by a general vision of the poetic art. I have no intention of presenting that general vision here; it would be too long and too complicated. But I should like to indicate, very briefly, why intelligibility is essential in all poetic matters, in what ways hermeticism is basically opposed to it, and the reasons why the poet must place limits upon any hermeticism that he might wish to practice.

Poetry, like the other arts, creates artificial objects—ones which do not exist in nature—with the aim of evoking, in whoever might contemplate those objects, emotions proper to those same objects. But if the objects are artificial and do not exist in nature, they nevertheless represent natural objects, and it is by these natural objects that the emotion of the contemplator is aroused. The tragedy of *Oedipus Rex* is the artificial product of its poet; but it represents a man like its protagonist, in circumstances that a man might have known, engaged in a humanly possible action; and if we feel a

420

certain pity for the Oedipus of the tragedy, it is because we recognize in him a man, circumstances, and an action that we might have known in life and which, in life, would have aroused that same pity within us. By bringing together the artificial object and a possible natural object, we have understood, and having understood, we have felt the proper emotion.

That is the basis for intelligibility in poetry. I should define it as the possibility of recognizing, in the work of poetry and through that work, a natural object (a man, a passion, an action) that belonged to or might have belonged to our experience as men. That intelligibility is the basis of our aesthetic emotion; for it is only to the degree to which we understand—either through feeling or through intellect—that we are able to feel an emotion that is proper and adequate to the object represented.

In traditional poetry, a great number of means and of devices were developed to assist us in understanding well, hence in feeling properly. The most simple method is that of the direct representation of the object: the poet names it, describes it, makes it visible. When Baudelaire writes "le ciel bas et lourd pèse," he uses this method of direct presentation; and when he adds, "sur l'esprit gémissant en proie aux longs ennuis," he identifies directly a part of the emotion that we are expected to feel. We thus have before us, at the same time, a visual image and the passion associated with the image, both presented without disguise and with perfect clarity. The other traditional method, that of indirect representation, might possibly seem to be more "poetic"; for it is the method of comparison, of analogy, of metaphor. It is indirect in the sense that, besides naming the object represented, it establishes a relationship between that object and another object that resembles it in one way or another. Thus Baudelaire completes the first line of his *Spleen* by adding, "Quand le ciel bas et lourd pèse *comme un couvercle"*; he compares, he adds another image, and when he later says "de l'horizon embrassant tout le cercle," he indicates what feature links the two objects and makes the comparison possible. By so doing, he enriches and complicates the visual presentation, he adds to the emotional possibilities that he will exploit in the rest of his poem.

The second method, that of indirect representation, is subject to a large number of variations. It may be used in passing, on a specific occasion, when one introduces the comparison or the figure that appears only at one place in the poem in order to provide, at that place, a visual image or a thought or a feeling. Baudelaire gives us an example in the same *Spleen:*

> Ainsi que des esprits errants et sans patrie
> Qui se mettent à geindre opiniâtrément.

Or one may use it as the basis for the whole poetic structure, creating what I call the "essential" or the "structural" metaphor. The poet who adopts this latter method chooses a basic comparison or analogy which is developed throughout the poem; thus Ronsard, in his "Mignonne, allons voir si la rose . . . ," develops throughout, as the organizing principle of his ode, the following proportional metaphor: the time of a day is to the beauty of a rose as the time of a life is to the beauty of a woman.

So far, complete intelligibility; for the method of direct representation, as it establishes a clear and simple relationship between an object and its expression, permits immediate identification and comprehension. The method of indirect representation, since it juxtaposes two equally clear objects, does nothing that might necessarily diminish that fundamental clarity. Thus we understand and we feel what we should understand and feel. However (and for reasons that I shall not examine here), modern poets since Baudelaire have found that there were artistic advantages in forsaking this traditional clarity for a greater and greater cultivation of obscurity, in abandoning intelligibility in order to move in the direction of hermeticism. For hermeticism, as I conceive it, is at the opposite pole to intelligibility. In modern poetry, it is a method that seeks to "close" the poem to the reader rather than "opening" it to him; it wants and works for unintelligibility.

As a consequence, hermeticism had to seek poetic means and devices that were new, perhaps even opposite, in order to replace clarity by obscurity, comprehension by incomprehension. This was an entirely legitimate aim, since through obscurity and incomprehension it sought to produce—and indeed did produce—new effects, reactions and emotions that were more subtle and more complicated than the ones that traditional poetry had called forth. Nevertheless, for the hermetic poet as for the clear poet, effects, reactions, and emotions were still important; therefore obscurity could not be complete, incomprehension could not be total. One could not have, in a word, integral hermeticism. In fact, an absolutely hermetic, absolutely incomprehensible poem would no longer be a poem; not understanding it (and I use "understanding" in the broad sense already indicated), one would feel nothing; it would be in impenetrable enigma, a riddle without solution. One might perhaps recognize in it a product of art, but not of the art of poetry; for the objects, the forms, the meanings and the feelings of poetry would be absent.

I suppose that, except in the cases of a few extreme dadaists, it did not take very long for the would-be hermeticist poet to discover that there were natural and necessary limits to his hermeticism. His poetry could not be without meaning—either for the feelings or for the intellect—and hence without possible effects upon the emotions of the reader. He could not manufacture hermetically sealed boxes that would contain—but how could one know what they might indeed contain? He needed therefore to open windows into his boxes, through which one might see, within, a poetic meaning and a poetic form—through which one could recognize an object or objects capable of producing an aesthetic effect. Rather than excluding all comprehension, each poem had to contain a certain number of elements, integral to its total structure, that would facilitate and insure comprehension.

In his search for counter-hermetic means, the hermetic poet could call upon certain devices that had been developed by his predecessors since the middle of the nineteenth century. For the hermeticism of the end of the century was not born full-blown in the farthest stage of its quantitative possibilities; it was the result of a long evolution that had developed simultaneously techniques for obscurity and techniques for clarity. All the movements in poetry beginning with Baudelaire (and maybe even before him) had participated in the evolution. This means that there are many kinds of hermeticism and that poets had experimented with a multitude of ways of producing them. In the same *Spleen* that I have cited, Baudelaire writes these verses in the last stanza:

—Et de longs corbillards, sans tambours ni musique,
Défilent lentement dans mon âme . . .

This is no longer direct representation; there are really no "funeral processions" in the "soul" of the speaker. Nor is it indirect representation through the use of a simple comparison; the poet has suppressed the "comme" and the "ainsi" that he had used previously. But we have before us another manifestation of the indirect method, a true metaphor where we understand that two objects are brought together but where both are not named and identified explicitly. What the poet means is that there is in the soul of the speaker a state of deep sadness, of silence, and of melancholy motion that is similar to what one would feel if one were to watch the passing of a real funeral procession. Since he speaks only of the procession and of the soul, the rest must be inferred; the reader must supply the two missing terms in order to complete the proportion.

To be sure, the true metaphor is a traditional device of poetry, used by all poets in all ages. But the fact that it fails to state certain elements, that it requires an inference on the part of the reader, that it demands an effort by our mind and our sensitivity, makes it especially useful to the hermetic poet. It suppresses something, and that is the first condition of obscurity; it permits an inference, and that is the basis of intelligibility. The more it suppresses, the more closely it approaches absolute hermeticism; but since, in the process of eliminating one clear indication after another, it must leave a sufficient number of elements to permit the inference, it never reaches the point of becoming the completely sealed box, the enigma. It is this true metaphor that is the basis of modern symbolism, one of the first forms of hermeticism.

We can see an example of such a metaphor—a fairly simple example—in Baudelaire's sonnet, *Recueillement*. If we look only at its superficial meaning, the sonnet is concerned with the arrival of evening, the falling of night that brings peace to a man who withdraws from the activities of the multitude. But as we look at it more closely, beneath the surface, we discover that it is concerned essentially with the approach and the arrival of death, bringing peace to the man who is willing to withdraw from life. How do we make this discovery? Through all kinds of signs, of pointers, of aids to understanding that the poet distributes throughout his poem. Baudelaire gives capital letters to certain words: Soir, Nuit; Douleur, Plaisir, Regret; Années, Soleil, Orient, thus showing that they must be given a special meaning. Especially, he multiplies the words that might be related to death: "mortels, bourreau, défuntes, robes surannées, moribond, s'endormir, linceul." There are thus in the poem the two normal parts of a metaphor, but only one of them is expressed, the other one is suppressed—not wholly, however, for the signs and the pointers remain, and these make inference and understanding possible. We therefore feel what we are supposed to feel in the presence of a poem about death.

Le Bateau ivre represents symbolism—perhaps I should say symbolist hermeticism—at a much more advanced stage, almost at a maximum. Once again, this is a poem based on an essentially metaphorical structure in which the symbol, the boat with its various adventures, is clearly expressed and fully developed, whereas the object symbolized, a man whose life would contain similar adventures, is not so expressed and developed. Of the four terms in the proportional metaphor, only the two that relate to a boat are expressed; the other two, relating to a man, are suppressed. But, once more, not entirely; if they were, the poem would be completely unintelligible as a symbol. Rimbaud uses signs and pointers that are more subtle than Baudelaire's, and since his poem is longer, he scatters them thinly through it. For example, the idea of "enfants," repeated four times and supplemented by a child's words and a child's thoughts, shows that one of the stages in a man's life that will be symbolized is that of childhood. The insistence on words like "victime," "noyé," "martyr," allows us to understand one of the aspects of the adventure. But above all Rimbaud assigns to his boat a set of sensations, of emotions, of passions that cannot properly belong to a boat (since it has none!), but that must belong to a man. "Impassibles, insoucieux, triomphants, regretter, amour, rêver, songer," to mention only a few, are passions and activities that are exclusively human; a boat that assumes them makes itself a symbol for a man. Indeed, it is through these passions that the boat's story becomes intelligible to us and that we feel the desired aesthetic emotions.

Symbolist though it may be, *Le Bateau ivre* permits us to penetrate its meaning, to arrive at the object symbolized, by means of the signs and the pointers that are common to any metaphorical structure. Hermetic though it may be, it does not remain unintelligible—its hermeticism is limited—and if we know how to discover the signs we shall find the meaning.

The two examples that I have just given belong to what I have called indirect representation. But there is also a hermeticism found in direct representation. The latter may be discerned not in symbolist poems, based on metaphorical structure, but rather in what I call "impressionistic" poetry. Even in a direct representation, the poet may become obscure by representing his object less than completely —that is, by suppressing something, either by combining two or more representations in such a way as to blur the distinctions among them, or by interrupting and dislocating the expression so as to make understanding difficult. The result is a shadowy and indistinct image, an impression rather than a hard line, and the resultant emotion has little definiteness and certainty. One may even reach the point where the emotional response takes precedence over understanding. Mallarmé achieves all these things in a poem such as *L'Après-midi d'un faune*. Its subject is indicated in the title; but nowhere does one find in the poem a complete and continuous description of the events of the faun's afternoon. On the one hand, to the narrative are added the faun's reflections and meditations, the next morning, about the afternoon's events—hence a simultaneous representation of two objects; and on the other hand, the narrative and the meditation are interwoven on a principle of constant interruption. Even if one were to separate the two parts and to reestablish the logical order of the meditation and the chronological order of the narrative, he would not have two complete representations; many details are lacking—much is suppressed—and the connections among others are hard to discern. The reader ends up with a doubt that is like the faun's own. In this case, what remains unknown is not the meaning of a symbol—there is no symbol in this poem—but rather the interpretation that should be given to an object that is presented vaguely and obscurely.

Nevertheless, Mallarmé's hermeticism in *L'Après-midi d'un faune* is far from being total; it is well within the absolute limits. If his poem becomes intelligible in large part, it is because he is once again generous with signs and pointers. First, he makes a typographical distinction between the two parts; the italics used for the narrative, the romans for the meditation, help us to make an initial separation, to know that there are two distinct objects. Next, the two parts are linked not only by a common subject, but also by a large number of words and images: "leur incarnat léger" of the meditation reflects "une blancheur animale" in the narrative, the reeds and the pipes of the narrative furnish most of the metaphors in the meditation. Finally, the fairly precise chronology of the narrative permits us to restore the order of the meditation, wilfully confused.

It is by the use of almost identical means that Mallarmé assures the intelligibility of his most hermetic poem, *Un Coup de dés jamais n'abolira le hasard*. He takes as his subject, not an adventure and the passions related to it (as in *L'Après-midi d'un faune*), but an idea, the one that he formulates in the barest way in his title. In order to transform that idea into a lyric poem (it would run the risk, if he kept to syllogisms, of becoming no more than a demonstration), he invents an action and an agent, a beginning and an end for that action; in addition, he creates three secondary comparisons that represent, through three other objects, the same idea. Action and objects make possible the necessary association, with the idea, of feelings and emotions. If Mallarmé had chosen, for his direct representation, a simple representation following a normal order, there would have been no problem of intelligibility. But because he wished to obtain certain effects, he chose to mingle the various strands of his idea, his action, and his comparisons, to interrupt each of them many times, to intercalate elements that seem to have nothing to do with the rest. He also adopted an extraordinary placing of the words upon the page, to contribute to the same effects. In a word, he did everything needed to make his poem hermetic; nevertheless, as a good poet, he showed his hand by certain signs and pointers that are completely adequate.

To express the central idea, there are two complete sentences, one used as the title, the other found at the very end ("Toute Pensée émet un Coup de Dés"). Even a first reading shows us that the title sentence runs through the poem, distinguished by a type-face that is used for it alone, but that its words are widely spaced out through the poem. Immediately, then, we recognize two keys to understanding: there are elements of continuity, sentences or parts of sentences, that appear in a broken or divided form; and these elements are identified by typographical peculiarities. We can quickly reconstruct some of these elements. After the word "jamais" (in large bold-face capitals) there begins, in small capitals, a long modification of the notion of a throw of the dice: "Quand bien même lancé dans des circonstances éternelles du fond d'un naufrage soit; le maître existât-il, commençat-il et cessât-il, se chiffrât-il, illuminât-il; rien n'aura eu lieu que le lieu excepté peut-être une constellation." It is this complex formula, presenting the ship in a storm, the ship's master who throws the dice, and the consequences, that introduces the action intended to illustrate the idea. After the word "n'abolira," and printed in a small italic type, the two comparisons that begin with "Comme si" prepare the introduction of another complete sentence (in large italic letters): "Si c'était le nombre ce serait le hasard." This last ends with the word "hasard" that also concludes the first sentence. Moreover, we find that there are other complete sentences—albeit much interrupted—that link the sentences already cited; and so we may reconstruct the following one: "Le maître, inférant que se prépare l'unique Nombre, hésite à n'ouvrir pas la main; celui, tentant une chance oiseuse, chancellera, s'affalera, n'abolira le hasard."

The same kind of linking between sentences and parts is made at fixed points, and the very place where the juncture is made is important; the "geography" of the structure is added to its chronology as an index for the mind that seeks to understand. This is another sign; we learn little by little to know it and it leads to new discoveries. Then there are parallel constructions and developments that facilitate understanding. I have already quoted the passage referring to the master: "existât-il, commençât-il et cessât-il, se chiffrât-il, illuminât-il"; the first words of the passage allow us to assemble and order correctly such words as: "Fiançailles, né d'un ébat, puérile, pubère, virile, vieillard, chenu, cadavre" as stages in a human life. "Se chiffrât-il" is explained by "énumère, un compte total en formation, le Nombre," while "illuminât-il" represents the transformation of the master (and of thought itself) into a "constellation."

In these ways Mallarmé multiplies his signs and his pointers. If he does much to make his poem hermetic, he does still more to make it intelligible. As an excellent artist, he recognizes the limits placed on hermeticism by our need to understand and to feel, and he borrows or invents or creates the means for assuring intelligibility.

Hermeticism is not a particular technique of the modern poet. Rather, it is an end that may be achieved in a variety of ways, either by the use of traditional devices or by the development of new variants upon those devices. As simple and direct a device as the simile or the overt comparison may, through understatement or suppression, become the basis for a hermetic presentation. As one passes from the simile to the metaphor, from the metaphor to the symbol, he may follow a single line of complication that presents a constantly increased potential for less-than-complete statement, hence for hermeticism. If one pursues instead the line of direct description, he may again discover possibilities for the imperfect or for the foreshortened statement (rarely, I think, for the misstatement) that lead to such hermetic techniques as "impressionism" or some of the other -isms of modern poetry.

In a sense, old and new devices of poetry may be diverted to the uses of hermeticism, provided only that the poet wishes to achieve the special effects that accompany a reduction in intelligibility. Modern poetry, of course, seeks many other effects, to which it adapts a great variety of procedures and methods. There is a constant interplay between the effects that the poet considers to be desirable and the ways he invents for arriving at those effects; so the "art" of poetry grows and its powers are augmented. But fundamentally the poet builds upon a small number of standard devices, with which he experiments as his inventive spirit dictates. These are the poetic means that represent basic relationships among the objects that he treats: comparison and analogy that distinguish likeness and dissimilarity, equivalence and opposition; relationships in time that bring the past into contact with the present, the present with the future; and always, the capacity of objects in the physical world to arouse—as they express—human passions and human ideas. In the last analysis, all "objects" are useful to the poet as they serve as means to represent the "passions," the "thoughts," the "feelings" and the "ideas" of men. His ends as a poet are the production of specific effects (appropriate to the given poem) upon thought and passion, and his means are such procedures as will evoke objects capable of producing those effects and will establish, with greater or lesser clarity, the link between the material world and the world of human feeling. One of the essential differences between the older and the newer poetry is the assumption on the part of the latter that "lesser clarity" makes possible a whole new range of emotional and intellectual responses.